The culture of consent

Mass organization of leisure in fascist Italy

The culture of consent

Mass organization of leisure in fascist Italy

Victoria de Grazia

Rutgers University

CAMBRIDGE UNIVERSITY PRESS
Cambridge
London   New York   New Rochelle
Melbourne   Sydney

Published by the Press Syndicate of the University of Cambridge
The Pitt Building, Trumpington Street, Cambridge CB2 1RP
32 East 57th Street, New York, NY 10022, USA
296 Beaconsfield Parade, Middle Park, Melbourne 3206, Australia

© Cambridge University Press 1981

First published 1981

Printed in the United States of America
Typeset by Maryland Composition Company Inc., Glen Burnie, Maryland
Printed and bound by The Book Press, Brattleboro, Vermont

Library of Congress Cataloging in Publication Data
de Grazia, Victoria.
The culture of consent.
Includes bibliographical references and index.
1. Leisure–Italy–History–20th century.   2. Rec-
reation and state–Italy–History–20th century.
3. Italy–History–1922–1945.   4. Fascism–Italy.
I. Title.
GV85.D43   306′.4   80-24361
ISBN 0-521-23705-X   AACR1

Contents

		page	vii
Preface		*page*	vii
1	The organization of consent		1
2	The politics of after-work		24
3	Taylorizing worker leisure		60
4	The penetration of the countryside		94
5	Privileging the clerks		127
6	The nationalization of the public		151
7	The formation of fascist low culture		187
8	The limits of consent		225
Notes			247
Abbreviations			245
Bibliography			291
Index			301

To Catherine and Jessica, dearest sisters

Preface

This book began as a political study of Italian fascism, with, as its central focus, the leisure-time organization or *dopolavoro* of the fascist regime. Inevitably it held certain social implications from the outset: I was concerned to understand how a regime that was so flagrantly anti–working class established any broad basis of legitimacy, and whether, in the process of consolidating its power, Mussolini's dictatorship had in any way succeeded in transforming Italian society. But, at the time I undertook the research, I shared certain commonly held assumptions about the totalitarian nature of fascist rule: awesome in its powers of manipulation and its capacity to infiltrate all levels of society, yet fundamentally removed from the daily lives of those on whom it was so violently imposed. Thus I initially conceived the study as an inquiry into the sphere of "high" politics, and of policy making, an analysis of the propaganda apparatus of fascism based on the examination of government regulations, party directives, and reports on the growth of the *dopolavoro* itself.

This assumption was immediately challenged as I began to sift through the trivia of bureaucratic orders, endlessly revised and updated, imposed on *bocce* groups, outing clubs, and choral societies, and to compare the seemingly petty accomplishments of small-town fascist functionaries with the omnipotent designs of the fascist state, as set out, for example, in the speeches of Mussolini. It soon became clear that the world of the *dopolavoro*, like the popular world in every class society, was viewed with condescension. For the fascists, the working-class social club, the neighborhood recreational circle, the village rendezvous, constituted the realm of "low" politics. The policies applied to them were never taken up in the high councils of state; and Mussolini, the great posturer, never deigned to have himself photographed at a company picnic or proletarian outing. However, as I discovered more about the deceptively apolitical mechanism of leisure-time organizing, I gradually understood the real political power of the modes of persuasion by which fascism had penetrated every domain of social life from industrial enterprise and city neighborhood to rural village. Its detachment from the clearly "fascist" activities represented by party service or propagandistic sloganeering made this depoliticized underside of fascism a decisive support for that consent to fascist rule essential to Mussolini's continuance in power over two decades.

In its final form, this book has become a political *and* social history of an institution of rule that, among others, was invented to mediate the sharp social and economic conflicts that resulted from fascism's intervention in an already deeply divided and unevenly developed Italy. As a mediating institution, the *dopolavoro* resembled the paternalistic schemes of an earlier era of capitalism, as well as bearing similarities to those social welfare services of advanced capitalism whose professed aim, outside of politics, has been to aid, support, and uplift a needy sector of the population or to redistribute the benefits of mass consumer society downward. The underlying political functions of these institutions in engendering consent have become especially apparent during the time this study was being written. In a decade in which economic crisis has met with surprising apathy and political mobilization has run side by side with mass acquiescence, the stabilizing effect of policies applied to apparently apolitical realms – those of culture, sexuality, family, and social welfare – could not be ignored. The outcome has been the realization that "cultural" politics, "sexual" politics, and "consensual" politics are part and parcel of politics proper, although with still much discussion as to the correct way to study, let alone confront, them.

From this perspective, the history of fascism's organization of leisure-time activities had to be conceived in its broader implications, through a process of comparison and contrast: between high politics and low; between fascist politics and those of other, less authoritarian regimes themselves struggling to stabilize their rule following the first "total" war; between specifically fascist modes of social organizing and the state social services and paternalistic voluntary institutions of liberal democracy; between the "Americanism" of the twenties and thirties at home and that received and utilized as ideology abroad; between, finally, the spontaneous expressions of worker culture and the manipulated motifs of a new mass culture. In this broader context, it has inevitably become a part of the history of the institutional and cultural transformations that occurred throughout Europe and America as the immediate corollary of the reconstruction of bourgeois states under monopoly capital; and which in Italy were especially distorted by taking place under a fascist dictatorship.

The order of the book follows, as far as possible, the logic of these problems: I have tried to give an account, not simply of the growth of a single institution, but also of its place in the changing policies of fascism. Chapter 1 summarizes the political and social implications of an institution of this kind, discussing the question of fascism's search for "consent" and the character of the mass organizations the regime developed for that end. Chapter 2 gives a synoptic history of the *dopolavoro*, from its origins in fascist syndicalist schemes for labor organizing, to its constitution as a full-fledged apparatus of state power. The next three chapters examine the impact of the *dopolavoro* on the industrial, rural, and tertiary sectors, on the working class, peasantry, and lower middle class respectively. They try to show how, in each instance, and in widely differing ways, the organization was utilized in the regime's attempts to forge responsive constituencies, blunt worker resistance, and gratify demands for consumption frustrated by its own wage policies. Chapter 6 assesses the way in which particular consumer habits and pastimes – mass sports, traditional games, amateur theatricals, film showings, and the like – were used to organize the Italian people into a public ostensibly above class: as audience, consumers, or participants, responsive, if not always enthusiastic, toward the regime's policies. In Chapter 7, the content of this diverse activity is examined to reveal the peculiar ideological synthesis that constituted fascist "low" culture: That this mixture was commonly known as the *cultura dopolavoristica* throughout fascist Italy only emphasizes the pervasive influence this single institution exercised within the society as a whole in the formation of a culture of consent. The concluding chapter explores the impact of fascist leisure organizing on the formation of mass culture in Italy, comparing this very contradictory development to cultural–institutional trends elsewhere in western capitalist societies between the two world wars.

The completion of this study was made possible by the generous assistance of a number of institutions and persons. The research for the dissertation that formed its original basis was carried out with a summer grant from the Council of European Studies and a fellowship from the Woodrow Wilson Foundation in 1972–3. Grants from the Research Foundation of the City University of New York and from the National Endowment of the Humanities enabled me to finish additional research in 1976–7. The writing was completed while I was a fellow in Italian Studies at the American Academy in Rome in 1978, and the preparation of the final manuscript was supported by grants from the Research Council of Rutgers University. In Italy, Dr. Costanzo Casucci and other archivists at the Archivio Centrale dello Stato were especially helpful in locating and interpreting essential sources, as were Professor Valerio Castronovo, Dr. Stefania Natale, and Signorina Albertina

Preface

Baldi. I also wish to acknowledge the help of the staffs of the Butler Library of Columbia University, the Department of Labor Library in Washington, D.C., the Biblioteca Nazionale of Florence, the Istituto per la Storia della Resistenza in Toscana, the Centro Storico Fiat in Turin, and ENAL, INA, the Dopolavoro of the State Railroads, and the Ministry of Communications in Rome.

The many questions about the meaning of the study raised by friends and colleagues in Italy and the United States have been very different; trying to answer them at all satisfactorily has made the work at times difficult, although always stimulating. Professor Fritz Stern was unfailingly supportive as the advisor of an earlier version presented as a doctoral dissertation in the Department of History at Columbia University in 1976, and Professor Robert Paxton made helpful suggestions for its revision. In its final form, this study owes much to careful readings by Professors Arno Mayer, Nicola Gallerano, Dean Savage, Molly Nolan, and Charles Maier and to discussions with Giulio Sapelli and Leonardo Paggi. The final copy, like several earlier ones, was typed with unstinting good humor by a fellow historian, Miriam Levy. Very special thanks to Anthony Vidler for help at once loving and wise.

Victoria de Grazia
New York City, March, 1981

1

The organization of consent

> The "normal" exercise of hegemony on the classical terrain of par-
> liamentary regimes is characterized by a combination of force and
> consent, which balance each other reciprocally without force ever
> prevailing too much over consent . . . In the period following the
> World War, the hegemonic apparatus cracked apart, and the exercise
> of hegemony became permanently difficult and aleatory.
>
> A. Gramsci, *Prison Notebooks*

The question of "government by consent" became for the first time
an overriding concern of political and economic elites in Europe as
they sought to reestablish the bases of their rule after the enormous
disruptions of World War I. With what authority could reconstruction
be undertaken after the great upsurge of labor unrest in 1918? On what
foundations could old governing coalitions be reconstituted as the sheer
numerical force of the left parties threw the exclusive liberal caucuses
into disarray? With what incentives could workers be induced to cooperate in retooling for peacetime production now that factory
councils and militant industrial unions pressed their demands for "democracy in the workplace"? Conservatives, liberals, and technocrats
naturally differed in their proposed solutions, debating the merits of
consultations and negotiated compromises with organized labor, more
active appeals to build responsive voter blocks, or a radical operation
of social engineering. But whatever the political perspective, it had
become clear that, with the end of the war, the era of laissez-faire
capitalism – of disorganized labor, rigid management hierarchies, long
working hours, and restricted consumption – was closed. The age of
employer absolutism, as the economist Luigi Einaudi recognized, had
ended. The economic, political, and social conditions of what liberal
observers called a "compulsive capitalism" no longer existed.[1] The
new age, that of an expansive, consumer-oriented, organized capitalism, called for rule by consent.

In the long run, the major possibility of building this consent depended on the degree to which traditional class alignments could be

1

The culture of consent: mass organization in fascist Italy

sidestepped and appeals for political support or social cooperation made on the basis of new, seemingly nonclass identities. Economic redistribution and changes in social stratification alone might make identification as, say, a consumer, or small property owner more compelling than that as a "proletarian." But the exploitations of these identities to form new political allegiances required that they be placed in a new frame of reference. To give a distinctively ideological cast to social experiences outside of the workplace – to unite "war veterans," "taxpayers," "sports fans," or "national citizens" – demanded the creation of a nationwide political culture that might persuade people that their shared goals transcended petty economic haggling, regional and ethnic disputes, or age-old social animosities. In short, the politics of the postwar era were premised on what might be called a "culture of consent" that, operating at all levels of the society, might play a decisive role in shaping those responsive though depoliticized mass constituencies necessary for the stabilization of advanced capitalist societies.

The effort to create such a supraclass national identity was not of course entirely new. Since the late nineteenth century, the "nationalization of the masses" had, in one form or another, been a constant goal of ruling elites.[2] In the years before World War I, liberal reformers had pressed for a modern civic culture by supporting the extension of paternalistic, usually privately run schemes to inculcate in the lower orders the duties of diligent work, service to the nation, and the proper exercise of the newly acquired right to vote.[3] In the postwar years, however, the terms in which the old dominant culture of "uplift" was conceived and organized were fundamentally transformed. This was partly in reaction to mass labor unrest and partly a response to the ever more complicated demands of an organized capitalism for workers to become disciplined consumers, as well as diligent operatives, conduct a "rational" family life, and use their leisure in an efficient way. It was also the result of advances in radio and film technology that created new, formidably powerful agencies of ideological influence. In the process of forming a new dominant culture with mass extensions, the old distinctions between a separatist "high" culture and bourgeois schemes for worker uplift were dissolved; the line between state intervention and public control and the private, parochial interests traditionally behind upper-class philanthropy was blurred; finally, with the addition of sports and amusements to attract and entertain the "masses," diversion was given equal weight with projects for skill training and moral improvement. Out of the new schools, agencies, and institutions of "high" and "low" culture, out of the changing

2

relations between the traditional and the new, and among popular, working class, folk and mass cultures, out of the fusion between the previously narrow sphere of politics proper and the ever broadening domains of ideological intervention, there emerged a distinctively new politics of culture. From the twenties on, as the sociologists of the Frankfurt School realized so presciently, this politics was to be as important to the stability of capitalist rule as the process of political decision making itself.[4]

This book studies the effort to form a culture of consent in Italy between the world wars: how Italy's fascist rulers were impelled to confront the inadequacy of force as their primary means of government; the methods they devised to translate a policy of persuasion into an entirely new cultural practice; and the institutional and ideological deformations that resulted from their systematic and dictatorial intervention in the development of mass culture in Italy.

Consent, however, is a term that has to be defined specifically in the context of fascist rule.[5] In Italy, once Mussolini had been installed in power in 1922, government did not have to face demands for democracy in the workplace, much less engage in debates about the legitimacy of parliamentary institutions. The breaking of the labor movement by *squadristi* violence and the subsequent outlawing of the antifascist opposition removed these from discussion. But the problem of consent intruded into fascist politics all the same. It can be identified, in the first place, with that vague perception, shared by many "fascists of the first hour," that the liberal state, by its failure to "nationalize the masses," was mainly responsible for the unruliness of Italian workers and the general disorder of Italian political life: For many fascist ideologues the overriding goal of their national revolution was to make the "masses adhere to the state."[6] But in the early twenties, the practical content of this slogan was so variously interpreted – as license for blackshirted thugs to beat workers into line, but also as some design for fascism to become "soul and conscience" of a new "national democracy" – that it can hardly be seen as representing any coherent concern or consistent program, much less as a totalitarian cultural policy.

In a second moment in the mid-twenties, the problem of consent presented itself in a more compelling way, in terms not so different from those faced elsewhere in Europe by liberal-democratic regimes in the process of stabilizing their rule. Mussolini had his own shaky conservative-fascist coalition to maintain, his own difficulties in balancing the conflicting interests of his major supporters in big business

3

and his many followers in the middle and lower bourgeoisie. To compete in world markets, Italian capital required at least as thoroughgoing a reconstruction as that proceeding in the rest of Europe by 1925; the costs of stabilizing the economy in the absence of any effective union movement were easily shifted onto workers and small consumers through wage cuts, accelerated work rhythms, high rates of unemployment, and austerity measures that, altogether, had the effect of pushing back the working class standard of living to prewar levels.[7] Yet without the disciplined support of these same "masses," the fascist leadership could not hope to pull the economy out of its chronic crisis; and without success in this endeavor, it could not expect to consolidate its own political base.

In this context, the need for a broader consent was brought home to the regime, a need that initially was very explicitly understood in terms of the regime's immediate economic priorities. Thus consent, for the production workers, meant a silent industriousness and acquiescence to pay reductions and speed-ups – no more could be expected from those whom Mussolini in 1927 characterized as the "generation of the irreconcilables";[8] for peasants, it meant an active involvement in "battles" to increase agricultural output in spite of price drops that under other circumstances would have sent them in precipitous flight from the land; for petty state functionaries, it meant political support, although their own professional status was being degraded with the rapid expansion of the tertiary sector. Consent thus acquired multiple specific meanings according to the responses demanded from different sectors of the society at different times. It can be said to have acquired a general meaning as well: as the sustained effort by the fascist regime to make the working population as a whole respond to and endure the terrible and contradictory pressures of a distorted economic growth taking place in a country in which the distance between government and governed was vast, regional differences sharp, and class and political divisions especially bitter.

The creation of this culture of consent in Italy was distinguished by the emphasis the fascist regime placed on mass organizing. This emphasis, although certainly exaggerated by the internal political dynamics of dictatorship, must be seen as a response to two basic conditions. First, fascism had to come to terms with its obvious inability to appeal to workers as *workers*. Insofar as political allegiance followed class lines, Mussolini's regime could never hope to outbid the left. What is more, any too-explicit appeal to workers as "producers," or any too-close imitation of old strategies of socialist or syndicalist labor organizing always carried the risk of reduplicating within fascism's own corporatist institutions the class-based division of leftist politics – something fascism had to avoid if it was to maintain the support of the traditional elites. Second, the fascist regime faced a real obstacle to developing appeals on the basis of nonworkplace identities because of the absence of what might be called the natural modes of producing mass culture: through the growth of consumption, the extension of the mass media, and increased civic participation in state institutions and in the voluntary associations of the dominant class.[9] Italian economic growth, largely as a result of the regime's own policies, provided little or no basis for the rapid expansion of a mass domestic market. Geared to developing basic industries, to manufacturing producer goods at the expense of consumer commodities, it would in no way satisfy the wants of the lower middle class, fascism's only spontaneous base of support, let alone support the creation of a worker aristocracy or prosperous small peasantry. Moreover, in Italy, at least until the mid-twenties, the mass media were still only minimally developed, and the standard of living generally so low, that the state itself had to support their growth before the regime could exploit them to inculcate the proper fascist virtues of discipline, obedience, and struggle. Finally, the fascists lacked any solid base of mediating institutions that could readily be converted to their goal of making the "new Italian"; for the liberal elites had largely failed not only to establish the basic social and ed-ucational instructional services of the modern capitalist state, but even to form the literate public that elsewhere in Europe was considered to be the natural underpinning of a conservative civic culture.[10]

Organizing thus became central to the fascists' effort to build con-sent: organizing to build an institutional base and to compensate for abysmally low levels of consumption; organizing to discipline the re-calcitrant and rouse the apathetic; organizing to prevent the accumu-lation of power in the fascists' own, sometimes menacing trade union federations; organizing, in sum, to mediate the sharp class conflicts and ideological divisions of Italy as it emerged into the era of ration-alized industry, with all of the contradictions of its part-feudal, part–small entrepreneurial, part–monopoly capitalist base. Moving beyond the casual manipulations of worker community and home life typical of laissez-faire capitalism, and the empirical and local practice of nineteenth-century paternalists, the regime's own efficiency experts, moral reformers, government planners, and political functionaries scrutinized for their susceptibility to organizing an entire range of social activities, from sports and entertainment to child-rearing practices. From the mid-twenties on, with the foundation of the fascist trade union organizations as state institutions and the establishment of new

The culture of consent: mass organization in fascist Italy

party and government agencies, the social and the private domains were inexorably drawn into the public sphere, to be opened in the process to political manipulation by the Italian political and economic elites.

Nonetheless, fascism's decision to organize the "masses" outside of its original, almost wholly middle and lower middle class constituency, matured very slowly. Like all of the Duce's policies, the impulse behind it was pragmatic, or, better, opportunistic. It was a decision that ultimately was forced on the dictator by the need to confront a still lively popular opposition to his rule; taken to appease the "second wave" revolutionists among the syndicalists and "intransigents" in his own party; and fundamentally conditioned by big industry's demands for "order and hierarchy in all social relations."[11] Without these compelling pressures, it is doubtful whether Mussolini would ever have exceeded his original conservative mandate. His government would have continued to rely on his movement's "destructive" powers to subdue labor rather than exercising its "creative" energies to build a mass constituency. It would have persisted in seeing its own syndicalist organizations as a sort of momentary affliction – what in 1923 Mussolini had called a "physiological need in the growth of fascism" – seeking instead some base of labor support through those "experts in organizing" within the reformist leadership of the old General Confederation of Labor.[12] In the early twenties, certainly, the sole intimation of fascism's later zeal for organizing, besides its lukewarm support for an Italian variant of business unionism, was its avowed intent to "make the masses adhere to the state."

Vague though this slogan was, it summed up with typically inflated rhetoric two widely shared perceptions about the character of associational life in prewar liberal Italy, myths of an imperfect past that were exploited by the fascists with their self-serving claims to be fulfilling the Risorgimento project of national unity. One was that liberal agnosticism had perpetuated a void between the state and the masses; the other, that this void had been filled by the antinational forces of socialism, bent on subverting national sovereignty by promoting an autonomous state within a state. These views found expression in various ways: in the complaints of a conservative liberal like Antonio Salandra, who decried the lack of "civic sentiment" among the Italian masses;[13] in the vehement denunciations by industrial spokesmen of workers whose "perceptions of the world" – unlike those of docile Anglo-American operatives – had been "deformed by expectations, aspirations, and superstitions totally extraneous to the economic functioning of society";[14] and, in a most comprehensive form, in the doomsday prophesying of Nationalists, like Alfredo Rocco, later the regime's foremost ideologue, who by late 1920 was predicting the imminent total crisis of the state as it "dissolved into a mass of particles, parties, associations, groups, and syndicates."[15] Whatever the differences among these views, the diverse interests they expressed, and the various solutions they implied, all shared a common perception: that a proper civic spirit was wanting and labor discipline entirely inadequate in the face of the competitive pressures on the resource-scarce Italian economy and the political ambitions of its leaders. For Italy to maintain its status among the great powers, for it to rebuild after war, for it to fulfill some immanent national mission, there was an impelling need for a strong authority to mobilize the nation's productive forces and to put an end once and for all to the "disruptive individualism" of the liberal polity and the "bolshevik anarchy" of the left.

These assessments of liberal "disorder" cannot, of course, be accepted at their face value; there was in fact no real vacuum between state and civil society in prefascist Italy in the sense that intermediate associations were lacking. Those that existed, however, as Rocco himself well understood, reflected the class conflicts of a rapidly industrializing society in far too transparent a way to act in what might be called a "Tocquevillian" sense; that is, as socially stabilizing, politically moderate forces.[16] The hundreds of bourgeois benevolent societies, the lay and ecclesiastical *oratori*, the secularized congregations of charity and the Catholic *opere pie* – the heritage of centuries of Christian almsgiving, of burgher and guild solidarity – frequently worked at cross purposes. Moreover, they were far too parochial in their effect to reestablish the influence of the Italian elites in the face of an increasingly politicized worker sociability.[17] Rather than suffering from a scarcity of institutions, civil society in prewar Italy, if we use the categories of liberal sociology, might be said to have become "overpoliticized" from the failure to develop one particular kind of mediating institution: the apolitical and intraclass civic association that in a now vast literature on voluntary associations is identified as the hallmark of a healthy liberal social order for its ability to involve citizens, regardless of class background or political belief, in common projects of self- and social betterment.[18] From another perspective, it could be said that the economic affirmation of Italy's new industrial elites had failed to find a corresponding ideological expression in their social and cultural agencies: Unlike industrial America, whose self-confident business leadership early affirmed its preeminence in civic society through the likes of Rotary clubs and the YMCA, the elites of old Italy, as the Italian marxist Antonio Grasmci observed in the early thirties, conserved their preindustrial institutional heritage in jesuitical networks and freemasonic allegiances.[19]

The failure in liberal Italy to develop what one reformer described as "more modern, effective, and rational" forms of social solidarity,[20] testified above all to the deep social and ideological divisions within the prefascist ruling class – between rural and industrial, Catholic and lay, liberal and conservative. Industrial growth in Italy had come later and been far less intense than in England or Germany; the business classes, ruling over insular company villages or settled in long-established towns, were never confronted with the overwhelming bleakness of the Manchesters or Liverpools or the menacing gap between riches and squalor that impressed a "class consciousness of sin" in the Victorian mind and, as Beatrice Webb suggested, inspired the British bourgeoisie to its displays of philanthropy.[21] Nevertheless, in Italy, after the turn of the century, in response to the rapid growth of the socialist movement, several prominent nationalists and liberal reformers had called for a complete overhauling of the institutions of private beneficence through the enactment of a nationwide Poor Law and the long-overdue reform of the state educational system.[22] But there could be no agreement on a single project: The socialists naturally resisted any additional state regulation, on the entirely legitimate ground that any measure justifying further government restrictions on associational activity was bound to be used by the prefects to harass socialist workingmen's clubs; the Catholics were equally opposed for fear that the liberals would use such means to curb church influence; while the industrialists too resisted, claiming that government regulation would infringe on private enterprise in addition to swelling what they considered to be already superfluous expenditures on social welfare.[23] Before the fascists could even contemplate developing any new institutional base for their own consolidation of power, they would first of all have to unify the Italian elites themselves around some single project of reform.

This unity was initially constructed, if only in a very superficial and negative way, in the bourgeois *jacquerie* led by the fascist squads in 1920–1 against the prosperous club life of reformist socialism. The primary target of this violence was the far-flung network of perhaps ten thousand party sections, unions, cooperative ventures, friendly societies, "popular" universities, reading circles, and so on, loosely grouped under the banner of Italian socialism. Though they were rarely the hotbeds of revolution the fascists claimed them to be, they had indeed given an enormous impetus to the worker offensive in the "red years" of 1919–20, as the centers of what can only be described as a socialist "counterculture."[24]

The flourishing club life of the industrial suburbs, artisan *borgate*, and rural towns of the northern agricultural plains was truly national when Italian politics as a whole was still parochial and personalized; democratic, when most Italians were excluded from the vote; genuinely popular when the public and private institutions of the liberal state were class-bound and exclusive. Membership, like that in the socialist party itself, extended beyond the industrial proletariat proper, which in 1914 still comprised under a fifth of the active population, to embrace many of the have-nots of liberal society: those who, as the statues of one rural club indicated, "for lack of sufficient means, must earn their living principally through labor in the fields and workshops, from small commerce, or from low-paid work as elementary school teachers, town clerks, and the like."[25] So field laborers and factory operatives mixed along with their families in the "peoples' houses" at the city edges, easing the split between urban and rural life; craftsmen and shop floor mechanics met in the town chambers of labor, uniting older traditions of artisan mutualism with the new militant mass labor unionism. In Italy, the socialist leadership exercised none of the stern regulatory authority used by German social democracy to define the operations of its auxiliaries. Consequently those functional distinctions of a "modern" and specialized kind – among party offices, trade union locals, theater groups, or mutual funds – remained for the most part blurred, with single associations comprising the entire range of social and cultural activity supporting the workers' struggle for emancipation – from aid to the sick and disabled and advice to emigrants to economic defense and political propaganda. Individually the circles had thus achieved a remarkable degree of autonomy by the "red years," and not only because of their basic self-sufficiency. In a very real way, they had remained outside of an admittedly still very inefficient bourgeois state, escaping attempts by the central government to control their conduct by refusing, as required by national law, to register their statutes with the public authorities.

In times of movement, this confusion of initiatives in single clubs naturally lent an extraordinary vitality to the worker advance; in times of reaction, however, it left the neighborhood meeting place, the rural circle, the small-town people's house highly vulnerable to attack. For the social and cultural life of workers was identified by local elites as being as much culpable for their "intransigent" conduct as their strictly economic organizations; the reading club and the local press were ultimately as threatening reminders of the fragility of bourgeois attainments as the explicitly economic pressure of the trade union local or the agrarian league. This explains why the social and cultural organizations of the Italian labor movement – the consumer cooperative, the recreational hall, the popular library, the uniformed gymnastic and bicycle squads – provoked such violent antipathy; and why the pillars of what one despairing reform socialist called that "marvellous construction . . . for a new world of civilization and justice" proved the first targets of the fascist bands, rather than the better protected, openly revolutionary communist sections.[26] Whether a more disciplined club life might better have resisted fascist attacks is beside the point; in the unequal battle that pitted paramilitary forces against defenseless peasants and workers, "the lorry against the *case del popolo*," the provincial outposts of the socialist movement fell one after another. By the end of 1921 the much-feared socialist state within a state lay in ruins.

Even when the working class associations had been smashed, the mixed forms of popular sociability they embodied remained a constant reference point for the fascists themselves: the models against which the newly emergent plans and politics of the modernizing fascist state had to be measured; and ultimately the structures onto which any new fascist system of mass organizing would be grafted. In the early twenties, certainly, fascism's reaction against the mix of economics and politics in working class associational life strongly reinforced its productivist concept of organizing labor. Whether this took the form of nationalist theorizing or came out of first-hand observations of worker club life by the provincial party bosses, the fascists' reasoning went much the same: The combination of political aspirations and economic demands in the socialist labor movement had confounded the ingenuous minds of the proletariat, leading it to make demands that the struggling Italian economy could not possibly sustain. To end this confusion, the fascists called for a new leadership for the working masses that would demonstrate the operations of what the syndicalist leader Rossoni called the "dinamica produttiva."[27] It would instruct workers in a simple lesson to the effect that nothing could be gained by causing Italy to lose her competitive edge in world markets and much could be won by supporting her economic aggrandizement through self-discipline on the job, moderation in demands, and whole-hearted cooperation with employers. In the corporate bodies that, for the fascists, would ideally replace parliamentary institutions as well as the organizations of an autonomous labor movement, labor and capital – the "active forces of production" – would finally obtain their direct and accurate representation. This corporatist model did not, however, take into account that only a fraction of the population was actually employed in the industrial-type enterprises to which it was best adapted, nor the many nonsyndical social and economic functions of the prefascist working class movement. But so long as there was no immediate prospect of implementing the corporations, as was the case in the early twenties, the fascist movement could ignore the complexity of working class associational life, together with a more fundamental dilemma: Insofar as any production-based organizing reflected the real economic interests of workers, it was inimical to capital; to the extent that it reflected those of business, it was odious to many workers.

The mid-twenties, however, saw a shift in fascism's labor policy from a simple strategy of "disorganizing" to a more sustained attempt, in Mussolini's often-repeated words, to "bring the masses into the state"; the focus on production that had characterized the fascist syndicalists' schemes in the early twenties was gradually extended to organizing outside of the workplace through the fascist party's auxiliaries. The initial incentive was economic. From 1922, Mussolini's rule had been graced by prosperity that was as much the result of the reopening of international markets as of his laissez-faire policies. By late 1924, however, Italy, like other European countries, faced inflation and increasingly competitive foreign markets. Elsewhere in Europe, the resulting monetary instability had exposed serious cracks in postwar governing coalitions, with the middle classes, identifying the causes of unsound currency in inflated wage schedules and unbalanced budgets, forming antilabor coalitions with big business.[28] In Italy, obviously, Mussolini did not have to appeal to any parliamentary majority, for elections were effectively abolished after January 1925. Nonetheless, by the middle of 1926, as the lira dropped to 155 to the pound sterling, the fascist dictator had become convinced that this regime would survive or fall over the question of sound currency; Mussolini, writing to his Finance Minister Volpi in August 1926, vowed he would disprove that "authoritarian regimes are incapable of saving depreciated currencies and overcoming the social role of the postwar period," this without having recourse to "ostentatious collaborations" to rally public support.[29] Acting on the assumption that police measures could handle any opposition, Mussolini committed his government to pegging the lira at *quota novanta*, or 90 lire to the pound, a goal that was achieved fourteen months later after a jolting deflationary crisis. Simultaneously, the regime stepped up its intervention in the economy to correct some of the imbalances that were identified as underlying causes of monetary instability: industry's dependency on imported producer goods and raw and semifinished materials, the lack of capital for industrial investment, the inadequacy of agricultural output to meet internal demand, and finally, the narrowness of the domestic market. Through a combination of tariffs, subsidies, tax incentives, and support for research and resource exploitation, the regime laid the basis for what recent studies of the fascist economy have characterized as a "dynamic though distorted" period of growth.[30]

The definition of what the economist Saibante characterized as the "fascist reorganization of production"[31] had both immediate and long-term implications for developing a specifically fascist strategy of mass organizing. In the first place, it created an immediate need for an institutional network that was both responsive to the government and had numerous local extensions. The revaluation crisis, experienced by industrial workers from 1926 to 1929 in the form of real wage losses of 25 percent, work speed-ups, and unemployment rates of 15 percent produced such a spate of strikes and other "demonstrations of illegality" that Mussolini was led to describe 1927 as a "particularly gray and difficult year" for his regime: For the dictator the crisis was indeed far worse than the "political–moral" one after the Matteotti assassination in 1924;[32] and perhaps it seemed so because he himself had been so confident of the efficacy of the strong-arm tactics that had reached their legal extreme with the passage of the special police laws of November 1926. What seemed to disturb Mussolini most, however, was neither worker agitation in itself, nor even the taunts of antifascists about the futility of coercive measures – "castor oil can't intimidate Wall Street and city bankers," "iron bars won't raise foreign exchanges"[33] – but rather, the negative response of most Italians to official exhortations. For Mussolini, as for his chief economic advisor, Minister of the National Economy Belluzzo (a wartime engineer at the Ansaldo Ironworks), the success of national retooling required "battles"; and battles for the lira, for grain, or for national savings could evidently not be won without what Mussolini in mid-1926 characterized as the "general economic mobilization of [Italy's] citizens as means and agents of production," meaning, as he further specified, the "real conscription, a real civic and economic recruitment of all Italians."[34]

In conceptualizing the kind of institutional transformation that had to accompany economic retooling, the fascists substituted the more current metaphors of industrial modernity for the vocabulary of wartime mobilization. Thus they appropriated the term "rationalization," which was commonly used throughout Europe by the mid-twenties to refer specifically to industrial cost-cutting. Used indiscriminately with other terms and techniques associated with the most advanced capitalist technology – Americanism, fordism, scientific management –

fascist rationalization denoted a state intervention to eliminate those inefficient, class-ridden associations that hitherto had prevented single managements from effective planning; the setting up of new, reliable institutions where government agencies were previously few or lacking; and, finally, the consolidation of the corporate organizations of the regime to promote labor-management harmony.[35] Rationalization was thus tantamount to that "rigorous organization" which Mussolini wrote to the inventor Marconi, was required in a country as "poor and densely populated as Italy . . . to resolve difficult problems rapidly, to avoid the waste of energy, money, and time."[36] In other words, as he told the Third Congress on Scientific Management, it meant "unity of command and direction, forbidding the dissipation of forces and energies" at the top;[37] and throughout the society it called for the alignment of all social relations to the needs of production. Whereas in the United States, corporate rationalization itself produced a sort of ripple effect through the surrounding community, and then swept American society as a whole with a wave of capitalist modernity, in Italy, the fascist regime, under pressure from big business and impelled by its own desire to discipline its capacity to cope with the complexities of a technological society, proposed the creation of the essential supports for industrial reorganization from the top down.

It was inevitable in this context that the initial development of the framework for fascist mass organizing was guided by the primacy of economics. Thus in 1927 the fascist party itself was turned from political activism toward engaging the masses in what *Critica fascista* characterized as the "greatest battle that the Nation had ever decided to fight."[38] The economic emergency was similarly used to justify the rapid consolidation of the fascists' monopoly over youth groups, worker leisure-time activities, the women's *fasci*, and the local associations for mothers' and children's welfare. The fascist syndicates too, now established as state institutions by the Law of 3 April 1926, constituted one more aspect of what the economist Gangemi described as the "regime's contribution to rationalization."[39] These bureaucratic measures, however, so self-consciously reflecting the existing relations of production in their concern to organize the Italians as "producers," still paid little attention to addressing the underlying sources of political instability that resided in the continued absence of any sustained participation by the working population in state institutions.

In the long term, the political economy defined by Italian fascism in 1926–7 not only precluded any real integration of workers and peasants through the economy itself, but also exacerbated class and social tensions. Government economic intervention, while supporting Italy's transformation from a half-industrial/half-agricultural country into a predominantly industrial nation, aggravated the decades-old imbalances in economic growth: between a few protected monopolies and the proliferation of small, unmechanized firms; between an efficient, mainly northern capitalist agriculture and the large stretches of semi-feudal landholding in the southern regions; between, finally, the increased productive capacity of a heavy industry supported by state subsidies and armaments contracts and a disproportionately narrow domestic outlet. The potentially equilibrating benefits of mass consumption were lacking, even while the Italian population suffered from all of the dislocations attendant on a normal capitalist development: from urbanization and a further enclosure of agricultural lands to growing concentrations of workers in big industries and government offices. The result was a profoundly unstable social system, which, in addition to assiduous policing, demanded a social intervention by the state at least as broad as that in the economy and political institutions.

The shortcomings of a productivist model of mass organizing were further exposed during the Depression; the corporate "superstructure," as Carmen Haider described it in 1929, "built on the lack of interest of the masses and applied only in its exterior forms," proved demonstrably incapable of containing labor unrest.[40] Threatened by the reports of renewed communist militancy and social Catholic activism, after rural tax revolts, strikes, and unemployment riots in the winter-spring of 1930–1, Mussolini called for the full-scale social mobilization of his regime: "If there are vested interests that act as obstacles, we shall smash them," he declared in October 1931, announcing the new fascist strategy of "reaching out to the people."[41] There were some within the party leadership, like the PNF secretary Starace, who initially conceived of this strategy along the lines of the Communist *agitprop*, as a fascist *political* action among the masses; though if the party had actually succeeded in finding the loyal clerk, student, worker, or peasant who would "proselytize among his fellows in the office, classroom, factory, or field" on behalf of the regime,[42] it would doubtless have realized the inappropriateness, indeed the danger inherent in agitational models of organizing. In contrast, "reach out to the people" was a strategy of pacification, of responding to small-scale social demands in a personalized way rather than by rallying workers around major political and economic issues. As the communist *Stato operaio* pointed out in 1932, it was a question of mobilizing the already existing fascist organizations: of "reminding the regime's own forces in the most emphatic way possible that their relations with the masses

The concert room of the Chamber of Labor of Torino, wrecked by fascist gangs on April 26, 1921; one of the more than three hundred working-class associations destroyed during the six-month fascist offensive against reformist labor movements mounted after November 1920. *Source: Fascismo, inchiesta socialista sulle gesta dei fascisti in Italia,* Rome, 1963.

constitute a real problem that could become still more serious if a truly revolutionary situation were to develop."[43] From late 1931, the fascist regime, at the same time as it stepped up its intervention in the economy by "socializing" capitalist losses, pushed the further extension of its mass organizations outside of the workplace into urban neighborhoods,

15

small towns, and even isolated rural areas. By the mid-thirties, along-side of the sprawling fascist syndicates and professional associations, there were, in addition to nearly 20,000 *dopolavoro* recreational circles, thousands of veterans' organizations, *fasci* for women, "rural house-wife" sections, Fascist University Groups, or GUF, *balilla* for little boys, Young Italian units for girls, and Wolf Cub circles for the smallest "new Italians." These were truly mass organizations, not only because of their several million members, but because they intentionally grouped people by sex, by social group, by age, and by activity to prevent any autonomous expression of class identity or class alliance.

Among these, the network of fascist recreational circles occupied a special place as the largest of the regime's adult organizations, the least overtly political, and the most variegated in its institutional forms. Cutting across all sectors of the society, its activities comprised vir-tually everything that in the twenties and thirties was defined as "mass culture." Precisely because it exploited social roles and needs outside of the workplace, the *dopolavoro* organization shows especially well, the means of ideological and social persuasion developed by fascism to build a responsive public among industrial workers, peasants, and salaried employees – that is, among people whose previous associa-tional traditions and economic treatment under one dictatorship made them strongly resistant to any explicitly political appeal.

The mixed character of its origins and the variety of functions it was called on to play made the *dopolavoro* organization from the outset a hybrid institution. In the course of twenty years, it was at one time or another a technocratic scheme, a fascist trade union recreation hall, a state regulatory agency, and a fascist party auxiliary. From one point of view, the organization was a hierarchically ordered bureaucracy under the direction of the Opera Nazionale Dopolavoro or OND; from another, a hodgepodge of several thousand disparate circles. The in-itiatives behind these local groups were both popular and elitist; per-haps one-half of the total in their first formation predated the fascist seizure of power, including not only the surviving working class clubs – ex-reform socialist, ex-democratic, and most rarely ex-commu-nist – but also the small-town bourgeois *circolo* and hundreds of peas-ant hang-outs; another sixth were run directly by industrial and commercial firms on behalf of their employees, or by the government ministries for their personnel; about a third, located primarily in rural areas, were established on entirely new bases by the fascist regime itself. A political organization insofar as it was directed by the fascist party, the *dopolavoro* was also a social service agency and at the local level the promoter of official cultural directives. The fascists themselves were divided as to the import of this multifaced institution: For technocratic reformers, it was the ultimate social engineering project, a nationalized YMCA as it was called by the "revisionist" Bottai;[44] for the Fascist party, an opportunity to undercut the competition of the fascist unions; for the irreverent, the fascist answer to Roman circuses – a "syndicalist Salvation Army," as it was described by Curzio Malaparte, "the consummate expression of a Candide-like optimism."[45]

How does one study an organization that is neither wholly political, nor social, nor cultural in any traditional sense, state promoted yet sustained by the participation of millions of members? The *dopolavoro* cannot be seen wholly from "above" as an agency of social or cultural control or social modernization, operating according to some clear-cut capitalist design: That would be to exaggerate both the coherence of fascist projects and the ease of their implementation. If we discount fascism's rhetoric of omnipotence, we find that its schemes were as much bounded by elite squabbling, provincial rancors, and the resistance of its subjects as any technocratic utopia from the Enlightenment to the present. A history "from below," on the other hand, while it may highlight the tenaciousness of popular customs and the undoubted persistence of class tensions, risks underestimating significant transformations in what might be called the "social location" of worker associations. The personnel, sometimes even the roster of pastimes of a single club, may be found to have remained virtually unchanged over a period of many years, even while the place of the group in the totality of social relations had been profoundly altered by being resituated in a more complex web of mediating institutions.

Nor can the history of the *dopolavoro*, as a *mediating* institution, be separated from the history of the relations between state and civil society. The fascist organization of worker leisure-time activities resulted from a balance between state intervention and private initiative that was entirely different from that prevailing in liberal democracies; and the ways in which national strategies interacted with local interests have to be taken into account in any analysis of the specific character of this fascist variety of mediating institution. Fascism had appropriated, and, of course, fundamentally transformed the idea of the voluntary nongovernmental social service organization; and the regime sometimes exercised significant political leverage to persuade businessmen that it was in their class interest to support an organization that in its exterior form and social functions was similar to those employer-supported voluntary associations that one American sociologist

17

has identified as the "community expression of the private enterprise system."[46] This sometimes forced intersection of interests meant that the *dopolavoro* was often called upon to perform double duty; as social mediator and disciplinarian of labor. While the former function was defined by the fascist regime itself, the latter was usually determined by the needs of local sponsors. In theory, the smooth-running corporatist state had eliminated all such petty distinctions between parochial managerial goals and the overriding interests of the nation – the patriotic citizen and the dedicated producer were one and the same. In fact, the economic priorities of business were not always compatible with fascist political objectives, nor the interests of local elites with those of the national government.

The lopsided character of capitalist growth under fascism, reinforcing the historically deep divisions between city and countryside, suggested a primary distinction to be confronted by this study: between the industrial sector and rural society. When large business corporations sponsored *dopolavoro* facilities in their enterprises, they were behaving much like paternalistic business employers elsewhere, but with one significant difference: In Italy, these social services were not only tools of personnel management, but also local extensions of the fascist mass organization. As such, the formation of these company groups, or *dopolavoro aziendali*, reveals at one level how employers became more favorably disposed to managing their personnel with techniques of persuasion; at another level, it reveals how a traditionally self-isolating industrial establishment recast its relations with the community and the state as a whole. In the Italian countryside, on the other hand, the recreational circles were conceived as a means for involving previously isolated rural inhabitants in a public life that increasingly was shaped by the exigencies of the industrial sector – an ambiguous purpose, as we shall see, since the regime also expected the village groups to reinforce the traditionalist culture of the peasant community as a support for fascist conservatism.

The regime was equally active in a third area of Italian society, one that cannot be precisely classified as "sectoral," although it encompassed a considerable number of people employed in the tertiary sector of the economy. This was the state administration itself, rapidly expanding after 1930 as the fascist regime greatly increased the regulating and coordinating tasks of government. The recreational associations in the public administration were parallel in importance to those considerably more numerous groups in industrial firms and rural areas, not primarily because they enrolled a quarter of all the members of the OND, but because in their high visibility they set the patterns of leisure consumption for Italy's growing "new" middle classes.

This study is not, however, solely concerned with the process and pattern of organizing. These are important only insofar as they provide indications of the regime's ability to engage mass participation, and thereby as a measure, however imprecise, of the aims and effects of fascist policies. The regime's own statistics on rates of membership are, at first reading, baffling figures, even ludicrous when one thinks of Salvemini's properly sardonic comments on the fascist mania for counting.[47] What did it mean that three million persons out of a wage-earning population of nearly eleven million (1936) were members; or, on the local level, that in a Tuscan hill town with 3,500 inhabitants in 1931, 128 persons were enrolled in the fascist recreational club? Such figures might seem insignificant, if not simply meaningless, unless several considerations are kept in mind. First, the fascists had not won the voluntary allegiance of most workers; they always confronted millions of exploited laborers, many of whom viewed the regime's policies with deep if ineffectual resentment; any significant degree of participation in fascist organizations is from this point of view remarkable. Second, the number of potential joiners was always more restricted than the figures on the active population aged eighteen or above would suggest; an organization that capitalized on the desire for recreation, without taking special compensatory measures, inevitably discriminated against the old, against women (especially married ones), and against family men, who could ill afford time off or the small expense for organized sports or outings. Finally, the meaning of nonparticipation itself is not at all clear: Rather than being diehard resisters against the regime, those who did not join, in the vast majority, were perhaps the most socially isolated, the least conscious of collective aims, and the least able to form any collective criticism of the regime.

If Mussolini's bombastic "all in the state, nothing outside of the state" is taken too literally, there would also be some difficulty in explaining the enormous variety of groups left outside of this avowedly totalitarian organization: the parish circles under the cautious leadership of Catholic Action, the dozens of new Rotary clubs, the private meeting places of bourgeois gentlemen, as well as the quantities of plebeian bars whose numbers, Mussolini boasted in 1927, had finally been reduced by 25,000 to 162,000![48] The fascists practiced what might be described as a "selective totalitarianism," although it was more pervasive than the "limited pluralism" of Franco's Spain and it had little of the compulsive thoroughness of the notorious Nazi *Gleich-*

schaltung, or "synchronization."[49] The Italian fascists were generally not inclined to expend excessive energy regulating groups that posed no obvious threat to their rule. Nor did they seek to extend state or party control into areas of civil life where a responsive audience would have served no immediate political or economic end. There was a clear pattern to what the fascists left alone – the bourgeois gathering place, the apolitical parish circle, the irrepressible street corner hang-out – just as there was a distinct pattern to what they destroyed, restricted, and controlled.

But what did participation mean if it is to be understood as more than a mere presence in the organization? Was it in any way to be equaled with that "consent" sought by the regime after 1926? Consent is sometimes defined as a favorable public opinion, something subject to being ascertained scientifically at the ballot box or by polling. The assumption that such opinions are freely given, if not freely formed, could never be sustained for fascist Italy; nor, as some recent studies of the regime have implied, is it possible to deduce from the personal charisma of the Duce or from the propaganda bombardments of the Ministry of Popular Culture the existence of a generalized consensus in favor of the regime.[50] In fact, the popular voice, so ebullient in the "red years," becomes silent with the suppression of the organized opposition after 1925, and except for two brief moments of protest in 1927–8 and 1930–1, it is almost entirely absent through most of the thirties. The institutional indicators of popular sentiment – strikes, work slowdowns and stoppages, as well as the miscellaneous "collective disturbances" recorded by the police – become increasingly difficult to read, not so much because they were filtered through the fascist apparatus of surveillance, but because they completely lacked the vibrancy they had when they were publicly known and open expressions of the workers' movement. Even the fascist government had only an approximate idea of people's attitudes toward the regime in spite of the constant flow of reports from Mussolini's "natural organs of information" – the prefects, quaestors, and royal *carabinieri* – and from the many new agents of surveillance – from freelance informers (*fiduciari*) to Bocchini's efficient OVRA. For every fascist functionary dissembled in some way, exaggerating, embellishing, or concealing, and few people were ever so foolish as to admit their true opinions about the regime. What finally makes the search for an "authentic" vox populi so futile is that the regime itself, for most of its rule, as long as it had some degree of cooperation, was perfectly satisfied with silence, no matter whether this masked indifference or disapproval.

20

Indeed the organization of consent cannot be equated simply with the molding of public opinion. Rather than the degree of extent of support for fascism, we must look for the social-institutional and cultural transformations that were brought about as a result of the fascists' search for a responsive public. The fascist intervention in leisure-time activities was most successful, as might be expected, when the social needs of the participants corresponded to the interests of local elites, the aspirations of the organized to the aims of the organizers. These points of contact were neither generated spontaneously nor easily maintained, precisely because of the dual nature of the organization – as a political extension of the state and as a social institution deeply embedded in civil society. While this tension was never fully resolved by the regime, some measure of equilibrium was attained by the mid-thirties through the artificial creation of a sense of overriding "national" identity. This identity was achieved at both a structural and an ideological level, on the one hand, by the appropriation of popular associational forms and ideological motifs, and, on the other, by the imposition of dominant institutions and beliefs.

Understood in these terms, the organization of consent may be identified as an essential aspect of the achieving of class hegemony. Here one speaks of hegemony in the way Gramsci uses it in the *Prison Notebooks* to signify the establishment of an integral form of class rule that exists not only through the economic preeminence and political might of the dominant classes, but also through the active involvement of subaltern groups in their social and cultural experiences.[51] In his reflections on the mechanisms of bourgeois rule in stabilized societies, the Italian marxist distinguished between the two superstructures of society on the basis of their exercise of different functions: on the one hand, civil society, which he defined as the "ensemble of organizations commonly called 'private'" – among which should be placed what in this study have been called mediating institutions – on the other, political society or the state apparatus, which has the function of "direct rule." In the former, classes contend ideologically to determine how the society should be organized, with the dominant groups succeeding or failing in creating support or consent for the established order; the latter functions to secure its acceptance by coercion or by the threats of force. In all societies, whether liberal-democratic or authoritarian, some balance is struck between coercion and consent, depending largely on the degree of cohesion and self-consciousness of the dominant social groups. In this sense, the organization of a culture of consent, as it is analyzed in this book, must be understood first of all as involving the self-organization of Italy's capitalist classes; a self-organization that was largely achieved under fascist leadership, first as a reaction against the postwar working class offensive, then through the incitements of the fascist political elites, and finally as a result of the process of mass organizing itself. The capacity of the regime to unify a hitherto fragmented ruling coalition around a common project was nowhere more visible than in its ability to engage thousands of business sponsors and middle class cultural organizers in a new kind of bourgeois voluntarism.

As it is presented by Gramsci, the concept of hegemony would, however, appear more readily applicable to the study of liberal-democratic regimes than to a fascist dictatorship, especially if the dictatorial apparatus of the state completely absorbs civil society, as "totalitarian" interpretations of fascism sustain.[52] For, as Gramsci held, true hegemony is ultimately generated in civil society by persuasion, through what might be described as a class struggle of ideas and institutions. In their search for consent, the fascists did in fact intrude into civil society; by using the state apparatus itself to legitimate their rule, they truly eliminated any meaningful distinction between force and consent. Nevertheless, the ultimate effectiveness of any state initiative as a means of legitimation depended on its capacity to take root in civil society. This ultimately meant involving local elites in the organizing effort; it also meant responding to the social needs of constituents to the point where the responsiveness of local organizations to fascist directives was even called into question. In some sectors, local businessmen and middle class professionals did indeed take advantage of this state intervention to (so to speak) redress the balance in favor of agencies of persuasion, to develop cultural institutions commensurate with their economic power. In these instances, we seem justified in speaking of the formation of a new hegemonic order – a precariously balanced one, to be sure, because of its high degree of identification with the fascist regime and with the state apparatus, but reinforcing nonetheless the interests of Italy's traditional elites in a stabilized capitalism. This fundamental transformation in the way in which political power had previously been exercised in Italy was thus supported by a change in the organization of the state itself: Even by the mid-thirties it was apparent that the narrowly based state of the liberal era, so strikingly precarious in its lack of effective mediating institutions, had become a more complex, resistant state, sustained by a capillary network of associations with vast powers of social and cultural persuasion.

To emphasize this noncoercive face of fascism might lead to conclusions that are as misleading as those which maintain that the dictatorships of the thirties constitute wholly different political and economic *systems* from liberal capitalist rule. It is true that the regime in Italy, holding power during the two decades most crucial to the transformation of capitalism from laissez-faire to monopolistic forms, exposed, by its authoritarian deformations, certain complicated hidden mechanisms of power, whose workings have come to be understood only gradually: through slow accretions of bureaucratic reform; the covert accumulation of power in the marketplace; and the innumerable apparently casual decisions of pluralist political systems. But that fascism is somehow inherent in all advanced capitalism, with its one-dimensional leveling, increasingly centralized bureaucratic apparatus, or interventionist political economy, is neither an assumption nor a conclusion of this study. Quite the contrary. At the point where the fascist and liberal forms of rule were apparently most similar, the distinguishing features of each stood in sharpest contrast. The major possibility of building consent in liberal-democratic regimes was bound up with a pluralist associational life, the expansion of consumption, increased social and geographic mobility, and the influence of the mass media, while in fascist Italy, it must always be remembered, force was both the premise and a constant threat. Under this shadow, the effort to build consent was state sponsored and mediated, but with insistent pressure, by fascist mass organizing.

2

The politics of after-work

The technocratic origins

As an idea, the *dopolavoro* was the American-inspired invention of a technocratic reformer. As an institution, it owed its origins solely to the political opportunism of the fascist movement's trade union organizations. First presented in Italy as a scheme for a company social service by Mario Giani, the former manager of the Westinghouse Corporation's subsidiary at Vado Ligure, it might have remained one of many similarly simpleminded "paper" projects for improving labor–management relations in the early twenties, had it not been for the need of the National Confederation of Fascist Syndicates to attract a worker following and assuage employers' fear of fascist militancy at the same time.[1]

For the early policy of fascism toward labor organization was entirely "productivist," based on the primacy of the workplace, utilizing the fascist unions where possible to gain the allegiance of the workers, and force where necessary to discipline them. At their most comprehensive, fascist schemes for the restructuring of the state envisaged the formation of corporations. Whether controlled by an authoritarian state in the version proposed by the Nationalists,[2] or assisted by "councils of experts" as preferred by the "revisionist" technocrats,[3] or simply consisting of the mixed employer–worker associations as urged by the syndicalists, there was little if any thought given to the organization of the workforce outside the factory or off the fields. The new national consciousness trumpeted by Mussolini and his followers was a producer's ethic, and it seldom or never addressed itself to the question of leisure time.

But the fascist syndicalists, led by the ex-revolutionary socialist Edmondo Rossoni, found themselves in an ambiguous position after Mussolini was installed in power with conservative support.[4] The socialist unions were still active, while their own capacity to attract workers was severely hindered by the need to operate within the parameters prescribed by the fascist leadership. They themselves had

24

hoped to utilize the well-tried techniques of labor organizing – strikes and labor slowdowns – gradually building up a national labor constituency to force the transformation of the state toward corporativism.[5] However, their appeals for "rule by corporations" were opposed by the business elites who supported the new government; calls for the workers themselves to take up a "struggle of expertises" were blocked by the PNF as inimical to the party's immediate interest in attracting support from the industrialists; attempts to satisfy worker demands were precluded by Mussolini's injunction against strikes in March 1923. Thus hemmed in by their own political ambitions, the syndicalists were forced to conciliate employers and seek to attract a worker following by more indirect methods. In the course of 1923 they rapidly assimilated Nationalist, technocratic, and business views on how to form the model citizen-producer, becoming "experts" on worker education, technical instruction, factory hygiene and safety, social welfare, and recreation.[6] Their programs now emphasized the class collaboration and increased labor productivity that would stem from proper vocational training, the restorative and morally uplifting effects of recreation, and the education of workers in the "national interest."[7]

The syndicalist dilemma was underscored most sharply by the passage of the first Eight-Hour Bill in March 1923: They were nothing if not embarrassed by Mussolini's enactment of a traditional socialist demand, now presented as a first "fascist" act of social legislation to appease the reformist General Confederation of Labor (CGL) and, hopefully, to attract some of its "organizing experts" into the fascist ranks. Unable to support wholeheartedly the measure, which in the event was only token in its effects (having the real effect of lengthening the working day while holding down wages),[8] syndicalist spokesmen concentrated on its implications for the use of leisure time. "Far more serious than the problem of work itself," stated Armando Casalini the day the bill was passed, is the "problem of after-work [*dopolavoro*]." The increase of free time implied its proper use on behalf of productive work; eight hours under fascism should not mean a "socialist Cockaigne where eight hours of work means three or four," or where workers frittered away their leisure in "politics" or the "banal imitation of bourgeois vices."[9]

In using the neologism of Mario Giani, coined in 1919 to denote his industrial welfare work scheme, this leading syndicalist spokesman was signaling his movement's interest in any proposition that might, under the guise of enhancing managerial efficiency, at the same time provide some tangible benefits for labor, and thereby render the fascist syndicalist program more appealing. Giani's original blueprint, distributed in some forty thousand privately printed circulars to industrialists in 1920, was, in its initial conception at least, hardly appropriate for union organizing. The recreational facilities the American-trained engineer proposed were no more than an update of the "cradle to grave" services favored throughout the history of company paternalism, from Robert Owen's New Lanark to Henry Ford's Sociology Department.[10] They were to be organized "scientifically" in keeping with the latest advances in management practice, and were especially recommended for accustoming workers to the discipline of "taylorized" heavy industries. In this form, his plan had in fact met with no response from business, and little initially from the fascist movement besides an empty promise of support from Mussolini's brother, Arnaldo.[11] Until March 1923 Giani's scheme was known only through his own indefatigable propagandizing, the small "institute" in Rome that he established in 1919, and his journal, *Il Dopolavoro*, founded with private funding in February 1923. The "fascist" content of his plan was evidently no more than a thin veneer of ingratiating polemic on an Americanizing frame: Giani's measures for worker uplift, so he claimed, had much in common with fascism's own effort "to bring about class harmony by the moral and physical improvement of its following."[12]

It was just this technocratic affect, however, that in March of 1923 attracted syndicalist organizers: Giani was invited to contribute to the movement's newspaper almost simultaneously with Casalini's editorial: Equally opportunistically he dutifully modified his plans to fit syndicalist theory. Casting his new *dopolavoro* in terms of organizing rather than of management, he transformed its image from a company personnel department into a trade union circle, or "center of uplift." No longer to be attached to a firm, this might be the center of recreation and instruction for an entire community or neighborhood, rural and urban. It should be self-financing insofar as possible, supported by membership dues in addition to contributions from well-to-do benefactors. In small towns, especially, it would be open to all residents regardless of their class, and not restricted solely to company employees. The programs of the circles consisting of "healthy" and "praiseworthy pastimes" would be selected according to "criteria of practicality, efficiency, and enlightened modernity"; they would be administered by trained "social secretaries" – familiar figures in American social engineering initiatives – careful to discourage frivolity. The ultimate goal was to convince workers that their emancipation would be achieved "not by struggle against capitalism, but by individual self-betterment."[13]

In this way, Giani's after-work institution emerged in its "syndicalist" version as a kind of recreational center, which while not dissimilar in form to the traditional workingman's club, still clearly bore the imprint of its Anglo-American industrial precedents. Giani's proposals, as Casalini had recognized, provided a ready answer to the syndicalists' urgent need to demonstrate special expertise in the organization of worker leisure. On 5 May 1923 Rossoni formally endorsed Giani's scheme; in the next several months Giani himself was invited to join the directory of the fascist Confederation, becoming coeditor with Casalini of the new syndicalist monthly, *La Stirpe*, and his institute was incorporated into the CNSF as the Central Office on After-Work.[14]

By December 1923, the fascist syndicalists had drawn up comprehensive guidelines for the establishment of what were now generally known as "*dopolavoro* circles." In its general structure, this project for a syndicalist *dopolavoro* embodied all the opportunistic tactics and contradictory ideals of Rossoni's organization. On the one hand, it displayed the characteristics of a class-based organization; definitively antisocialist, it nevertheless conformed closely to the prefascist structure of working class associational life. Thus, in keeping with the democratic traditions of Italian workingmen's clubs, its administration would be elected by club members and a union representative (replacing Giani's "trained social secretary") would serve as a liaison between the group and the provincial headquarters of the Fascist Confederation. But unlike the socialists, who for decades had struggled to free worker associations from bourgeois sponsorship, syndicalist organizers were encouraged to involve local notables in the activities of the new centers; this seemingly was to be less for the edification of the workers themselves than to "enlighten the ruling classes with a sense of their responsibility and interest in bettering the lower classes."[15]

The most visible difference with respect to the socialist clubs was of course political. Socialist club life had been informed by a mobilizing conception of politics; and recreational activities, however mundane, were all explicitly manifestations of the movement itself. In the fascist circles, by contrast, class politics of this "traditional" kind were to be actively discouraged; instead, Rossoni proposed "education" in the most paternalistic sense of the word. The *dopolavoro* center was thus designed first of all to "attract and entertain" workers by promoting their "moral, physical, and intellectual improvement . . . without boring them"; at the same time it would instill in them the idea that "work is a sacred duty to the nation and to themselves." Such efforts on behalf of class collaboration were, of course, hardly disinterested: There was indeed a strong tension between the pacifying notion of a "center of uplift" and the barely concealed hope of using the *dopolavoro* to mobilize on behalf of the syndicalists' "revolution." If, as Rossoni maintained, its primary function was to provide CNSF officials with an opportunity "to make greater contact with the masses, thereby enlarging their sphere of propaganda," almost inevitably, in the event of a syndicalist offensive, the fascist recreational circle would itself become highly politicized.

In practice, the first groups were set up not in industry, where the competition with the left was sharpest and where the syndicalists most desired a base, but as a piecemeal process in the rural areas of the Po River basin, where Rossoni's unions had recruited a huge peasant following largely by intimidation. The earliest "fascist" recreational circles were thus no more than replacements for the old socialist clubs in the former strongholds of reformist socialism, where from late 1920 the *squadristi*, with backing from agrarian employers, had been especially active. The first *dopolavoro* on record was set up in July 1923 at Ponte all'Olmo in the province of Piacenza by Count Bernardo Barbiellini Amidei, the chief of the local *fascisti*. After ravaging scores of socialist associations in the spring of 1921, Barbiellini had established his own "peace," levying tithes on landowners, building up the fascist unions, and finally reopening the "ex-subversive" groups under syndicalist auspices. By 1923, he was the undisputed arbiter of the life of the province: His cohorts, "those same *squadristi* of yesteryear," as they were portrayed by the fascist deputy Acerbo on a visit to his home province in September, "were now dedicating themselves to social work and worker education and presided over cultural, educational, and welfare associations of singular importance."[16]

By far the largest number of *dopolavoro* sections – reportedly more than 100 with 13,000 members by mid-1924 – were located in the agrarian province of Novara, likewise a former bastion of reformist socialism. Unlike Piacenza, it had suffered relatively little damage from the "punitive" missions. The directors of the flourishing local cooperative movement, concerned to retain their influence and to preserve their associations from destruction, had quickly succumbed to fascist threats and accepted the protection of the syndicalists.[17]

In urban industrial areas, where the fascist unions faced entrenched hostility from production workers, the pace of organization was far slower. But in February 1924, Luigi Lojacono, the provincial secretary of the syndicates of Liguria, which drew their main strength from a large membership among dock workers, announced the opening of the headquarters of the Dopolavoro of Genoa. Lojacono, an experienced organizer who had founded the first Fascio d'Educazione Sociale in Milan in 1919, was unabashedly elitist and the statutes of his *dopolavoro* were aggressively paternalistic. On no account was the worker "to be left to his own devices in his free hours." The activities offered by the organization, including outings and sports, in addition to traditional pastimes such as choral singing and amateur theatricals, were designed to "instill in the workers a consciousness of the nation, a sense of duty, and a desire for harmony between labor and capital." The Genoese Dopolavoro was open solely to syndicalist members; those workers who were employed in sectors not yet controlled by the fascist unions would be issued temporary cards.[18]

Whereas in Piacenza and Novara the *dopolavoro* had forcibly replaced preexisting socialist circles, and in Genoa the impulse behind its foundation was clearly intraunion competition, in Naples, the major center of syndicalist activity in the South, the new institution expressed the desire for social camaraderie among a petty bourgeois constituency that was at least partly made up of war veterans. The Naples Dopolavoro, inaugurated in March 1924, was sponsored by Duke Andrea Carafa D'Andria, the general consul of the fascist militia, and included a lawyer named Oriani and the veteran Captain Arturo Sorrentino among its founders. Its statutes, acclaimed by the Central Office for their suitability to the Neapolitan environment, recalled certain Masonic oaths in their proposal to "impart an admiration for Beauty, a love of Righteousness, the need for Truth, and the discipline of Justice" among its members. However, unlike the traditional lodges, or the *circoli dei civili* common in the South, or the "sterile academies and so-called popular cultural associations" execrated by the Neapolitan syndicalists, the *dopolavoro* claimed to offer a practical education. This endeavor was to be supported by such modern facilities as a popular library containing reading materials on local industry and furnished with a slide projector, "intellectual refreshment centers," special bulletins on culture, sports, and a social service fund – all of which were to be financed by contributions from banks and industries, special fund-raising benefits, and membership contributions. Benefactors were to pay 3,000 lire initially, and not less than 500 lire in annual dues; sustaining members 100 lire and then 50 lire per year; ordinary members, that is, "true and proper workers," 1 lira or approximately 8 cents monthly. Membership was compulsory for all persons enrolled in the syndicates.[19]

In the short term the syndicalist circles generally met with indifference, if not with outright hostility from labor. Given any choice at all, workers remained faithful to their old meeting places. The old clubs indeed proved more resilient than the syndicalists had anticipated. Associations identified with the left were still the object of sporadic fascist violence after 1922, and from 1923 increasingly subjected to harassment by the public authorities. Nevertheless, in the relative calm that followed the widespread devastations of 1920–1, it was not uncommon for the modest "wine circles" of the rural north to reopen, while in a few of the more tranquil urban neighborhoods, the members of the *case del popolo* cleaned up the debris left by the squads and quietly undertook new subscriptions to refurbish the devastated premises. Indeed, the number of cultural and recreational associations on the revolutionary left even appears to have increased in 1923 as antifascist militants – the communists and maximalist socialists, in particular – responded to worker demand for sports, while at the same time seeking an apolitical camouflage for their gatherings. By the spring of 1923, despite the arrest of the greater part of the Communist party leadership, the police reported a suspicious growth in the number of sports clubs and outing societies associated with the APE (Associazione Anti-alcolica Proletaria Escursionistica) and the APEF (Associazione Proletaria Educazione Fisica), identifying the nuclei of reconstituted Communist party sections in many of the new groups set up in Milan, Turin, Naples, and several small cities. In Florence, as the communist mechanic Tagliaferri recalled, men and women no longer able to meet in the neighborhood *case del popolo* headed into the surrounding countryside "with the pretext of an outing, which was then in great vogue," going toward Settignano and Castel di Vincigliata, beyond Ponte all'Asse, into the forest of Terzzolina or up to the wooded hillsides of Fiesole, where they were finally able to debate the serious organizational problems faced by the party as it was forced into semi-clandestine activity by the fascist repression. On 14 July 1923, in an effort to support and unify these often spontaneous initiatives, the internationalist faction of the Socialist party (the so-called Terzini), in cooperation with the Communist party, founded a new weekly, *Sport e proletariato*. The bulletin had reached a circulation of 9,000 by December 1923, when the office of the press where it was printed in Milan (together with *Stato operaio*, *Sindacato rosso*, and other movement publications) was ransacked by fascist squads.[20]

The syndicalists had anticipated, of course, that their projects for worker uplift would meet with employer approval and that support from bourgeois benefactors would compensate for their inability to attract a spontaneous following among factory workers. Certainly employers in advanced industry had become convinced of the virtues of welfare work. With the restoration of employer authority in the factories after 1921, the managements of the Fiat automobile plants, Westinghouse, Michelin, the huge public utilities enterprise SIP, as well as textile firms and steel companies with well-established traditions of company paternalism, took advantage of the worker defeat to institute a wide range of social services in their firms.[21] But these were intended to reinforce managerial authority in the workplace and to undercut any form of union organizing, whether by left-wing unionists or by fascist syndicalists. Few employers seriously contemplated the cooperatively run facilities that, in the fascist syndicalists' view, would have "safe-guarded the workers' dignity and prestige" by guaranteeing them "the opportunity to express their own preferences and undertake their own initiatives."[22] Indeed, the syndicalist *dopolavoro* aroused some apprehension, especially among agrarian employers; it "looked too much like the red-tinted consumer cooperatives and wine circles traditionally organized by the proletarian masses," recalled A. Nicolato, the fascist *federale* of Pavia and a major landowner in the province.[23] Not until it was divested of its ties with the trade unions after 1925 would the *dopolavoro* gain a more receptive hearing from business.

The belief that the fascist labor organizations could effectively compete with the free labor movement, even with the advantages of government protection, was finally dispelled during the election campaign of the spring of 1924. The CNSF was particularly anxious to make a good showing in the first legislative elections held since the fascists had come to power. By emphasizing their concern for reformist initiatives aimed at improving work conditions, syndicalists hoped to broaden their voter appeal. Accordingly, they increased their propaganda for the *dopolavoro*. The day before the vote, on April 5, the press office of the CNSF furnished an overall panorama of its groups. The list was hardly impressive: In addition to the *dopolavoro* at Novara, Piacenza, Genoa, and Naples, it listed four at Turin, one at Leghorn, six at Lucca, one each at Padua, Avezzano, and Ferrara and a number of sections planned for the continental South and Sicily.[24]

The elections proved an enormous defeat for the syndicalists. Parliamentarism, compromise with business, and competition with non-fascist unions had brought them no closer to the corporatist revolution. Only 22 syndicalist deputies to the Chamber were returned, out of the total 374 seats contested, and the victory of the socialist FIOM during the spring shop floor committee elections confirmed beyond doubt that the industrial working class remained staunchly antifascist.

Even the more easily intimidated rural laborers were restive; wildcat

31

strikes during May in the most powerful of the fascist trade union federations at Bologna called into question the CNSF's ability to control its own disgruntled following in agriculture. At the third meeting of the National Council of the Corporations, convened on 23 May 1924, the syndicalists agreed that the time had come for the state to intervene on their behalf by sanctioning a single compulsory national union, with sole power to bargain with employers. To force the issue, a more radical group within the movement, critical of Rossoni's temporizing, began arguing against further collaboration with employers and for recourse to militant action.[25]

The ambivalence of the syndicalist position in mid-1924 inevitably affected the status of the *dopolavoro*. Giani was well aware that if the syndicalists abandoned methods of persuasion in favor of direct labor action against employers, his project would be placed in jeopardy. The *dopolavoro* needed ample funding that could not be afforded by the Corporations; yet as a union auxiliary it was precluded from "accepting charitable handouts." It demanded expert personnel, not rabble-rousers, systematic organization inspired by "modern criteria," not haphazard improvisations. Inevitably the ex-business manager Giani sided with the moderates in the CNSF leadership (including Rossoni) against the growing militancy of the union locals. "Our institutions," he emphasized in his special report to the May conference, "have to repudiate the obsolete methods of the popular universities and the demagogic incitements of subversive circles."[26] In July 1924 he began to press the government for legislation in support of a new national welfare agency that, unlike the existing social service organizations – the Red Cross, the National Commission on Emigration, the National Fund for Social Insurance, and the National Insurance Institute – promised to reach large "masses of the humble" through its numerous local sections. The assassination on September 12 of Armando Casalini, Giani's major ally in the syndicalist movement, made his requests for government support more urgent.[27]

The syndicalists, too, took advantage of the weakening of Mussolini's coalition government in the crisis following the fascists' murder of Matteotti in June 1924 by suddenly reversing their earlier position of autonomy with respect to the state apparatus. The CNSF leadership now called for the government to suppress altogether the antifascist labor movement and to enact legislation to regularize their own position within the state. In this context, Rossoni was now disposed to support Giani's call for government sponsorship of a nationalized *dopolavoro* network. A resolution calling on the government to set up a "national agency for after-work" that would develop "a complete set of measures for reeducating the laboring masses of all Italy" was passed by the CNSF directorate in late October 1924 and presented formally to Mussolini by Rossoni the next month. Such an agency was thought to complement the syndicalists' organizing efforts in every way. It was assumed that the government would still have to rely on their organizing talents, that the local sections would remain in their hands, and finally, that government patronage might be exploited to take over groups that previously had escaped their control.[28]

Mussolini, aware of the opportunity to demonstrate the regime's interest in the "social question," immediately authorized the clerical-moderate Minister of the National Economy, Nava, to draw up appropriate legislation for a national agency in consultation with Giani.[29] In early April 1925 the syndicalists stepped up their own pressure for the agency, now with the argument, presented by the national secretary of the CNSF, Pezzoli, that hundreds of politically suspect associations had been closed down after the coup of January 3 and their vacant premises were free for the taking. The syndicalists, in an unusual display of legal-mindedness, wanted clearance to occupy them, especially because the sports season was about to open and the opposition parties might still try to regroup the clubs in competing federations. Knowing Mussolini's greed for self-publicity, Pezzoli urged that the announcement of the new legislation be timed to coincide with the Fascist Labor Day. This argument apparently stuck a responsive chord, and on April 21 the Council of Ministers approved the bill in draft form.[30] But Mussolini, always the consummate opportunist, had the decree authorizing the foundation of the Opera Nazionale Dopolavoro signed into law by the King on May 1, although the traditional worker May Day festivities had been formally banned since April 1923.

The nationalization of leisure

The establishment of the National Agency on After-Work in the form of an *opera*, or paragovernment foundation, in effect announced the regime's implicit policy of arrogating a wide range of social welfare initiatives to the authority of the state rather than to the fascist syndicates or Fascist party. This particular juridical formula offered a number of distinct political and legal advantages, not the least of which, in the context of the Matteotti crisis, was the possibility it afforded of seeming to undertake a "corporatist" reform of the state, while actually postponing it until Mussolini felt more secure in his own position. An already established precedent, the *opera* had been the form taken by the leading Catholic charitable undertaking for immigrant Italians (the

Opera Bonomelli) and by the national foundation for war veterans (the Opera Nazionale Combattenti, or ONC) established in 1917. It thus carried overtones of charitable uplift and heroic nationalist endeavor, at the same time evoking images of the collective civic work of medieval community in the *opera del duomo*. Beyond this, its quasi-autonomy from the state administration proper allowed it a great flexibility with regard to its financial arrangements and its relationship to local private and public initiatives.[31]

Thus with the *opera* the fascist government was already positing a very close coordination of national policy with locally sponsored initiatives, although originally this was conceived more as a technical-administrative control rather than an overtly political intervention. The utility of this form of organization was demonstrated by the foundation in quick succession of the Opera Nazionale Maternità ed Infanzia (ONMI) in December 1925 and the Opera Nazionale Balilla (ONB) in April 1926: The former was to set up and guide provincial committees to care for mothers and infants in the context of the regime's campaigns to increase the birthrate; the latter, taking charge of the youth groups developed haphazardly under PNF auspices since 1921, was to provide for the civil education and physical preparedness of Italian youth. In the case of the ONMI and the ONC, which by their very nature had limited constituencies, this original character was retained throughout the fascist period, whereas the *dopolavoro* and youth groups, under the OND and ONB respectively, with vast potential memberships, would rapidly take on the structure of mass organizations in response to the regime's need to consolidate its rule in the precarious economic climate of the late twenties.

The Opera Nazionale Dopolavoro was thus presented initially as above politics: an executive agency responsible to the Ministry of the National Economy, which, since the abolition of the National Labor Office in 1923, had supervised labor affairs. Its policies were to be formulated by an administrative council made up of representatives from the state ministries, delegates from member associations, and experts. Its president, together with a counselor-delegate assigned to perform executive functions in the president's absence, were nominated by Mussolini in his capacity as President of the Council of Ministers and were appointed by royal decree.[32] As if to confirm the OND's suprapolitical character, Mussolini named Emmanuel Philbert, Duke of Aosta and cousin of the King, as its first president. The Duke, an ardent fascist supporter, had achieved national renown for his showy command of the Third Army in the Great War; his proclaimed willingness to take charge of this "eminently moral and patriotic" mission,

34

to lead his subalterns in peace as he had in war, would, it was hoped, attract patrons for this still colorless bureaucracy.[33] The less conspicuous Giani, who had since resigned from the secretariat of the CNSF, was named counselor-delegate and until April 1927 acted as the OND's executive officer in the Duke's frequent absences from Rome.

Although Mussolini's government was now openly dictatorial, the OND's own authority to manage worker sociability was initially very limited. The founding statutes defined the agency's general mission as "promoting the healthy and profitable occupation of workers' leisure hours by means of institutions for developing their physical, intellectual, and moral capacities." But in itself the OND possessed no real organizing powers, other than those that came from its legal right to confer certain fiscal privileges on worthy local institutions by recognizing them as *enti morali*, or charitable foundations, and from its capacity to form provincial committees in support of local activities, to provide discounts on certain equipment and services, and to publicize the services of benefactors. Its extremely modest endowment of one million lire (approximately 140,000 dollars) further tied even these endeavors to the vicissitudes of public sponsorship, private donations, and membership fees.[34] Since its authority extended only to the coordination of already existing institutions, its base of strength was inevitably bound to be only as wide as these initiatives themselves. Its mandate did not even include the autonomous jurisdictions of those *dopolavoro* groups set up under special laws in 1925–6 for government employees in the national railroads, post and telegraphic services, and state tobacco and salt monopolies.

Nevertheless, freed of syndicalist patronage, the *dopolavoro* could more readily seek backing from private enterprise. To appeal to potential supporters in business, Giani stressed the advantages of an "apolitical" and "productivist" organization of worker leisure. The programs for worker "uplift" proposed by the agency reflected a self-evident national interest in maximizing production. This, he claimed, transcended partisan politicking – whether in the form of antinational subversion from the left or irrational political pressures from within the fascist movement itself. Properly managed "after-work" would, Giani argued, significantly increase workers' output by providing those healthful activities that would restore them for labor. Moreover, it held in itself the possibility of producing a totally reformed citizen-producer by allowing for the reduplication within civil society of the models of competitive capitalism developed in the firm. The OND, according to Giani, thus intended to "discipline and strengthen" local associations by organizing "peaceable competition" at the neighborhood, municipal, provincial, regional, and finally national levels; in this way, it would promote a "fusion of characters, of spirits, of regional tendencies into a new 'national' type, more fully representative of our ancient and glorious stock and more conscious of its duties to the nation."[35]

This powerfully productivist appeal, combined with the conservative form of the *opera* and the trapping of royal patronage, very quickly legitimated the OND in the eyes of established elites. In the course of 1926 business leaders and local notables who had earlier shunned syndicalist overtures endorsed the government agency, contributed to its endowment, and attended the gala celebrations that marked the inauguration of each new provincial commission – though few, until put under pressure by the regime, actually invested in recreational centers of their own. The commissions themselves were invariably headed by prominent businessmen and aristocrats, as well as by fascist party dignitaries: at Turin by Edoardo Agnelli, the son of Fiat's director; at Pisa by Count Rosselmini Gualandi; at Novara by the big landowner, Count Vitaliano Borromeo; in Rome by the ex-nationalist PNF *federale* Ugo Gugliemotti; by Giovanni Giuriati at Venice; Costanzo Ciano at Leghorn; the *ras* Carlo Scorza at Lucca; and the fascist deputy Francesco d'Alessio at Potenza. Much of its appeal lay in the self-styled modernity of the initiative: Augusto Turati, who was to become the secretary of the PNF in April 1926, writing to potential benefactors in his capacity as chairman of the commission of Brescia, emphasized its similarity to "institutions that have been functioning for years in America, England, and Germany, where the field of social welfare is far more developed than in our country."[36]

But the OND's image as a nonpartisan philanthropic endeavor proved also to be a political liability in a country that after 1925 was rapidly undergoing "fascistization." Experienced organizers stayed with the fascist unions, and in the north-central regions, where the syndicalist *dopolavoro* had taken hold, they sometimes refused to cooperate with Giani's new appointees. Nor did Giani's conception of the OND easily attract fresh talent from the Fascist party. More preoccupied with social engineering than with bureaucratic aggrandizement, Giani had no tolerance either for fascist "intransigents" or the many "opportunists" who rallied to fascism once it appeared on the way to recovery with the Matteotti crisis. His notion of capable public servants – including ex-members of the Catholic Popular party and other nonfascist though conservative supporters – was inevitably galling to party aspirants jostling for position in the expanding fascist bureaucracy; his demand for a rigorous "technical" selection and scrupulous attention to the "moral and political credentials" of applicant associations slowed the pace of organizing. In the end, Giani's exhortations to an indifferent officialdom for support were bound to antagonize. On repeated occasions, he importuned Mussolini for greater cooperation from the state ministries, for authorization to use military property for athletic events, even to compose an official anthem for the *dopolavoro*, requests that irritated rather than ingratiated; the last was turned down by the Duce himself with a peremptory, "I am not a poet."[37]

With the passage of the Syndical Laws on 3 April 1926, the OND rapidly became the focus of rivalry between Rossoni's Corporations, whose power had been considerably reinforced by their legal recognition as extensions of the state, and the Fascist party, which felt increasingly deprived of a vanguard role as Mussolini recovered strongly from the Matteotti crisis. Although no longer autonomous, the fascist syndicates were unified and well organized; since 1925 they had controlled the reconstituted cooperative movement (ENIC), as well as the influential worker welfare institution, the Patronato Nazionale d'Assistenza, founded by Rossoni in June of that year. Numerically they surpassed the old reformist CGL; and with a membership of 2,800,000, more than double the size of the Fascist party, they were the regime's largest single organization by 1927.[38] The party, on the other hand, was on the defensive: The legal suppression of the opposition, the elimination of national elections, and the establishment of a national police reduced its repressive and containing functions while the personal dictatorship of Mussolini worked to subordinate it to the legal authority of the state.[39]

In this context, the OND, with its large potential membership and local extensions, naturally assumed a political importance, and especially to the party secretary Turati, himself a former labor organizer in industrial Brescia. The imminent possibility that the OND would be placed within the new Ministry of Corporations spurred him to intervene actively in the selection of a new executive officer under the figurehead position held by the Duke of Aosta. While Giani argued for this position to be held by the undersecretary of state for the Ministry of Corporations, at that time occupied by Mussolini's innocuous subordinate Count Suardo, the party pushed strongly for somebody from its own hierarchy – preferably its secretary. Mussolini, always working to prevent the accumulation of power in any one sector, agreed with Turati: Having appointed the astute "revisionist" Bottai to the Ministry of Corporations, he named the party secretary vice-president of the OND on 11 November 1926.[40] Within three weeks, Turati ordered the provincial *federali* to take "political responsibility" for the organization, leaving the OND solely in charge of administrative matters.[41]

The complete party takeover of the organization required, however, the resignation of Giani, who despite his weak political position was still held in respect by Mussolini and supported by the Duke of Aosta. Apprised by Mussolini of the "delicate situation," this self-styled "Condottiere and Educator of Soldier-boys" resigned the presidency in early April 1927. Immediately the government named Turati as the Duke's successor. His protector gone, Giani was ousted within six weeks. His final appeals to Mussolini were pathetically in character: He wished to set up another "autonomous technical institute," this time to act solely as an "information center" on the progress of after-work in Italy and abroad. They went unheeded. Banished from public service despite a personal plea from the Duke, he died three years later. Turati's brief epitaph praising Giani as a "disciplined, intelligent, faithful, and honest comrade" was the last and very oblique official mention of the managerial origins of this institution. Starting with Turati's administration, it was invariably to be described as a "typically fascist" innovation.[42]

The party takeover

During the three years of Turati's administration the OND was transformed into a full-fledged auxiliary of the Fascist party; decision-making powers formerly divided among president, counselor-delegate, general director, and administrative council were assumed by Turati himself as "special commissioner";[43] the headquarters in Corso Umberto I were expanded and reorganized; propaganda and publication were increased; and the full hierarchy of local, provincial, and national boards of direction was overhauled. Whatever the qualities of its leadership – which, as in the case of the ingratiating party man, Enrico Beretta, who directed the central offices from December 1929 to July 1935, consisted of a law degree and close personal ties to his fellow Brescian, Turati[44] – the image fostered was one of rationalized bureaucracy; the reporting procedures, hierarchical command structures, and statistical reviews all testified to this obsession. With the expansion of the central administrative staff to thirty people in 1927–9, special offices for accounting and archives, membership, statistics, and inspection were created as the first step in a massive recruitment drive.

The program departments themselves envisaged the OND's involvement with a totally integrated range of social services: instruction (divided between popular culture and vocational training), artistic education (with subsections for amateur theater, music, cinema, radio, and folklore), physical education (including sports and tourism), and assistance (concentrating on housing, consumer affairs, health and hygiene, social insurance, and company recreational facilities).[45] Such an all-embracing structure implied a far broader and deeper commitment by the party to the organizing of worker recreation and welfare than had previously been indicated by the syndicalists or the government.

Supporting the development of these programs was a battery of expert advisors and professional propagandists. "Technical commissions" composed of specialists in each area (all "authoritative citizens of flawless moral and political conduct") were set up to advise functionaries on content and policy. A new 5,000-volume staff library was established based on Giani's original multilingual collection and a press bureau organized to compile reviews and statistical reports and to collect news on foreign endeavors. At the same time the publication program of the OND itself was expanded. The weekly news-sheet *Il Dopolavoro*, with a circulation of over 32,000 directed to party officials, government, and local institutions, was supplemented by a montly *Bollettino ufficiale* in 1927, that instructed functionaries in the art of using orchard gardens, choral societies, and theater groups for organizing purposes. By the end of 1928, these publications were absorbed into new organs: a monthly bulletin for cadres and a weekly for general membership. This last, called *Gente nostra* (Our People), was a glossy illustrated review, with feature articles on culture and news on the progress of the fascist sports and recreation movement. Modeled on the popular *Corriere della Domenica*, its circulation reached 115,000 by 1939.[46] Altogether these innovations confirmed that in policy at least, Turati's intention was to transform a relatively modest parastate institution into a party auxiliary with a mass audience.

In the shift from social welfare agency to national "movement," the effectiveness of the local boards was central. Constituted under the party *federale* in each provincial capital, they brought together representatives of fascist employer and syndical associations and public authorities. As in the national offices, local voluntary "technical commissions" gave advice on programs, whereas the work of administration was entrusted to a salaried secretary or president approved by the party secretary. The secret of fascist efficiency, noted the official handbook, "lies in hierarchical order, with appointments invariably being made from the top down."[47]

The provincial boards were responsible for supervising all the local after-work organizations, not only the neighborhood or village *dopo-*

lavoro sections founded by the OND itself, but also the growing numbers of circles that, either voluntarily or under compulsion, took out membership in the national organization after 1927. The boards also mediated relations with the employer-sponsored recreational groups.

At the lowest level of this national hierarchy was the local *dopolavoro* circle. In its internal organization, it reproduced exactly the structure of the central directorate. Supervised by the secretary of the local *fascio*, administered by a fascist-appointed president, it was counseled by a board that, ideally, would be composed of the town secretary, the municipal medical inspector, the elementary school teacher, the fiduciary of the women's *fasci*, and representatives from the local fascist unions and employers' association. Rural sections would include a delegate from the "traveling school of agriculture" (*cattedre ambulanti*) and from the forest militia. Guided by national directives and assisted in their day-to-day operations by the appropriate *tecnici*, the local *dopolavoro* groups, or "meeting centers," in the words of the official handbook, would offer their members "new opportunities for culture, recreation, and physical education, according to their tastes and local means," in addition to "proper care for their patriotic education."[48]

With only a small paid staff, the success of the so-called *dopolavoro* movement inevitably depended on its capacity to recruit volunteers for the day-to-day activities. The presidents who ran the circles, the members of the directory whom they consulted, and the technical collaborators who directed cultural programs, provided medical care, or organized outings all served voluntarily. But fascism had inherited from the liberal state a middle class little concerned with such activity, and without much sense of its extended class interests. Demagogic appeals to the "sense of class mission" of this "technological bourgeoisie" along with reassurances that volunteer work would not force it "to renounce its high status in the hierarchy of Italian society" apparently failed to encourage its involvement with the OND. Consequently, at the beginning of 1928 the regime began to offer gold, silver, and bronze medals and "diplomas of meritorious service" distributed at "solemn ceremonies." The effectiveness of these pompous symbols as incentives to voluntarism was much reinforced by their recognition as points toward promotion in the civil service. The position of "consultant" to the OND, as well as to the Balilla and OMNI, gradually acquired a certain social prestige; after all, it bore none of the stigma of overt political servitude that many professionals sought to avoid.[49]

Relying on the professional qualifications of these volunteers for the development of its programs locally, and dependent on the central party administrative apparatus, the OND was neither a purely state-sponsored social welfare agency concerned with the delivery of services nor a completely spontaneous mass organization based on voluntary membership. This hybrid quality was reflected in the ambiguity of membership itself. "Members" were evidently not participating in an organization that was democratically responsive to its membership; yet the fiction of "voluntarism" was essential to gain any real support. Recognizing this contradiction, the regime tried to solve it by semantics: in November 1926 the *soci* or members of the OND created by the founding statutes, became suddenly *aderenti* or joiners. Such "joiners" could not expect legally to have any say in the operations of the organization. Thus were the persistent demands by fascists and nationalists for the masses to "adhere to the national state" reinforced in word at least.[50]

Throughout Turati's tenure the original technocratic aims of the OND were maintained. The administration's goals, like those of the syndicalists previously, were directed toward production. The party, mobilized in the "battles" for stabilization of 1926–7, was concerned to present itself as a new political force for the transformation of Italy into an industrial power: Its auxiliary naturally fitted into the scheme. The OND's special task was the promotion with "unified criteria and methods, of programs for rationally utilizing workers' spare time."[51]

As a government agency, intimately involved with the workings of local society, the OND was in a unique position to further the rationalization of the corporative state. On one level it was an executive agency of state economic planning working closely with the Ministry of National Economy and cooperating with a proliferation of parastate agencies concerned with the regulation of small industries, national insurance, consumer information, and the domestic silk industry. At the same time it could disseminate a wide variety of information in the localities from advice on the fine points of fascist labor codes and pension plans to aid in filling out complicated bureaucratic forms. It was thus a kind of "representational" institution standing between state and local society, disbursing wisdom and (reciprocally) "interpreting the needs, sufferings, and diffuse aspirations of the anonymous masses of the humble," ostensibly to "enlighten" the policies of government agencies and employers.[52]

In the exercise of this mediating function, the OND was gradually to distinguish among the specialized "needs" of its different constituencies. In industry, after-work would serve as an instrument of personnel management – an "antidote to the damaging effects of mechanization and the automation of the work process," as a representative

The culture of consent: mass organization in fascist Italy

to the 1927 International Congress on Scientific Management maintained.[53] In rural areas, it would contribute to "a more pleasurable" life by providing certain modern amenities and educational opportunities. The new meeting rooms would act to blunt the traditional hostility of the peasant to the state – no longer would government be personified by *carabiniere* or tax collector or military recruiter, but by the benign agent of *dopolavoro* uplift. Now the peasant would hopefully "collaborate spontaneously, increasing the prestige (of the state), adopting its laws and defending its structures from any attempt at social subversion."[54] In the tertiary sector, the OND would act to soften the degradation of office work and bolster the shaky economic and social position of the petty functionary, not quite "intellectual," no longer "proletarian."

These increasingly "functional" definitions of its task in different sectors of the economy were supplemented in the late twenties by a new concern for the organization of women. Encouraged by a regime that actively supported the elimination of women from the industrial work force to relieve the tight job market and counter falling birthrates,[55] the OND developed two kinds of programs: for working women and for housewives. Rest and recreation rooms in factories, home economics courses, instruction in first aid, hygiene, and nursing, as well as propaganda for the "moral elevation" of women in fascist society, were to assist the female labor force to fulfill a "more active and responsible mission" as workers and mothers.[56] Housewives, on the other hand, were to be instructed in judicious household management. Experts at the Third International Congress on Home Economics, cosponsored by the OND and the Fasci Femminili in Rome in November 1927, estimated that more than 60 percent of the household budget regularly passed through women's hands; fascist austerity measures demanded its wise expenditure. "Teaching women to understand that they are the pivot of the family, that they must economize time and effort to dedicate the greatest time possible to their children's education is a fundamental social task," stated Belluzzo, Minister of the National Economy, at the Rome Congress on Scientific Management in 1927. Although Belluzzo was clearly echoing Frank and Lillian Gilbreth, the American exponents of household rationalization, the fascist program was more concerned with the formation of binding social obligations than with any emancipatory potential for women.[57]

The obvious contradictions of this policy, at least with respect to working women, were most evident in the organization of the recreational programs themselves. The place of the private sphere in fascism's naively productivist division between work and after-work was unclear: It was simply assumed that a well-organized *dopolavoro* would solidify the family. But the primary intent of a *fascist recreation* – to restore workers after their fatigue in the field or factory – by no means necessarily encouraged time spent in the home. Quite the contrary: If the relaxing diversions from home life recommended by organizers were merely a continuation of a traditional mode for male workers, they were not for working women, who were still expected to fulfill their primary roles as wives and mothers in the household. Yet the cooking classes, sewing lessons, and home economics courses that reinforced a traditional domestic vision of women's "special needs" were hardly designed to restore women after their work. In fact, a majority of the hundred thousand or so women members enrolled in the OND by 1930 seemed more attracted to the sports, outings, movies, and amateur theatricals directed primarily to male members. Yet it was precisely the dangers inherent in these modern leisure pastimes – "the adoption of spendthrift habits, the multiplication of expensive needs, the abuse of consumerism and pleasures of every kind, a false understanding of social well-being" – that, together with female employment, were commonly identified by misogynist fascist ideologues as the leading cause of the deplored decline in the birthrate.[58] Inevitably, a basic conflict was raised between what was thought proper for women "in the national interest," and what women saw developing around them and perhaps even wanted for themselves.

In practice the OND never confronted this dichotomy. Accepting a functional division between leisure activities for men and those for women, it acceded to the requests of the Fasci Femminili for the right to organize women in separate *dopolavoro* sections, a move intended to compensate the women's auxiliary for the loss of its girls' groups to the ONB in late 1929. Far from emancipating women's leisure activities from a male-dominated bureaucracy, this action by the party secretary consigned them to a women's group that clearly defined the public role of women in a traditional way, from the point of view of a genteel and beneficent bourgeoisie. The Fasci Femminili were in no way set up, as the *dopolavoro* centers at least claimed to be, to organize working women with any real sense of their social needs, much less of their double burden as "producers" and "pillars of the household." The inherent conservatism of this move was underlined by the hearty approbation it received from the Catholic hierarchy, which manifestly preferred the heightened competition of the women's *fasci* with its own lay union of Donne Cattoliche (UDCI) to any continuation of the promiscuous mixing of sexes within the fascist *dopolavoro*.[59]

Out of this practice and its theoretical justification, a number of themes became clear by the late twenties. Leisure was, in the first place, presented as apolitical. The "statist" polemics of the Nationalists provided principles that related leisure to the welfare of the nation; the technocratic schemes for social management supplied rules for its practical organization. No longer seen as an "end" in itself, leisure was now construed as a "means" of improving the worker in the national interest, curing the defects of proletarian character, teaching workers not to kill time, and instructing them in the virtues of "self-discipline," "self-control," and "fair play" – those much mythicized "Anglo-Saxon" qualities seemingly so sorely lacking in the Italian working class.[60] But at the same time workers now – at least in the token terms of the fascist Labor Charter of 1927 – had a *right* to organized leisure activities, something the fascists were quick to contrast with the "Quakeristic and pietistic philanthropy" and "debilitating largesse" of liberal paternalism.[61] The actual administration of leisure was still conceived in strictly managerial terms: The extension of techniques of labor management to social relations would lead, as one proponent enthusiastically claimed, to a veritable "taylorization of leisure." Even as the work process was timed, measured, and divided into single tasks to maximize output, so now the activities of leisure might be analyzed, taken apart, and reassembled as efficient restorers of the workers' energies. The *dopolavoro* would be to leisure what scientific management was to work: "the scope," remarked G. Di Nardo, "is exactly the same, the difference solely in the methods used."[62]

Coordinating the circles

Against every rationalizing scheme, every "totalitarian" project for the smooth extension of after-work programs into all sectors of social life, stood the resistance of a still-active worker sociability. The number of clubs and circles that had survived the fascist terror, legal harassment, and the enforcement of the "special" Public Security Laws of November 1926 was surprisingly large. When the PNF took control of the OND, a preliminary survey revealed that some five thousand amateur theater groups, music and choral societies, sports and outling clubs, reading circles, mutual aid societies, and "popular universities" were still outside its purview; an equivalent number would be uncovered in the next two years.[63]

Certainly, many of these associations had simply not been considered sufficiently political to warrant any special attention from public authorities. Others, identifiably antifascist, had managed to escape detection through skillful subterfuges or administrative oversight. In some instances clubs simply reopened, chameleon-like, under new guises, or their members, in an attempt to escape police surveillance, took up residence in innocuous-looking cooperatives or mutual aid societies. On occasion, they would change their names, abandoning those of political heroes or slogans that immediately identified them with socialist or democratic traditions. Thus the railroad workers' circle, Sempre Avanti! (Ever Onward!), closed down for the first time by the prefect in January 1925, reopened a year later under the name Cordiality. Seeking to maintain a low profile in order to keep the sodality intact, members even tried to discourage their more vocally socialist comrades from frequenting the premises. It was not uncommon for groups simply to eschew all overt political activity and claim that they were adhering to their original *ragione sociale*, which, as set out in the statutes, called for mutual aid and recreational pursuits.[64]

The campaign to eradicate these survivals and finally to bring all working-class clubs under fascist control began in November 1926, when Mussolini assumed personal charge of the Ministry of the Interior. Condemning *squadristi* tactics as "anarchistically sporadic" in their effects, Mussolini called on the government's prefects to assume complete charge of the "moral and political order" of the provinces. In the next few months, prefects and party functionaries closed in on clubs, drinking societies, and sports circles: The decree-law on associations of January 1924 was strictly enforced against any clubs financed by worker contributions suspected of "abusing public confidence" or having "endangered public safety or order"; and the existing communal and provincial laws were interpreted broadly against infractions such as unlicensed liquor sales, dancing, and card playing after hours.[65]

Against this concerted action by public and party authorities, the clubs found few avenues of escape. The fate of the Varese Cordiality Club is typical. The neighborhood *fascio* had long coveted its premises for use by the fascist organizations and had repeatedly complained to the prefect that the club members were "antinational" and "impeding the progress" of the local fascist movement. In 1928, citing the presence within the association of "former socialists posing a threat to national institutions," the prefect ordered its premises confiscated and immediately delivered to the local fascists.[66] Even when a club membership was clearly apolitical, such as that of the Cup Society among railroad workers at Novara, the prefects would act, and especially if the society was competing with fascist institutions. "While of no usefulness," the prefect reported of the Novara circle, "and failing to improve its members, it causes people to desert the premises of the OND instituted by the national government and the regime for the express purpose of reconciling the interests and controlling the needs and pastimes of the various categories of workers."[67]

While closing down a club was relatively easy, the confiscation of its property and premises was legally complicated; even more so was the appropriation of this by the OND – an organization that considered itself the natural heir to such property. For the Laws on Public Security did not stipulate what should be done with "subversive" property, save that it should eventually devolve to the state. Local government authorities thus had to adjudicate among a number of claimants: the local chapter of OMNI, the fascist trade unions, the PNF, the Balilla, the local "congregation of charity," as well as the OND. Turati's efforts to make the OND the "legal" heir, by requesting that the prefects cite the January 1924 law on working class associations in their action against individual circles, were unsuccessful; it was held that such action would open the way to legal recourse by club members.[68]

The regime, ever careful of the fiction of capitalist legality, even when closing circles on the most spurious of motives, was especially reluctant to have such matters brought before the courts; the process of confiscation was entered into therefore only when the property was of particular value or political importance, as was true of the grand Casa del Popolo of Rome or the elegant Spreti Palace, the former residence of the socialist municipal administration of Ravenna; or as a punitive measure against particularly recalcitrant groups like the workers' *circolo* of Dongo, Como, which refused to consign its financial records to the prefect, even after half of the members were finally persuaded to join the OND in 1930.[69] Buildings were also confiscated in those very rare instances when the original proprietors actually abandoned the premises. The worker members of the Casa del Popolo of Borgo Isola in Vercelli province, founded in 1919, had repaired the devastated building after the fascist squads burned out its interior in 1921, reopening it in 1923. But as the regime consolidated itself, and after repeated attacks by fascist gangs, some members decided to emigrate, some went underground, and some simply left the circle, making it as clear as possible that they had never belonged to it or participated in its activities. They abandoned a large and, as the prefect noted, unmortgaged building.[70] Although such confiscations were relatively rare – the fascists would always prefer the method of exacting "donations" of property to avoid legal complications – the ex-subversive properties were of considerable value; in 1933–4, before the big surge in fascist constructions, they made up one-third of the value of the OND's real estate buildings.[71]

The political significance of this transferral of property was nevertheless clear both to the former socialist proprietors and to their new fascist owners. The case of the Casa del Popolo of Rome became in this way a final *cause célèbre* for the maximalist socialists and a crude triumph of fascist legality. The president of the Workers' Society, which had housed the Rome section of the PSI, as well as the federal chamber of labor, was Costantino Lazzari; as the former secretary of the Socialist party and leader of its maximalist wing, he was in a position to mount a strong legal defense against the fascists. On 19 November 1925 the prefect of Rome had dissolved the association and the police occupied the premises. Lazzari, with legal counsel from the socialist jurist G. E. Modigliani, immediately petitioned the Ministry of the Interior to overturn the prefect's ruling. When this attempt failed, he filed suit against the prefecture for "abuse of power" and "violation of the law." A special recourse to Victor Emmanuel III was turned down by decision of the Council of State on 16 August 1926. On December 3, while Lazzari sought to prolong the lawsuit through appeals, the property was confiscated, according to section 245 of the Law on Public Security. In 1927 a final appeal to the high court was turned down, and the following year the property was ceded to the OND. Finally, in May 1929, the administration of the OND, having outgrown its office in the Fiano Palace, took up lodging in the grandiose *belle époque* edifice in Via Capo d'Africa in the working class district of Celio.[72]

By far the more frequent practice for bringing recalcitrant associations into line was by "coordinating" their governing boards. Between 1926 and 1931, when the last 700 holdouts were reportedly "duly absorbed and transformed" under OND auspices, as many as 10,000 groups were registered with the national offices; a "delicate and important task," as it was described by Beretta in 1931, that had been accomplished "not without conflicts and resistance."[73]

"Coordination" (*inquadramento* or, sometimes, *coordinamento*), a term equivalent to the Nazi's "synchronization" but which in Italy was reserved almost exclusively for worker associations, was an elaborate procedure that began when the club administrators were instructed to "apply" for membership in the OND. This meant literally that they were both obliged to join under threat of confiscation and well advised to orchestrate at least a modest display of enthusiasm at the prospect. Thus it suited fascist purposes to retain at least a fiction of democratic procedure until after the society was registered. The group's presiding officer or the acting commissar appointed by the prefect convened a general assembly of the membership to vote in support of the application. There was of course no need for a quorum or the support of a two-thirds majority as was prescribed by the clubs' democratic statutes for such extraordinary measures. The motion in favor of application was declared valid at the workers' circle of Bagno a Ripoli (Florence), although it received only 20 votes out of a possible 250 in its support.[74] Once the vote was taken, the official in charge forwarded the election results to the provincial board, together with a list of the members actually purchasing the five-lira cards. He was personally responsible for providing written assurances that all of the society's members were of "good moral and political sentiments," and that prospective cardholders – numbering at least a third of the total club membership – were at least eighteen years of age and bona fide workers or salaried employees.[75]

The review of applicants' political credentials was, in appearance, strict, and especially so in the late twenties, while the regime was trying to rout the last remnants of the antifascist opposition. Turati demanded "political faith" as the "essential prerequisite" for joining; "subversives or even disguised opponents of the regime must not find sanctuary in the *dopolavoro*."[76] The enforcement of this directive was inevitably uneven. Only an unusually well-regimented fascist federation, like that of Ravenna, could insist that all members of applicant associations have "all of their cards in order" and have demonstrated "obedience to the regime and respect for its laws."[77] In other cases the regime had to rely on the fealty – or opportunism – of those nuclei of fascist sympathizers that, by the mid-twenties, could be found in even the "reddest" of associations. The several thousand members of the Pignone Union of Florence, formed in 1889 by local foundry workers, had fought off two fascist assaults in 1921; yet by 1924 the prefect of Florence had forced them to take in a profascist veterans' group by the simple expedient of demanding compliance with their statutes, which guaranteed hospitality to any bona fide neighborhood worker association. The fascists nevertheless still comprised a minority within the organization; and it was not until the November laws were passed in 1926 that the fascist group, led by the notorious *squadrista* Lorenzo Gambacciani, expelled the leading antifascists for "indegnità politica," held new elections – which it easily won – and imposed a new fascist statute barring all former "subversives" from joining. Renamed for a local fascist "martyr," Nicola Bonservizi, the old Pignone union was subsequently reinaugurated as the center of the fascist neighborhood associations of Oltrarno.[78]

Even when there was no such blatant coercion from within, the pressures to submit to authority were enormous, if only to preserve the association from official harassment and terrorist reprisals. Since there was no provision for individual membership – although membership cards did become transferable after 1927 – there was always pressure from within the group itself to ensure the political moderation of comrades in the interest of the collective membership. Some members might still refuse ostentatiously to purchase the cards, but few in the end would leave the association voluntarily; they recognized that by giving up participation altogether they would cut themselves off from the companionship of their fellows and bolster the largely artificial authority of the hand-picked fascist administration.

Once a circle was enrolled in the OND, it was divested of its statutes and symbols. The old clubs, priding themselves on their hospitality, had placed no restrictions on joining, provided that members were working people from the area; the fascist statutes imposed by the provincial boards invariably called for "complete political and moral reliability" as criteria for membership.[79] The traditional statutes had stressed democratic procedures for decision making and the responsibility of the president and governing board to the membership; the new regulations called for a president who, appointed by the *federale* or by the secretary of the local *fascio*, was personally responsible to them rather than to club members for the conduct of activities. Finally, the clubs were divested of their traditional banners, the "lighthouse and lodestone" for the masses, as the socialist Linda Malnati had called them, with their symbolic representations of union, fraternity, or the artisan crafts. In their place, the OND stipulated a regulation banner (which might be purchased, if it could not be assembled by a "committee of patronesses"), a voluminous tricolor embossed with the seal of state and OND's own eclectic emblem with its vigorous Savoyard eagle and fascist lictors superimposed on a landscape of fertile fields and smoking factories.[80] When all preparations were completed, the premises were reinaugurated with a new fascist ceremonial, attended by local clergy and public authorities.

Although numerous acts of resistance to fascist takeover can be documented, it would be mistaken to assume that all, or even a majority, of the associations subjected to this process had put up any strenuous fight against "coordination." In May 1927, for example, the Church hierarchy had agreed to dissolve the Catholic national sports federation (FASCI); the local groups were left "free" to decide for themselves whether to join the OND. Many must have followed the secular groups and done so; for joining was a way of preserving fraternal bonds. Official protection promised respite from harassment, a tempering of antagonisms between fascists and nonfascists, a return to habitual routines, and perhaps even a small token of official favor in prompt action on a liquor license or a subsidy.

Not every club was selected by the OND, nor was every "popular" circle put through the arduous process of coordination: Although all had to register, the distinction was made between those clubs that had been officially and completely entered into the national organization and that had the full right to call themselves *dopolavoro* and those that were simply recorded as "dependent." Insisting on this distinction, Giani, as early as 1926, had noted that a large number of groups tried to appropriate the adjective "national" to describe their activities, which were in fact of "scant social value" and of "dubious artistic merit." Turati, too, would have liked to consider the rush of applicants after May 1927 as "a gesture of homage" to the OND, but closer scrutiny cast doubt on the "organizational seriousness" of many; "joining," he complained, had frequently become "no more than a means of bolstering precarious finances or concealing dubious or improvised political faith by exploiting the name of an institution of the regime."[81] By the end of the decade some 4,221 institutions had been declared "dependent" on the OND, while 2,700 had been fully incorporated into the 6,863 new *dopolavoro* sections (see Table 2.1).

The expansion of membership under Turati was more systematic than in previous years, but groups for the constituency primarily aimed at by the founders of the *dopolavoro* – for industrial workers – were still in the minority. Only 15 percent of the total 11,040 listed in October

Table 2.1. *OND association membership between 1926–29*

	1926	1927	1928	1929
Dopolavoro, including municipal and neighborhood	300	1,454	2,550	5,010
Company *dopolavoro*	260	504	1,259	1,670
Dependent associations	504	1,075	2,445	4,221
Women's *dopolavoro*	—	—	—	183
	1,064	3,033	6,254	11,084

Source: BLPS, 31 July–31 December 1930, p. 161.

1929, some 1,670, were sponsored by private employers and state-run services and industries as agencies of personnel management. In industrial areas, for example in the maritime center of La Spezia, workers still remained "suspicious of and indifferent to" the organization, according to the party *federale*. In Genoa, similarly, the *dopolavoro* had "not developed among the working masses as expected," reported a fascist fiduciary in August 1930. The workers were still "attached to their own mutual aid and recreational associations in which they continued to meet and find their accustomed pastimes."[82]

Compounding the effects of this natural resistance was a decided lack of enterprise by local functionaries; at Genoa "effective propaganda" was lacking, inducements were not actively offered, and petty regulations were often enforced so as to "persistently hamper" the efforts of theaters, recreational circles, and sports. The functionaries were in many areas indifferent. They had shut themselves up in their offices, though even the slightest contact with workers in the old circles would immediately have demonstrated "how much remained to be done to win over the minds and hearts of the workers to the regime."[83]

Only the salaried workers appeared to respond to the membership appeals of the late twenties: in 1929 they formed by far the largest membership group – over 40 percent of the million and a half members. For this urban lower middle class, with its shorter working hours and higher pay, the five-lira card was apparently a worthwhile investment, especially when its possession was accepted as prima facie evidence of loyalty to the regime, a desired attribute for bureaucratic promotion.[84]

Reach out to the people

In the late twenties, the goals, programs, and general tenor of the OND were still remarkably productivist: its recreational activities and their justification were shaped by the ever-stressed need to mobilize the population on behalf of the regime's economic battles. This wholly utilitarian ideology of leisure, inherited from the early origins of the *dopolavoro*, now permeated all of the OND's projects, whether for rural or for industrial use. But such purposefulness was an inadequate response to the social effects of the Depression crisis: soaring unemployment, the widespread adoption of short time, and wage cuts. The renewed threat of communist "subversion" and a resurgent Catholic activism were patently unsusceptible to being countered by calls for sacrifice in the national interest; economic distress and lack of work could hardly be assuaged by reminding workers of their ennobled status as producers in the corporative state.[85] The OND, organizing the free

51

time made available no longer by a guaranteed shorter work week but by severe economic dislocation, was now called upon to emphasize the distractive benefits of leisure as diversion from political opposition to the regime's economic policies; while at the same time it began to perform the very real service of distributing aid to the indigent.[86]

Late in 1931 Mussolini began a campaign to mobilize all of the regime's auxiliaries to cope with the economic crisis: "Reach out to the people," he exhorted, "assist those groups of the population with the greatest wants." This "populist" direction, in fact, brought no significant changes in the political economy of fascism – certainly not in the redistribution of wealth or in the restraints applied to private enterprise. But it did lead to a far more pronounced effort on the part of the state and the party to intervene systematically in the social life of the nation.[87]

"Reaching out to the people" in practice took two forms: a sizable relief program, provided by public distribution of fuel and bread under the auspices of the party's Ente Opere Assistenziali, or EOA, together with public works projects, which in 1935 had employed about half a million of the several million unemployed; and, second, an intense though increasingly depoliticized activism on the part of the regime's mass organizations. Party headquarters were ordered to remain open day and night, and fascist functionaries, as Mussolini admonished his cohorts through a widely publicized "note" to Parenti, the free-living *federale* of Milan, were to adopt an entirely new populist style – no more nightlife or theatergoing; travel on foot or by motorcycle rather than in chauffeured cars; plain "black shirts of the revolution" at public occasions instead of top hats and fancy dress; a full day at the office listening to "the greatest number of people possible" with "the utmost patience and humanity"; finally, visits to working class neighborhoods on a regular basis to make "physical as well as moral contact" with the working population.[88]

The OND had already been prepared to respond to the regime's new understanding of the role of its mass organizations by Achille Starace, who on 18 October 1930 was appointed to succeed Turati as special commissioner. As special party commissar at Milan in 1929, Starace had demonstrated his intuitive grasp of the special social uses of the *dopolavoro* organization; while purging the PNF of the populist *federale* Giampaoli and 9,000–10,000 of his followers, Starace had sought to pacify the city's restive proletariat by making its *dopolavoro*'s programs cheaper and "more congenial to the habits and mentality of the working population." Within ten weeks of his appointment, he convened the first national meeting of OND organizers, at which he announced the imperative need "to penetrate still further among the masses."[89]

Appointed national PNF secretary on 7 December 1931, Starace retained his leadership of the OND and continued to demonstrate his personal interest in the organization: Contemporary critics were both amused and appalled by the pride with which the new party chief pronounced himself the "impresario of the greatest theatrical enterprise in Italy and perhaps the world."[90] In a very real sense, he was not referring solely to the spectacular shows of the OND, but to the entire party apparatus. Clearly the OND, under Starace's direction, was being enlisted in the shift, which had Mussolini's full support, toward a "party of a new kind," one that would become a sophisticated agency of social mediation – a depoliticized means of reaching groups not responsive to an overtly ideological appeal. The "circus" created by Starace, deplored by old guard revolutionaries and technocrats alike, was no mere exercise in choreography, as Bottai would have had it: This was confirmed by the new party statutes of 1932, which reminded members of their duty not simply to subordinate themselves to the state, but also "to put themselves at its service, to become its agents," in order to bring the masses into the state.[91] To this end, the PNF's ban on new members was lifted, greatly expanding its pool of cadres and its mass extensions. Thus the *dopolavoro*, which hitherto had been described as "an auxiliary" of the PNF, now became an organization "dependent" on the party and "directly responsible" to its secretary.

For Starace, the OND represented one of the regime's most effective instruments for the carrying out of Mussolini's new populist policies: At the 17 December national meeting of OND functionaries at Palazzo Littorio, he stressed the fundamental importance of the organization as an "effective tool of assistance and propaganda among the masses." Starace ordered an extension of assistance programs for which the local clubs too should remain open day and night and an increase in the number of excursions – one of the cheapest of all possible organized diversions. He also announced plans for a giant national gymnastics contest for the forthcoming celebration of the tenth anniversary of the regime.[92]

The essential component of Starace's program was diversion: By abandoning the effort to generate the skills and values of a technological society in the memberhsip, and by espousing more sports and other pastimes "favored by the masses," the OND could lay claim to be responding to popular demand. Even though the official rhetoric would have had little appeal to the membership, the frenetic activity sponsored by the recreational organizations might have the effect of literally removing the worker from politics: "Our *dopolavoristi*," explained the fascist consul Nicola Leuzzi, head of the 6,000–member Rome Transit Company Dopolavoro, "even if they do desire, no longer have the time to hang out in the cellars and taverns, to allow themselves to be seen in places of ill repute or associate with pernicious types."[93] In his 1933 pamphlet on OND programs, Starace devoted only three pages to technical instruction, whereas sports were allocated a total of twenty-five pages.[94]

Under Starace's leadership, the OND devoted increasing attention to organizing industrial workers and rural laborers, neither of which had been among its "natural" constituency of salaried employees or brought in in great numbers by the coordination of the circles in the twenties.[95] In February 1931 Starace ordered the provincial OND functionaries and party *federali* to put greater pressure on industrial employers to support party initiatives in the community, as well as setting up recreational facilities of their own in the vicinity of their firms. At the same time, beginning in October 1931, party functionaries were urged to initiate a "more active and rapid movement to penetrate the rural masses." In both of these sectors the *dopolavoro* was recommended as a device for pacifying labor unrest. The *federale* of La Spezia, for example, in the wake of the local navy yard walkouts of March 1931, directed industrialists to set up recreational facilities as the first step toward restoring order. Similarly the strike-prone agricultural day-laborers or *braccianti* of the northern provinces, with their history of sympathy for communism, were primary targets: They would, Starace prophesized, benefit greatly from centers that offered them "moral and material uplift."[96]

In its drive for membership the OND leadership now tended to abandon coercion altogether. Announcing the new policy, Starace proclaimed: "Membership should be a voluntary and spontaneous act."[97] As opposed to the quasi-obligatory membership in the trade unions and other professional organizations, this lack of compulsion ostensibly opened the *dopolavoro* circles to those who, although not especially supportive of the regime, might simply want to take advantage of the recreational benefits it offered. Although the OND leadership maintained the fiction of screening applicants for political undesirables, in practice from 1931 on, an expanding membership was given the higher priority. Now, more than ever, it was possible for a worker to practice a selective hostility for the regime's institutions. In the former "red" city of Turin, a party fiduciary remarked in 1931, although the workers were still antifascist and openly antagonistic to the ineffectual fascist trade unions, there existed a "more decisive orientation toward the *dopolavoro*," with a "natural and spontaneous participation not seen in the past."[98]

After 1932, membership picked up rapidly, rising from 1,744,000 in that year to 2,376,000 in 1935. That year the entire organization comprised just under 20,000 local groups. By far the greater number of these – 64 percent – were regulation *dopolavoro* clubs, organized on a territorial basis, with city-center groups accounting for 29 percent, village sections for 19 percent, and neighborhood and rural district centers for 16 percent. Private enterprise ran 13 percent, the state service organizations 2 percent, and the remainder was taken up with affiliated chapters. Membership was increasingly drawn from manual workers, and by 1936, with the pick-up in industry and the increased enrollment of agricultural laborers, this constituency comprised nearly 70 percent of the total membership. This meant that in Italy as a whole, 20 percent of the industrial labor force and 7 percent of the peasantry was enrolled in the OND, in addition to the "near totality" – 80 percent – of state and private salaried employees (Table 2.2).[99]

The social and political importance of an organization the size of the OND cannot, however, be measured totally in terms of the membership; equally vital for the regime were its large complements of functionaries and volunteers – not only in the process of organizing but also in terms of their own involvement in the social and political life of the fascist state. With its full-time salaried staff of 700 and over 100,000 volunteers at the provincial and local levels,[100] the OND ex-

Table 2.2. *Division of OND membership by salaried employees and manual workers, 1926–36*

Year	Salaried employees	Manual workers	Total
1926	164,000	116,000	280,000
1927	289,000	248,000	537,000
1928	437,000	445,000	882,000
1929	524,000	921,000	1,445,000
1930	528,000	1,093,000	1,621,000
1931	674,000	1,097,000	1,771,000
1932	675,000	1,099,000	1,774,000
1933	725,000	1,201,000	1,926,000
1934	795,000	1,312,000	2,087,000
1935	805,000	1,571,000	2,376,000
1936	864,000	1,921,000	2,755,000

Source: OND, *Annuario*, 1937.

ercised a critical social function, offering upward mobility and status to its petty bourgeois functionaries, and an equally important political role by satisfying the aspirations for national service harbored by "fascists of the first hour." This amassing of OND personnel in a great variety of functions contributed in no small way to the "self-organization" of the Italian bourgeoisie that took place largely through the vehicle of the expanding fascist bureaucracies in the late twenties and early thirties. A process that in other countries was effected through the rapidly expanding business sector, in Italy it was primarily concentrated in the state offices and party organizations of the regime.

There were three levels of functionaries in the OND: the top bureaucracy; professionals like the lawyer Beretta, its general director from 1929 to 1935; or disciplined "fascists of the first hour" like Corrado Puccetti, a former party *federale* and MVSN official who served in the same post until 1939.[101] These were joined by the ex-prefects, pensioned-off career functionaries from other services, professionals with multiple job obligations, and political appointees rewarded by the regime with bureaucratic sinecures, at least some of whom – according to the fascist government's own inquiries – apparently found a rich fount of graft and speculation in the OND.[102] The second echelon, serving on the provincial boards as special commissioners or inspectors, were more professionalized: Some were old guard fascists, some new bureaucratic managers. Rino Parenti, the president of the 250,000-member *dopolavoro* of Milan from 1931 to 1933, was typical of the former: A first-rate organizer, entirely malleable in the face of authority ("a watered-down fascist," as his colleagues described him), his greatest asset was an unquestioning devotion to the party and to Mussolini. With a good record from the first days of the fascist "revolution" and an intuitive sense of the "systems best suited to lifting the morale of the masses," he proved uniquely able to unify "fascists of the first hour" and popular classes within the *dopolavoro* – all of this without giving offense to Milanese business circles.[103] Emilio Battigalli, on the other hand, appointed OND general director in December 1939, was an engineer; too young to have been a *squadrista*, he began his career as a neighborhood fiduciary at Pescara and came to national attention as the president of its efficiently run *dopolavoro*. The nearly five hundred paid positions in the provinces, together with hundreds of others on the payroll of local organizations, similarly provided a means of professional advancement for many of the young lower middle class. Little academic or special technical expertise was required; only membership in the party and administrative effectiveness, as judged by enrollment increases, numbers of activities sponsored, and punctuality in turning in reports.[104]

At the third, and in terms of local organization, the most important level were the volunteers. As a group they included the entire spectrum of bourgeois and petty bourgeois occupations: In the towns, doctors, lawyers, engineers, and other professionals served on the local boards; in rural areas, pharmacists and small businessmen.[105] In the sections themselves, and especially those located in villages and small towns, "intellectuals" in the broad sense of the term inevitably played an active role, adding to their traditional functions as scribes and docents for a semiliterate population, entirely new functions as interpreters of the emerging mass media and organizers of mass culture. Their profile, as described by the journalist Emilio Radius, departed little from that of the proverbial, humanist petty bourgeoisie prominent in the Italian provinces – "educators of modest extraction, teachers at the Popular Universities, actors in amateur theatricals, conferenciers, fine-phrase-makers, autodidacts, men about the town and village," with the added novelty of course of the "retired *squadristi*."[106] Personally more prestigious than their fellow members perhaps, and unquestionably more ambitious politically, these volunteers were distinguished as a group from other members by their mandatory party card. Whatever their real allegiance to the regime, these functionaries were by virtue of their own small aspiration for upward mobility bound to serve its interests. Neither the "passionate" agitators feared by fascist technocrats of the early twenties, nor the "disinterested" experts they had advocated to staff fascism's corporate organizations, they were the true mediators of the regime's social policies. So completely did the OND rely on the professional qualifications of these volunteers[107] that inevitably their social origins and their own ideological formation in the rhetorical academicism of the Italian educational system would powerfully condition local initiatives, sometimes contradicting, more usually reinforcing the cultural directives of the regime.

Rallying the nation

By late 1935, when Mussolini's regime attacked Ethiopia, the network of *dopolavoro* sections, along with the other fascist mass organizations, was entrenched enough to be seen as a primary means of rallying the population for the war effort. In fact, the regime began to mobilize the *dopolavoro* sections well before the opening of hostilities. On 20 June 1935, it instituted the so-called Fascist Saturday, ending the work week on Saturday at one o'clock, with the afternoon being reserved for "instructional activities," especially those of a "pre-military and post-military character." From late September, local groups were directed to take part in the hundreds of preparatory rallies in factories, neighborhoods, and villages that culminated on the eve of the invasion of Ethiopia on 2 October 1935 in gigantic nationwide demonstrations. The eight-month campaign, lasting until May 1936, when the foundation of Italy's East African Empire was celebrated with a new round of national rallies, provided a striking demonstration – and perhaps the only clear one of its kind – of the entire fascist mass organization in action as the recognized agency of the regime's propaganda. *Dopolavoristi* at the Fiat plants melted down their gold and silver trophies for the war cause as did those employed in the naval shipyards at Palermo, while workers of the Galileo Machine Works at Florence contributed four gold ingots to the national cause. Working class women in the neighborhoods of the Turin "barriers," the Milanese industrial suburb of Sesto San Giovanni, in the proletarian neighborhoods of San Lorenzo, Porta Maggiore, and Garbatella in Rome donated their marriage rings to the "plebiscite of gold," along with thousands of "rural housewives" in the Varese, the Po Delta, the provinces of Tuscany, and the rural districts of the Mezzogiorno. Neighborhood associations collected tons of scrap metal for the war effort, while rural clubs set up rabbit hutches and beehives, raised chickens and planted grain for the domestic "battle of autarchy" to defend Italy against the League of Nations' sanctions.[108] So clear was the response in the months between October 1935 and May 1936 that the antifascist opposition had to remark – disconsolately – on the apparent unanimity of support for the regime, the spontaneity of popular outrage at the announcement of the League of Nations' sanctions against Italy, and the extent of public acclamation for the foundation of the Empire in May. According to clandestine communist organizers, the regime, "at least for the moment," had successfully "rallied [*fanatizzato*] vast numbers of petty bourgeois as well as a not insignificant segment of proletarian youth."[109] For antifascists who had anticipated that the Ethiopian adventure would prove the regime's undoing, public response was particularly surprising: The enthusiasm generated by victory, reported the socialist Rodolfo Morandi to the PSI's Paris headquarters, had a "remarkably fortifying effect on the regime."[110]

Propaganda alone could not have accounted for the regime's ability to penetrate so many areas of Italian society that, because of geographical isolation, cultural resistance, or political tradition, had hitherto been impervious to government appeals. From the vantage point of the mid-thirties, it is clear that, since the fascists came to power in 1922, the relations between state and civil society that prevailed in liberal Italy had been profoundly modified. In the same way that the strategic ends of taking power had originally brought about the transformation of fascism from anarchic movement to a nationally based party, so the goal of maintaining power had finally led the regime to bring about major structural changes in the state apparatus itself. Looking back, however, it is clear that these changes were in no way the calculated result of an across-the-board application of any of the unitary projects put forward by syndicalist, revisionist, or nationalist theoreticians in the early twenties. The rigidly centralized bureaucracy of the OND, like that of the PNF, the trade unions, or the mass organizations for women and youth, corresponded to the authoritarian structures of state intervention favored by the nationalists. However, in its final form it was the result of what might be called a specifically fascist practice. Between 1922 and 1935 this had been developed less from any totalitarian application of a single political scheme than through the gradual and often uneven attempts on the part of Mussolini's regime to mediate dominant social interests and respond to diverse social and geographical environments.

3

Taylorizing worker leisure

From policing to persuasion

For large-scale industrial enterprise in Europe and America, there was nothing especially novel, much less "fascist," about setting up facilities to regulate the leisure of workers. The services recommended by Mussolini's regime to assist, educate, and uplift the "masses" differed little from the Sunday schools, night classes, "truck" stores, and company housing that, since the mid-nineteenth century, had been founded by paternalistic employers to root the transient peasant-laborer, enforce shop-floor rules, and train unskilled workers for increasingly complicated factory operations. The notion that businessmen should invest in community institutions as well was also entirely familiar to the post-1900 generation of industrial philanthropists whose patronage for parks and playgrounds, for the YMCA and for settlement houses was inspired by the realization that the formation of a modern industrial workforce – of loyal citizens, as well as disciplined operatives – demanded industry-wide cooperation and systematic intervention outside of the firm. In all respects Giani's own initial conception of the *dopolavoro* organization was indeed no more than a transposition of these increasingly common business practices into the Italian environment. Italian industry, he had presciently realized in 1919, had reached a critical stage of development following its hasty expansion during World War I: one in which firms were rapidly growing in size, management was becoming separated from ownership, and improved technology was being applied to rationalize industrial processes. If employers were to confront at all effectively the problems of labor management engendered by a unionized labor force; if they were to succeed in the "taylorization" of their enterprises to compete on the tight international markets of postwar Europe, then they too had to follow the British and American example: relinquishing the parochial policing techniques of the first phase of industrialization for a more systematic and "persuasive" management practice.

In postwar Italy there were, however, powerful obstacles to the adoption of such a policy of persuasion – as Giani himself had experienced first hand in 1919 when Italian employers simply ignored his first appeals for their support. The first and the most fundamental was the dualistic character of Italian industry itself, with its few dozen large technologically advanced firms, its relatively small number of medium-sized enterprises, and its scores of thousands of marginal, family-run concerns. The sense of the giant modern firms that they stood alone in the wasteland of Italian economic backwardness had fostered an attitude toward labor management that was at once insular and dependent. Protected by the state with tariffs and subsidies, they pursued a short-sighted, "go-it-alone" policy to satisfy their immediate needs for a stable and skilled work force. So the great textile magnates of the North constructed self-contained, despotically run company villages to break in their peasant-worker recruits, whereas the machine and metallurgical employers simply exploited a cheap and vast supply of unorganized labor, tapping the still vital artisan traditions of Italian craftsmen. Warding off any social legislation as too costly a burden for latecomers to industrialization, business employers expected the state to assume all of their social costs as well: for the education, instruction, and above all for the policing of the working class. Relying on the political authority of the central government to maintain their privileged place in the nation, Italy's fledgling industrial leadership before 1914 had failed to develop any of the new institutional mechanisms that would have guaranteed it a national cultural influence at all commensurate with its burgeoning economic power.[1] Inevitably, after the war, as individual employers began to see the advantages of industrial reform as a means of bolstering their position in the face of militant unionism, it was too late: A powerful associational movement, built on self-help traditions of craft communities, supported worker resistance against the blandishments of company paternalism.

For the fascist regime to gain industry's support for the *dopolavoro*, there thus had to be a transformation in business's relations with the state itself, as well as a thoroughgoing change in the attitude of individual employers toward their workers. Yet the coming to power of Mussolini had at first reinforced the old political barrier to industrial reformism.[2] If the state could still be relied on so absolutely to do industry's bidding – as did indeed seem the case after the *squadristi* broke the labor movement and Mussolini repealed Giolitti's social insurance laws in 1923 – there was certainly no need for employers to seek any new social solution to labor-management conflicts. In the aftermath of the "red years," the immediate restoration of management authority in the firm and a return to business as usual were of paramount concern to employers; and both, seemingly, could be achieved

The culture of consent: mass organization in fascist Italy

by severe repression alone – by the dismissal of strikers and black-listing union militants, and by playing the fascist syndicates and the socialist unions against each other. The resistance of employers to reformist initiatives was supported, at least implicitly, by the new president of the Confindustria, Antonio Stefano Benni, one of the first Milanese employers to use fascist vigilantes to break strikes. Under his leadership, after January 1923, neither the Confindustria nor its journal, *Organizzazione industriale*, discussed with any enthusiasm the proposals for welfare work or for *oeuvres sociales* that in the United States and elsewhere in Europe were gaining an interested hearing.[3]

Indeed, the experience of those Italian employers who took advantage of labor's defeat to experiment with an American-style company paternalism, demonstrated that in the face of worker resistance a purely parochial effort to reconstruct personnel relations was bound to fail. The Fiat Company, for example, had followed the advice of its prominent consultant Professor Mario Fassio; from 1922 on it allocated large sums to support "an enlightened and pragmatic" company policy aimed at "diverting workers from the political arena into an economic-professional one."[4] Even after the victory of the socialist FIOM in the first shop-floor delegates election in the spring of 1924, Agnelli had reasserted his commitment to company welfare work. But his million-lire donation to Fiat's Workers Mutual Fund itself precipitated a new strike, the workers protesting "management's abuse of authority" and its "constraints on the free will of the workers" imposed by the condition of mandatory enrollment.[5] A new plan by Agnelli, which had the Fund placed under a bipartite administration the following June, was similarly frustrated when the workers elected all communist and socialist delegates. Only Agnelli's recourse to public authority and the intervention of the Prefect of Turin were able to enforce the Fund's reestablishment in 1926 under a more pliant delegation of fascist syndicalists. If the giant Fiat failed to win over the workers with "enlightened" management, other industrialists could hardly be encouraged.

Not until mid-1925 did the fascist government even begin to bring pressure to bear on employers to institute some measure of reform. In May 1925, following the prolonged metallurgical strikes of February–March, Mussolini himself opened a campaign for what he called a "more enlightened policy" that would lead to "greater tranquility in the factory, greater productivity, and a better chance to beat the competition." "Intelligent capitalists," the Duce emphasized, "gain nothing from misery; that is why they concern themselves not only with wages, but also with housing, hospitals, and sports fields for their workers."[6] With these glib remarks, the Duce for the first time publicly supported a corporatist solution to labor-management conflicts: one in which the self-reform of industry was to play at least as important a role as the imposition of legislative controls. In this, Mussolini was indirectly at least supporting Mario Giani, who that very month had become the de facto head of the OND and the government's chief expert on industrial reform. For Giani, "the retrograde ideas of certain industrialists" were "particularly anachronistic in light of present-day concepts of the national interest." In the fascist regime, employers could no longer expect to conduct business as if it were a "strictly private affair."[7]

Giani knew his ex-colleagues in industry too well to believe that the OND could do much more than document as clearly as possible the advantages to employers of a well-rounded program of social services. Above all in Italy, any convincing argument had to be made on economic grounds: "Given the present state of opinion," the *dopolavoro* would have to justify itself as a "profitable activity," he recognized, and not, as he preferred, as a "social obligation with no concern for cost." Drawing a blatant parallel between the care of men and that of machines, he argued that the "greater well-being of personnel would have favorable effects on output, in the same way that the maintenance of the mechanical plant tended to increase the efficiency of production."[8]

Such exhortations to managerial self-interest, at least in the first two years of the OND's existence, failed to convince most employers that laying out large sums for social services was economically profitable. Those companies that provided their employees with extra services tended to confine their offerings to sports, neglecting vocational training, cultural activities, and the health and hygiene measures that Giani considered so fundamental to an integrated program of company services. At least some of these firms, Giani complained, were giving the management reform movement a bad name by running their personnel offices in a "rudimentary and empirical way," performing disciplinary functions with "inquisitorial and police methods that ma[de] them distasteful to the employees." Moreover, few displayed any willingness to cooperate with the government agency, although Giani conducted an "assiduous campaign" to convince employers that "the state had no intention whatsoever of invading those fields already cultivated by industrialists for the benefit of their employees." By the end of 1926, only a hundred companies – with a mere 17,710 employees – had registered with the OND.[9]

Beginning in 1925, however, employer attitudes underwent a striking change. Abandoning their insular defense of the firm against the inroads of public authority, employers began cooperating with government and party agencies. Following the enactment of the Syndical Laws of 3 April 1926, the Confindustria, reassured by its juridical recognition as a state institution, had naturally publicized its compliance with the spirit of class collaboration they embodied. But the willingness of businessmen to translate vague corporatist concepts into practice was ultimately determined more by economic conditions than by mere political expediency. The reorganization of industrial enterprise, which began in 1926 with the economic downturn and accelerated rapidly after 1927 as business sought to readjust to harsh deflationary measures, prompted employers to experiment with a more professional management practice.[10] Industry's "first year of social participation," as the Confindustria later called 1927,[11] was also marked by serious labor unrest as workers responded to wage cuts, threatened layoffs, and changes in factory organization with strikes, work stoppages, and slowdowns. Although the number of strikes was by no means significant in terms of the total workforce, nor by comparison with the massive strikes of metallurgical workers in March 1925, it demonstrated that neither the final disbanding of the free labor unions, nor the assiduous policing of the workforce could stem resistance, much less guarantee the cooperation required to taylorize the production process.[12]

Employer interest in testing new techniques of labor management was further reinforced by those government officials who saw that enlightened industrial management might help to stabilize the fascist order. Speaking before the Roman section of the National Fascist Association of Industrial Managers in January 1928 in his capacity as undersecretary of the Ministry of Corporations, Bottai pointed out that the number of joint stock companies had more than quadrupled since 1913, rising from 3,030 to 13,800 in 1928. As business management acquired a broader role in industrial policy, social responsibilities were correspondingly greater: The growth of the enterprise had to be accomplished "as humanely as possible by involving the worker in the operations of the firm." Management should not only "command" workers, but also "persuade" them; it should not simply "manage," but also understand and acknowledge the employees' "efforts."[13]

In theory at least, there were several means of "persuasion" available to employers. Most were familiar with the much-discussed example of fordism, and the apparent ease with which Ford, using his "doctrine of high wages," had accustomed his workers to the highly standardized work process of his Detroit plants. Italian employers, however, discarded such a solution outright. The industrial engineer Carlo Tarlarini summed up the case against fordism. American industry, he conceded, might well afford the luxury of high wages: abundant capital had facilitated mechanization; a broad domestic market had rendered standardization profitable; finally, labor was relatively scarce – in itself an incentive to higher wages – and was considered to be a potential consumer. In Italy on the other hand, capital was scarce, machinery expensive, and the domestic market narrow; above all, labor was cheap and abundant. Although the panoply of social services associated with fordism could be contemplated, incentives to accept rationalization in the form of higher wages could not.[14]

In Tarlarini's view, "the task of persuading the masses" to accept the new work systems should "naturally lie with the workers' Corporations." After all, the socialist unions in 1919–20 had posed no objections to rationalization provided it was accompanied by shorter working hours, higher wages, and a union voice in determining clocking systems and piece rates; the fascist syndicalists were certainly pliant bargaining agents by comparison. But employers had no intention now of involving them in what was considered a "technical question," subject solely to management authority. The syndicalists, they feared, would try to make it an issue in order to regain a foothold within the plant, especially as their power to bargain over wages and hours was now being further curtailed by the imposition of national contracts. This fear was not unwarranted; for the syndicalists, as we shall see, did indeed seek a voice in determining piece rates and fringe benefits to compensate for wage cuts and heavier work rhythms.

To preempt the fascist unions, employers instituted their own schemes of compensation. Among the first such initiatives and a forerunner of the more systematic programs of the late twenties was the "Liverani plan," a commodity distribution system invented by Ferdinando Liverani, general secretary of the powerful Lombard Consortium of Machine and Metallurgical Industries and general counsel to the Confindustria. His scheme called for a wholesale distribution network that combined the functions of the municipal provisioning board (the traditional provider for popular subsistence in times of scarcity) with the managerial prerogatives of the company store. The first seventy-one of these discount outlets were opened in Milan in August 1926: underwritten by participant firms, they provided employees with basic commodities such as rice, pasta, tomatoes, soap, and coal.[15] According to Liverani's calculations, workers buying all of their supplies at the outlets and paying with scrip deducted from their paychecks saved an average of 16 percent over retail costs; not surprisingly, the system was first introduced to counter worker demands for wage increases. Not only that: It was Liverani's view that the enhanced purchasing

65

power that resulted from worker patronage at the over 500 established outlets by late 1926 could even be used to justify further wage cuts. Beyond its purely economic benefits – provided at no extra cost to employers because operating costs were covered by profits – the plan, so Liverani explained, afforded numerous benefits of a "moral nature": It would teach workers how to calculate costs and deal with credit, and unlike the consumer cooperatives of socialist fame, it would foster "solidarity between classes and social groups in a practical way."[16] Liverani's own contention that the "psychological and social climate created by fascism" accounted for his plan's prompt success seems fully justified. It was immediately endorsed by *Popolo d'Italia* for its role in "educating the worker to dedicate his earnings to his family" and "fortifying the sentiment of collaboration between industrialists and workers";[17] Mussolini himself supported a similar plan when, overriding the demands of the Union of Fascist Metallurgical Workers of Turin for a wage increase, he urged Fiat instead to donate a million lire to Turin's Alleanza Cooperativa to enlarge its discount food operations.[18]

The most important indication of the shift toward policies of persuasion within industry was the rapidly increasing popularity of the social provisions developed under the name *dopolavoro*. By mid-1927 numerous management reports collected by the OND suggested that large enterprises had begun to treat recreation and assistance as Giani had hoped: as an "integral element of rational and efficient industrial organization." Thus the management of the ILVA Steel Mills of Genoa now endorsed the *dopolavoro* for "contributing to the productive efficiency of workers," whereas that of the Steel and Iron Works of Novi Ligure recommended it for "raising the dignity, moral personality and self-esteem of the workforce thereby causing it to feel the need to collaborate with other classes."[19] These initiatives were given official support by the Confindustria, which in 1927 established an Office of Welfare Work in its Rome headquarters and began publication of a new journal, the *Assistenza sociale nell'industria*. The Confindustria's own technical publication, the *Organizzazione scientifica del lavoro*, even claimed scientific evidence in support of industrial welfare work: A "rigorous analysis of data and numbers had demonstrated the unquestionable effectiveness of recreational centers, sports fields, and worker housing in increasing efficiency and productivity." The publicity it gave to the exaggerated claims of engineers – that well-placed charts and pamphlets on taylorism, company newspapers, and rest areas for workers could actually obtain the "moral consent" of labor for speed-ups and stretch-outs – could not help but intrigue cost-conscious managements.[20]

The acceptance of the *dopolavoro* as an "organizational norm," especially in large firms, as OND officials frankly admitted in late 1927, was "determined by practical motives in the majority of cases rather than by considerations of a humanitarian character."[21] The movement was led nationally by those very large firms engaged in rationalizing their plant, which, by virtue of their reorganization and expansion, had rapidly consolidated a monopoly position in their sector of the market: from the General Electric Company of Milan (CGE) in the electro-mechanical field to Gualino's Snia Viscosa and the Chatillon Company in synthetic textiles. In 1927, at Cengio, Italy's largest chemical dye factory instituted its *dopolavoro*, thus marking "a further step in that collective and individual action of political regeneration" that had first begun in 1921 with the vigilante action conducted by the owner's son against striking workers.[22] The following year Montecatini, the giant petrochemical conglomerate, announced that 9,000 of its employees had been enrolled in the OND; by 1937 one-half of its 180 affiliates reported social services of one kind or another enrolling 44,500 out of its 50,000-person payroll.[23]. Between 1927 and 1929, while nearly doubling its total sales, the new synthetics concern, Chatillon, inaugurated five sections in its subsidiary plants at Vercelli, Rhô, Chatillon, and Ivrea.[24] In 1929 Commendatore Bolognini of the STIGE Gas Works of Turin presided over the opening of the Dopolavoro STIGE, proclaiming it to be the "keystone of the action of concentration and rationalization in the natural gas industry."[25]

Fascist welfare capitalism

Although many large-scale employers were prompted by purely utilitarian considerations to pursue a more open-handed welfare policy, others, who either had not experienced serious labor unrest or were accustomed to relying on public authority to maintain order in their firms, remained impervious to the new spirit of corporate solidarity. There were also the thousands of smaller enterprises, severely squeezed by the economic recession and sometimes victims of the big-firm mergers; in these enterprises, social services represented a costly if not superfluous expenditure. Even when the larger concerns had made ample provisions for their own employees, they naturally were little inclined to extend assistance to the general public, through private charities or, as was demanded of them with increasing frequency, through party facilities established to propagate an image of fascist beneficence. A general spirit of "voluntarism" was still wanting. Too often, as Mussolini noted in 1928, commenting on Benni's incessant demands for wage cuts, industry's idea of class collaboration "resembles the collaboration of the noose with the hanged man."[26]

Business's uncooperative attitude was patently unacceptable in view of the regime's demonstrated willingness to compromise with organized industry on virtually every aspect of labor policy. The legislative acts and social principles formulated in 1926–7, although not infringing on management control in the enterprise or burdening industry with weighty contractual agreements or costly state-sponsored social programs, were after all premised on the self-reform of organized industry and its abiding cooperation with the state. The industrial community was now exhorted to accept social responsibilities corresponding to its expanding power in Italian society. Addressing the first assembly of the renamed "Fascist" Confindustria in June 1928, Mussolini reaffirmed that the "fordist" policy of high wages would not be implemented in Italy; in turn, however, the regime expected industry to abandon its traditionally parochial view of its own interests: "The horizons of the fascist industrialist must embrace other aspects and manifestations of social life."[27]

It became the PNF's responsibility to make certain that industrial employers, once assured of their power in the corporatist state, did not in fact lapse into their habitual shortsightedness. In a speech carried prominently in the national press in June 1929, party secretary Turati complained that employers too often treated the PNF as a "mere reflection of their interests," although – as it was well known – the party was "above and beyond all interests." The PNF now intended to demonstrate that it was the mediator of the capitalist system as a whole by inspiring in employers who previously had been guided purely by "egotistical motives" a "sense of collective concerns."[28] Persuasion was used to enlighten powerful firms, like Fiat, as to their duty to cooperate with state and party agencies: Its management was finally convinced to enroll its office employees' association (AIF) and its workers' sports group in the OND in March 1928.[29] Intimidation was used against small firms – the food processing enterprises and printing companies of Ravenna province, whose owner-managers were virtually compelled to set up facilities for their workers after being warned by local party functionaries that it was in their best interest to comply with OND directives.[30]

The net result of nationwide propaganda, well-calculated political pressure, and outright threats was a general and rapid increase in the company services where purely economic calculations appear not to have been a determining factor; that is, in firms with 250 or fewer employees, where such expenditures represented capital outlays not usually compensated for by expected increases in worker productivity. In just two years, from 1929 to 1931, the number of firms claiming *dopolavoro aziendali* rose by over fifty percent from 1,660 to 2,938, and by 1936, forty-three percent of the approximately 6,000 firms employing 100 or more persons had facilities of their own. Moreover, 600 medium-sized firms (those employing from 51 to 100 persons according to Italian census data) had enrolled their personnel in the OND, all this in years when the economic crisis had led employers in other nations to institute a reduction in similar kinds of company services.[31]

Party pressure also played a significant role in obtaining business aid for party-sponsored programs outside the firm. In the case of family enterprises, party functionaries exercised what was tantamount to a compulsory voluntarism. Persistent demands for donations to relief work organized by the party-run EOA, or Ente Opere Assistenziali, party construction projects, and seaside and mountain colonies for children provoked small businesses to complain that contributions were solicited in an "intimidatory and vexatious way."[32] Large firms too were subject to party demands. The Terni Steel Mills had provided generously for its own employees by building company villages, sports fields, a swimming pool, and several food outlets. But during the first year of the Depression, it had completely ignored the province's numerous destitute. To subsidize the EOA, the *balilla*, and the provincial *dopolavoro*, the *federale* had thus imposed a tithe, amounting to a day's pay annually deducted from workers' pay and a matching contribution from management.[33] As late as 1937, we find the PNF's administrative secretary Marinelli writing to Guido Donegani, the head of Montecatini, requesting that the conglomerate assume the costs of building a *casa del fascio* in the commune of Lecore Signa (Florence), where Montecatini's subsidiary Dinamite Nobel was located. Although Donegani protested that only 34 of the company's 2,500 employees lived there and the company had previously constructed a party seat where the majority resided, he acquiesced: Montecatini subsequently contributed 22,000 of the 50,000 lire requested.[34]

For the most part, however, little pressure of a personal nature was required. Since the foundation of the first *fasci*, industrialists had made substantial if surreptitious contributions to the party federations. After 1928, when the Confindustria openly sanctioned industrial donations to the PNF, they were given far greater publicity and were more frequently directed to social assistance than to outright political activity.

Corporate contributions were thus a major source of subsidies for party work during the Depression. The Confindustria itself regularly contributed huge sums: 18 million lire in 1931, 21 million in 1932, 24 million in 1933, 28 million in 1934, and in 1935 – the last year of extensive party relief work – a total of 35.5 million lire.[35] Single corporate giants, including Fiat, Pirelli, Montecatini, and Snia Viscosa, made similarly large donations. Fiat, among the firms most noted for their beneficence, besides contributing 50,000 lire to the construction of the Casa Balilla of Turin in 1929, donated 500,000 lire to the Winter Relief Fund in 1930 and underwrote a party campaign to finance a vacation colony for workers' children in 1932, while making substantial annual donations to welfare work and the yearly celebrations of the Befana Fascista.[36] Agnelli himself made what Fiat publicists described as a "personal gift" of 3 million lire to Mussolini on the occasion of the proclamation of the Empire. Montecatini – not to be outdone – claimed to have distributed 18 million lire for charity in 1936 alone, of which 1,500,000 lire took the form of a gift to Mussolini in honor of the same event.[37]

Since the first year of the Depression, the fascist leadership had acknowledged that industrialists were fulfilling their responsibilities to the corporate order. The "industrialists have done their duty," Mussolini solemnly affirmed before the National Council of Corporations on 9 June 1930. "We need not reprove them for anything: there has been a strong and praiseworthy increase in all kinds of assistance."[38] Bottai too, formerly a staunch critic of industry's resistance to corporate discipline, now extolled its support for party relief work as displaying a "spirit of voluntarism worthy of the highest praise."[39]

The management of social services

This "spirit of voluntarism," like that behind welfare work in Europe and the United States, was in individual enterprises interpreted entirely by management. Even though 467,058 industrial workers, a fifth of the entire OND membership, were enrolled through company plans, it was agreed that industrial services did not "lend themselves to standardization." Each employer was therefore declared "free" to organize such initiatives as were "compatible with his financial situation and suited to the aspirations, tasks, and needs of his personnel."[40] Naturally, there were some external pressures, beyond the routine directives announcing discounts or publicizing provincewide or national activities. Turin's fascist federation, for example, would have much preferred for Fiat to hold mass rallies in the city's center, whereas Fiat, more concerned with output than offering occasions for such

70

blatant propaganda, wisely demurred,[41] knowing that nothing risked alienating workers more than forcing them to spend their half-day Saturday rest in boring fascist ceremonials. Usually, barring particularly blatant abuses by management (which, in the absence of effective grievance mechanisms, had to be brought to the attention of party

Workers' children in balilla uniforms for the Befana Fascista at the Saint Gobain Chemical Works of Pisa. *Source*: OND, *I dopolavoro aziendali in Italia* (Rome, 1938).

71

authorities and trade union officials in an informal way),[42] company welfare plans were formulated and carried out at the complete discretion of management.

In an effort to ensure that employers would implement an "organic" program of services, the OND had, however, planned to set up its own network of professional social workers.[43] But it was preempted by the PNF, which founded its own school of social work at San Gregorio a Celio in 1928 and used its political clout to reach an informal agreement with the Confindustria to place graduates in its member firms. Ostensibly the social workers' tasks were nonpolitical: to publicize safety and hygiene measures, provide family counseling, familiarize workers with fascist social welfare legislation, and especially to help them fill out the numerous forms required to release any of its benefits. But a party-sponsored school afforded few guarantees of disinterested professionalism. Social workers wore the uniform of the Fascist party and acted as social go-betweens for the fascist federations. According to Guelfo Gobbi, editor of the Confindustria's monthly *Assistenza sociale nell'industria*, the so-called *assistenti* had thus been able to introduce workers to party notables, to organize celebrations of the "Birth of Rome" in the presence of local authorities, and to supervise the inaugural festivities of new company recreational halls.[44]

Nor was party-run social work necessarily efficient. In fascist Italy there were no nationwide campaigns of the kind organized by the

The central headquarters of the Fiat Dopolavoro. *Source*: OND, *I dopolavoro aziendali in Italia* (Rome, 1938).

"There exist no miracles, only your labor": Mussolinian realism in the conference room of the Fiat Dopolavoro. *Source*: OND, *I dopolavoro aziendali in Italia* (Rome, 1938).

OND's Nazi counterpart, the *Kraft durch Freude*, and promoted by its "Beauty of Work" Office in 1935–6: to replace ugly tumbledown fences with "dignified" enclosures, to paint delapidated factory facades, to conceal unsightly buildings with trees and shrubs, or to transform untidy factory yards into orderly recreational areas. "Actions," like those sponsored by the "Beauty of Work" with its frenetic sloganeering – "Good light – good work," "Clean men in a clean factory," "Happiness on the bench means higher productivity" – were foreign to fascist social workers.[45] Indeed their contact with actual factory conditions must have been highly sporadic if in 1937 only 200 party-certified assistants made the rounds of over 800 plants, 650 of which had in excess of 500 employees. Whether such lethargy was caused by party inefficiency or by the school's location in Rome, far distant from any major industrial center, can be debated. Superficial even in its policing functions, this party-sponsored, management-administered system may well have inhibited an especially pernicious interference in workers' private lives; but it also obstructed any advances in preventive health and job safety measures under the regime.[46]

The absence of any systematic national coordination of private in-

73

itiative led to considerable variation in the expressions of company
paternalism: What an employer offered and how it was presented depended not only on the business philosophy of a particular firm, the
degree of mechanization and modernity of the plant, the size and sex
composition of the labor force, but also on the employer's own views of
fascism. A "typical" company *dopolavoro* is thus hard to identify
among enterprises ranging in size from the tiny family-run firm employing at most a handful of workers to the highly mechanized plants
employing thousands. Probably very few of the approximately 100,000
concerns employing 50 workers or less had their own recreational
facilities, since only 600 firms with 100 employers or less were recorded
as having any social services at all. If their workers (who comprised
a quarter of the industrial labor force) participated at all in fascist-
sponsored recreational activities, they did so on their own initiative,
through neighborhood groups or through the associations that occasionally were set up by the fascist unions. Mechanized firms with more
than 100 employees were atypical in size, though they employed sixty
percent of the labor force; and just under half of these – 2,600 according
to Confindustria statistics for 1937 – had facilities of their own.[47]

Although this diversity makes it difficult to construct a general
"model" of the operations of the *dopolavoro* services within industry
as a whole, their functioning nevertheless remained fairly constant
within specific sectors of industry. Thus, in a mass-production industry
such as Fiat, the institution of the *dopolavoro* reinforced a natural
tendency of management toward strict discipline; in the new capital-
intensive industries such as the public utilities, electrical, and chemical
enterprises – more receptive to American management science – the
organization took on a strongly corporatist character; in the traditional
labor-intensive firms, textiles and food processing plants, it was treated
as an extension of older-style company paternalism.

Corporate fascism at Fiat

The social services at Fiat, Italy's largest enterprise, were the pride
of its management: Each phase of plant reorganization and expansion
from the postwar reconversion to peacetime production to the inauguration of the enormous new complex at Mirafiori in 1939 was accompanied by a corresponding growth in the company's welfare and
recreational facilities. By the end of the thirties, Fiat had the largest
dopolavoro and the most munificent social services of any firm in
Italy, representing an investment of hundreds of millions of lire and
serving 57,000 employees and their 150,000 dependents.[48]

Since 1919–20, the Fiat Company had been the foremost "Americanizer" in Italian industry. In response to the militant network of neighborhood clubs and political groups of the Turin working class, Agnelli had supported the development of an alternate system of reformist initiatives: from the ILO at the international level and the YMCA in the community to a range of programs for worker recreation and social welfare in his own firm. Not until the collapse of the workers' movement after the September 1920 factory occupations had Fiat's management been able to implement its own initiatives, no longer in the context of liberal reformism, but as extensions of a powerfully authoritarian system of labor control. With a discretion reflecting the circumspect planning of Fiat's American-trained managers, the company in 1921 had established a cut-rate food store and credit program that quickly attracted a growing clientele too preoccupied with inflation to dwell on the motives inspiring this apparently disinterested gesture. Using this opportunity to approach workers outside the factory gates, management had soon convinced some that "demonstrations were not the only kind of distractions available after work."[49] In February 1922 the company proceeded to organize a worker sports group, and the following month it opened the Fiat professional schools to begin training a new generation of skilled workers to replace those fired for political reasons the previous year. These efforts "to make workers' lives easier on the job and off" had yielded such promising results, according to the 1922 stockholders' report that justified their high cost, that management expected to "continue and perfect them."[50]

From their first introduction, Fiat's social services were conceived as integral elements in the production process, and they closely paralleled its transformation. The first services had thus been instituted in 1920–2, with the reorganization of the assembly line, whereas the inauguration of the new headquarters for Fiat's recreational programs in 1928 coincided with the adoption of the Bedeaux system.[51] In 1932 the operations of the *dopolavoro*, as the recreational programs were called after 1928, were considerably expanded once more; this time it was in response to Agnelli's decision to pacify worker discontent arising out of the Depression without recourse either to disruptive political purges or to the mediation of the fascist unions, whose reentry into the affairs of his firm he had hitherto resisted successfully. Following a series of management directives to the plant floor supervisors, enrollment in the *dopolavoro* doubled in 1932–3, so that by the end of the year some seventy-five percent of the 30,000 Fiat employees had been enrolled. Membership was further increased after 1933, when a pickup in production enabled Fiat to begin rehiring. The supervisory problems posed by the unprecedented growth in the workforce over

75

the next two years – which would bring the total Fiat payroll to 45,000 by 1935 – apparently motivated the Fiat management to request and receive a special dispensation from the OND that allowed it to enforce enrollment. In November 1933 Fiat announced that it wanted a "totalitarian" participation in the *dopolavoro*: In other words, all workers had to join, the fee of 1 lira per month being deducted from their paychecks.[52]

Initially no more than outgrowths of personnel services, the two recreational groups, one for office employees and the other for production workers, soon required an internal machinery of their own; in 1928 they were reconstituted as a separate department with its own president, secretariat, and directory. Unlike the vast majority of such company groups, the Fiat Dopolavoro was managed by professionals, in the early twenties by the German-trained director of Lingotto, Ugo Gobbato, an industrial engineer, as was his successor Ernesto Vandone, the president of the Dopolavoro from its inauguration in March 1928 to September 1935. Vandone was succeeded by Aristide Follis, the former head of Fiat's Italian sales division, whose skills in merchandising apparently made him well qualified to head the organization in its mature phase.[53] The directory, composed of management representatives from eleven Fiat *sezioni* and several affiliates in and around Turin, was designed to allow the maximum flexibility in planning sports and cultural-recreational pastimes at the plant level. This "concept of decentralization," as it was characterized by Vandone, was further promoted by establishing "small distinct groups" within the plants themselves, thereby encouraging "an agility of movement that the great bulk of the work force ill permitted."[54] Implicitly at least, he also acknowledged that the "soviet-type" system – so admired by Russian worker-delegates visiting the Fiat plants in 1931 – was best suited to exploiting for company use the traditionally close-knit shop organizations in the individual Fiat plants.[55]

To coordinate the day-to-day activities within the plants themselves, Fiat gradually built up a vast network of worker-delegates or *fiduciari*. The term had been applied originally to the worker-elected shop-floor delegates who had been denied legal recognition in accordance with the Vidoni Palace agreements of 1925. The *dopolavoro fiduciari* – 300 in 1933 and 600 by 1937[56] – were in contrast appointed by office managers or shop supervisors. Besides relaying company policy to employees, they performed some of the tasks formerly handled by shop-floor delegates, such as ascertaining the needs of their fellows and referring special problems to the appropriate job supervisor or service office. Although workers lacked any formal say in administering the company welfare services, management was nonetheless provided with a means for probing worker needs and involving them in semimanagerial functions. In this way it was able to assure the good functioning of the *dopolavoro* while avoiding the potentially dangerous forms of shop representation personified in the shop-floor delegates.

Although the term *dopolavoro* was used frequently to designate all company facilities not specifically covered in labor contracts, some of Fiat's social services were not in fact administered by this department. The Workers' Mutual Fund, for example, reorganized in 1928 in accordance with the new national metallurgical contracts, was run by a bipartite commission of trade union and management delegates. Monthly contributions by management and workers (3.50 lire for men, 2.50 for women, and 1.75 for personnel below age eighteen) paid for sick days, pregnancy leaves, medical treatment, and pharmaceuticals. In addition, the Mutual's reserve fund, consisting of work fines and management donations, served among other purposes to subsidize the vacation camps at Chiavari and Marina di Massa, where workers' children passed month-long summer holidays. Membership in the Salaried Employees' Mutual Fund was in contrast voluntary. Participants paid from 1 to 4 lire monthly, depending on the plan they chose, with additional funding derived from management grants and fines. Besides providing generous coverage for sick days – 10 lire daily for the first ninety days and 20 lire daily for the next ninety and an indemnity of 1,000 lire to beneficiaries in case of death – the fund underwrote all but 150 lire of the costs of children's vacations.[57]

Fiat's highly developed training program had not been incorporated into the Dopolavoro either, because of its major importance in plant operations. The Fiat schools catered to two categories of workers and were organized accordingly into two distinct sections: a three-year training program for apprentices – the sons of workers and employees with "notable ability and desire to learn" – and a year-long adult school open to workers between the ages of twenty and thirty who desired to secure promotion.[58] Besides these schools, Fiat set up courses in photography and languages for *dopolavoristi* in 1934. A special Fiat school, administered by one of Turin's established night schools, provided additional courses in office work, languages, accounting, and shorthand.[59]

Company housing, a standard service in isolated rural areas, was apparently considered superfluous, given that the majority of the Fiat sections were located near worker residences in the crowded neighborhoods of the Turin *barriere*. However, a cooperative housing society founded by several Fiat workers in 1923 undertook at its own initiative to build a group of twenty-four family dwellings on a site near the Lingotto works that had been conceded it on favorable terms by the Fiat management. The members made down payments of 10,000 lire, with the remainder of the costs covered by monthly installments of 60 lire over fifty years. Technicians and other employees at the Lingotto plant constructed a second group of houses consisting of sixteen two-family villas at a nearby site in 1927. Otherwise, Fiat simply leased land to the city, which, through the Istituto delle Case Popolari, constructed three groups of standard multistory apartment dwellings giving preference to Fiat workers. Plans for the Mirafiori Section, which opened in 1939, called for low-cost housing extending around the sprawling suburban plant. It was only at the rural Villar Perosa Ball-Bearing Factory, one of Fiat's original establishments, that the firm actually founded an industrial village in the old style, with Agnelli himself as *podestà* and residents comforted by cradle-to-grave services.[60]

The sense that Fiat workers belonged to a privileged close-knit community was imparted most notably by the recreational facilities the company sponsored, which in their munificence far outshadowed those readily available to the Turin middle class. The headquarters of the Dopolavoro inaugurated in 1928 in the presence of party authorities and town dignitaries – though without the participation of the syndicalist functionaries, who, invited at the last moment, refused to attend[61] – was situated on the right bank of the Po River. The palatial two-story building surrounded by an elegant esplanade accommodated a buffet, a spacious assembly hall, committee, game, trophy, and storerooms, in addition to a large boathouse and men's and women's dressing rooms complete with thirty showers. The elite status of the Fiat employees was further demonstrated by such amenities as three tennis courts, boating (with sixty boats and eighteen training skiffs), a skating rink, an outdoor theater, and a children's playground.[62] The company also built a gymnasium in Via Marochetti with indoor tennis courts, and a large sports field in Corso Stupinigi and at Fossata, and five smaller playgrounds in outlying worker neighborhoods. For trips outside the city, it opened a ski lodge at the nearby Alpine resort at Bardonecchia in 1928, a resort that offered room and board for 200 persons and hosted up to 1,000 persons for day-long excursions.[63] Vacation camps, with space for 2,500 children in 1936, were located at Chiavari and at Marina di Massa, where the renowned Torre Balilla – a futuristic multistory dwelling designed by V. Bonadè-Bottino – was inaugurated in 1932.

Upon payment of the obligatory 4.5 lire for a membership card and a monthly 1-lira fee, workers obtained access to recreational pastimes surpassing those available to the vast majority of *dopolavoristi*. The Fiat Dopolavoro sponsored sections for all of the games supervised by the OND, and in addition, many of the competitive sports assigned to CONI. By 1928, 450 persons were enrolled in the boating clubs including 50 women, who had their own special section. Tennis players numbered 100, of whom 60 were women. Besides the twenty-three sports groups, there was an outing society that had eight buses at its disposal, an automobile excursion club, a motorbike and cycling group, and sections for theater, indoor games, music, family excursions, and a special office handling discounts and credit facilities.[64]

Fiat sports, unlike those found in the majority of *dopolavoro*, were highly competitive. Promising athletes were recruited for the Italian Olympic Committee, CONI, with the aim of grooming the best for international meets. Soccer tournaments were held regularly among the various plants, with teams competing for the coveted Agnelli Trophy. Besides building up one of the top-ranking professional soccer clubs, the Juventus, management trained its teams for outside competitions. Vandone, noting in his annual report that the Fiat teams in 1933 had won only 5 national, 12 regional, and 5 provincial contests, exhorted them to make a better showing in the future.[65] Fiat sports did indeed keep pace with the accelerating rhythm of national athletic events in the thirties: In 1937 the Fiat teams – in addition to engaging in 650 intramural events – took part in 34 national championships, 102 regional competitions, and 71 provincial contests.[66]

Cultural pastimes were equally an object of management concern, as Fiat remained sensitive to the fact that it was dealing with a work force that still conserved a strong sense of its identity as vanguard of this first mass-production industry in Italy. Management in fact perpetuated the mystique of the Fiat workers as a worker elite at the same time as it sought to convert the old political radicalism into acceptably conservative social and cultural pursuits. Workers were praised for their concern for politics, demonstrated, in Fiat's view, by the fact that an estimated half of the Lingotto workers regularly purchased newspapers upon leaving work. "Science and technology are at home at Fiat," noted *Bianco e rosso*, the Fiat house organ, commenting in 1934 on the enthusiastic response to the new Hoepli bimonthly publication, *Sapere*.[67] Management regularly sponsored tours of the Fiat plants to give personnel a grasp of the whole production process, from the hydroelectric generators to the foundries and the motor-vehicle assembly plants. Workers were also encouraged to express their individuality in purposeful ways: "To create," went the announcement for the first Fiat show of arts and crafts and small inventions in 1931, "that is the greatest desire of those who work all day, all of their lives to produce what has been conceived by others.''[68] Besides giving employees "an opportunity to cultivate their minds and abilities," the show had an ulterior purpose in fostering worker interest in improving the production process. Indeed, immediately following the opening of one show, the Dopolavoro set up a special counseling service to advise employees on obtaining patents for after-work inventions.

Bianco e rosso, delivered monthly to all employee homes, was evidence of management's estimation of the generally high cultural level of the Fiat work force. The eight- to sixteen-page newspaper, containing reports on national and world events in addition to sports, cultural pursuits, and company news, was far more sophisticated than the national *Gente nostra*. Its literary page carried reviews of Proust and Thomas Mann as well as the short stories of Ardegno Soffici and other representatives of the fascist literary vanguard.[69] *Bianco e rosso* also broke the fascist press's censorship of good news from Russia with reports on the progress of the Riv Moscow, Fiat's contribution to Soviet industrialization, which, while paying tribute to the achievements of Soviet society, probably did little to cheer those Fiat workers who clung to the vision of revolutionary Russia as the unsullied heartland of international communism.[70] *Bianco e rosso* even permitted itself an occasional, if benign, piece of antimanagerial humor:

> Manager to worker: Congratulations, Antonio, on your thirtieth year of service to the firm.
> Worker: Yes, sir . . .
> Manager: From now on, as a sign of our appreciation you get to be called Mr. Antonio.[71]

In addition to numerous cultural events – three operas, four orchestral concerts, twenty band performances, eight choral presentations, four operettas, twenty-four dramatic works, and twenty films in the first half of 1933 alone,[72] Fiat also provided its workers with a 10,000-volume library, which was run, as described by an ILO observer in 1928, by a "conscientious and disinterested" staff. The library, as indicated by the 1928–34 catalogue supplement, carried relatively few fascist works. New acquisitions consisted overwhelmingly of eighteenth- and nineteenth-century European classics, including Voltaire's *Candide* (which was condemned by the Church), technical and scientific works, and a good selection of writings of the international literary vanguard – Maxim Gorky, Jack London, and John Dos Passos, all books which, if not altogether unfamiliar to the OND's functionaries in Rome, would undoubtedly have been judged inappropriate for a general readership.[73]

Beyond its function as the Fiat house organ, *Bianco e rosso* also served as a vehicle for fascist propaganda. The fascist rhetoric of Fiat emulated the "futuristic" image of fascism – an image personified by Italo Balbo, who, following his first transatlantic flights in 1932, visited the Fiat workers to thank them for their contribution to fascist Italy's aviatory might. Fiat's fascism was imperialistic, stressing the connection between expanded production and Fiat's contribution to the war in East Africa. It was profoundly militaristic, equating in 1935 the proletarian elite employed at Fiat with the front-line soldier in battle for Italy's empire.[74] Always it advocated a military-like discipline, consistent not only with an orderly society but also with the rigorous organization necessary in a highly mechanized mass-production firm.

It is in a sense ironic that in the thirties Agnelli, that "fine Giolittian liberal" as Mussolini had earlier described him, espoused what was in essence the most imperialistic version of fascism. Yet this is not to say that Fiat's president did not continuously strive to prevent the Fascist party and especially the fascist trade unions from entering his firm. While pursuing what was in intention a policy of autonomy, the firm itself was transformed into a microcosm of the regime, with its own detachments of blackshirts in the Cohort 18 November, its own 1,000-member section of Giovani Fasciste, its 2,500 uniformed Donne Fasciste, several premilitary formations enrolled in the Gioventù I-taliana del Littorio (including *pre-aeronautiche, marinaretti,* and pre-tank troops)[75] and, not least of all, its own highly regimented *dopolavoristi* – the envy of many party functionaries, who lacked the resources and management skill available to Italy's most powerful corporation. Fascism of this kind, organized to strengthen the production process, was fully compatible with a personnel management system that had long ceased to refer to the ostensibly "liberal" managerial techniques of fordism – its original inspiration – espousing instead a peculiarly authoritarian administrative system premised on strict hierarchy and harsh discipline.

The American plan at SIP

Whereas Fiat, together with other heavy industrial concerns, had to deal with entrenched traditions of labor militancy, the public utilities recruited a labor force with little or no experience in autonomous labor organization. Fiat was faced with the problem of transforming a class-conscious mass work force into a worker elite, isolated by its privileges from other segments of the working population. The public utilities in contrast employed a large yet highly differentiated work force ranging from its urban office staff to unskilled laborers in outlying hydroelectric plants, and were confronted with a more complex task in engendering a single and overriding sense of corporate unity.

The management of the Piedmontese Hydroelectric Company or SIP, one of the largest of Italy's new postwar conglomerates, was perhaps the most self-conscious emulator of American-style management policies of any Italian firm. Like many of Italy's new public utilities, SIP drew on American technology and the American finance market.[76] Its general director, Gian Giacomo Ponti, had studied with the inventor Steinmetz and completed his training at the Edison Company of New York. American capital was borrowed to expand company operations and to underwrite the new corporation in 1918. In reorganizing the business, Ponti had begun to introduce the forms of American personnel management: in 1922 a company newspaper, a sports group in 1924, and a company pension plan in 1925. These initiatives were by 1926 grouped under the offices of the SIP Dopolavoro or DAS, which by the late 1920s served over 6,000 employees in offices and plants spreading from Turin to Bologna.

Sincronizzando, the SIP newspaper, was the first of its kind in Italy, although in style it remained unabashedly American, carrying jokes in translation, American illustrations, and even – for the edification of SIP employees – the loyalty pledge exacted by an American public utilities company:

> If you work for me, in heaven's name work for me loyally. If you are paid a decent wage, work for me with dedication. Speak well of me and the firm, defend me and think of the firm as a second family, for an ounce of devotion is worth a pound of intelligence.[77]

Ponti's injunctions and comments, a regular gesture, suggested management's benevolent concern for employee welfare. At the SIP, or so *Sincronizzando* would have had its readers believe, management and staff worked in closest collaboration. Office work, in contrast to factory labor, was carried out in a humane and informal environment with all personnel, however humble, working side by side in the public interest. The management evidently wanted this ostensible camaraderie to continue off the job as well. Recreation, in Ponti's view, was to serve as a true leveler: "We have never allowed our *dopolavoro* to take on an aristocratic air that might have alienated and humiliated our closest associates, nor a saloon-like atmosphere that would have repelled our most distinguished functionaries."[78] As a matter of company policy, management and lower-grade employees shared the same leisure organization, unlike most other industrial firms, where separate activities – if not totally separate facilities – were set up on the well-accepted principle that their tastes, if not their means, were entirely dissimilar. When planning its *dopolavoro*, SIP had attempted to "conform to the habits of both"; accordingly, it had established a "single modest, decorous, and serene standard for all." This was intended "to improve the habits" of the clerical personnel, or "associates" (to use Ponti's euphemism) while toning down the habits of the managerial staff, which, according to Ponti, were "still inclined toward the luxurious and profligate habits of the wartime period."[79]

Ponti himself, as if seeking to reproduce the democratic atmosphere of the American office, relentlessly exhorted management and technical cadres to participate with clerical personnel and workers in after-work activities, something they seemed little inclined to do of their own accord. "Nothing," he affirmed, "pleases me more than seeing engineers joining in card games with their workers, and supervisors, without the slightest trace of affectation, pausing affably with their staff and workers, taking part in their conversations, and not occasionally in their leisure pastimes as well."[80]

Although joining the DAS was never made compulsory, taking out membership was nonetheless emphasized as a test of the employee's goodwill toward the firm. Not surprisingly, most employees complied: By 1928, half of the staff was enrolled; in 1930, a total of 4,241 or 71 percent.[81] Employees were further expected to participate with a proper "communitarian spirit." It was not enough, Ponti wrote, "simply to improve one's own physical and spiritual capacities" while engaging in the company-offered pastimes: "He who fails to strive for intellectual and moral solidarity with all members of the same *dopolavoro* is neither a good *dopolavorista* nor a good citizen of the corporate state." The DAS was clearly conceived as forming good *citizens* as well as good *workers*: "We would be committing a vain if not pernicious act," Ponti stressed, "if we failed to give the nation healthy and cultivated workers or citizens lacking an associative spirit, understood in the most fascist sense of the term."[82]

Whereas the Fiat management had emphasized the importance of a technological "futurist" culture, the DAS evoked that eclectic ideological mix so typical of "petty bourgeois" fascism, consisting of a "healthy sensible culture, of one's artistic tradition, one's own history and its evolution across the past – a culture formed in close contact with the process of production yielding at once the consciousness of a producer and that of a citizen aware of his civic functions in the social mechanism."[83] The DAS's recreational program likewise recalled that prompted by the OND at the national level: beauty contests for children, the plays of Goldoni, excursions, and sports. That it so closely resembled that of the OND reflects the similarly heterogeneous constituency to which each was appealing. SIP had its own "new working class" of white-collar employees and workers. By playing on its novelty and distinctiveness with respect to traditional factory labor, it sought to impart a new sense of corporate allegiance, thus duplicating the rhetorical motifs of the OND within the confines of the firm.

Neopaternalism in the textiles industry

Personnel management in the textiles industry differed markedly from that found in more mechanized branches of industry; typically labor intensive, and with an average of sixty workers per firm, it had the highest labor concentrations in Italian industrial establishments. The "human factor" was thus a primary determinant of productivity, and increasingly so during the interwar years as the leading manufacturers rationalized work methods, thereby requiring a smaller labor force but a stricter work discipline to enforce the fatiguing work rhythms. Unlike other branches of industry, textile firms generally had small clerical staffs. What is more, the labor force was predominantly female: at 77 percent, nearly four times the overall average in Italian industry. Workers were also unusually young, with more than a quarter of the total nineteen years old or under. Roberto Tremelloni described it in 1937 as a "young, agile, cheap, yet unstable work-force,"[84] one that demanded a management attuned to such specific needs as room and board, child care, and special paternal guidance for women and youth alike.

The leading cotton and wool manufacturers were by far the most experienced company paternalists, with solid traditions dating back to the latter half of the nineteenth century. In the past, however, their practice had evolved out of individual efforts by owner-managers to stabilize the work force and cement loyalty to the firm. By the mid-twenties, however, the fashion for experimenting with personnel management methods, together with the desirability of breaking in new workers in rural areas, led many to adopt or at least contemplate a more calculated approach to problems of labor discipline.[85]

With the development of hydroelectric projects, it was no longer strictly necessary to build plants in isolated rural areas near water power. But the trend nevertheless continued, supported by what textile engineers called "economic-eugenic reasons" for decentralizing industry. According to G. Bullo, the location of new plants in rural areas would lower food costs and protect the workers from the evils of an urban environment.[86] In an industry with a turnover estimated at some

60 percent annually among the first generation of workers, housing, food provisioning, religious, recreational, and educational services were seen to be vital. The well-planned textile village promised to yield results equal to if not greater than those employers had obtained simply from close surveillance of the work force: "The enterprise itself," in Bullo's words, would "systematically, rationally and rapidly generate a lively labor-force, selected, qualified, skilled, fully trustworthy, and of highest individual and collective productive efficiency."

This peculiar mixture of old-style company paternalism and more systematic personnel administration, found in a company town like that constructed by the Marzotto Wool Firm at Valdagno in 1926, was similarly present in all aspects of personnel management in textiles. For one expert quoted in the *Bollettino della "Laniera,"* the so-called "psychotechnic selection" of the efficient wool-worker consisted of "eliminating the lazy, the drunk, and those lacking any specific skill, who curse from morning to night against the ill fate that doomed them to labor against their free will."[87] When the company provided workers with accommodations, the organization of recreation was often placed under the supervision of the person in charge of room and board. In many plants such tasks were handled by Salesian or Franciscan nuns;[88] at the Nocera plant of the Manifatture Cotoniere Meridionali, founded in 1924 and among the most modern in Italy, they were administered by the daughter of the plant manager. Generally speaking, the operation of the *dopolavoro* was guided by a puritanical, primitive, and occasionally brutal attitude toward discipline. For the management of the Nocera plant, it proved of "inestimable value": The "patient education of every day and every hour" had rendered "even the most riotous and intransigently undisciplined girl . . . not only obedient to the norms of civic life, but also a convinced advocate of the utility and efficacy of the system . . . with a strong disdain for rural existence and little inclination to return to her peasant home."[89] Described elsewhere, the Nocera Dopolavoro appears to have consisted solely of worker dormitories where rigid rules and house discipline transformed rough and refractory peasant girls into paradigms of civilized working-class virtue: "No longer girls dominated by their instincts and ignorance, but fresh bunches of roses exuding vitality."[90]

In response to inquiries into their social services, many textile firms cited worker housing. Each of two factories of the Valli di Lanzo Cotton Mills of Piedmont housed 100 women workers. The Strambino Cotton Mills similarly provided dormitory space for 200 of its 650 employees, whereas the Borgosesia Wool Works accommodated 400 of its 2,000 workers in large barrack-like buildings.[91] The Marzotto

Wool Firm, to cite an exemplary case, opened a new worker village in 1926 that provided complete services for 1,200 employees. This "brave new world" in the foothills of the Venetian Alps was complete with worker housing supplied with such modern amenities as electricity and indoor plumbing, renting at the modest annual rates of from 200 lire to a maximum of 1,000. It provided a full range of services from the company store to the company-supported church. But it was the *dopolavoro* that especially impressed visitors. According to the English cooperativist Karl Walter, it was "as spacious and well-appointed as any American athletic club and made the RAC [Royal Athletic Club] look stuffy – a great swimming pool, tennis courts and gymnasium, glass-enclosed in winter under a single span of roof so high that you forget it, with tiers of dressing cabins and showers and spectators' galleries, a cafe, card room, billiard room, bar, theater, writing room – all on the same scale, furnished in the steel-and-glass style." What impressed him above all was the comprehensiveness of Marzotto's "generosity"; for nearby he found a "model" clinic, a "model" maternity home, a "model" old people's home, and a "model" créche, in which "not only the beds and tables and chairs of its many rooms were graded in size for the many groups of uniformed infants and toddlers, but also the modern lavatory furniture."[92]

Although the company towns may have differed little in conception from their nineteenth-century counterparts, their more comprehensive planning secured for their managements a greater degree of control over employees. Rents were generally paid a month in advance and in all cases deducted from the worker's paycheck. Severance from the company led almost immediately to eviction from the company housing. The Borgosesia Wool Company, which prided itself a magnanimous employer, gave a worker a maximum of fifteen days to find other lodging.[93] Workers often became heavily indebted to the company stores, thus limiting their mobility and curbing any desire to make trouble with the company. Workers attended the company church; and their children went to the company school and, as was the case at Marzotto, Borsalino, Rossi, and other leading firms, to the seaside and mountain camps for summer holidays. Management control was all the more effective because the mutual aid societies and workers' circles, which had broken down the isolation of the nineteenth-century factory towns, were now banned,[94] restoring employers' monopoly over their employees' lives.

Textile employers, although relatively generous in satisfying basic needs for bed and board, were notably less open-handed and inventive in supplying workers with recreational facilities. Marzotto, Borsalino,

Paolo Mazzonis, Cantoni Coats – to name the leading textile manufacturers – matched in quality and quantity the provisions made by the more progressive heavy machine manufacturers for their employees. Otherwise, having furnished a common room or a nursery, most employers seemed to feel that they had discharged their responsibilities. After all, the needs of an unsophisticated and largely female work force were perceived as relatively primitive compared to those of a more politicized, urban, male work force. Employers were little inclined to disrupt unnecessarily the insular life of their firms by introducing the unfamiliar and frivolous distractions of urban leisure.

Even the most innovative textile employers conceived of appropriate worker pastimes in a traditional and austere way. The sober paternalism of nineteenth-century Catholic ideology was frequently simply updated with fascist politics. The worker feast days, first instituted to break the monotonous routine of the work week, were celebrated with a new fascist gloss. The Weavers' Festival (Sagra dei Tessitori) originally conceived by Baron Alessandro Rossi in the 1880s to commemorate the artisan weaver, was reinaugurated in 1932 as a fascist holiday "to commemorate a new form of austere collaboration between labor and capital."[95] In the course of the thirties the prizes formerly granted to especially devoted employees were combined with the award of the fascist Star of Merit. The awards ceremonies, like that held yearly by the Borgosesia Company to confer its Papà Magni award (which consisted of a small premium in company stock, as well as the fascist Star of Merit), were inevitably the occasion for paternalistic soliloquies. When the president of the Gutermann Silkworks at Perosa, Argentina, thus honored a seventy-six-year-old worker with sixty-six years of service to the firm, he reminded the assembled workers "how much fascism cares about the destiny of the working masses." By virtue of fascism they had "been educated to a higher and nobler sentiment; to consider their labor not merely as a social necessity but also as a patriotic duty, indeed one of the most patriotic acts possible in this complex modern society."[96]

Textile firms collaborated in full with the fascist regime – the Crespi management for example boasted of the "assiduous personal attention" devoted by Crespi and his sons to fascist and patriotic propaganda in the plant[97] – but the fascism they espoused seemed less militaristic than the imperialist rhetoric at Fiat and less petty bourgeois than that of the SIP. Textile employers had already evolved a coherent corporate philosophy drawing on social catholic traditions; embellished with the motifs of fascist patriotism, it served equally to sanction management authority and to reinforce discipline in the firm.

The erosion of fascist trade unionism

How did the workers themselves react to such a comprehensive system of management-sponsored social organization? Italian employers, perhaps not surprisingly, were silent about worker response, except insofar as it was positive. Yet we know that outside of Italy, employers had difficulty making workers cooperate with noncompulsory company welfare schemes and especially with those bringing no tangible economic benefits. Workers disliked socializing either with their superiors or their fellow workers after working hours, at least under company supervision, preferring to leave the factory premises and choose their friends freely. Any especially visible philanthropy was considered demeaning, and activities over which the worker had no say were regarded with suspicion. "Industrial betterment," as one leading American businessman told the original "social engineer," William H. Tolman, "should be gone into very cautiously . . . let the employees themselves show a desire for something more and a willingness to help accomplish it," he advised. "It would be very easy to wreck industrial betterment work by overdoing it."[98]

The silence of Italian employers on this issue contrasts with the candid appraisals of their colleagues in liberal democracies and must be explained in part by their need to present in a positive light the achievements of firms often cooperating closely with the fascist dictatorship. This alone would ensure that any resistance on the part of employees would be minimized. Beyond this, supported by a government always ready to use force, the question of worker "cooperation" was in a sense a moot point. Business employers, least of all, could accept the notion of voluntariness that was spelled out in OND directives and necessarily implicit in the constitution of the territorial group, which lacked any power to enforce participation.

Yet sources other than employers, including the reports of fascist syndicalists as well as communist militants, suggest that company-sponsored social services encountered no serious resistance. Was this the result simply of the opportunism of workers who had no alternatives and nothing to lose? The answer is more complex. The regime, by instituting the *dopolavoro* in all areas of national life and by propagandizing such initiatives as a worker right, merely supported by company largesse, had in a sense succeeded in giving this originally *private* managerial operation a *public* character that made it more acceptable to workers. So long as there was no visible alternative to these benefits – the fascist neighborhood groups were less well equipped and more politicized – nobody, least of all communist militants, would suggest that workers refuse them. Workers may well have remained suspicious of employer motives, and, as we shall see, were encouraged in their suspicions by fascist trade unionists. But the socialization of industrial welfare work under fascism made it more difficult for them to identify the reasons for this management largesse or to counteract the subtle forms of dependency on employers that a service of this kind inevitably engendered.

But such benefits did not blind workers to their low wages or their nearly total loss of bargaining power. Workers at Fiat, according to an informer's report in 1937, repeatedly complained that Fiat's "lavish expenditures" on sanatoria and assistance would have been better spent on wage increases.[99] Although they lacked any specific means for voicing their complaints against the *dopolavoro* – since it was not covered by contract – workers occasionally protested against the practice, tolerated by the OND in the late thirties, of enforcing enrollment by deducting dues from paychecks.

The attitude of fascist syndicalists toward company welfare policies is far easier to gauge than that of workers: The bitter criticism of such measures amply testified to their effectiveness in further undermining trade union authority. By the latter half of the twenties the fascist unions had clearly lost their battle for integral corporativism. The conclusion of the Vidoni Palace agreements, by which de jure recognition of the shop-floor delegates was eliminated, resulted (according to Gino Giugni) in the trade unions being "deprived of any organic relationship with the factory or the world of production."[100] With the enactment of the Rocco Laws, syndicalists lost the strike as a bargaining weapon, while the subsequent "unblocking" of the industrial confederation in November 1928 destroyed the national unity required to defend wage levels. The widespread introduction of piecework systems accompanied by changes in skill rankings and methods of calculating wages further eroded their bargaining position. Contract negotiations now took place on unfamiliar terrain. Management experts versed in the new work systems had the upper hand in dealing with the older generation of syndicalists, who, in keeping with the traditions of Second International unionism, focused on the skilled worker categories. They were also at an advantage in bargaining with the new generation of union bureaucrats, trained in the sophistries of corporate law, yet often ill-acquainted with the practical workings of the plant.

Nevertheless, the syndicalists seemed to regard their loss of bargaining power and inability to defend wage levels as mere tactical concessions rather than as resounding defeats. What rankled most was to find that both state reforms and management initiatives were usurping those accessory functions they needed to organize their own constituency. The Giordani project, proposing government regulation of trade union mutual funds, presented before the Chamber in April 1929, provoked the first public reaction from the trade union leadership. If the project was made into law, affirmed Malusardi, secretary of the Turin Federation, it would constitute "another step toward removing altogether the ethical functions of the syndicalist movement."[101] The unions had already "lost any direct influence over the *dopolavoro*, that is, over the educational and recreational aspects of worker organization." The professional schools, too, formerly under syndicalist guidance, had been handed over to the state. Malusardi feared that once assistance was removed, the syndicalists' functions would become "purely contractual and economic," like those of the socialists, who – as was well known – had focused on "satisfying material aspirations and needs." Malusardi was forced to acknowledge, however, that the respective bargaining powers of the two organizations were very different: The socialists had recourse to extralegal tactics whereas "today's unions have to act with legal methods . . . " If in addition they were deprived of accessory functions, they would lose "all possibility of organizing the masses in our associations and instilling in them a sense of solidarity and nationhood."

The syndicalists reserved their sharpest criticism for industrial employers and especially for the noncontractual and therefore nonnegotiable benefits afforded by company social services. Debate at the First Interprovincial Congress of Fascist Syndicates, held in Milan on 1 July 1929, focused on management social provisions. For Cuzzeri, the outspoken delegate of the fascist metallurgical workers, the food outlets were "an economic anachronism, bolstering management authority in the workplace."[102] He further claimed that the *dopolavoro* was deliberately being used by employers to undermine trade union power in the firm. Fioretti, the president of the CNSF, acknowledged that the food outlets "facilitated the policy of wage slashing" and he deplored the "estrangement" between the trade unions and *dopolavoro*, which in his view should "never have taken place." But when he sought to reassure the delegates that this "estrangement" would readily be overcome, since the trade unions had been granted permission to distribute *dopolavoro* membership cards, he was interrupted by shouts from the floor: "At Milan, that's not what's happening," and "The company sports groups have got to go!"

Reverberations from this disorderly debate were subsequently felt at the meeting of the Central Intersyndical Committee convened on July 6 at Palazzo Viminale. Mussolini himself, presiding over the meeting, took the occasion to denounce the "demagogic tone" of the Milan Congress.[103] The Confindustria, he held, had "no personal interest in maintaining the food outlets." "If the syndicalists didn't want them," he felt certain that "the industrialists would be delighted to eliminate them without a word of regret." The *dopolavoro* on the other hand was in Mussolini's opinion "among the most vital and important institutions of the Regime." The syndicalists themselves were to blame for causing the "estrangement" and "tending to underestimate its significance." Bottai, seeking to mediate, emphasized that "the trade unions wanted to clarify its relationship with their organizations precisely because they recognized its importance." Benni, in reply, reaffirmed the Confindustria's viewpoint, defending management largesse and claiming in no uncertain terms that the fascist unions, as always, were quite simply unappeasable: "If industrialists do something useful, they say it's done with the workers' money; if they do nothing at all, the syndicalists call us bastards."[104] Benni made an especially adamant defense of the workers' sports groups – the management initiative that had aroused the loudest protest from the trade unions. In his view, they served not only as a "stimulus to the spiritual life of the worker," but also to "foster competition among firms, with great benefit to productive output."

Faced with Benni's forceful argument for the productivity of company paternalism, Fioretti could only respond rather lamely that such measures were in any case the workers' due. Therefore they should not be construed merely as the product of the "liberality or paternalism of employers."[105] Any further clarification would have required a political confrontation of a magnitude that the syndicalists were disinclined and unable to engage in. No further opportunity to debate the issue was afforded in any case: The provincial intersyndical congresses that had provided the original forum for this last polemical outburst were subsequently banned.

From the early thirties, the syndicalists fought a rearguard action against what the fascist union leader Ugo Manunta described in 1932 as the "evident trend among the greater part of Italian industrialists to transform the factory into the monopolistic center of worker life."[106] The employers' immense strategic advantage, especially in the company towns, forced the fascist unions on the defensive; but it also made them "try harder," so to speak, to avoid any suggestion that their militancy had been dulled by management handouts. Thus, when Karl Walter asked the secretary of the union local at Marzotto whether management's "generosity" had any "ulterior motive or at least some embarrassing ulterior effect," he answered boasting: "Well, we won a case against them last year for 700,000 lire."[107] Nevertheless, most syndicalists would have agreed with the fascist union organizer interviewed by *Lavoro fascista* in 1931, who insisted that to "conquer and convert the doubtful, it [was] absolutely necessary to approach the workers when their nerves were relaxed," that is, after work.[108] Compulsory meetings did not yield the desired results; these could be obtained solely by what the CNSF commissioner Bruno Biagi described as "daily contact, vigilant interest, and constant attention to those needs and requests which fall outside of normal trade union activities."[109]

For all of their efforts to engage workers outside of work, thereby reuniting recreational pastimes with economic demands, the syndicalists proved ineffectual. The most active union members were those workers with experience in the prefascist associations, whereas young workers took out union membership because they were compelled to do so. But instead of participating in the union, they joined the *dopolavoro* and passed their spare time in sports[110] – an understandable preference in view of the scant prospect held out by the syndicates for ameliorating worker conditions.

Syndicalist criticism did in the end, however, bring a few nominal concessions from the regime, none of which amounted to the joint administration of company welfare programs envisaged by the fascist trade union leadership. The party order of 1929 allowing the unions to distribute *dopolavoro* membership cards remained on paper, as did a 1934 circular enjoining employers to allow trade union delegates to serve as consultants on the boards of the company groups. In the late thirties the pliant president of the CNSF, Tullio Cianetti, boasted of the greater cooperation between the two organizations.[111] But this cooperation was limited to promoting worker exchanges with the German Labor Front and to organizing holiday excursions. When finally in 1939 the OND was placed temporarily under trade union supervision and Capoferri was named special commissioner, the trend of the preceding years was not reversed. The *dopolavoro*, together with the social services associated with it, had become permanent fixtures in industry. Formal concessions from the top did little to restore the syndicalists' presence in the factory, nor the powers of which they had been divested during the previous years of fascist rule.

In the United States, hegemony, as Gramsci reflected, was "born in the factory and required for its exercise only a minute quantity of professional political and ideological intermediaries."[112] In Italy, by contrast, where business had traditionally exercised its influence through the state apparatus rather than through the institutions of civil society, employers had to be persuaded, and occasionally even compelled, to accept "social responsibilities" commensurate with their expanding economic power. Swayed more by profits than by political considerations, they doubtless would have preferred a thorough de-politicization of industrial relations to government intervention in support of initiatives on behalf of worker welfare. Yet it was tacitly recognized that the very conditions enabling employers to exercise this new power over their dependents were entirely created by fascism: from the breaking of worker resistance against management paternalism to the monopoly profits that in tiniest part were reinvested in social services. For most of the interwar period, there was in fact no incompatibility between the *technical* aspects of the *dopolavoro* – as an agency of personnel management – and its *political* functions as an outpost of fascist mass organization. This was well understood not only by fascist leaders, who depended on business entrepreneurship for the most vital sections of their local *dopolavoro* groups, but by industrial spokesmen as well. The business firm, as the Confindustria's president Benni affirmed before the Fascist Chamber of Deputies in 1931, "is the primary and fundamental corporate entity," where "the concept of collaboration in its spiritual, economic, and productive significance must be achieved, understood, and felt." Social assistance, he stressed, should be construed "not as paternalism, but as an especially political and humane effort to root the fundamental principles of the corporate order ever more firmly in the minds of our workers."[113]

4

The penetration of the countryside

The "civilization" of the countryside by dominant urban cultures has been a constant process since the beginning of industrialization. Hastened from the early nineteenth century by the rapid spread of capitalist market relations, emigration from the land, universal military conscription, and the growth of state education systems, it has virtually been completed in the twentieth century by mobilization for "total" war, mass political movements, and the influence of the mass media. Fascism was in power during an especially crucial moment in this long process: when Italian agriculture was, so to speak, at the crossroads. Although half of the active population was still employed in agriculture in 1921, contributing over one-third of the entire national income, Italy was rapidly becoming an urban-industrial nation: From the mid-twenties on, the rural economy was being put under severe pressure to yield more agricultural surpluses, savings, and markets for industry. At the same time, central government was acquiring a formidable capacity to penetrate rural areas by means of the new networks of mass communication.

The fascists were nonetheless deeply ambivalent about using this power. Condescending toward the superstitions and oddities of the superficially understood world of the Italian peasantry, they were at the same time convinced of the superiority of its conservative rural values. They understood that agricultural reforms called for a vigorous mobilization of backward rural areas; but they resisted any thoroughgoing modernization out of deference to the traditional landed elites and for fear that the ensuing rural landflight might swell already high rates of unemployment.

Any fascist social organization was bound to reflect this deep ambivalence, and especially a preeminently urban industrial form like the *dopolavoro*. Although the first fascist recreational circles had been founded in rural areas, as Rossoni's unions had sought to take over the reform socialist peasant leagues of the Po valley in the early twenties, the OND itself evinced no real interest in furthering their work until 1930-1. When the OND did finally begin to step up its organizing

94

effort, it discovered two unexpected obstacles. First, country equiv-
alents of city forms of sociability were not always what they seemed
to be: In the small towns and villages of the Mezzogiorno and Sicily,
the *circolo* was just as likely to be a bourgeois club as a proletarian
one. Second, the rural elites were usually still confirmed users of traditional modes of rural labor management: paternalistic sharecropping
arrangements especially in the central-northern regions, mafia bullying
in the South, firings and evictions everywhere. Consequently, party
and government intervention had to be especially energetic if the institution was to take root, with no guarantee of success; for the initiative
behind it always tended to respond more closely to the interests of the
urban industrial bourgeoisie or the central party apparatus than to the
concerns of rural proprietors, not to speak of local peasant custom.

Fascism's defense of rurality

From the early twenties on, Mussolini's government had been urged
by its conservative supporters to secure itself a broad social base by
establishing a firm alliance between the urban middle classes and Italy's
ten million peasants. According to the country's leading agronomist,
Arrigo Serpieri, the industrial proletariat was "incorrigibly hostile" to
fascism, whereas the plutocracy, despite its protests of loyalty, was
by nature "politically indifferent" and therefore "unreliable in the
extreme." The peasants, on the other hand, "long absent from political
life," had been "partially awakened in the last few years." Socialism,
he pointed out, had established strongholds only in a few provinces of
the North, whereas the Catholics had made inroads in areas of Piedmont, Lombardy, and Veneto. But most of the northern countryside
offered a "virgin terrain" for fascist "cultivation" and "all or almost
all of the Mezzogiorno with its vast peasant masses was open to any
and all new political initiatives."[1]

As Under-Secretary of Agriculture from July 1923 to June 1924,
Serpieri had urged the government to secure this peasant following by
undertaking a comprehensive program of agricultural modernization.
This policy, aimed at stimulating agricultural output while reinforcing
rural social stability, was necessarily to be differentiated by region.
For the north-central regions with moderately well-developed zones
of capitalist farming, Serpieri advocated a laissez-faire approach with
incentives for increased agricultural efficiency and some protection for
those industrious smallholders whom he regarded as model rural citizens. In the underdeveloped South, by contrast, he urged the adoption

of a kind of fascist Stolypin plan; this would have encouraged the division of the vast unproductive *latifundia* with their thousands of wretched agricultural workers, forming in their stead stable farms cultivated by a new class of thrifty, productive, and socially conservative small proprietors.

The far-reaching land reforms needed to create this rural base were not, however, forthcoming from the fascist government. Mussolini, although supporting in theory the spread of small holdings "when and where they could increase national wealth," was more swayed by considerations of his political base. Beginning in early 1923 his government sought to appease the large landowners with several measures, including the repeal of the Visocchi and Falcioni decree-laws of 1919–20 ceding uncultivated lands to peasant cooperatives and the ouster of peasants from lands occupied since 1919. Subsequently, in May 1924, Serpieri's bill calling for government-sponsored land reclamation projects (*bonifica integrale*), backed by the power to expropriate unimproved lands, was abandoned in the face of strong opposition from large southern landowners.[2]

Not until 1926, when low agricultural productivity was conclusively identified as a major cause of the economic instability leading to the depreciation of the lira, did the regime develop a sustained interest in rural affairs. Except in the North, where market-oriented capitalist farming was prevalent, agricultural methods were still remarkably primitive. Few landholdings were mechanized and the use of chemical fertilizers was slight. The small yield produced by most cultivators, frequently on scattered strips occupied with short tenancies, was consumed locally; overall in the early twenties, no more than half of the gross annual output went to market. Since the war, cereal imports had accounted for 15–20 percent of the nation's annual trade deficit – and in 1924, 40 percent as a result of the disastrous harvest.[3] Such low agricultural productivity had not only reduced the role of the rural sector in capital formation, but by contributing to the decline of the lira, had actually hindered efforts to obtain badly needed loans abroad. Moreover, impoverished rural markets had restricted outlets for industrial products, thus accentuating industry's dependence on competitive foreign markets. Fascist officials and industrial leaders, preoccupied with stabilizing the economy, now emphasized the crucial functions of agricultural improvement for industrial progress. The "maximum development of agriculture," as Mussolini noted in prefacing Belluzzo's *Economia fascista* in March 1927, "signifies the maximum development of the national economy and especially those industrial concerns . . . tied to agriculture."[4]

Fascism's agrarian program, as it evolved after 1925, combined the regime's overriding concern for the stabilization of industry with various expedients to buffer the countryside from the worst effects of this policy. The impact of monetary deflation on the rural sector was especially harsh; there, as Adrian Lyttelton has noted, the 1926–7 crisis was not "merely a passing disturbance but a real turning point."[5] The trend toward the dispersal of landholdings was suddenly reversed as the many small farmers who had purchased land on credit during the inflationary period since the war were forced to sell. Southern agriculture producing specialized crops for export was doubly afflicted by the sharp deflation and by the prolonged fall in world agricultural prices from the mid-twenties on. Government policies to alleviate the crisis, as well as to stimulate agricultural output, had a mixed effect. The law of 6 June 1926 authorizing the sale of common lands, the December 1928 integral land reclamation act, and many other incentives to "rational" farming all favored the further mechanization and commercialization of the market-oriented production located mainly in the Po River plains and valley. But protectionist measures on cereals and sugar, aimed at reducing foreign imports by increasing the domestic supply, tended to reinforce the traditional extensive cultivation methods common in the more backward southern regions. So although agricultural productivity increased overall, and significantly in the North over the following years, in the Mezzogiorno it stagnated. The lopsided character of Italian growth was thus emphasized, at the same time as the relative weight of the rural sector as a whole declined with respect to industry.

To sustain such a contradictory policy, the regime had to intervene at a number of levels. First of all, it sought to stimulate agricultural output. According to Serpieri, it was in the context of the "battle" to produce more grain opened in the summer of 1925 that Mussolini first spoke of "mobilizing the huge rural army spread out through the Italian countryside." At the July meeting of the Committee for the Battle of Grain, the dictator called for "propaganda and persuasion" to "penetrate the vast masses of silent and industrious peasants." The peasants now had to produce more and more efficiently; and all fascist organizations were expected to prepare themselves to support this "exceptional exertion of the collective will."[6]

More immediately, the regime had to somehow pacify rural unrest. As agricultural prices dropped after 1926, unemployment in the countryside rose, former smallholders were reduced to either tenant or sharecropper status, and land values fell, in some areas of the North by as much as 50 percent.[7] Protests from farmers, voiced by prominent fascist leaders on behalf of their constituents in the Po valley provinces, brought a qualified response from the government. Following the themes of Mussolini's Speech of the Ascension of 26 May 1927, fascist propaganda began to defend rural virtues against the dangers of urbanism. As if to give symbolic force to the regime's claim to be protecting the humble denizens of rural Italy from the oppression of industrialism, Mussolini himself abandoned the cosmopolitan suit of the "Americanizer" in favor of the sober garb of "first peasant of Italy." In line with the Duce, fascist ideologues took up the theme of the noble *rurale*, much as earlier Italian imperialists had mythicized the Abyssinian native.

Over the long term, the regime had to confront one inevitable consequence of agricultural crisis: peasant migration off the land, reportedly increasing in many mountainous rural districts by late 1927. In the past this landflight had ultimately found outlets abroad. Since 1921, however, the United States, formerly the primary destination of emigrants, had been virtually closed off to Italians, and Mussolini, for reasons of national pride, discouraged departures to northern Europe. As emigration abroad declined – from 614,611 persons in 1920 to 201,219 in 1921 to an annual average of 120,000 for 1921–30 – the landflight threatened to spill over into the cities.[8] Yet Italy's industrial expansion, never sufficiently vigorous to absorb rural overpopulation, was itself at a standstill in 1927. Given that the major investments were being made in capital-intensive industries, and that concentration and rationalization were actually eliminating positions in the labor-intensive textile firms, it was unlikely – as the Minister of Finance Volpi pointed out in 1928 – that even when industry began to rehire, sufficient new jobs would be created to employ rural immigrants.[9] But if jobs had existed – or could have been created by a public works program – a growing urban population called for costly investments in housing and social services that the government had no intention of undertaking. On the contrary: To restrict consumption, it deliberately sought to confine the reserve labor force in the impoverished rural areas where it could be maintained at the least social cost. Finally, as every public official recognized, it was far easier to control an isolated rural population accustomed to abysmally low standards of living than to placate a volatile and unemployed urban labor force.

Under pressure from agrarian employers who complained that their cheap labor was leaving the land, the fascist leadership in November 1928 launched an antiurbanization campaign under the slogan "Empty the cities." Mussolini urged that "every means, even coercive ones," be used to "promote an exodus from the cities, to prevent the desertion of the countryside, and to impede the waves of immigrants into the towns."[10] Legal measures, starting with the decree of 24 December 1928, which authorized the prefects to deport unemployed laborers to their places of origin, followed on 9 April 1931 by legislation blocking all unauthorized migration outside of single provinces, culminated in 1934 with a general law against urbanization.

Coercive measures, however, offered only a limited solution to what promised to be a complicated and enduring problem. The number of industrial jobs grew at a rate of less than 50,000 annually; by 1938 only 525,000 new openings had been created in firms employing two or more persons. Meanwhile, there was an unsurpassedly high number of live births especially in the poorest rural areas (approximately 28 per thousand or 1,112,900 annually for 1921–39), encouraged by the regime's ideologically motivated demographic campaign.[11] The pressures on the land were thus greatly augmented, despite the critical shortage of arable soil, growing property concentration, and persistently low agricultural prices.[12]

Fascism, as Serpieri commented, "although authoritarian," could certainly not impose a "new feudal bondage" to keep the peasants on the land.[13] In any case officials familiar with rural misery knew that no police measures could restrain a determined peasant from finally reaching town. Antiurban propaganda was to no effect either: For the peasants – as one OND functionary pointed out – fully understood the hardships of urban existence; in compensation they knew – whether from military experience, short visits, or hearsay – that city life offered attractions that were altogether lacking in their isolated rural homes.[14] If the regime hoped to curb the landflight, it had to develop a policy of introducing into the countryside, if only in part, the amenities of modern industrial society: decent housing, schools, and of course some counterpart to the varieties of urban leisure.

The fascist policy of intervention in the countryside, first sketched out in 1927, thus had to combine two quite contradictory aims: agricultural modernization on the one hand, and the conservation of rural community on the other. "Ruralization," as this policy came to be known, meant first of all an ideological defense of rurality that masked the real subordination of the countryside to the urban industrial world. Inevitably, it also involved far-reaching structural changes: above all, new institutions had to be established that were at once responsive to the national state, while reinforcing the "timeless," the "traditional," and the "harmonious" in rural social arrangements. In this sense, ruralization implied the kind of support fascism sought from the peasantry. Consent meant above all malleability: to respond when the occasion warranted; and, otherwise, to remain a reservoir of good faith and stability in a rapidly changing world. Political support was a negligible concern, for by 1927 fascism had no need of an electoral base, and force, far more successful in the rural areas than in the towns, had virtually eliminated the vulnerable Catholic and socialist rural networks. Economic mobilization was seen in any case as the peasantry's main "political" contribution to the consolidation of fascist rule, as well as the primary means of its involvement in national life. The 50,000 *rurali* trucked into Rome in 1928 to celebrate the "victorious outcome of the first round of economic battles" marked, in the words of Serpieri, the "beginning of the tangible and lively participation of the masses of rural Italians in the political life of the nation."[15]

Uplift for the peasantry

Ruralization, however, presupposed already existing organizational ties with the countryside, and these were still either extremely weak or entirely lacking in most rural areas in 1927. Fascism had acquired a peasant following in only a few northern provinces in the early twenties: in Ferrara, for example, where politically inexperienced rural laborers had responded to fascist promises for property, profit-sharing in rural enterprise, or ready job placement; and elsewhere in Emilia, among sharecroppers and tenant farmers hiring occasional field hands, who rallied to the PNF out of fear of the socialist leagues. With the revaluation crisis, however, many of these formerly enthusiastic party supporters deserted the PNF in protest.[16] The fascist syndicalists meanwhile found it difficult to maintain discipline and membership levels in the unions. Although they claimed 700,000 members by 1925, many had been forcibly recruited from the rural sections of the reformist CGL, whose membership had plummeted from 889,000 to 15,000 since 1920; thousands of other peasants were summarily enrolled by fascist recruiters in the South in 1925–6.[17] The OND itself had an insignificant number of peasant members by 1927 – 60,000 or 11 percent of its enrollment. Of these, three-quarters came from Piedmont, Lombardy, Venetia, Emilia, and Tuscany, all north and north-central regions where the fascists had capitalized on the socialist defeat (see Table 4.1). The rural environs of Rome and the southern regions of Apulia and Sicily accounted for most of the other peasants enrolled. The wretchedly poor agricultural region of Basilicata reported the least – a mere 39.[18]

Fascism's appeal to the peasantry began on an inauspiciously crude economic note. Economic mobilization was the subject of the first

Table 4.1. *Dopolavoro members in agriculture, 1926–1932*

Region	Population active in agriculture[a]	1926	1927	1928	1929	1930	1931	1932
Piedmont	743,791	7,696	20,243	24,487	58,569	61,988	81,526	81,973
Liguria	160,515	1,502	2,469	4,032	9,150	6,945	12,475	15,536
Lombardy	755,505	3,148	9,580	11,451	28,687	28,013	30,005	30,317
Tridentine–Venetia	149,634	270	779	2,548	5,828	5,198	7,775	7,542
Venetia	892,176	1,724	4,312	8,282	11,865	18,805	22,325	21,386
Julian–Venetia	151,022	1,008	1,831	3,078	3,542	5,272	5,881	10,042
Emilia–Romagna	845,691	1,351	3,510	6,276	24,285	25,246	29,297	27,698
Tuscany	564,453	1,061	3,653	6,633	20,657	22,696	28,251	27,100
Marches	355,993	471	1,432	3,012	5,047	8,750	8,317	7,119
Umbria	182,408	298	595	1,730	2,511	6,964	8,918	7,384
Latium	329,027	1,087	2,669	6,673	9,493	7,159	7,383	8,778
Campania	599,332	831	1,734	4,335	10,784	12,201	12,626	12,902
Abruzzi–Molise	417,316	68	107	1,841	3,743	4,893	3,733	3,555
Apulia	492,196	1,004	1,832	5,320	12,416	7,445	6,612	6,348
Basilicata (Lucania)	141,390		39	732	1,684	1,625	4,673	4,068
Calabria	406,272	324	928	3,571	1,684	11,370	10,888	9,055
Sicily	702,665	1,186	3,967	7,418	19,654	23,101	31,449	29,403
Sardinia	210,955		461	791	1,798	4,948	3,733	3,555
Totals	8,168,876	23,309	60,141	101,210	236,816	262,610	333,599	335,102

[a] According to the 1931 census

Source: O. Vitali, *La popolazione attiva in agricoltura attraverso i censimenti italiani* (1881–1961) Rome, 1968, Table 3, pp. 190-198: OND, *Le realizzazioni e attività dell'Opera Nazionale Dopolavoro*, Rome, 1933.

OND circular addressed specifically to the rural areas. On 21 December 1927 Turati ordered the provincial boards to "harmonize" their activities with the regime's recent directives on ruralization. Specifically, this meant setting up agricultural training courses, "in the interests of the national economy." The courses themselves, Turati emphasized, were to be "practical" in scope, stressing production, and not "theoretical." To assist the local boards, the central office promised to make appropriate arrangements with state agencies such as the National Silk Board to send instructional material on the cultivation of mulberries, silkworm raising, rabbit breeding, beekeeping, and chicken farming. Turati announced that the central office could already provide not only illustrated pamphlets and charts, but also kits containing models of the silkworm metamorphosis, sample mulberry shrubs, and small quantities of silkworm eggs for experimental breeding.[19]

This petty economism, quickly abandoned by the OND when dealing with what it considered to be more sophisticated urban constituencies, remained a hallmark of policy toward the peasantry. No special bureau, similar to that acting as a liaison with industry, was set up to deal with rural affairs. And no fascist functionary ever presented himself as a leading theoretician of "rural" welfare work. As a result, any central planning tended to be haphazard and far more responsive to government demands than to the prevailing conditions in rural society. Thus no special measures were taken to finance the rural groups: The provincial boards were simply instructed to procure financial aid from municipal governments, local agricultural consortia, agrarian associations, and sympathetic industrial and commercial firms. Only staffing was recognized as needing expertise, because so much stress was placed on vocational instruction. In 1927, therefore, Turati had instructed communal *dopolavoro* groups – that is, those established in small towns – to include in their administrations the directors of the local "traveling chairs of agriculture." By late 1929, however, this measure seemed insufficient and Turati requested assistance from the National Fascist Syndicate of Agrarian Technicians.[20] Aid from agricultural engineers and agronomists did indeed play a significant role in formulating programs in the northern provinces. But elsewhere, and especially in the South, the task of developing programs – or simply of recruiting members – was handled indiscriminately by special OND commissioners, syndicalist organizers, the regular staff of the provincial board, or even by the *federali* and prefects.

A national rural program was nonetheless formalized by 1930, and was modified little in the following decade. The OND's overriding aim in the countryside was to "harmonize the rhythm of agriculture with the tempo of science and modern civilization." Said less pretentiously, it was to make the country more agreeable to live in and to try to raise peasant morale. It was observed that agricultural workers frequently saw their work as "sheer drudgery" rather than a "serene necessity"; they felt oppressed by their sense of social inferiority, demoralized by the want of even the most basic necessities, and were resigned to living in abject conditions. The fascist solution was moral uplift combined with technical know-how. Once apprised of the benefits of living in the open air and instructed to take best advantage of their surroundings, the peasants themselves would work to enhance their productive and social efficiency.[21]

Despite such an opportunistic mythology, the dominant concerns of rural programs continued to be strictly utilitarian. Organized activities were above all to stimulate agricultural productivity. Organizers were advised that work-related exercises like plowing contests and wagon-loading competitions were conducive to "awakening the proper spirit of initiative in the rural classes."[22] Beyond this, there was much discussion of extending the urban media into the countryside through traveling theaters and cinemas, and especially by means of the radio. Radio broadcasting for a peasant audience was contemplated as early as 1927. But it was only in March 1933 that a special program entitled the Farmers' Hour (L'Ora dell' Agricoltore) finally began transmission on a regular basis with Saturday evening and Sunday morning broadcasts containing crop quotations, technical information, and cultural programs of a more general appeal. Not until the following June, with the foundation of the Ente Radio Rurale, were more systematic efforts initiated to place radios in rural schools and *dopolavoro* circles.[23]

Why was the OND so slow in pressing for the introduction of these urban cultural forms into rural communities? The answer lies partly in the evident risk of stimulating rather than appeasing the peasants' taste for the amenities of town life. Farm employers were especially alert to this danger. When the National Fascist Confederation of Agriculturalists first endorsed the institution in 1929, it urged that its activities serve as a way of disabusing peasants of their "envy" for industrial workers. In particular, it advised trips to factories to show them "what life was like working indoors all day, amidst a great stench, always doing the same thing under an iron discipline."[24] Fascist functionaries, acknowledging the legitimacy of this concern, found a solution of sorts by recommending that the peasantry be only partially exposed to urban mores: "to protect these oases in the midst of universal neurasthenia," the organization had "to filter or denicotinize

103

The culture of consent: mass organization in fascist Italy

all novelty so that it reaches the peasant in the least toxic form possible."[25] Education, as one organizer stressed, was to provide "a modest yet solid set of notions to students who subsequently would pass their lives in the countryside; it should not distract them from the land nor delude them that they can go on to pursue urban professions."[26] Another functionary, acknowledging that movies of any kind were guaranteed to gather a crowd in rural areas, recommended: "Cinema . . . yes, but of a rural kind, instructive films such as newsreels rather than detective thrillers or romantic films made of bourgeois trash; the radio . . . yes, but still better *Il Trovatore* or *La Traviata* played by the local band in the marketplace."[27] In the end, the OND's vision of appropriate pastimes for its peasant members conformed precisely to the propagandistic image of an idyllic rural world, with celebrations of peasant festivities and *sagre* – work-oriented cultural forms – manifesting the solidarity of the traditional peasant community.

The geography of organizing

The "penetration" of the countryside, as is suggested by the phraseology of fascist functionaries, began in the towns where rural policy was formulated. Initiatives thus depended largely on the concerns and strength of the urban-based *dopolavoro* boards, and especially on the vitality of their contacts with the province's agrarian elites. The importance of this cooperation must be underscored: It was at least as crucial to the success of the *dopolavoro* as that of industrial employers. When their concerns echoed the regime's own, the local landowners gave it an impetus that would otherwise have been lacking; moreover, they provided the technical information on rural affairs that was indispensable to effective planning. Enterprising fascist functionaries, or the spirit of initiative of single small rural entrepreneurs might overcome the reluctance to innovate of powerful agrarians, it is true. But it was their attitudes – negative or positive – that ultimately backed – or blocked – the drive to institute these new urban forms of rural management.

Even with equally resourceful provincial boards, the unusually diversified rural landscape would have led to significant variations in the impact of rural organizing. Success or failure was determined by many conditions, some reaching well into the past, others more immediately dependent on the effects of fascist agrarian policy. Such factors as the proximity of the rural areas to the towns, peasant political custom, literacy levels, land tenure, and patterns of rural habitation, and especially the generally deplorable economic conditions of the peasantry under the regime, could either facilitate the work of rural organizers or doom it to failure. What makes any strict sociology of this pattern so difficult is that the *dopolavoro*, although so eminently adaptable to local needs, was itself an urban form, carrying with it essentially extraneous meanings – positive in the North as centers of citified recreation, negative in the South as outposts of modern bourgeois political organization.

Where then did the fascist rural organization take hold most strongly? According to the OND, a pervasive "*dopolavoro* consciousness" was to be found solely in Piedmont and Lombardy, which together accounted for a third of the 335,000 rural *dopolavoristi* in 1932 (see Table 1). These two northern regions, with their densely populated, generally fertile agricultural zones, closely linked to urban centers by good roads, were considered to be ideal terrain for fascist organizers. Peasant illiteracy, a veritable blight in more southern regions, amounted to less than 5 percent of the adult population. Well over half of the Piedmontese peasantry, 66 percent or nearly double the national average, owned their own land, the majority being small proprietors engaged in livestock breeding, wine, and silk production.[28] Lombardy, like lower Piedmont, was noted for its productive large-scale commercial farming of rice, wheat, corn, and tobacco. The great estates, extending through the upper Po valley from the Piedmontese provinces of Novara and Vercelli through Pavia, Cremona, and Mantua in the Lombard lowlands, were run by capitalist leaseholders and employed hundreds of thousands of migrant laborers.[29]

The provincial boards in Lombardy and Piedmont, and especially those located in the lowland provinces, began with a further advantage in that they were able to capitalize on preceding traditions of peasant organization. The first *dopolavoro* in the area had in fact been built out of the socialist cooperative movement; in Novara alone in 1924 the fascist syndicalists had reported 13,000 members from 110 former socialist associations.[30] The rigorous "coordination" of these groups in the mid-twenties must have driven away many peasants, because the combined rural membership for the two regions amounted to no more than 10,000 in late 1927. Although fascist organizers would have preferred to start anew, they found, at Pavia at least, that any organization that was "artificial" or "imposed" was bound to lead an "ephemeral existence." Consequently, rather than competing with the groups to which the peasants were obviously tied by "reasons of affection," they limited themselves to conducting periodic checks on their "moral and political renewal."[31]

Favoring new initiatives, especially in the more industrialized provinces of Turin, Vercelli, Novara, Milan, Brescia, and Varese, was unquestionably the unity of the local bourgeoisie. This was manifested in the presence of the well-established urban boards, backed by the powerful *dopolavoro aziendali*, and in the pressure coming from the large landowners to establish special offices for rural affairs. As a result, urban functionaires had ample resources at their disposal and they were motivated to pay attention to the surrounding rural areas.

By the end of the twenties, they faced trouble on two fronts: from the mountains and from the plains. The 1927 crisis in agriculture caused many small farmers and *coloni* in the mountain zones to lose their land. Fear of unemployment apparently deterred no one from coming to the towns, because many peasants, already accustomed to seasonal labor in industry, knew that relief measures for the urban destitute were generous by rural standards. Police measures to stem the flow proved so ineffectual that by the early thirties the depopulation of the Piedmontese mountainsides was described as a "veritable demographic disaster."[32] By the spring of 1930, the migrant labor force of the lowlands rice fields began organizing against wage cuts that reduced their seasonal rate by 20 percent. The strikes among the women rice-weeders in 1930–1 were so widespread and prolonged, and the reappearance of communist militants so ominously reminiscent of the agitation of the "red" years, that landlords, public officals, and fascist functionaries were galvanized into action.

Thus it was only in mid-1930, following labor disturbances in the Lomellina rice fields, that the fascists in the province of Pavia began to address the problem of organizing migrant workers at all systematically. Before then, functionaries had devoted their time either to admitting ex-socialist associations into the OND, more than a hundred of which had been looted and closed by the agrarian squads in the early twenties, or to trying to organize the dour sharecroppers and *coloni* of the hill areas. The decision that the *braccianti* were more "needy" and would consequently be more receptive to the *dopolavoro* was apparently well taken. Already in October 1930, the province's *federale* happily reported to PNF headquarters that the new groups were "depopulating the local hostelries" causing vociferous complaints from their owners.[33] From 1931–2 on, the Pavia board, with support from the fascist unions, the *fasci femminili*, and employers' organizations, set up rest stations for transient farmworkers in the outlying rural districts. By 1937 Pavia had an unusually well-developed network of associations, some 282 altogether, including 72 rural sections; and more than half of the province's 45,000 members were peasants.[34]

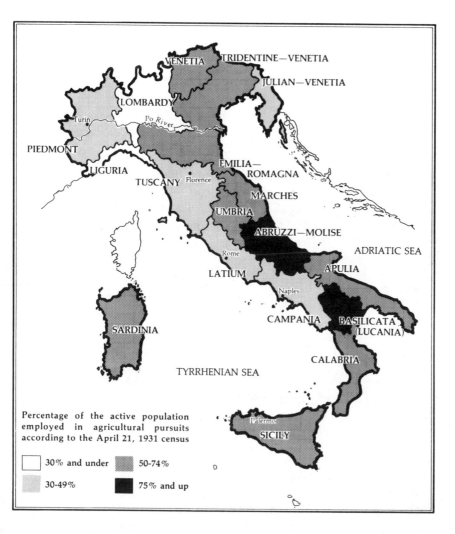

Percentage of the active population
employed in agricultural pursuits
according to the April 21, 1931 census

30% and under   50-74%

30-49%   75% and up

Membership in agricultural areas. Percentage of the active population employed in agricultural pursuits according to the census of April 21, 1931: Lombardy, Liguria, under 30%; Piedmont, Julian–Venetia, Tuscany, Latium, Campania, from 31% to 49%; Venetia, Tridentine–Venetia, Emilia–Romagna, Marches, Umbria, Apulia, Calabria, Sicily, Sardinia, 50% to 74%; Abruzzi–Molise, Basilicata (Lucania), 75% and over. Percentage of the active population in agriculture (according to the 1931 census) enrolled in the Dopolavoro in 1931: Sardinia, Basilicata (Lucania), Calabria, Abruzzi–Molise, Campania, Latium, Marches, Venetia, Apulia, under 3%; Emilia–Romagna, Tridentine–Venetia, Lombardy, Tuscany, Umbria, Julian–Venetia, Sicily, from 3% to 6%; Liguria, Piedmont, 7% and over.

107

More than the mere pacification of unrest, the institution of the *dopolavoro* was intended to rebuild peasant communities by giving their former inhabitants some reason to stay on the land. Success in such an endeavor naturally demanded special conditions in a country in which nearly two-thirds of the peasantry lacked land of their own. These circumstances were perhaps best illustrated in the prosperous northeastern Lombard province of Varese, whose *dopolavoro* was often cited as a paradigm of efficient organization. By the mid-twenties Varese province with its 382,462 inhabitants was in fact predominantly industrial: Just under 15 percent of the active population was still engaged in agriculture, although many of the workers in the textiles and machine industries of Busto Arsizio and Gallarate were first-generation city residents and still retained close ties to the land. With unemployment already exceptionally high, and confronted with a notoriously strike-prone work force in the textile factories, the public authorities sought at all costs to forestall further immigration and, if possible, to encourage workers to return to the land. After 1927, with support from the local landowners and industrialists, they undertook efforts to promote new forms of peasant profit-sharing through the *consociati* contract, a variant on sharecropping. They also encouraged investment in agricultural enterprises, especially in livestock breeding.[35] Beginning in 1928, haltingly at first and thereafter with what the Varese agronomist Luigi Mattei described as an "organic program," they actively supported the establishment of new rural recreational centers.[36]

The province's first rural *dopolavoro* was founded in 1928 at Bariola, a rural *frazione* of Caronno Milanese, a town of 5,000 persons. Not until 1930, when peasants began to abandon or neglect their fields to seek employment in Busto Arsizio, did the provincial board decide to stop this "unhealthy trend" by setting up four new groups on the edges of the city where the peasants owned their land.[37] These were well attended; their membership at the year's end numbered 680 persons. Thereafter, the number of rural recreational centers grew rapidly: to fifteen in 1931, twenty-four in 1932, thirty-eight in 1933, forty-seven in 1934, and sixty-seven in 1935. By 1936, the board's special commission on rural affairs reported a total of eighty-two recreational centers, with an enrollment of 10,200, or almost a third of the 28,822 persons active in agriculture.[38]

The popularity of these groups was apparently due to the combination of novel urban recreational pastimes and aids to agricultural improvement they offered members. It was the former, conceded Mattei, the technical advisor on rural affairs, that first attracted peasants to the centers. The Varese Dopolavoro equipped all of its groups with radios, many of which were donated by industrial concerns. It also sponsored its own traveling cinema and library and, at various times during the thirties, hosted a truly special event: the elaborate performances of the Thespian Prose Cars. But the numerous courses in agrarian techniques, the thousands of acres of experimental growing fields, the annual agricultural fairs and competitions also boosted enrollment since, as Mattei stressed, the prizes and other benefits were restricted only to those members in good standing with the PNF and *dopolavoro*.

In its effort to spur rural productivity, the Varese Dopolavoro was remarkably successful. Already in 1928, Varese had won the OND national competition for experimental orchard-gardens by sponsoring 15,000 hectares (approximately 33,000 acres) of intensively cultivated plots using a fifth of the province's total cultivated surface. By 1936 hundreds of such plots, marked by special OND plaques, bordered town edges, railroad beds, and roadways.[39] Although political propaganda appears otherwise to have been subdued, these served in themselves as continuous reminders of the regime's beneficence, as well as of the apparent progress of agriculture under fascist tutelage.

The flourishing attendance rates were due, as Mattei himself recognized, as much to the attractiveness of the program as to the relatively prosperous state of the Varese peasantry. Less than 3 percent of the population was illiterate, and many peasants had prior contacts with urban life that favorably disposed them to seeking out the amenities offered by the *dopolavoro*. Although the number of rural proprietors had dropped 10 percent since 1930, some 60 percent – almost double the national rate – owned their own land in 1937; 26 percent were sharecroppers or tenants; and only 14 percent were day laborers.[40] Peasant properties were generally small (80 percent were under 25 acres, of which 37 percent were under 6.6 acres); nonetheless Varese's farmers, when given sufficient incentives, could be induced to take advantage of agricultural instruction so as to improve their holdings. It is also likely that the absence of sharp economic divisions among the rural population – few of whom were particularly affluent – favored full community participation in the rural centers. All categories – owners, tenants, and day laborers – were equally represented in the association's membership.[41]

A highly commercialized agriculture did not always ensure the success of the rural *dopolavoro*, even when organizing conditions were otherwise favorable. Where neither peasant landflight nor rural protest was sufficiently threatening to arouse the attention of the provincial boards, fascist penetration into the countryside was both slow and superficial, and entirely insufficient to overcome the accentuated division between town and countryside caused by the impoverishment of the defenseless rural labor force. Before the *squadristi*'s "expeditions" in 1920–2, the large rural proletariat of the agrarian provinces of Emilia and Romagna was by far the best organized in Italy. Yet even in the late thirties, after seemingly energetic recruitment campaigns, membership tallies never corresponded to the renowned traditions of sociability and self-help of the Emilian and Romagnuole peasantry. The reasons must be sought both in the attitudes of local agrarians who had supported the fascist squads and maintained a hand in the day-to-day management of the provincial federations, and in the miserable conditions of existence of the peasant laborers.

The experience of the *dopolavoro* in the Romagnuole province of Ravenna confirmed that where landless peasants comprised the vast majority of the cultivators, as was true in most of the Emilia–Romagna provinces, rural membership remained low.[42] Ravenna's fascist federation began with an unusual advantage in the Po valley: In the summer of 1921 the *caposquadristi* Balbo and Grandi had marched on Ravenna with 3,000 armed fascists, successfully occupying the entire province.[43] The "patrimony" of the numerous republican and socialist peasant circles thus passed more or less intact into the hands of the fascists, who in 1926 took up residence in the Spreti Palace, the former home of the city's socialist administration. The Ravenna Dopolavoro, founded in 1926, was unusually strict about policing the remaining "subversive" holdouts: No new members were permitted to join the OND unless "all of their credentials were in order" and they had demonstrated "obedience to the regime and respect for its laws."[44] By 1929, the federation boasted that more than sixty associations had been "coordinated." Apparently few of their former members were allowed the privilege of joining the OND, for total enrollments for the province amounted to no more than 2,416 persons at the year's end.[45]

Once Ravenna's federation had secured control over all of the existing workers' associations, it proceeded to organize the province's numerous farm workers. At the Dopolavoro's second congress, held in May 1930, its president – the *federale* Renzo Morigi, an agronomist, major landowner, and Olympic gold-medal marksman – announced plans for a membership drive to begin as soon as the 35,000 *braccianti* were gathered for the spring planting; its aim, according to Morigi, was to "dispel forever the memory of the wine circles." To attract potential members, organizers were instructed to promote a "variety of useful and productive pastimes" and, in addition, to plan a major outing of *rurali* to Rome to pay homage to the Duce. Morigi also established a special fund to supply radios to rural groups. Purely in

terms of membership tallies, the campaign was unquestionably successful. Between October 1929 and the end of June 1930, the federation
managed to recruit 6,017 new members bringing the total to 13,053, or
nearly double the previous year.[46] However, about half of this new
membership came from the ranks of the Fascist Union of Agricultural
Workers, an organization that the *braccianti* had earlier been forced
to join so as to qualify for job placement.

Even after political restrictions on membership were relaxed, the
federation never approached the 50,000-member goal it optimistically
set for itself in 1932. Hard-sell campaigns appeared to little effect, as
Morigi's personal tour of all of the *fasci* in the countryside around
Lugo during the spring of 1933 showed. At each stop, he exhorted local
leaders to set up recreational facilities for the farm workers; wherever
possible, he also arranged for showings of the film *Le gioiose giornate
del decennale*, although whether this celebration of the tenth year of
fascist rule served the desired purpose, which was to attract new members, seems most doubtful. Lugo's historian, Rignani, recalled that the
close-ups of those "simpatico club-carrying louts" merely reminded
people of when they had been beaten up and purged with castor oil to
familiarize them with the Duce's systems of persuasion. Overall membership actually dropped by nearly 2,000 between 1931 and 1934 despite
the federation's repeated warning that it would "tolerate no excuses"
from those refusing to renew their cards. Through 1936, enrollments
fluctuated around 11,000–12,000, no more than a third of which were
from the countryside, and the rest from Ravenna, Lugo, and other
provincial centers.[47]

What were the reasons for this failure beyond the obvious rawness
of the class conflict in Ravenna province? One frequently cited obstacle
to recruiting farm laborers was financial, although the Ravenna *Fascio*
itself was quite prosperous. The province's Federation of Agricultural
Employers gave such "scant encouragement" to the organization that
even Morigi, although a member and a staunch friend, had publicly
criticized it in 1930.[48] Now that they no longer had to contend with a
militant farm workers' movement, the capitalist leaseholders who ran
the large estates were reluctant to contribute to their seasonal laborers'
welfare. Smaller employers hiring casual laborers were even less inclined to give aid since their own economic circumstances were often
precarious. In Ravenna, as was true elsewhere in northern and central
Italy, landowners preferred more individualist solutions for dealing
with the rural labor force. The favored solution, encouraged by the
regime itself with its policy of *sbracciantizzazione* (or "deproletarian-
ization"), consisted of setting up the peasant laborer on the land as

a sharecropper, thereby restoring the traditional paternalistic bond between landowner and cultivator.[49]

It is nonetheless doubtful that financial difficulties were the only reason for the Ravenna Dopolavoro's faltering initiatives. More simply, it lacked any real incentive to establish circles for *braccianti*; they were too impoverished to merit attention as consumers or savers and, for lack of land of their own, they had no use for technical instruction.[50] The agrarians themselves saw no need to improve agricultural methods, for they prospered as a result of the subsistence wages they paid their workers and the protective tariffs imposed on sugar and grain. Moreover, the Ravenna federation apparently sensed the futility of expending excessive energy on converting the province's peasants to fascism – even with the "low-key, healthy, honest and well-intentioned propaganda" that Morigi had recommended his organizers use when approaching diffident rural laborers.[51] Apparently it was far too troublesome to insist that field laborers spend even 2.5 lire out of their meager thousand or so lira annual income on another useless card. Rather, the federation wisely invested its resources in its bustling urban associations – a veritable "showcase" of leisure organization, as it was acclaimed by *Gente nostra*.

Although the town's *dopolavoro* circles supplied their audiences with movies, outings, and other amenities of the new urban leisure, the Federation abandoned the rural workers to their abysmal poverty. In this way the fascist organization had the effect of accentuating rather than bridging the gap between the urban centers and the outlying rural districts. The meticulously constructed associational life of Ravenna's "municipal socialism" had tended to eliminate the social and economic differences between rural and urban workers by uniting them in a common political organization; its fascist successor, tended to restore the deep divisions between town and country. Indeed, the new leisure not only failed to compensate for the sharp decline in rural wages, the absence of job security, and the destruction of the workers' associations, but paradoxically became yet another index of the very real drop in the standard of rural life under fascism.

Fascist organizing was ultimately more successful in the neighboring region of Tuscany, which, like Emilia–Romagna, was predominantly rural, although its numerous large landholdings were usually farmed by sharecroppers as opposed to the capitalist leaseholders employing *braccianti*. The sharp rural class divisions, exploited so effectively by the agrarian fascist squads in Emilia, were lacking in Tuscany. To subdue the *mezzadri*, the notoriously violent Tuscan fascist movement had relied to a far greater extent than in Emilia on recruits from the towns.[52] When the peasant associations had been vanquished, the cities once more became the centers of fascist activities: The now silent countryside was generally ignored, except by fascist intellectuals who extrolled the sober virtues of the Tuscan *rurali*. The provincial boards, through the early thirties, catered almost exclusively to an urban clientele, which, in centers like Florence, consisted primarily of petty bourgeois. Not surprisingly, in 1932 only one-fifth of the region's 138,000 *dopolavoristi* were classified as peasants, and many of these, as suggested by the rosters of the Florence Dopolavoro, were drawn from the former *case del popolo*, mutual aid societies, and cooperatives that fringed the major urban centers; their main function, according to accounts carried in the Florentine Fascio's *Il Bargello* in 1934, consisted of giving economic relief to their peasant-worker members.[53]

Although Tuscan *mezzadri* generally fared badly after 1927, as share-contracts were renewed on unprecedentedly harsh terms, the decline in their standard of living was less than that experienced by the chronically underemployed migrant *braccianti* in neighboring Emilia. Consequently, it was not unusual for villagers to organize themselves to enjoy the benefits normally extended by the OND to its urban constituents. The Cutignano Dopolavoro, one of the liveliest of 87 rural groups located by 1936 in moderately prosperous Pistoia province in the lower Arno valley, had been founded by twenty-five local residents eight years earlier. Its first president, Cherubino Ulzoga, a middleman by profession, was an energetic fund-raiser whose major ambition was seemingly to solicit a donation from the Royal Family for his club. His plans to acquire a building, as well as a truck, furnishings, and a bank acount for the group were realized in 1930 through contributions from the local public authorities, wealthy vacationers, and several benefit fairs. In spite of its intraclass patronage, the club's membership was overwhelmingly peasant; rising steadily, it included 128 of the town's 3,500 inhabitants by 1938.[54] The clubhouse, consisting of a common room with a radio-phonograph and a small game room with a bar, hosted the kinds of activities one might expect in a rural backwater: regular Sunday gatherings to listen to market quotations, weather forecasts, and other news broadcasts during the "Farmers' Hour," band rehearsals for a twelve-piece group, an annual costume parade at Carnival, and a children's party at Epiphany. But once or twice a year, the club took advantage of its national affiliation by sponsoring a major outing: to Piombino in 1931, where the group visited the Seva blast furnaces and took a boat trip to Elba; in 1932 to La Spezia, where members visited the battleship *Giulio Cesare* and the naval museum; in 1933 to both Florence and Genoa; and in 1934 to the Etruscan museum and alabaster works at Volterra.

From the perspective of its composition and activities, the Cutignano Dopolavoro had all of the attributes of a voluntary association, freely formed and with a self-selected membership. In one sense, it was just that: for without the initiative of a Cherubino Ulzoga and the constancy of his fellows, there would have been no sustained fascist recreational program in this particular town. It was in fact this very real spontaneity combined with the intraclass backing it received and its responsiveness to national programs that made such a group the ideal fascist mediating institution.

But fascist intervention could as readily be a hindrance to voluntary action as a stimulus. Bureaucratic regulations and policing discouraged the informal gatherings, the quasi-clubs set up near a tavern from which one could fetch wine, some chairs, and a table, drink more cheaply, play cards, and chat. Yet these ad hoc off-shoots frequently constituted the basis of more formal associations. The presence of police and party loyalists, always ready to interfere, further foreclosed at least one goal – politics itself – which until the fascists came to power had been a powerful magnet for peasant gatherings, certainly as much as wine consumption or agricultural improvement. Finally, the publicity for urban diversions set standards that were difficult for peasant groups to meet. This was especially true when the pace of activity was set by an outside organizer, as was true in Albarese (Grosseto), whose *dopolavoro* was founded by the engineer Enzo Fedi in the course of government reclamation projects in the Maremma swamplands. The 120-member group had flourished for a year or so while it was directed by Fedi. In 1932–3 it won the provincial *bocce* championship, the bicycle tour, and the light athletics league contest. However, as soon as he left, the club lost its momentum. As membership dropped to 98 persons, some of the remaining members formed an amateur theatrical group in the hope of attracting new participants. But for want of adequate quarters, the theater group was forced to perform outdoors – and this became cause for further demoralization. By 1934, the club had lost 40 members; and thereafter, perhaps like many similar rural groups, it led a struggling existence, with only the most sporadic contacts with the national organization.[55]

These difficulties were compounded in the Mezzogiorno and the Islands by the effects of fascist rural agrarian policy on southern society. Far from mitigating the traditional dualism between North and South, fascist policies in fact accentuated it at a number of levels. The regime's protective tariffs not only perpetuated the primitive methods of cultivation of the *latifundia* but even fostered their extension to lands that formerly had been profitably given over to livestock breeding, wine production, and fruit and olive cultivation. The further division of the common lands, combined with the constant turnover of small holdings among an impoverished peasantry, fostered the age-old unproductive speculation in land.[56] Although improved communications bound northern towns and countryside closer together, roads and radios in the South barely penetrated the rugged mountainous interiors above the coastlands. Finally, the political system itself, as a reflection of the conservative social relations reinforced by fascist economic policy, aggravated the already profound differences between northern and southern rural society. Thus, while north-central Italy was subjected to the Fascist party apparatus – itself a response to the political clashes of the nation's most industrialized areas – southern political life remained embroiled in the faction-ridden, personal clientele relations that, in the end, obstructed the establishment of the "party of a new kind."

The absence of any significant tradition of modern bourgeois self-organization was perhaps the most difficult obstacle to organizing faced by the fascists in the South. The "great fear" that had driven the rural bourgeoisie of the Po valley to join the Fascist party in 1921–2 had, in the Mezzogiorno, been limited to a few enclaves of socialist organization in Apulia and southeastern Sicily in the environs of Ragusa and Syracuse. Elsewhere, the dominant classes remained organized in the hundreds of liberal, "demo-liberal," or "demo-social" clubs that traditionally had determined political alignments in the South. Subversion, as the fascist syndicalist newspaper *Lavoro fascista* pointed out in 1929, was a "readily identifiable and easily dispatched antagonist" when compared to the pervasive "political misconduct" (*malcostume*) and "inefficiency" for which these factious groups were blamed. In the North, fascism had only to seize control of the state to make its power felt; in the South, it had to "impart a sense of the state, to replace passive obedience with conscious discipline."[57] In the North, the OND had to measure itself against the proletarian association; in the South, first of all, against the bourgeois "circle."

Until the twenties the *circoli dei civili* or *circoli dei capeddi* had been the virtually unchallenged class organization of the southern elites.[58] Many traced their origins to the *carbonari* societies, the masonic lodges, or the national guard units formed during the struggles for Italian unification. Their peculiarly archaic forms virtually unchanged amid the general political apathy, they had gradually been assimilated into national politics as electoral agents for the liberal parliamentary groups. Frequently, they were also the sole meeting place outside the parish or public squares; when they were not, there was constant bickering and occasionally violent clashes with rival bourgeois cliques or with the Catholic groups, veterans' leagues, and workers' societies formed since the war. Membership in the circles, deliberately restricted to enhance its value, betokened great personal prestige and high social status in the town; for the circles, in a society of scarce resources, were reserved for leisured men – the "hats" (*capeddi*) – whose secure economic position as landowners, merchants, and free professionals enabled them to pass their time in conspicuous fraternizing. Within the circles favors were dispensed, municipal taxes assessed, communal lands assigned, and litigations settled. At election times, the clubs flourished, manipulating the vote, arbitrating factional disputes, and finally distributing the electoral spoils. The small-town notables above all prided themselves on their power to mediate relations between the central government, personified in the prefect, and their own personal clienteles among the town's inhabitants.

The clubs had represented a convenient ally for the fascist government during the early twenties. The southern *fasci*, which proliferated following the March on Rome, were frequently installed in their premises. Given sufficient incentives, the circles also supported the government's National Bloc in the 1924 elections, recruiting votes for the ruling party much as they had done during the Giolittian period. With the elimination of electoral politics after 1925, however, the fascist government could begin to dispense with the services of the clubs. Indeed, these formerly expedient allies now proved a liability as the regime sought to extend its own party organizations into the South. Although the clubs had been willing to support the government in Rome, they were totally disinclined to cooperate with the modern mass party organization that fascism was seeking to introduce into the Mezzogiorno. Their power of patronage, invaluable in terms of their own prestige, was challenged by fascist organizers, who, if not emissaries from the North, were themselves social parvenus or representatives of rival factions eager to ally themselves with the PNF to strengthen their own political position.

Despite the elimination of elections, stringent laws specifically directed against freemasonry, and a ruthless campaign against the mafia conducted by Mussolini's personal emissary, the prefect Mori, in 1925–6, the southern notables still retained their considerable local power in the late twenties.[59] When the energetic Roberto Paternostro was appointed *federale* of Palermo in 1928, he noted that the circles

were once again "proliferating in small towns." As always, they constituted a "major font of factionalism," which now "hindered the extension of the syndicalist movement and the membership drive for the
dopolavoro." Efforts to curb their activities, by forcing them to enroll
in the OND or Federation of Italian Excursionists, were failing. The
circles, in Paternostro's words, had "few scruples about joining,"
although their readiness to do so was unabashedly "fake and diversionary"; once inside the party organizations they persisted in their
"usual disputes and dealings."[60] In the South Sicilian province of
Ragusa the party "as understood in the North" was still nonexistent
in 1928, according to the prefect. Numerous associations with "ostensibly recreational and cultural aims continue[d] to survive on the fringes
of politics," "camouflaging their activities with a pro-fascist line." So
great was their "mania for power" and so deeply rooted their "individualistic conception of protection and patronage" that they not only
obstructed the consolidation of the fascist organizations but also their
very formation.[61]

In these circumstances, similarly noted almost everywhere in the
South,[62] the *dopolavoro* – as the fascist organizational structure most
resembling the traditional circle – was conceived as having far more
overt political functions than it had in the North. To subdue the circles,
the *federali* or the prefects charged with "normalizing" provincial
politics would force them to enroll in the OND or in the FIE, even if,
as would frequently turn out to be the case, they simply pursued their
previous activities under the banner of fascism. Some of the more
inventive *federali* even contemplated using the party apparatus to rationalize local political struggles: that is, to make local institutions
reflect class divisions in a clear-cut way. So in 1928 Paternostro ordered
all of the party secretaries of Palermo province to establish a single
fascist circle and a single *dopolavoro* in each town or village. The
fascist "circles" were to include all persons belonging to the PNF or
to the fascist militia, that is, all of the local bourgeoisie, while the
dopolavoro were to "absorb, not simply enroll" all worker societies.[63]
That same year, the OND's special envoy to Sicily, an ambitious man,
proposed to reopen under the auspices of the OND all of the 187 circles
previously closed down by the acting *federale* Turchi. For "social
reasons," he explained, the clubs would be divided into two broad
categories that, in his view, corresponded to the prevailing class divisions within the society. The former would include the bourgeoisie:
"technicians, intellectuals, clerks, etc."; the latter, "workers of all
kinds." All of the circles would assume a public character in that their
costs would be defrayed by the local town administrations at an annual

rate of 30 lire per resident member. Already, he announced, a notable victory had been won by the regime: To the jubilant applause of the local populace, he had forced the exclusive Prince of Piedmont Club of Vittoria to open its doors to a lower-class public. Numerous other *circoli dei civili*, over the protests of their members, were similarly being subjected to the new order.[64]

Elsewhere in the South, the PNF conceived of using the *dopolavoro* itself as a means of undermining the traditional patronage system. For this purpose the OND special commissar Carlo Lodi had been dispatched to Potenza in 1930 by Mussolini's close collaborator, Ottavio Dinale, who at the time was prefect of the province. In his missionary zeal, Lodi personified the "fascist of the first hour" whose revolutionary fervor, the PNF thought, would best be expended in the South. At Potenza, Lodi was to contend with Don Vito Catalani, a former ally of the Nittian liberals, who, as described by Lodi, was a "fascist of the last hour" adamantly opposed to all those "working for the success of the fascist revolution." Despite the abolition of elections, Catalani, his family, and his friends still dominated the town administrations; the fascist *federale*, according to Lodi, was his personal pawn. In Lodi's plan, the *dopolavoro* would be the spearhead of his attack on Catalani's clan, by "demonstrating practically and tangibly to the peasants what the Fascist Revolution had to offer them." As a first step he ousted several dishonest party secretaries; he set up new *dopolavoro* sections in sixty-four municipalities; he forbade the waste of approximately a million and a half lire annually on fireworks and professional bands for celebrations of patron saints' days; and finally he bolstered the finances of the organization by securing it an additional income of 150,000 lire per year. His labors near completion, he reported that the *dopolavoro* now had "top priority" in the province; his efficiency had "logically exposed" the old politicians' incompetence in managing this and the other institutions of the regime. The "masses of workers," he concluded optimistically, were now "being drawn to fascism," thus breaking the ties of patronage that had bound them to the clientele organizations of the traditional elites.[65]

But this missionary zeal on the part of fascist government functionaries was in the end frustrated by the regime's own support for local clientele systems. By the mid-twenties, the government had come to rely on the most conservative elements in Sicilian society. As the prefects restored order, wage levels dropped; and as the project for the reform of the *latifundia* was abandoned, the great landlords recovered their confidence. Consequently, their willingness to manipu-

late the fascist functionaries and ultimately resist effective fascist penetration was greater than elsewhere in the South. When the new
federali, prefects, or special party, trade union, or OND commissaries
arrived in the late twenties, they provoked only short-lived upheavals
in local political life. Draconian decrees were issued closing down the
circles, local party bosses swore allegiance to the regime, the clubs
were enrolled *en masse* in the OND, and membership figures swelled.
Having imposed at least the appearance of normality in the province,
the functionaries – like the *federale* Di Belsito at Palermo – could write
back to party headquarters that the *dopolavoro* was making good head-
way, "despite the tremendous odds of the environment."[66] Membership figures would indeed appear to have borne out their optimism.
Palermo province reported 22,841 *dopolavoro* members in 1929 and
23,623 in 1930, surpassing in membership the Varese *dopolavoro*. Similarly high enrollments were claimed for all of the other Sicilian provinces, with rural members purportedly accounting for nearly a quarter
of the total (23.4 percent) compared to the national average of only
15.8 percent.[67]

Subsequent inspections by party officials immediately revealed the
utter superficiality of the work of even the best intentioned of their
predecessors. A despairing report from the party inspector Leone Zannardini tells us that the "old order had been completely restored" in
Messina by 1930. The moment the special party commissar Turchi had
departed from the province, the new *federale* Catalano, a local medical
doctor – under the sway of ex-parliamentary deputy Michele Crisafulli
Mondio, a leading landowner and former ally of the fascists – had
allowed the old political cliques to resurface. Twelve of the fifteen
masonic lodges of Messina city had reopened, party life in the small
centers had atrophied, and the inflated membership rosters of the *dopolavoro* were proven to be "wholly fictitious."[68] The political revolution from above, carried out in Ragusa province while Turchi was
acting *federale* in 1928–9, was similarly short-lived. Turchi's successor, *avvocato* Luigi Lupis, proved to be a pliant agent of the big landowners, who had promptly permitted the old circles to reopen within
the framework of the OND. The Prince of Piedmont Club of Vittoria
was thus able to expel the members it had acquired under duress in
1929, thereafter reestablishing itself as the dominant power in municipal
politics.[69] At Palermo, too, despite the prefects' vigorous struggles
against the mafia, the local *fascio*, it was reported in 1932, "existed
solely to recruit members." Otherwise it had undertaken no new activities whatsoever. The *dopolavoro*, as a result, "left much to be

desired'': most people took out membership "solely to obtain discounts at the movies, while in the provincial centers the sections had degenerated into gaming circles.''[70]

This protracted struggle within the bourgeoisie inevitably obstructed the disciplining of the worker-peasant clubs – to a degree that was inconceivable in the North, where local notables were more or less unified behind the fascist federations. Small-town circles, torn this way and that by the squabbling elites, responded by being obstinately malleable, professing deference to orders' as a political art to avoid obeying them. The membership of the Circolo Pio X of San Salvatore Fitalia in Messina province, like so many similar sodalities, had understood by the mid-twenties that the change of regimes meant that it needed a new patron. Initially it had misread the situation by asking the Minister of the Interior to become its new honorary president in 1926, although it did display a certain collective good sense by voluntarily dropping the words "Christian Democratic" from its name. By 1929, at least thirty members had become fascists, according to the club's president, A. Musarra, and the town's ex-mayor; as clear proof that the others were "sympathizers and very faithful to the regime," he cited their contributions to Bread Day, Flower Day, and Red Cross Day, their participation in all patriotic and fascist festivities, and their unanimous vote of "Sì" for the regime during the March 1929 plebiscite.[71] It was Musarra's arch-rival, the town *podestà* and secretary of the *fascio*, who in April 1929 decided that the circle should be enrolled in the OND. In a preemptive move, Musarra urged his followers take out membership on their own, and one-third applied as required. But their application was turned down by the special Sicilian OND commissioner, who, justifiably suspicious of Musarra's maneuvering, now wanted unanimous enrollment – a demand, in Musarra's account, that was simply unrealistic because there was "no work and the means were wanting." At this point, Messina's prefect stepped in; convinced that Musarra was doing his best to embarrass the town *podestà* – as indeed he was – he closed the circle and confiscated its property, a temporary expedient (the club later reopened) and an action that did little to bolster the OND's prestige in the town.[72]

Faced with such complex personal animosities, the regime more usually concluded by accepting some token expression of obeisance. The Dopolavoro of Montalbano Elicona (Messina), inaugurated in November 1931, was formerly the town's Società Agricolo-Operaia founded by small proprietors, tenant farmers, and common laborers in 1889. Until 1929 the society had an unblemished political record, at least according to its president, Giuseppe Pantano; momentarily allied with the Democrazia Sociale in the immediate postwar period, it had opposed the socialists and at no time in the past had given trouble to the public authorities. Of its members, 75 were war veterans; and by 1929, 37 were enrolled in the PNF, 7 in the militia, 50 in the OND, 12 in the trade unions, and 1 member even belonged to the directory of the town *fascio*.[73] Nevertheless, the fascist trade union delegate complained that on various occasions he had gone by the clubhouse to proselytize, and each time he found it empty though he had forewarned the president of his imminent arrival. Moreover, it was the prefect's view that members were politically apathetic: They used the club solely for "personal and utilitarian purposes, rarely taking the initiative in propagandizing their support of fascism." Although the club met hurriedly to vote itself into the OND in February 1929, the action came too late, and the prefect ordered it closed down.[74] So it remained, despite petitions to Mussolini and the Minister of the Interior, until November 1931, when the OND commissioner announced its reconstitution as a *dopolavoro*. Pantano, who alone in the town apparently possessed the requisite prestige needed to head the "new" fascist organization, once more assumed its presidency. According to the commissioner's reports, Pantano and about a hundred peasants and workers voted their "unchanged devotion to the PNF" and their "readiness to defend the cause of the fascist revolution by any means." The inaugural ceremonies, in his words, were greeted with "great enthusiasm by the working classes and by the entire citizenry."[75]

The exasperating and ultimately futile attempts to discipline the circles inevitably exhausted energies that might otherwise have been spent on organizing new recreational programs. Official statistics indicated that by 1937 all of the Sicilian communes and numerous rural *frazioni* possessed facilities of their own,[76] and some structure may well have existed. For the typical southern *dopolavoro* clubhouses – rented or built with local materials and labor and consisting of little more than a covered space – required minimal expenditure. But these were rarely supplied with radios or reading materials, or sponsored the organized pastimes common in the North. Perhaps the most memorable occasion in the association's life turned out to be its inauguration, when the town's citizenry turned out together with local notables, church dignitaries, and government and party officials for the blessing of the banner. Otherwise, the *dopolavoro* led an uneventful existence punctuated several times annually by the celebration of the patron saint's day and fascist and patriotic holidays.

In all Italy, Basilicata had to be the least auspicious terrain for organizing the *dopolavoro*. This south-central region was in one respect

121

only a showcase for the regime. Its prolific inhabitants were repeatedly extolled for having the highest or, as Mussolini put it, the "most fascist" birthrate in Italy – 39 per thousand. Next to Calabria, Basilicata also had the highest rate of permanent emigration abroad. Industry was practically nonexistent in the area: About 70 percent of its half-million population lived off the land – as tenants, proprietors, or day laborers working tiny scattered strips in Potenza province and, in Matera, as day laborers employed on the great *latifundia* extending from the arid hills down onto the vast malarial plains of the coast.[77] Precisely because Basilicata was so notoriously impoverished and perhaps to demonstrate that its high birthrate was not incompatible with a decent tenor of life, the regime regularly dispatched conscientious functionaries to the area.

The mission of Carlo Lodi to Potenza, who had claimed success in thoroughly revamping the organization of fascist recreational clubs in 1929, apparently lacked a follow-up. Until the *federale* Lacava – scorned by Lodi but respected by government authorities as a "perfect gentleman" – was replaced by the more enterprising Filippo Rautiis in 1934, the undeniable obstacles to organizing in the area were not even identified.[78] Under orders from Starace to expand *dopolavoro* activities, Rautiis discovered that sufficient funds were lacking to build even the most rudimentary facilities. The biggest obstacles, however, derived from the "character" of the population, with "its obsession with caste distinctions" and persistent refusal to abandon the circles that were divided by profession according to time-honored tradition. Women, moreover, were "totally absent" from theater performances, outings, and other *dopolavoro* manifestations.[79] Under Rautiis's guidance, membership rose from 3,609 in 1934 to 7,829 in mid-1935 including, he proudly noted, 549 women. Activity was sustained at least through 1937, when 8,691 members were reported for the province.[80] It is unlikely, however, that more than 2,000 to 3,000 were peasants. Nearly a fifth of the city of Potenza's 25,000 population inhabited miserable damp underground dugouts or *sotterrani*, lacking in the most rudimentary hygiene facilities;[81] in the almost inaccessible hilltowns, conditions were so primitive as to discourage even the most callous offical from hawking cards.

In 1934, fascism was still a "chimera" in the neighboring province of Matera according to the *federale* Sandicchi: In the twelve years since the March on Rome, in the seven since Matera had become a separate province, "nothing, absolutely nothing, had been done to give the local people a tangible sign of the fascist era." As elsewhere in the South, Sandicchi found that the "energy of the local *gerarchi*" had

been "totally absorbed in exasperating struggles for each other's mutual destruction."[82] The party was lacking in cadres because the "best
men emigrated to the major towns to enter into the bureaucracies or
professions, leaving behind only the *cagoiani* [former followers of
Nitti], or those who had otherwise been compromised in previous party
struggles."[83] Communications, too, posed an enormous obstacle: The
roads were so poor and the distances between the rural villages so
great as to exhaust even the most energetic organizers. Beyond this,
funds were short; and unless substantial financial assistance was forthcoming from Rome, it was impossible to build the necessary facilities.
In this setting, the *dopolavoro* was almost incongruous. The passage
of the OND's traveling theater or Thespian Car, in Sandicchi's words,
had made an "enormous impression."[84] However, as he wrote to
Starace, he could not envisage developing a sports program. Agricultural laborers lived in "primordial" conditions, housed – as another
observer noted – in "caverns dug into the rock, row upon row like the
cells of a beehive, receiving light and air only through the low door-
ways."[85] Despite his efforts, enrollment for the province amounted to
only 1,660 persons at the end of 1935; and in 1937, notwithstanding
the OND's insistence that all municipalities have their own centers,
eleven of Matera's miserable villages still lacked any meeting place at
all.[86]

Whether increased assistance from the OND could have facilitated
the expansion of the *dopolavoro* in these conditions seems doubtful.
The OND in fact provided special subsidies to the southern federations;
but these were irregular and in any case failed to compensate for a lack
of local initiative.[87] The rural towns in most cases were too impoverished to construct their own facilities, much less to sustain any degree
of organizational activity, whereas affluent townsmen – small-town
mecenati who might be prevailed upon to donate a radio, or furniture
– and rural landowners generally preferred the more traditional forms
of personal patronage to impersonal donations to party-sponsored welfare initiatives. Given the milieu in which the party was operating in
the South, it was likely in any case that more substantial outside funding
would simply have constituted a new fount of graft and a further source
of contention among rival cliques.

In the last analysis, however, it was the fascist regime itself that
obstructed the work of its reforming functionaries. Even the most
energetic organizers like Lodi and Rautiis at Potenza, Sandicchi in
Matera province, or Sellani in Sardinia attacked no more than the
outward manifestations of power of the clientele networks in the
"masonic mentality" and "factious squabbling" of their members; the

real source of their strength lay in the semifeudal social-economic relations of Southern rural society, under attack in the immediate postwar years by peasant leagues and cooperatives, fully restored after years of assiduous economic protectionism by the fascist government. The fundamental incompatability between, on the one hand, the reactionary effects of fascist agrarian policy, and on the other the efforts of the "party of a new kind" to build itself a mass base, was understood at some level by fascist functionaries assigned to the South – though virtually all labored under the illusion that fascism could finally reform itself. So Pirretti, prefect of Matera in the late thirties, finishing yet another pessimistic assessment of the "state of the province," urged that laws be passed to break up the great rural properties – *laws*, he stressed, and not the usual "extemporaneous, half-baked, demagogic improvisations." Land reform, in his view, would finally eliminate the *nouveau riche* landowner and the "intransigently reactionary feudal lordling"; it would free the miserable tenant farmer from the exploitation of the *latifondista* and the middleman. The peasants set up as independent smallholders, their ties to clientele systems broken, the "residues of the old world" finally swept away – then and only then would the political energy formerly expended in "hate, vice, and indolence" be released for "building a new political order."[88] Such, in 1939, was a fascist bureaucrat's utopian project.

The intractable hinterland

The OND had already understood its accomplishments fell far short of its ambitions when it reviewed its forces at the opening of the Ethiopian campaign. Organizing the countryside, in Starace's words, had proven "slow and difficult." By his estimate 3,479,200 small proprietors, tenants, sharecroppers, and common laborers were eligible to join: 1,662,660 in the North; 536,300 in the central regions; 847,800 in the continental South; and 432,500 from the Islands. According to Starace, only 572,180 peasants or 15 percent of the total had thus far done so. The OND's rather evident failures were, in Starace's view, due less to the organizational shortcomings than to the peasant's innate reluctance to join. The *rurali*, he complained, "when not simply apathetic or recalcitrant, were little inclined toward any form of organized activity."[89] Nonetheless, there was the implicit recognition that the fascist hierarchy had been seduced by the simplicity of its own "ruralist" slogans. Experience had demonstrated that the will of the organizer could not triumph over such formidable obstacles as impoverishment, illiteracy, and the lack of cooperation of local landowners.

The penetration of the countryside

Not perceived failure but rather new needs ultimately prompted the OND to develop a new rural "strategy" between 1936 and 1937. Economic autarchy, adopted as an explicit policy in the wake of the League of Nations sanctions, presupposed agricultural self-sufficiency; and the attainment of that goal required a far greater mobilization than had been hitherto contemplated. Consequently, for the first time in early 1937 the OND began to scrutinize the rural topography more systematically to determine the approriate forms for rural organizing. The new master scheme devised by Puccetti in June 1937 divided rural Italy into three general zones, each defined by its pattern of peasant habitation and each serviced by the appropriate model of *dopolavoro*: the *dopolavoro frazionale* for Zone A of rural centers or urban agglomerates; the *dopolavoro di casale* for Zone B, where peasants resided in scattered homesteads; and the *dopolavoro di corte* or *masseria* for Zone C, consisting of the grouped farmsteads common in the Venetian–Paduan plains and large southern estates.[90] Of perhaps greater importance than these remarkably mechanistic directives were the agreements the OND concluded in July 1937 with the National Confederation of Agriculturists, whereby the latter finally agreed to press its members to support rural groups, both by defraying their costs and persuading their employees to attend.[91]

The momentum set up by the mobilization for the war in Ethiopia combined with sustained pressures from the national organization led to a spectacular increase in OND rural facilities and membership after 1936. During the war period alone, enrollment grew by 200,000. By the end of 1936 the OND reported 3,767 rural organizations and an increase in rural membership to 720,554.[92] OND activity increased commensurately with the formation of victory gardens, the organization of rural technical courses, and the distribution of huge quantities of rabbits, chickens, mulberry seedlings, and silkworms.

Even with this full-scale mobilization, the OND was only partially able to surmount the barriers that hitherto had obstructed its efforts to assimilate the peasantry into national political and economic life. The imbalance between North and South was not eliminated; as the OND itself admitted, the overwhelming majority of new associations continued to be set up in the north-central regions.[93] So while in the North agricultural modernization accompanied and indeed spurred the introduction of new political structures into the countryside, in the South a conservative agricultural structure – reinforced by the regime's own policies – finally prevented the regime from establishing a base of its own. The *dopolavoro* in the South served simply as a gathering place, its members frequently without even a card as token sign of

125

allegiance to the regime. Far from being the "spearheads of a new order," as the zealous Lodi had envisaged, the circles were inconsequential outposts of the state, tools of local factions more often than agencies of the regime. Their presence may well have suggested to local inhabitants that something had indeed changed in Rome, but perhaps only that the alien forces of government had become more obtrusive and complex.

Overall the fascist organizational network had a wider geographical extension than that of either the Socialist or Italian Popular parties in the immediate postwar years. Nonetheless, it is doubtful whether it could claim a broader base of peasant support than that achieved by the two mass parties in 1920–1. The very existence of the new associations in formerly isolated rural areas engendered a familiarity with the central government that was previously lacking; and the unaccustomed attention from party authorities perhaps impressed politically inexperienced peasants with its novelty. But contact between the regime and the peasantry was never sufficiently sustained to generate anything more than passing enthusiasm, whereas the enduring day-to-day misery sufficed to dispel fascism's illusory promises for a better life.

5

Privileging the clerks

The "new" lower middle class has commonly been identified with the emergence of mass culture, as its leading consumer if not its actual creator. Through the thirties, at least, salaried workers generally had more spare time and disposable income than the vast majority of production workers; they were also inclined to participate more actively in the dominant culture as a means of reaffirming a middle class status. In Italy, however, in the years between the wars, the clerical labor force was still so small in number, so deeply divided by the different terms of employment in the private and public sectors, and so poorly paid that it could hardly keep up appearances, much less set standards of cultural consumption for an emerging mass public. Moreover, it was of such recent formation, beginning its rapid growth with the expansion of state intervention and industrial enterprises during the war years, that the definition of its social place – somewhere between free professionalism and traditional proletariat – was still a wide-open question.[1] How this group would be situated – whether it would be treated as mere clerical labor, or elevated into a new middle class – was the major problem that the regime had to address when it sought to organize the more than three-quarters of a million clerks, small functionaries, and uniformed service workers in the state and private sectors.[2]

The after-work sections developed for this salaried personnel, about two-thirds of whom were on the payroll of government and parastate offices, offered an exceptionally original solution. The use of the *dopolavoro* to organize clerical and manual labor alike gave the appearance of treating all of the working classes or *classi lavoratrici* equally, whereas in fact, the groups were instituted in such a way as to break the solidarity between "brain" and manual work that, briefly, had been achieved in the labor struggles of the postwar years. As an organizational form, the *dopolavoro* appeared to have none of the proletarian connotations of trade unionism, though it could provide some of its economic benefits. As such it appealed especially to the growing number of clerks, technicians, and sales personnel with little previous organizational experience, offering them an institutional means through which to define their new social identity, or at least articulate their perplexity and anguish about their dependent status, precarious economic situation, and routinized work patterns. By assiduously publicizing the activities of these employee clubs, many of the most active of which were located in Rome or in other major cities, the regime moreover successfully identified the cultural habits of the "white collars" as the proper national standard for the expenditure of spare time. What this group lacked in real social weight – because it still constituted only 5 percent of the total labor force – or in economic power as consumers, it made up for in a state-conferred social status: This came from being identified publicly as the most active participants in the official mass culture. The fact that 650,000 of these employees were also on the government payroll, and were thus associated by public opinion with the conduct of state affairs, made it possible for the regime to exercise an unusually powerful and direct role in setting the patterns of cultural consumption of the middle classes as a whole.

Fascism's "new" middle class

The importance of this officially organized leisure time for defining the social place of Italian salaried employees can be better understood if we take into account not only the income, working conditions, and contractual power of the white collar labor force, but, as importantly, the unusual social and political pressures that were placed on the group under the fascist regime. For lack of a labor aristocracy, or any cohesive body of "disinterested" experts – whose formation had been sought by fascist technocrats in the early twenties – the regime expected its own employees to perform the social and political functions of a middle class; in addition to carrying out their regular duties as state servants, they were also expected to act as social mediators between the political elites and the working population as a whole, by serving as vigilant cadres and volunteers in the PNF's numerous local agencies. Yet employment in the civil service was in a very real sense unfree labor; like white collar workers in the private sector, state employees performed routinized tasks; and although many held technical diplomas or university degrees, they were equally dependent, if not on the marketplace, on executive fiat and the vicissitudes of state finance.[3]

The fascist government had initially sought to reconcile this basic contradiction by singling out the civil service for privileged treatment. The fascist "ideal" of the civil service, as Mussolini told postal workers on 6 November 1923, consisted of a "few well-cared-for employees" who, once freed from worries about the "inexorable necessities of existence," would "take pride in their mission and function."[4] The civil service codes, adopted in November–December 1923, granted state employees special juridical status, as well as authorizing separate and unusually preferential contractual arrangements. From 1923 to 1930, the civil servants received larger salary increments than any other single employee category – a policy, the fascists then boasted, that was achieved without any increase at all in government expenditure because the total state personnel had been reduced from 544,000 in July 1923 to 514,000 in mid-1929 by firings, attrition, and a freeze on any new hiring.[5]

This policy of giving state employees preferential economic treatment could not be sustained for long. With the onset of the Depression, the regime began to rehire on a massive scale; between 1929 and 1939, the state payroll increased by one-third as the police agencies, party and corporative bureaucracies, military establishment, and social welfare and economic planning offices absorbed thousands of new employees, many of whom were redundant from the outset as the fascists too picked up the much-deplored habit of their "demo-liberal" predecessors of using the state as employer of last resort for out-of-work degree holders and war veterans.[6] For financial reasons, as well as to give some credence to the fascist notion of "equal sacrifice," the civil service could no longer be treated to the same economic privileges of the relatively small civil service of the twenties. In 1930 and 1934, state employees were subjected to the same across-the-board salary cuts as were imposed on industrial and rural laborers. It is true that real salaries increased all the same, by some 3–4 percent during the time fascism was in power, while real wages declined overall by 15–20 percent. Nevertheless, salary cuts, together with the uneven distribution of the increments in favor of the upper grades, accentuated the misery of the low-ranking C and subaltern employees, at the same time exposing the dependent status of even the uppermost ranks of functionaries.[7]

If the civil service had constituted just any group of salaried workers, the unrest these cuts provoked by the early thirties would probably have passed unnoticed. However, at the same time as the economic gains of the civil service were being whittled away, the regime required its increasingly more active cooperation, as interpreters as well as administrators of government policy. With the complete subordination of the party to the state apparatus, who else but the civil service could be relied on to give the creative support the regime needed to implement its strategy of "reaching out to the people"? Without the active collaboration of competent officials, how else could it reach outlying areas to set up its own party agencies and institutions? From late 1931, the regime thus sought to mobilize the bureaucracy, as a "civil militia," much like the "soldiers in plain clothes" whom the Nazis sought to create through their Restoration Act of the Civil Service of 1933: "as disciplined and devoted to duty as the nation's armed forces."

Any such political mobilization naturally called for a change in fascism's own attitudes toward the political responsibilities and attitudes of government personnel. Until the early thirties, the regime had seemed perfectly satisfied with mere tokens of political obeisance from its employees; although it had long cast off any pretense that hirings and firings were taking place according to criteria of efficiency or merit, it never acceded to pressures from its "intransigents" for a thoroughgoing political purge. It may well be, as Mussolini sustained in 1925, that the majority of employees had indeed "conducted themselves well"; political firings in 1923, together with the threat (expressed with Mussolini's customary delicacy) of "driving out any remaining mangy sheep" had quickly ended any political resistance.[8] But no fascist at all familiar with the bureaucracy was so credulous to think that government personnel had truly been "fascistized" or that the "pusillanimous" habits of the old liberal bureaucrats had disappeared. Short of replenishing the bureaucracy with entirely new personnel – something that was never seriously contemplated for lack of competent cadres of its own making – the regime sought to revolutionize the bureaucratic mentality: So, the "slow-moving black-frock with his mutterings and complaints" would be transformed into a "true servant of the public welfare and the apostle of the highest national duties." To achieve this transformation, the regime evidently had to provide some incentives; the "prestige" that ostensibly came from performing "indispensable tasks" in the corporative state evidently gave insufficient motivation.[9]

The rewards of civil service

The ambiguous social status of civil servants was, however, further reinforced by their complete lack of contractual power under fascist labor legislation. The Committee of Eighteen charged with drawing up the preliminary draft for the corporate laws passed in April 1926 had advised the regime to distinguish between the uniformed personnel in the railroads and other public services (including the post and telegraphic system and government monopolies) and the state office employees; the former, by virtue of their proletarian character, were to be granted the right to organize in state-run syndicates, whereas the latter, as "intellectuals" with only slight traditions of union organization, were to be excluded from this privilege. But the nationalist Rocco had argued that the mere existence of any kind of syndicate for civil servants would have implied that organizations could exist outside of the corporate state, influence its action, and maybe even subvert its interests. In keeping with this authoritarian logic, the law of 3 April 1926 banned any kind of civil service union. In theory, the fascist civil service codes protected government employees from the arbitrary personnel practices of previous regimes by regulating promotion, pay, disciplining, and retirement policy. In fact, dependents of state and local government, the railroads and other government agencies, together with the personnel employed by public charities and other public laws bodies were now to be entirely subject to executive fiat; they could neither engage in collective bargaining nor even apply to the fascist labor courts for arbitration of disputes.[10]

This ban notwithstanding, the fascists could not ignore the strong traditions of public service associationalism that were being consolidated when the fascists came to power. By late 1921, almost 90 percent of the 550,000 state employees had joined some kind of local or national organization. This vast movement had taken two basic forms. The militant trade unionism of the railroad and postwar workers in the uniformed services and among employees in the state mines, salt, and tobacco manufactures had a reformist socialist orientation and identified itself with the proletarian class organizations in the private sector. The professional groups, on the other hand, consisting of sundry national and local unions, federal chambers, and associations, had grown out of the traditional *associazioni di impiegati* formed from the turn of the century among government functionaries and private employees for purposes of mutual aid and recreation; although their purposes were mainly economic, they also demanded the right to criticize government procedures and to support political parties.[11] To have ignored this movement would have meant denying what Rocco and other nationalists characterized as the "modern" and "inevitable" tendency of groups to associate; more important, it would have entailed disbanding the fascists' own groups among railroad and postal functionaries, teachers, municipal doctors, and state office employees, established in the early twenties in order to gain a foothold of their own in the public administration.[12]

Accordingly, the regime allowed for what Rocco, with typical juridical sophistry, defined as "associations for purposes of assistance"; personnel in the judiciary and the Ministries of the Interior, Foreign

Affairs, the Colonies, and the Corporations were excluded even from this benign form of organization. The Railroad Employees' Association, which had developed out of a militant contingent of fascist functionaries organized since 1922 in the Associazione Nazionale dei Ferrovieri Fascisti, was the first to be recognized on 3 April 1926. In the next several months, Mussolini approved the constitution of the Fascist Teachers' Association (divided into five sections from the primary school to the university level), the Fascist Association of Public Employees (AFPI) for dependents of the central and local state administration, the Fascist Association of Postal and Telegraphic Employees, and finally the Fascist Association of Employees in the State Industrial Enterprises.[13]

But even this highly controlled associationalism could not be tolerated for long. In March 1931 the PNF, renewing its battle against "indifference" and "anti-fascism" in the public administration, tightened the control it had nominally exercised over the Associations since 5 February 1927. Their national secretaries were immediately replaced by party fiduciaries selected by the PNF secretary, who were empowered to appoint even the local section leaders. In September 1931 a single monthly bulletin, *Forze civili*, replaced the occasionally polemical news sheets formerly published independently by each of the services.

The PNF's decision to set up such an extraordinarily unwieldy organizational structure – even to the point of insisting on a single news bulletin for personnel as diverse as the fastidious Roman bureaucrat and the hard-laboring railroad trackman – can only be explained by its determination to eliminate even the last residues of the old "spirit of category" within the various branches of the civil service. The establishment of a unified association with no regard for divisions either by rank or function – which were in fact being accentuated and codified by the civil service laws of 1923 – already tended to eliminate any possible solidarity along job lines. The PNF's attempt to efface the identity even of the single services in turn laid the organizational bases for developing an entirely new corporate image, common to the civil service as a whole, with the state alone as its primary reference point.

Although they were completely devoid of representational powers, the associations performed some residual representational functions. *Forze civili* readers could learn from the fiduciary Dr. Antonio Luigi Farina's article on the "limits and forms of associative action" that the associations existed in the recognition that employees were "citizens and men whose rights, needs, and aspirations had to be articulated."[14] The local groups held periodic meetings to discuss wages, hours, and employment conditions, and presumably conveyed the results to higher authorities. All questions involving the status, promotion, and transfer of individual members were handled by the local offices of the associations. These could also provide legal advice on technical questions, although not before courts of law. Finally, as completely "disinterested" parties, they were also empowered to conciliate disputes.[15]

The main function of the fascist "association for assistance," beyond testing political loyalty by checking on who joined and who did not, was to deliver services. By the early thirties, the state employees' groups had used their good offices to gain a whole range of benefits for their constituents, from the establishment of the Italian Consortium of Manufacturers or CIM in 1927 – the petty functionary's version of the fashionable La Rinascente department store chain which supplied office employees with the latest styles in clothing and household items – to the several thousand low-cost housing units built under the supervision of the state agency INCIS. In this emphasis on the provision of services, the fascist associations recalled the preunion *associazione per impiegati*. But the services supplied by an authoritarian state to a clientele just on the edge of mass consumption were of course more inclusive than those that could be obtained by the mutualism of struggling local groups. Moreover, the way in which these services were delivered underscored the truly reactionary character of the fascist organization of civil service employees. Not only did the regime seek to eliminate any residual class identification by organizing civil servants on an entirely different basis from manual labor, but it also sought to prevent the consumer demands of this relatively well-paid sector from coalescing with or in any way influencing those of the mass of workers. The prefascist salaried employees' associations had always maintained that their noneconomic demands – for decent housing, efficient provisioning, and low-cost public services – coincided with those of the "consumer pure and simple"; that is, they identified their own social demands with the public interest, seeking to "advance the consumer demands of the middle classes and of the people as a whole" through the electoral process and by organized pressure in local communities.[16] The fascists, by contrast, treated such social services as the exclusive perquisite of government employment; any improvements were the result of a corporatist pressure – by the category and for the category. In this way, the isolation of the civil service from the working population as a whole was greatly reinforced. At the same time, state employees were singled out as a specially privileged corps of consumers within an emerging mass market, to be served with a dispatch and care that was denied all other groups in the working population.

In a structure so bound up with the delivery of services, the organization of the *dopolavoro* perfectly complemented the civil service association. The first in the public administration, the Dopolavoro for railroad employees, had been founded in October 1925. Subsequent legislation provided for the institution of groups for dependents of the state-run tobacco and salt works in May 1926 and employees of the postal and telegraphic services in July 1926.[17] By the mid-thirties, virtually all of the half-million state dependents had access to recreational facilities; some through the municipal *dopolavoro*, which catered primarily to civil servants and dependents of local government, the majority through membership in the more than 500 sections organized in the state administration itself.

Although in theory the *dopolavoro* and the employees' associations were separate, in practice the two, unobstructed by the "syndical" conflicts between management and unions in the private sector, had tended to merge their activities. It was not uncommon for the local groups of the associations to sponsor their own *dopolavoro* sections. Even when the administrations were kept clearly separate, as was true in the railroads, the two organizations were mutually accommodating, promoting activities and publicizing the progress of the local groups as if they were all part of one monolithic fascist movement. Of course, it was to the associations' advantage to claim credit for the services provided by the ministries themselves; the regime in any case prevented any effective organization of civil servants except in the sphere of consumption; what's more, the *dopolavoro* circles were far more active than the associations; how much more can be suggested in spatial terms – by the inconspicuous side-door entryway of the Railroad association at the palatial Dopolavoro of the Railroad at Rome, in which the Association was housed by the benevolence of management.

The recreational groups for government employees, like those set up in private enterprise, differed according to the sector in which they were operating. Broadly speaking, two quite different types can be distinguished: An "industrial" model located in the autonomous state enterprises (*aziende autonome*), which ran the railroads, the telegraphic, long-distance telephone and postal services, and the state monopolies and included about a third of all government personnel; and a "club" model, located in the administrative offices proper, in the central ministries and local state bureaucracies, and in an increasing number of parastate agencies and semiautonomous administrative bodies, includ-

134

ing the national petroleum agency (AGIP) and the various state insurance groups like INA and INFAIL. The former were set up by the general directors of the administrations primarily to maximize the efficiency of their large contingents of manual workers; and they operated under independent charters granted by special legislation, at considerable expenditure and with careful attention to planning. The *dopolavoro* sections operating according to the "club" model were, by contrast, frequently formed at the initiative of the personnel itself, with only a limited initial financial support from their managements. Free of any explicit managerial objective, these operated with a far greater degree of autonomy.

In the one case and the other, the *dopolavoro* was treated by management as a perquisite of service with no syndicalist connotations whatsoever. In the "syndicalist state," ironically, it was as if this nonsyndical form were accepted as the natural mode of organizing the *impiegati*; no bargaining, and certainly no labor struggle; no petty haggling over wages, hours, and job security, but rather the provision by a benign management of services consistent with their relatively elevated status as intellectual workers and modest consumers. Above all, by banning trade unions in the public sector, where the majority of the intellectual workers were employed, it set a singularly important precedent. Civil service unionism in other industrialized countries always set a highly visible example for employees in the private sector.[18] The absence of this example in Italy could not help but be detrimental to the development of a union consciousness within this category as a whole.

Making the model railroad corps

The Railroad Dopolavoro was the first to be established in the public administration, and after 1925 it had quickly grown into the largest and most heavily subsidized of all of the recreational groups in fascist Italy. By the late thirties it had 274 sections and 134,000 members. This extraordinarily rapid growth reflected at once the particular character of the railroad personnel and the special preoccupation of the regime with the efficient administration of train services. The very nature of employment in the railroads, with its frequent transfers, exhausting tours of duty, and lengthy assignments, sometimes in isolated country branch lines, demanded auxiliary services – hostels for stopovers, cafeterias, supply stores, and recreational facilities. Traditionally such needs had been at least partially met by the employees themselves, through their mutual aid societies and cooperatives and, after the turn of the century, in the conviviality of union clubs and socialist circles, whose persistent survival into the mid-twenties persuaded the railroad administration of the urgency of developing an alternative.[19] This effort was entirely supported by a regime that had quickly understood that no technological achievement quite so impressed bourgeois opinion as much as an efficiently run railroad system. Accordingly, from 1922 on, it made a special effort to modernize the railroad system – a totalizing effort that involved the establishment of the Ministry of Communications in April 1924 headed by Costanzo Ciano during its entire first decade, a several-billion-lira investment in equipment and lines, the rationalization of work procedures, and, of course, efforts to form a new-model railroad man.[20]

According to Italian railroad officials, the improved attitude of the personnel accounted more than any other single factor for the transformation of the railroad system from a symbol of "demo-liberal incompetence" into the "mirror of the nation's progress" under fascism. The 130,000–140,000 employees who remained after the political firings of nearly 50,000 persons in 1923–4, attrition, and additional layoffs of 16,200 persons in 1932, were subjected to an entirely new personnel policy. This acknowledged the need for a dual leadership of the huge staff, at once political and technical. The Azienda continued to be personified in the figure of the general director, who, as under the old regime, was entirely responsible for the day-to-day conduct of business; it was he whom subordinates held responsible for the often unresponsive bureaucracy, the military-like discipline, the inflexible rules, and the demanding work schedules. The new minister, on the other hand, although responsible for general policy and claiming credit for any positive innovations in the service, was considered above blame for specific employee grievances. Ciano, a World War I naval hero, equally at home in industrial and fascist circles, expertly and self-consciously exploited this advantageous position. He was at once a severe disciplinarian who promised to be "inexorable toward those who failed in their duty" and a tough paternalist; his assertions of "affection and respectful devotion" for his men and promises of generosity for work well done, led even the most skeptical to perceive him as the "father of a great family."[21]

Company policy favored a stable, small, and relatively well-paid staff, at least until the mid-thirties, when the administration submitted to political pressures and began hiring unemployed veterans of the fascist wars in Ethiopia and Spain. Thus the part-time personnel, which had made up a quarter of the total work force in the early twenties, was reduced to a mere 3 percent by 1931, while with the suspension

Privileging the clerks

of new hirings and the greater seniority of those already employed, almost all full-time personnel had advanced to the upper levels of their pay scales. Consequently, the railroad personnel as a whole had a higher rate of pay than any other single category within the civil service, even if the overall average was lower as a result of the large number of ill-paid manual laborers. Although the average pay declined, as was true for other civil service categories, this was more than compensated for by a significant increase in fringe benefits. Already in 1929, the sums spent on pensions, indemnities, uniform allowances, and medical and health services amounted to fully 20 percent of the total per capita expenditure on personnel, or double the sum spent in 1913–14.[22] In addition, the railroad administration significantly expanded those paternalistic initiatives dispensed as compensation for the special conditions of duty in the railroads: The Opera di Previdenza, founded in 1913, supplemented severance pay, paid out indemnities for death in service, and provided subsidies for hardship cases, including the Helena of Savoy and Victor Emmanuel II Foundations to assist employee children, especially orphans, an important function in a service that frequently became a family tradition; the *provvida* to supply low-cost food and fuel in the main division centers and fill special orders in isolated branch lines; and finally, the 3,000 new low-cost rental and cooperative housing units for employees.[23]

With the establishment of the Dopolavoro in October 1925, the railroad administration implicitly recognized that organized sociability too constituted a very real need for employees subject to frequent transfers or serving in isolated areas. Although the organization was financed and managed by the railroad administration, it was generally considered to be the regime's contribution to the well-being of the personnel, instituted as a result of Ciano's benign intercession. Ciano was in fact entirely responsible for formulating the legislation establishing this first state-run *dopolavoro*, although his argument in favor of a subsidy of 800,000 lire annually plus a 10-lira contribution per employee – that the service would "predispose employees spiritually and physically to a more productive labor"[24] – was certainly a familiar one. In any case, the Railroad Dopolavoro was organized with such an exacting professionalism that few of its members would easily have characterized it either as a tool of personnel management or an agency of fascist control. The central office, established in late 1925 in Rome, naturally had some contacts both with the personnel office and the Fascist Association of Railroaders. But the Dopolavoro had its own autonomous offices and staff headed by a high-ranking administration appointee, and it was counseled by a central commission including a delegate of

137

the personnel, selected from the Fascist Association, that met at least once a month.

What could this central office offer to personnel who already had strong traditions of associational activity and therefore required little special incentive to socialize? First of all, it gave the hundred or so local groups that already existed in 1925 some measure of protection: Those circles that failed to file for "recognition" with the central office within six months did so at the risk of having the administration "disinterest itself in their conduct," thus exposing them to the heavy-handed interference of the Fascist federations.[25] Beyond this very guarded "moral" support, the administration sustained local initiatives by establishing what Dr. Fasciolo, the Dopolavoro director, described as "special and dignified" facilities that were also "strictly economical in terms of rent, maintenance, and management."[26] Between 1926 and 1936, the railroad administration spent over twenty million lire on conversions and new constructions; the main expenditures were for new buildings at Bologna, Rome, Leghorn, Rimini, Bari, Brindisi, Florence, and Genoa, all designed by the state railroad's architectural office under the direction of A. Mazzoni and R. Narducci (both of whom were influenced by the regime's official architect, Piacentini) and were executed with technical proficiency in a variety of distinctively fascist styles: from the trim functionalism of the Florentine Dopolavoro just adjacent to Nervi's modernist station of Santa Maria Novella, to the temple-like opulence of the huge Roman center with its eclectic iconography of caryatids, columns, and *fasci*. At least a dozen of the 270 facilities set up by 1936 – those located along the main lines – were veritable recreational complexes with thousands of members. The Railroad Dopolavoro at Bologna, for example, situated at the crossing of the trunk lines to the central and southern parts of the country, had a main headquarters in the town center, in addition to a second major facility in the vicinity of the Azienda's worker housing at the city limit. This was situated in a huge park with a fountain and several thousand trees and was equipped with a 3,000-seat movie theater, a giant outdoor stage, and eight *bocce* and four tennis courts. Even the smaller groups were well equipped. By the mid-thirties, practically all had small libraries and radios (153 had gramophones as well) and 200, or three-quarters of the total, had movie projectors of their own, seventy-five of which were sound models.[27]

In the end, however, the character and quantity of activities were determined by the energy of the local membership. When a circular arrived, publicizing the availability of, for example, a model rabbit hutch or special seed and fertilizers or novel theatrical texts, some enterprising member would respond. In this essentially voluntary way, small stages were built and amateur theatricals performed (often with the stationmaster's wife taking the lead female roles), darkrooms were set up, outings were planned, and new films were ordered. In small towns especially, the new circles were seen to be a "breath of life,"[28] social centers open to all railroad employees, the day-to-day conduct of which seemed free enough, conditioned rather than controlled by the desire of the section presidents – the stationmaster or his assistant, the ranking office functionary, or the depot head – as well as of the membership to avoid the disturbance that might be caused by idiosyncratic cultural choices or eccentric social behavior.

The agency's "watchful care"[29] over its staff acted to set the personnel of the uniformed railroad services distinctly apart from other worker categories. A modern enterprise operating in a generally backward social context inevitably tends toward self-sufficiency, it is true; but this tendency was strongly encouraged by the railroad administration, not only in the technical administrative aspects of the service, but also in the area of employee recreation as well. Not only did the Railroad Dopolavoro have its own separate recreational facilities – in this it was similar to Fiat or any other large private firm – but it also had its own circuit of competitive athletics, with its own national rallies and prizes. In many respects, this isolation had a more insidious effect on worker solidarity as a whole than did the isolation of the former worker vanguard at Fiat, for the *ferrovieri*, like medieval masons, had provided an important link among workingmen, especially in politically backward areas. As it was, under fascism, the worker categories in the railroad service were cut off from the working class as a whole, not only by virtue of the elimination of their unions – which had been a mainstay of the reformist CGL in the postwar labor struggles – but also by the formalization of their leisure under the auspices of the Railroad Dopolavoro.

It is doubtful, however, that such privileged treatment converted the skeptics – detachment from the mass enthusiasms of the regime in such a self-sufficient structure may well even have cultivated a certain critical spirit, articulated by the next generation of railroadmen if not by their subdued parents. According to Italo Briano, author of the three-volume *Storia della ferrovie italiane*, who during his own twenty-five years of service from 1917 to 1942 had passed from apprentice to inspector, the majority of railroadmen had a nuanced understanding of the meaning of fascist largesse: "Nobody cared for the great boasting which went on in that period, attributing to the regime, and to it alone, everything that was accomplished: a truly imposing body of works, it is true, but that was realized above all by the spirit of discipline and sacrifice of the entire class, and not by the exclusive merit of a political oligarchy."[30] In the end, they would have preferred a structure that was democratically run and "apolitical." Nevertheless, they accepted what was offered with "enthusiasm," in Briano's words, "not looking at the plate, so much as its content." This logic was certainly not without ambiguities. As Briano himself recalls, the modernization of the service under fascism strongly reinforced the *esprit de corps* of the railroad personnel, and they, perhaps more than any other single category, appreciated first hand a certain kind of technical–administrative progress that unquestionably took place under fascism. Although many railroad men may have been uncomfortable with fascist bombast that once more elevated the railroad system into a political symbol – "once hothouse of irreverence and insubordination to the state, today temple of devotion to the nation and to duty" – most would nevertheless have approved of Ciano's image of the service as a disciplined, modern corps "as reliable as the army of the Piave and Carso."[31] With the passage of time it was of course easy to forget the social price initially paid for this progress – or the political repression that was its necesary concomitant and which could not give way to the "apolitical" system many might have preferred.

It is doubtful in any case whether the regime actually ever sought to fascistize thoroughly the railroad employees, and certainly not by means of the *dopolavoro* associations. "Politicking" was not encouraged by the central administration because it disrupted work routine, and members of local groups themselves discouraged overtly political events as opening old rancors and disrupting comradely relations among colleagues whose political differences were already declared. The administration itself logically preferred to stress service traditions. Even if it occasionally distributed gratis fascist books and journals, it gave its far more enthusiastic support to the circulation of the railroad *Album of Honor*, for example, or to the *Album* of wartime gold-medal winners from the state railroads. For the regime too, the professionalism of the railroad man, his pride in the service was more important than any repoliticization of the work force. Making the trains run on time was in a very real sense as necessary to the prestige of fascism, if not more so, than affirmations of political loyalty to the regime.

Cultural uplift for the bureaucrats

Government offices were not generally subject to the same administrative imperatives as the private sector, and because their managers were not directly accountable for employee efficiency as measured by output or profits, they were naturally unresponsive to the kind of productivist arguments in support of social services that found so receptive an audience in business enterprise or in those state services, like the railroads, that were organized according to industrial criteria. The state bureaucracy nevertheless faced personnel problems that were closely bound up with transformations – and the lack thereof – in the nature of bureaucratic labor during the period between the wars. The "discipline of respect," to use sociologist Michel Crozier's phrase, which had regulated personnel relations in the nineteenth-century bureaucracy, had been undermined by new hirings, changing administrative procedures, huge salary disparities, and, finally, by the change of regimes itself; yet the "discipline of efficiency" of the rationally organized twentieth-century office hierarchy had hardly begun to be established.[32] In this context, the need for mechanisms for building staff solidarity on an entirely new basis was particularly acute.

From the early twenties on, fascist reformers had understood that bureaucratic inefficiency was a leading cause of employee demoralization. Anachronistic work methods had a particularly debilitating effect on the brightest and most energetic young functionaries. Ettore Lolini noted in 1923: After a few years of performing routine duties with no bearing on their professional qualifications, they abandoned their studies and lost all capacity to conceptualize, convinced that "academic qualifications, culture, and intelligence" were all "nonvalues," or even detrimental to their careers, because they were frequently associated by superiors with independence of mind and character. The rationalization of office work, Lolini had hypothesized, would not only render government business more efficient, but also improve employee morale. Standardization of office procedures and specification of tasks within the various departments, together with the mechanization of a few basic tasks – using the telephone, for example, rather than handling business in person – would speed up clerical operations, as well as freeing administrators and executive officers for more imaginative tasks in the area of policy making.[33]

Belatedly, on 16 August 1926, the fascist government under the pressure of the stabilization crisis finally passed the first legislation calling for the "introduction of accelerated work methods" in the state administration. Except in a very few ministries, however, such as the Ministry of War, in which the pressures for a more efficient management were particularly compelling, administrative procedures never underwent any significant rationalization under fascism. Advocates of reform, from the ex-Finance Minister Alberto De Stefani, who headed

141

The culture of consent: mass organization in fascist Italy

a special parliamentary inquiry into the bureaucracy in 1929, to Bottai, who in his journal *Critica fascista* repeatedly demanded official action against the "graphomaniacs" in the central administration, were in the end obstructed by bureaucratic inertia. Just as in industry, the availability of low-cost labor reduced economic incentives to reorganize the work process: The greatly increased use of part-time employees (52 percent of custodial, maintenance, and other menial jobs in 1925; 91 percent in 1931) actually blocked efforts to select and train personnel. Moreover, the abolition of activist employee unions interested in trading off improved productivity for salary increments, the lack of any effective public criticism of bureaucratic muddling, and finally, the resistance of senior civil servants who considered "taylorism" like all other "isms" to be a threatening innovation to be avoided at all costs, eliminated effective pressures for reform.[34] There was, consequently, little change in the old routines of government office work.

On the contrary, the overall condition of work appeared to have much worsened for the majority of state employees. True, average pay had increased relative to that of industrial workers. But disparities in stipends had grown enormously, so that a division chief who had earned on an average 4 times as much as his clerical staff in the entire decade 1911–20, and only 2.4 times more in 1921, was by 1930 earning a comfortable 4.6 times as much.[35] Moreover, the military-like reorganization called for by the fascist codes of 1923 had completely removed internal mechanisms of solidarity by imposing a hierarchy of discipline more appropriate to a blindly devoted army in the field or, in De Stefani's approving characterization, to a monastic order.[36] Unlike the army, however, exemplary performance of duty was not necessarily rewarded; diligence, understood as obedience and tractability, was a quality superiors prized more than initiative, and career advance and salary increments depended almost entirely on seniority – if positions in higher ranks were open at all – or on the accumulation of additional appointments. A structure of command that conferred high-ranking functionaries with nearly total power over their subordinates, together with the political pressures that undermined the security of position normally associated with bureaucratic employ in Italy, marked government employees, as an acute observer G. Pischel noted, with a "sense of oppression and depression" that combined together in a "deep inferiority complex."[37]

In this context, it was naturally in the government's interest to encourage such an organization as the *dopolavoro* to build a new basis for service solidarity. Yet the very institution of recreational groups in the central state offices took place at a far slower pace and more haphazardly than in private enterprise or in the state service, not only because of bureaucratic lethargy, but also because management assumed that salaried workers could not be treated with the same rigid paternalistic authority displayed by industrialists toward their personnel. They had to be attracted to join, convinced that the circles responded in some way to their needs; and their needs, certainly, were more difficult to satisfy than those of production workers. Singularly individualistic and family-oriented, often isolated in the *villine* of new garden suburbs just outside the old city walls, or else, as was common in Rome, inhabiting the anomic eight-story suburban *palazzi* constructed by INCIS for state employees, functionaries tended to seek out their own amusements and were, at least initially, disdainful of the collectivist plebeian connotations of the *dopolavoro*.

If personnel offices or administrative departments wanted their recreational groups to be a success, they thus had to be especially attuned to the wants of their employees. The office employee, as the director of personnel of the Banca Popolare of Milan advised colleagues, wanted "a decorous tasteful ambience, with a genteel atmosphere," a variety of amusements equal in quality to those available on the market, though at lower cost, opportunities to develop his culture suited to his educated tastes and temperament, not boring lessons; finally, he wanted to realize enough savings through the *dopolavoro* to have more recreational independence.[38] The underlying assumption, in other words, was that even joining the *dopolavoro* to take advantage of the low-cost services it offered, the white collar worker remained an individual, a consumer with free choice in the marketplace in addition to being a producer of services.

The seemingly casual way in which the *dopolavoro* sections were established in the central bureaucracy, usually at the initiative of some middle-ranking functionary, certainly catered to this sense of social individualism. Nobody could readily argue that the initiative was controlled by management and that employees were therefore unfree in their leisure time. The fact remains that for lack of personnel departments in government offices, the initiative *had* to come from within the bureaucracy itself. The most effective advocates, usually enterprising division chiefs or section heads, exploited intraministerial rivalries, playing on their personal familiarity with their superiors in the ministerial directorates to request subsidies and accommodations for recreational services on behalf of their colleagues and subordinates.[39] By the mid-thirties, these rivalries among the state ministries, exacerbated by the competition from the conspicuously activist groups in parastate agencies such as INA and INFAIL, had led to an escalation of staff demands as well as to an informal definition of what constituted the appropriately decorous facilities for state functionaries: headquarters in the vicinity of the central offices, a floating dock on the Tiber River, a beach house at Ostia or nearby Castelfusano, and perhaps even a country hostel in the Alban Hills. Dominated by senior functionaries, they promoted a highly articulated structure of collegiality that, precisely because it was internally constituted rather than imposed from without, proved a more powerful mechanism for enforcing conformity than any agency openly sponsored by management.

The directors of recreational groups in the public administration, lacking any of the scientific pretensions of management in industry, proposed a more rudimentary function for their organizations: that of simple togetherness. In the interest of staff solidarity, the senior functionaries in charge inevitably had to address the problem of the disparity of economic treatment between the well-off administrative officers and the miserably paid clerical and custodial personnel. Especially when there were large numbers of low-grade civil servants, as was true in the Ministry of the Interior and the Presidency of the Council of Ministers – the staffs of which had grown significantly under the dictatorship – it was important for the recreational group to assist personnel in keeping up appearances, so to speak, rather than encouraging the kind of conspicuous socializing that went on in elite ministerial offices such as the Ministries of War or Finance, which had a greater proportion of high-ranking civil servants. Although it sponsored a full range of activities – the group outing to Naples and Capri on 14 June 1935 included 600 of the 1,560 members – the Dopolavoro of the Presidency of the Council, which merged with that of the Ministry of the Interior after 1935, had as its main function, according to its director Mario Carta, to assist "as tactfully as possible" the category C and subaltern personnel who made up a quarter of the office's 1,850 dependents; nearly 40 percent of the budget for the years 1934 to 1939 was thus spent on assistance, mainly in the form of clothing, school books, the seaside holiday camp Michele Bianchi at Nettuno, and the "utilitarian gifts" distributed on the occasion of the annual children's party of the Befana. Beyond this assistance to employee children, who apparently could be aided without humiliating their parents, the Dopolavoro supplied a range of admittedly "modest" services – medical advice and discounts, a refreshment center near the offices, a barbershop, as well as assistance for C-grade employees preparing examinations for promotion – in other words, all services helpful to maintaining a middle-class status, while at the same time "giving tangible evidence of the watchful and ardent solicitude with which the regime looks after the private lives of government workers.''[40]

At its most successful, the employees' *dopolavoro* combined the social exclusiveness of a private club with the pseudo-egalitarianism of a fascist institution. "Close-knit and carefree" was how the Dopolavoro of the National Insurance Association (INA), a parastate agency, was described by its directors. Located in the heart of Rome at Via Veneto, 89, it claimed to offer "first-rate entertainment" to a "lively and intelligent public" with none of the vices of the decadent bourgeois habitués of the classy though very unsavory spots on the rest of the avenue. The organization itself was independent of management, although it was headed by high-level functionaries; and from 1929 on it was entirely self-financing, its revenues coming from activities and interest on loans granted employees by INA's mutual aid association. The Dopolavoro's managers were strikingly image-conscious, with the knowledge that the group's attractiveness to outsiders added to the prestige of INA's own staff of 1,200.[41] In fact, the mannered elegance of the central headquarters – with its wood-paneled 2,000-volume library, well-equipped gymnasium, billiard room and theater – the stylish floating dock on the Tiber, and the vast summer resort at the Lido of Rome made INA's *dopolavoro* a social reference point for Roman functionaries. At major cultural soirées, during which intellectual luminaries like Pirandello and Marinetti provided entertainment, leading fascist dignitaries mingled with high civil servants on a *tu à tu* basis.

This is not to say, however, that the availability of services in itself guaranteed participation, or that potential members were free from pressures to join, whether from management or from colleagues: Such pressures may have been subtle, though they certainly weighed as heavily on the individual employee as any flagrant management coercion. More than any company newspaper published by management, INA's monthly bulletin, *Famiglia nostra*, demanded conformity, playing on both petty bourgeois status fears and the anxieties about security of subalterns in the company hierarchy. Responding to every shift in the PNF's line, it insistently exhorted its readers to join the party, always intimating that INA's management were personally close to fascist leaders (especially to the president of the National Employees Association, Aldo Lusignuoli) and that the INA Dopolavoro was itself the object of special attention from the hierarchy of the Fascist Federation of the Urbe. For INA's director, Eugenio De Simone, attendance, not only membership at the well-appointed headquarters, was

an "obbligo morale" for the staff. To encourage employees to participate, the Dopolavoro's administration presented an image of exclusiveness: Allusion to events that only group insiders could know about,
the use of nicknames for those who wrote for *Famiglia nostra*, and
publicity for those who took part in the house-sponsored teams and
theater groups, all suggested that only the best and brightest employees
belonged. The administration was not above using far cruder tactics
as well: *Famiglia nostra* had no compunction about singling out an
"unnamed twenty or so persons" who were "too snobbish to attend,"
and another twenty who had the "wrong attitude," coming only rarely
and merely "to show off or to have themselves photographed." The
INA Dopolavoro finally demanded a real physical and moral conformity as well. From February 1933 on, a new column entitled "Speronata"
(Spur) began publication, designed to "castigate the ugly and ridiculous
habits, the foolish irresolution, and inane pretensions that arise and
flourish in white collar ambients." The line between rough male camaraderie and bullying conformism was always exceedingly thin in the
malign comments on incongruous behavior, physical prowess, and
personal appearance, in the prescriptions for an aggressively masculine
and modern deportment for the new-model man of the tertiary, decked
out in his Oxford shirt, martingale jacket, and knee britches, and combining, in the words of one INA functionary, a "consummate snobbism
with frank cordiality."[42]

More than any single service, organized leisure presented office
employees with a means of articulating a new social image. In spite
of their relative economic privileges, government workers experienced
the ideological crisis felt elsewhere by "white collars" as they became
a major component of the labor force. The changes in work routine
under fascism probably do not justify speaking of their "proletariza-
tion." But their traditionally privileged status was exposed to subtle
pressures of all kinds. In a regime that had elevated productivity into
a national virtue against which the relative worth of occupations could
be measured, the *impiegato* was naturally sensitive to accusations of
"parasitism," as well as to those other "commonplaces," as they were
characterized by one unhappy functionary, that dismissed the "employee class" as a whole as "mindless and stupid."[43] Civil servants
could not have been insensible to the criticisms of fascist reformers,
who, if they had had their way, would indeed have made the bureaucracy truly accountable and responsive by reducing the personnel to
what one critic approvingly described as "human merchandise in the
market of the public administration."[44] Nor could they have been
especially comforted by fascism's broadened definition of what con-

stituted productive labor. Properly speaking (in fascist parlance), civil servants as well as employees in banks, insurance companies, and some businesses continued to figure as "brain workers." In journalistic usage, however, this term referred more commonly to technical cadres (engineers especially); whereas in social practice the definition of who was an intellectual – traditionally broad enough to include anyone who by education or vocation performed ideological functions – had become still more restrictive. Thus the fascists' own organization of "brain workers," the Sindacato dei Lavoratori Intellettuali, founded in 1922 and reorganized in 1931–2, clearly identified the status of intellectual with certain professions: teachers, journalists, publishers, writers, and artists. Excluded from this category were all functionaries, even though their social backgrounds and academic preparation were practically identical with those of free professionals, and they were perhaps prevented from practicing what they considered to be their true vocation by the impossibility of finding the prescribed employment.

Cultural uplift for these categories was thus not only the most direct mode of acquiring the values of bourgeois society, but also the essential means of affirming a bourgeois status. The modestly paid *impiegati*, under the fascist regime, like the Parisian *petit fonctionnaire* studied by Crozier in the mid-fifties, above all wanted to participate in high culture and "felt profoundly humiliated at being excluded."[45] For such employees the cultural activities offered through the *dopolavoro* – amateur theater, poetry readings, discounts for tickets to the opera – were at one level a restorative: "an energetic antidote" to the "monotonous office routine" that "so dreadfully levels intelligence."[46] The afterwork organization allowed for the formation of an entirely new cultural–social figure, the part-time intellectual, frequenter of amateur theatricals, artistic soirées, and lessons on learned subjects. By going to the help of these intellectuals, the *dopolavoro*, in the words of INA's theater "expert" Piero Raghianti, had accomplished the "miraculous": it had shown them how to improve themselves through leisure-time pursuits.[47] It is no wonder, given employees' defensiveness about their intellectuality, that they were resentful of the stinting attention *their* cultural institution, the *dopolavoro*, received from professional intellectuals: "a virgin and attractive subject," as it was characterized by one INA functionary, that was too often neglected for studies on the syndicalist, that is the *proletarian*, organizations of fascism.[48]

More concerned to reaffirm their position as intellectual *manqués*, employees generally failed to develop a modern corporate identity in a new ethos of public service. Fascists frequently spoke of the need for a "spiritual renewal" of the bureaucracy. But by this they meant greater responsiveness to the regime rather than any improvement in the bureaucracy's responsiveness to the general public. Unlike uniformed personnel, the civil servants employed in government offices were, as agents of the fascist state, protected from the public. The cult of authority did not tolerate the diatribes against the lethargic, frequently abusive officialdom that had filled Italian newspapers under liberal regimes. An ethos of public service was insistently demanded only of certain categories of public employees working in state and municipal services. The directors of municipal tram systems, unlike government functionaries, were of course directly responsible to the public and were therefore naturally sensitive to the complaints of bourgeois customers subjected to the "ironic, inappropriate, or worse yet, exceedingly vulgar phrases" uttered by employees in response to their complaints about bad service. In efforts to discipline personnel, the managements of the municipal tramways of Turin, Milan, and Rome used the news bulletins of their *dopolavoro* (which, like those in the state services, were strictly management operations) to invite the public to denounce instances of rudeness, as well as to publish letters of customer praise for meritorious service. In the context of *dopolavoro* activities, they also established rosters of honor for politeness and special awards for "zeal" in service. The *Dopolavoro* of the Rome Transit Company, a particularly authoritarian agency, even sought to develop its own "decalogue of the ticket-agent," an initiative that yielded unsatisfactory results, according to its organizer, Engineer Calzolari: Not only did only 22 persons participate in the contest (out of a total membership of 5,000), but the answers they gave about the virtues of loyalty, dedication, respect, and so forth, were so vague as to suggest that they lacked the slightest comprehension of the true meaning of being a ticket-agent.[49]

In forming a new image of themselves after work, some salaried employees did nevertheless begin to articulate their own understanding of the contradictions in their social status. Inevitably this definition was bound up with what was perceived as the positive psychological import of fascism. The sense of negative commonality of a social group that felt itself neither worker nor bourgeois was expressed in the false logic of contrasts: the old against the new; the life of the worker against the life of the functionary; the standard of living of the unprotected employee in liberal democratic nations against that of the privileged fascist functionary. The pre-fascist *travet*, if INA's more outspoken employees were to be believed, had been caught in the "iron-like discipline of bureaucratic rules" and ground down into complete mediocrity; in the collapse of his "spiritual life," all that was "lofty, intense, profound, eternal, and modern was destroyed, leaving behind only the most elementary cares: sleep, food, work, home, office, streetcar." But this "human machine" had been transmogrified by fascism: endowed by the corporative economy with "dignity, recognition, and responsibility," the clerk had become a futurist, with an entirely new psychological and physical dimension:

> Today, finally, there is geometry; in place of the curved, the composite, the rococo, there is the straight, the rigid, the schematic; in place of intellectual insipidness and syrupy speeches, the cubist solidity of ideas and the reckless courage to express them . . . Today, no more reading Sallust, Aretino, and Loyola, rather an understanding of Caesar, Farinata, and Oriani. Today, we leave behind the abject uniformity of browsing herds to jump into cars, trains, and ocean liners; motors gunning, sirens howling, commands shouted out, dazzling distances, sea blue-green, landings at bustling ports, palaces that crowd out to meet us. Today, mealtimes are shifted to march in column. The division head steps out of his bureaucratic Olympus to take up position beside the office boy; this is a new style of human sympathy . . . The spiritual, instead of the material, culture, even only "after-work," instead of the rigidity of mechanical manual gestures, quality instead of quantity, the book instead of the bottle, the gun instead of cologne water, guts instead of tact . . . the sense of the State, of the collectivity, instead of the sole feeling of Mister Me.[50]

This sense of solidarity remained nevertheless an expression of a new-found camaraderie *after work*. As for work itself, no false consciousness blurred the salaried dependents' sense of the degradation of the office routine and their feeling that they too, like manual laborers, lacked the freedom of choice shared by free professionals, employers, and rentiers. Unlike industrial workers, however, who in their company newspapers would not have been allowed to express their sentiments – even had they been so inclined – employees were allowed to vent their anguish, even if it was in an entirely aestheticized way. "Pink forms, white forms, blue forms," as the therapeutic poem of INA's Riccardo Di Segni went, "To pass my life amidst you is my destiny / I endure this, my fate." Dreams of change, of escape or glory were all mere illusion. "You are my reality / Pink forms, white forms, blue forms."[51] The *dopolavoro*, in this context, was quite explicitly a distraction, as it was perhaps for workers too, though without the emphatic ideologizing. "Only when I am in our home in Via Veneto do I succeed in forgetting everything," confided one functionary in 1932, "the crisis, the fact that fortune never comes knocking at my

149

door, although I play the lottery every week, the worries. I succeed in distracting myself, living for the moment, the thought of tomorrow disappears, or at least seems like something far off, of secondary importance."[52] In this form – anguished and resigned, conforming and escapist – the occupational ideology of the new middle class of clerks and functionaries was not simply tolerated but would, as we shall see, gradually become a dominant motif of an official *cultura dopolavoristica.*

6

The nationalization of the public

The formation of an overriding national identity, as the fascists well understood, depended at least as much on the relations of classes with each other, as on the relations of the mass of citizens to the central state. The establishment of a national agency like the OND even contained a certain risk: that it might become a further source of social division by revealing the very uneven levels of consumption, diverse associational and cultural traditions, and inequality of privileges among its numerous special constituencies. In its rhetoric and many of its programs, the OND was thus especially concerned to emphasize its role as the organizer of a unified public – a new national base for the regime and a counter to the regionalistic and class-based associationalism of the past. Although OND directives were, as we have seen, highly specific in their sectoral and local application, they were linked by common policies toward the formation of a seemingly egalitarian though definitively "low-brow" national cultural identity.

The most far-reaching of these were concerned with the attempt to manipulate those tendencies, endemic to capitalist development, that would potentially cut across class and regional lines; such were the expansion of a mass consumer market and the growth of the mass media. Fascist organizers were able to capitalize on the fact that the development of a mass consumer market in interwar Italy demanded regulation to compensate for the highly unequal levels of consumption. By using the *dopolavoro* as an instrument of advertising, and a controlled market outlet, they were able to turn this apparent disadvantage toward the support of the regime's claims to a supraclass identity. Similarly, the state support of the mass media, otherwise hindered in its development by the backwardness of the economy, was utilized to further the creation of a truly "national" audience for the regime's ideology.

On the level of recreational pastimes, Mussolini's dictatorship worked in a number of ways to promote a national consciousness. In the first place, it appeared to democratize access to events hitherto the province of an elite, providing services in the form of discounts and

151

special group events in areas over which it had no actual control, such as professional theater and commercial film distribution. The regime was further faced with a range of traditional pastimes, deeply rooted in popularity and custom, that threatened to retain their prefascist, oftentimes antifascist social and political connotations. Accordingly a systematic attempt was made to appropriate their popularity for fascist ends by absorbing their forms into nationally standardized patterns. This process inevitably tended to break the ties that had previously bound worker sociability to socialist and democratic politics. Finally, in its development of sports and outing programs, the regime strongly emphasized local participation that, through provincial, regional, and national networks, was intended to build up a new "Italian" identity. In each area of activity commonly associated with the idea of "mass leisure," whether entertainment, sports, or outings, the process of intervention was similar: the OND served to coordinate and mediate those large-scale tendencies that in liberal–democratic nations were the direct result of capitalist development. In Italy, the emergence of this "mass leisure" was thus closely tied to the specific ends of the fascist regime.

Toward a public of consumers

The organization of the public as consumers was, of course, a highly problematic undertaking under fascism, not only because of the sharp economic differences within the *dopolavoro* membership, but also because of the overall constraints on popular consumption itself. As a general policy, however, it was to become crucial to the legitimization of fascist rule. Open access to the marketplace was a potential social leveler, and state intervention on behalf of small consumers would compensate in some degree for the negative effects of wage policies on the working class standard of living. Control over consumer habits offered the state a mode of rudimentary economic planning, whereas advertising and the sale of what might be described as "social goods" – for example, clocks, and more especially radios – provided it with a means of social and political education. Further, the organization of consumption was in itself an important way of building membership. The *dopolavoro* card was thus advertised as a money-saver, a "discount coupon for the benefit of worker categories," and the public was invited to join in order to share in a consumerism already generated by the small commodity booms of the twenties and the first appearance of wide-scale advertising. "If you lack a card," the Florence Dopolavoro claimed, "you lose daily opportunities to save money."[1]

In defining what it classified as the "modern" social needs of its membership, the OND was naturally concerned to balance the promotion of consumption with a sense of necessary and justified self-control on the part of the consumer. Although in the regime's idealization, the typical *dopolavorista* would have no lack of basic necessities, he also would have no desire for conspicuous consumption. His consumer habits were most commonly described as "modest." To encourage further such *restricted* consumption, the OND placed strong emphasis on a hierarchy of suggested expenditures, from the household to the club facilities themselves, balancing these with a range of inducements for the worker to save and contribute toward his social security. Each expenditure was calculated to satisfy a legitimate want while reinforcing the social order. Household goods would permit the expression of individuality whereas the "cult of the home" would support familial stability. Investment in savings and insurance plans would guarantee a secure future as well as instill a sense of "order and responsibility" in the saver; not incidentally, the resulting funds would contribute to national capital accumulation. The "collective" consumerism encouraged in the *dopolavoro* would not only offer improved recreational facilities, at a saving to the national agency, but would also enhance club solidarity with a sense of ownership.

The household unquestionably took priority over the clubhouse as a focus of expenditure. Over a fifth of the more than 15,000 "agreements" that the national agency had concluded with retailers, national discount chains, and wholesale concerns by 1930 were for household items.[2] Their sales were boosted by a series of exhibitions that set the standards for the typically "decorous" home that were then reinforced by the OND's own advertising in *Gente nostra*. The first exposition for "economic home furnishings" was held in Venice in 1927; it was judged so successful by the public and by economically depressed artisan producers that the next year the OND sponsored two national competitions for "rational furnishings" in cooperation with manufacturers from the Fascist Association for Small Industries, the Confindustria, and the Fascist Federation of Artisan Communities. The results, especially designed with "attention to price, artistic taste, solidity, and practicality" to maximize "the sense of well-being of the popular classes at the least possible cost," were displayed in three regional fairs at Milan, Florence, and Naples, and subsequently in a national show, advertised as the first of its kind in the world, in Rome in January 1929. Sales were reportedly high; Florence alone, with its large petit bourgeois membership, claimed a turnover of 100,000 lire in the first three days of the exhibition.[3]

The culture of consent: mass organization in fascist Italy

Parallel to these efforts to stimulate consumption, the OND consistently emphasized the need for its members to participate in its plans for savings and social insurance. In a period of declining real income this policy might seem contradictory; in fact it responded to the peculiarly dualistic nature of the Italian economy, its incipient consumer market offset by the enforced diversion of capital away from commodity production and into heavy industry. The OND was not even concerned to promote thrift for the sake of future consumption, but more simply as a measure to supplement the inadequate social security coverage provided by the state pension and workingmen's compensation benefits;[4] a measure that would, besides, add another source for government investment programs. Thus the intervention of the OND facilitated the flow of savings into state coffers in an economy where savings and mutual benefit societies were just in the process of being integrated into national capital markets; the funds from mutual aid societies "coordinated" after 1926 were usually converted into government bonds, as were savings generated by the new *dopolavoro*. The regime's own subsidies for industrial recovery, its huge expenditure on the Ethiopian war, and its investments in colonial settlements in North Africa were largely supported by the vastly increased small savings that followed the 1927 stabilization of the lira, as well as by workers' contributions to fascism's new national pension and insurance funds. The postal savings booklet invented by the OND in 1930 was explicitly designed to underwrite this effort by "tapping even the smallest saving."[5]

Emphasis on saving and thrift could also act as a powerful "social educator." The so-called clock system, enthusiastically endorsed by the OND as the "most practical plan for modest savers," would, in these terms, surely have met with the approval of the first generation of industrial paternalists. Each subscriber to this special savings plan, devised in cooperation with the Alta Italia Insurance Company, was supplied with a combined clock and piggy-bank, which unless "fed by daily tokens of foresight" varying from 1 to 10 lire a day, ceased immediately to tell the time. This veritable miniaturized "panopticon" was advertised as a "perfect social educator"; a fictional clerk, Giovanni, was portrayed in publicity as entirely rehabilitated from his incorrigible lateness by the use of this one gadget. Not only had he gained a "clock, piggy-bank, punctuality, and the comfort of a secure future," but he had also earned praise from his bureau chief for his new-found diligence.[6]

This mechanical reinforcement of individual morals was the complement of the *dopolavoro* environment itself. OND advertising set

The nationalization of the public

modest but apparently accessible standards for the well-equipped club-house. It seemed, from the insistently repeated refrains of *Gente nostra*, that no self-respecting group could do without a radio, a phonograph, or a stopwatch for its sports; sections might even aspire to purchase their own sewing machine or movie projector, perhaps making use of the apposite soccerball-shaped savings bank specially commissioned by the OND or the *fasci*-decorated clocks *cum* piggy-banks advertised in the fascist press.

The single most advertised item for group consumption was, however, the clubhouse radio. In Italy, as in Western Europe generally, advances in broadcasting technology and mass production methods during the interwar years had transformed the radio from a specialty item with a limited audience into a major commodity of industrial production and one of the most important sources of popular entertainment. During the fascist era, the number of radio subscribers increased from an estimated 27,000 in 1926 to over one million at the end of 1939. Yet for all this, the radio was by no means a household item in Italy – the cheapest Marelli radio, advertised at 600 lire with a 114-lira annual government tax, was priced well above the average monthly wage of an industrial worker. Italy altogether had only one-quarter the number of radios in France, one-eighth the number in Great Britain, and one-thirteenth that in Germany.[7]

The high price of individual radio ownership would, in the free play of market forces, doubtless have restricted the growth of the listening public even further. The regime, however, viewed the radio as a major cultural and propaganda force: a means – as Starace accurately perceived – of "introducing the sounds and rhythms of industrial society into the rural world, and of assuring continuous contact between the state and the outlying rural areas."[8] Consequently, the OND sought to compensate for the limited availability of the radio to the individual consumer by sponsoring contests to encourage radio manufacturers to develop low-cost radio receivers, by holding shows to present "popular" radios, and, finally, by promoting "group listening" within the local sections. As a measure of fascist largesse the OND had initially conceived of distributing radios free of charge. But only one such propagandized mass distribution is recorded (of 100 radios in 1930). Failing this, it relied on private initiative, pressing manufacturers to supply radios to the *dopolavoro*, urging provincial boards to request donations from local benefactors, and, most commonly, by advising groups to purchase their own sets, exempting them from the purchasing tax and the payment of the annual licensing fee.[9]

The policy, despite the high priority accorded to it by the regime,

155

was less effective than might have been anticipated. By 1937, 8,795 of the sections, under half of the total, reportedly owned their own radio sets. The number of persons with access to them, estimated at 840,824, was admittedly large; but it was still less than a third of the entire membership.[10] The regime nevertheless benefited doubly from a promotional effort that had the effect of partially compensating for its own restraints on popular consumption. It was able to satisfy a demand that if left unfulfilled would have deprived the regime of an important means of propaganda and social communication, and, in addition, it was able to reap at least a reflected credit for this new consumer experience. Whereas for the urban middle classes the radio provided just another source of entertainment, for the public of the *dopolavoro* it frequently represented a unique and novel diversion; the ritual of listening to favorite broadcasts built up camaraderie and thereby the solidarity of the organization itself.

Although per capita purchasing power was low, the sheer size of its 2.5 million-person membership made the OND a powerful market force that, with proper guidance and restraint, could be and often was manipulated on behalf of the regime's "economic battles." The potential of the 20,000 sections as "organs of propaganda for commerce and industry"[11] was readily grasped by a number of manufacturers. In 1930, Giovacchino d'Orio, ex-director of the Gillette factory, who had set up his own national razor company to "emancipate Italy from foreign servitude," explained that he had decided to use the *dopolavoro* as outlets and the *dopolavoristi* themselves as salesmen rather than spend vast sums for advertising; this, he claimed, constituted a "more logical, more efficient, and cheaper method" of marketing his product. The savings derived from his public-spirited decision would naturally go toward reducing costs for the consumer.[12] Major manufacturers advertised directly through *Gente nostra*, and some, like the Necchi Sewing Machine Company, provided easy installment terms to customers whose credit rating had been approved by the provincial boards. Still other firms distributed special discount coupons through the presidents of local sections, sending along samples and advertising materials as well. Organized to handle merchandising, some of the more affluent urban groups soon looked more like commercial *gallerie* than fascist gathering places: "Never-ending streams of people," according to *Gente nostra's* description of one Roman *dopolavoro*, passed by "the row of lighted show windows in which objects of all kinds were on display, each carrying a sign indicating the price, the number of credit payments necessary, the kind of down payments possible – all that is necessary to get what one wants without too many sacrifices . . ."[13] Responding to this expanding market, some industrialists even developed a special range of products to be sold under the brand name "Dopolavoro," from the economy-sized packages of wool yarn marketed by the Rossi Company to patent medicines and cigarettes. The "ideal smoke of the *dopolavorista*," the low-cost product of the State Tobacco Monopoly (ten for 2.5 lire), was elegantly emblazoned with the Discobulus and inscribed with the initials of the OND.

As an official agency, the OND's consumer messages inevitably possessed an authority that was lacking in commercial advertising, and workers who might not be able to afford to consume commodities on an individual basis were nevertheless encouraged by such publicity to identify their interests with the products of their labor and to equate their own economic well-being with that of the nation. Manufacturers advertising in *Gente nostra* rarely missed the opportunity to evoke patriotic themes when publicizing their goods: The Vulcain stopwatch, like the "New Italy," was "solid – precise – beautiful";[14] Olivetti's "patriotism" consisted in selling a "typewriter that [was] not only Italian but also equal in quality to the best foreign models."[15] The motifs of pocketbook, patriotism, and the workers' stake in production were interwoven so as to intimate the close ties between individual security and national security. When Radio Marelli presented its product to the public, it explained that the company had willingly made the huge capital investments required to mass manufacture radios, so as to "emancipate the national economy" and not incidentally "to provide employment for thousands of workers." Marelli advertising was striking in its attempt to differentiate the new worker–consumer, whose interests were tied to the nation, from the old *rentier*–consumer, whose "innate snobbism" had made him disdain industrious national labor for decadent foreign wares. Such persons not "only committed a crime against the nation" but in addition got "a bad buy," in contrast to those Italians "who loved their country and demonstrated it by showing their preference for Italian products." As workers themselves, Marelli concluded, the *dopolavoristi* certainly "should be the first to recognize that the construction of every radio requires an average of fifteen worker-days, with the result that every purchase of a foreign radio in Italy means the unemployment of ten [*sic*] workers for one day, or of one worker for ten days."[16]

If Radio Marelli's calculations of labor value were baffling, its message was nonetheless quite explicit: Italian workers had an active and direct interest in defending the national economy. It was their vigilance alone that could protect their jobs from foreign competition. Unemployment was not the fault of the Italian employer, who, side by side with the workers, was defending Italian industry from cutthroat competition. The blame for unemployment was readily shifted onto those unpatriotic affluent who purchased foreign commodities. "Many Italians act against the best interests of their own country," another Marelli advertisement pointed out. "If only one of the many committees set up to study the means of decreasing unemployment would conduct an inquiry and publish the names of those who purchase foreign goods, this could be persuasively demonstrated."[17]

Such an officially sanctioned ethos of consumerism, totally out of proportion to the actual ability of most workers to consume, worked logically in favor of the fascist organization. By setting itself up as a mediator between the marketplace and the consuming public, the OND was in an especially favorable position to convey to its members the impression that the wants stimulated by an expanding commodity production were actually being satisfied as a result of benign official intervention. Because the OND arranged its discounts directly with the retailers and manufacturers and the membership gained access to them by showing their *dopolavoro* card, the organization could claim quite plausibly that its constituents were the beneficiaries of preferential treatment. By the early thirties, in fact, the term *dopolavorista* was closely identified with the growing number of thrifty savers and small spenders whose status in fascist society was defined not by their relationship to production as workers, but by their access as consumers to a slowly developing national mass market.

In its efforts to involve the *dopolavoristi* in the national economy, the OND was confronted, however, with a fundamental obstacle posed by the fascist regime's own wage policies. Although there existed an advanced sector of the economy with all of the characteristics of consumer society – the capacity for mass production, advertising, chain retailing, and installment buying – there was as yet no fully responsive public of consumers. The numerous discounts offered by the membership card were in the end slight in the face of the reduced purchasing power of most workers and the high costs of goods caused by monopoly pricing and fascist protective tariffs.

With the onset of the Depression, the OND leadership appeared to recognize the virtual impossibility of promoting more subtle and lasting forms of integration through access to an expanding consumer market. In the twenties Italy's *consumer* consciousness was still not an economically viable alternative to *class* consciousness. At best the regime could offer the promise of the modest trappings of economic participation. At worst there was the positive danger that advertising and the alluring images of consumer goods might arouse expectations that could not possibly be satisfied under the prevailing social system. Advertising, with the sole exception of the radio for collective listening, disappeared from the pages of *Gente nostra* after 1932; and the voluntary savings programs, to which only 13,000 persons had subscribed by 1931, were discontinued. Starace attributed this absence of popular foresight to the "lack of a solid and widespread understanding of social insurance among the working masses."[18] More likely it reflected their overriding concern with day-to-day subsistence.

Under Starace's leadership, organizers shifted their attention to public relief and to satisfying the needs of a Depression-weary public for simple diversions. As a result, they increasingly stressed not the consumption of commodities, but the consumption of leisure itself.

The democratization of access

By promoting the development of the mass media and commercial entertainment, the fascist regime was able fully to exploit their novelty in a society where only a narrow elite had been able to enjoy their first manifestations. Using the appeal of the new media to exercise an increasingly powerful influence over popular recreational habits, the regime both expanded accessibility to them and developed its own versions for popular consumption. Although not strictly under the control of the OND, the cinema and professional theater were nevertheless susceptible to a form of "democratization," as hitherto exclusive entertainments; their opening to a new wider audience became, from the late twenties on, a central focus of fascist policy.

The cinema, as medium par exellence of the new mass leisure, never possessed quite the mystique of the more traditional theater and opera. Yet for the majority of Italians in the twenties, movie-going was still a luxury and movie houses were largely inaccessible. In 1929 nearly three-quarters of Italy's 7,623 communes still lacked movie houses of their own; and over 60 percent of the 3,180 movie house were located in the northern region. More than 80 percent of the tickets sold still cost over 2 lire, making movie-going a rather costly and very infrequent pastime.[19]

Because the very novelty of movie-going made it a status item, especially among the urban low-middle class, discounts on tickets were among the first benefits associated with the *dopolavoro* card. In 1927 the OND brought pressure on the General Director of Taxes to reduce by 10 percent the luxury tax paid by commercial movie houses and passed on to their customers. That same year, the OND concluded its first agreement with the National Association of Movie Producers, obtaining a 50 percent reduction on fifty seats at each performance. In 1929 it struck a new bargain for its members, whereby ticket prices were reduced by 25–35 percent on all performances except premieres, Sundays, and holidays, with no limits placed on the number of seats.[20]

The commerical film industry proved cooperative on discounts, but it was uneasy about any plans to set up an alternate movie circuit. Although the OND had indeed expected to use the new entertainment technology as the "mainstay of its program of education and recreation for the working masses,"[21] it had to take into account the threat posed by its organizations to the developing commercial film network. To "avoid the discontent of cinema owners and to eliminate all possible competition that might damage the interests of commercial movie houses," the OND enjoined its sections from showing films on holidays or in open-air theaters wherever there was a regular movie house, and to show only educational films, documentaries, and propaganda shorts furnished by the OND or the government-owned documentary agency, the Istituto Luce. For entertainment, a comedy film of no more than one act might be shown.[22]

The OND's willingness to accommodate the demands of the movie industry inevitably slowed the development of its film circuit. Not until 1934 did it organize a special rural traveling cinema, thus bringing the first movies into the Italian countryside. Thereafter its expansion was quite rapid. By 1937 the OND reported a well-developed traveling cinema consisting of thirty-eight film trucks equpped for silent films and fifty-six with sound projectors. Its urban network, which was comprised of 334 permanent theaters and 288 summer movie programs with a total of 170,856 seats (1937), supplemented the commercial networks by offering what were for the most part weekend or holiday showings.[23] Their repertory appears to have differed little from that of the regular movies, because the OND never developed its own film distribution system: Apart from the documentary films obtained from the Luce Institute, which were also obligatory in commercial movie houses, the local circles, like the commercial theaters, acquired the bulk of their films from private distributors.

The OND likewise had no jurisdiction over professional theater, and as a matter of policy it was cautious about infringing on the potential public and profits of commercial entertainment.[24] Theatergoing especially was considered a symbol of bourgeois cultural privilege, and no other medium expressed so well the cultural pretensions of the fascist old guard – of Mussolini himself, who tried his hand at playwriting alone and in collaboration with G. Forzano; of Farinacci, who was an acclaimed author on the fascist-controlled amateur theater circuit; of

Starace, less talented, who was nevertheless an enthusiastic theater-goer and theater organizer – although, according to contemporary gossip, his main enthusiasm was reserved for the actresses.[25] The OND nevertheless hesitated to press for any substantial innovation in the organization of high theater, even though the "democratization" of the resplendent municipal theaters and the glossy productions of the commercial circuit would doubtless have demonstrated fascist egalitarianism in a particularly dramatic fashion. Provincial boards at Turin, Florence, Milan, and Naples concluded occasional agreements with local theaters, setting aside special matinees or full-dress rehearsals for *dopolavoristi*; the Royal Theater of San Carlo of Naples, for example, honored the fascist policy "reach out to the people" in February 1932 by offering a 50 percent discount on balcony seats.[26] Managers generally seemed reluctant, however, to experiment with popular-priced theater tickets; the professional theater, already in crisis as a result of the competition from movies and the unfavorable economy, feared that its traditional public would be disturbed by the influx of a new mass audience.

Professional theater houses were "democratized," so to speak, for the first time during the Ethiopian campaign, when the OND in co-operation with the Ministry of Press and Propaganda (later Minculpop) organized the famed *Sabato teatrale*. The inauguration of special Saturday matinee performances in January 1936 – at the height of mobilization – was well timed, securing the regime the benefits of maximum propaganda. Ticket prices were truly popular: from 1 lira for balcony seats to 3 in the orchestra; leftover seats, of which there were apparently few, were to be distributed free to families with relatives in East Africa.[27] Prices were reduced once again in 1937 to ½ lira and 2 lire respectively.

The novelty of the event and the extensive publicity announcing the performances generated a large audience. Some 400,000 persons attended the first round of special performances held between January and May 1936, packing the formerly exclusive municipal theaters – including the Reale d'Opera of Rome, the Carlo Felice of Genoa, La Scala at Milan, the Regio at Turin, and the Massimo at Palermo. The public, which initially had included relatively affluent *dopolavoristi*, was strictly limited by subsequent OND directives to low-income groups: workers, clerks, low-level state and private employees, and pensioners with incomes under 800 lire per month.[28]

For all the publicity it received, the *Sabato teatrale* marked no radical innovation in the organization of the theatergoing public. The special performances amounted to no more than three or four per season,

161

and the *dopolavoristi*, although allowed access to the formerly sacrosanct houses of bourgeois municipal culture, were strictly segregated
from the regular audience. No effort was made to abolish price dif-
ferentials in tickets; the new mass public was taught, like the old, to
accept the traditional hierarchical pattern of the orchestra, loge, and
balcony seats. Little attention was given to organizing the public in the
neighborhoods, or to transporting the professional theater groups out
of the inaccessible theaters into the popular residential areas. The
Florence Dopolavoro was unique in that local organizers experimented
in 1937 with bringing theatrical performances and orchestra concerts
to the industrial suburbs; notably to the Galileo Machine Works at
Rifredi.[29] Although this last experiment received ample publicity as an
example of fascist egalitarianism, it was rarely emulated; doubtless
employers objected to such superfluous disruptions in production, as
did the workers themselves, because their pay was docked for the
duration of the frivolities.

The OND demonstrated that it could be truly innovative only when
freed of its concern for the prerogatives and profits of commercial
entertainment. In 1929 it established a new traveling theater company
of its own. Inspired by Gioacchino Forzano, artistic director of La
Scala and joint collaborator with Mussolini on various literary projects,
the mobile theater, or Thespian Cars, drew on the experience of itinerant troupes and the skill and personnel of professional companies.

The three Thespian Prose Cars, together with the Lyrical Car for
operatic performances established in 1930, were designed expressly to
impress their provincial audiences with a "sense of the miraculous."[30]
During the spring and summer months, when the "brigades" made
their annual "propaganda tours" through the provinces, they employed
a thousand persons: scores of actors and opera singers, entire choruses
and orchestras, stagehands and sound technicians, together with the
drivers of the buses and two trucks that carried equipment for a "technically perfect" 890-square-meter theater with seating for 3,000–6,000
persons. Within a few hours after the troupe's arrival at their destination, the designated clearing was transformed with the aid of 130
hired hands (300 in the case of the Lyrical Car) into a "temple-like"
structure: a double stage covered by a specially designed Fortuny
dome, which simulated a stage of infinite depth and allowed for special
effects – starry nights, rainfall, waves, and the like. Long rows of seats
radiated out from the stage, followed by tiers of bleachers accommodating a public estimated at some two-thirds of the population in
the towns visited. When necessary, in Turin, Milan, and Rome, the
amphitheater could hold up to 10,000 persons.[31]

For weeks before the passage of the caravans through the provinces, the bulk of OND communiqués, often signed by Starace himself, were exclusively given over to planning the routes and mobilizing the audiences. Tickets, which were initially fairly costly, perhaps to impress the public with the cultural significance of the event, were lowered in 1934 to assure maximum public participation; in the case of the Prose Car, by 50 percent, so that seats cost 4 lire and the bleachers 2. The Lyrical Car, offering full-dress performances of *La Bohème, Cavalleria Rusticana, Aïda, The Barber of Seville, Tosca,* and *Norma,* was always more exclusive: Prices for the inaugural performance of *La Bohème* at Torre del Lago, Puccini's birthplace and a fashionable resort area, ranged from 50 to 5 lire. Until 1934, when prices were reduced by 20 percent, seats cost 15 lire for the orchestra, 10 in the loges, and 4 in the bleachers.[32]

An impressively large public was reached as a result of this rare coordination of national and local initiative. The Milan Brigade in 1930 held 116 performances in sixty municipalities for a public of 228,000 persons; the Florence Brigade toured eighty-three towns in central Italy in the same year, performing 108 times before a total audience of 292,000. The Sassari Brigade visiting sixty municipalities in the South and the Islands, performed 124 times before 303,151 spectators.[33] Shifting itineraries so as to pass through as many provincial centers as possible, by 1936 the Thespian and Lyrical Cars were reaching about a million spectators a year. The effectiveness of these spectacular visits as propaganda tools for the regime apparently well justified their high expense. Ticket sales covered only a minimum of the expenditures: In 1933–4, at the depth of the Depression, the OND was spending over a fifth of its annual net expenditures, by far the largest single item, on the Thespian Cars.[34]

Although evidently restricted by its respect for commercial profit, this policy of democratizing access to new leisure pastimes did in the end create a new mass audience for theater, the movies, and radio. Party functionaries present at the more spectacular new events never lost the opportunity to preface or conclude a performance with a eulogy to the Duce and the fascist order. But it was the novelty of the event itself that was calculated to strike a responsive note: The OND-sponsored performances, often simply because of their infrequency and stunning newness, left an indelible impression on their audiences, especially among a rural population habituated to the slower rhythms of a nontechnological society. Presented as special events and experienced collectively, they dramatically punctuated otherwise uneventful lives.

The culture of consent: mass organization in fascist Italy

The itineraries of the entertainment caravans were planned well in advance; careful organization assured the active participation of the public in the towns through which they passed; abundant publicity ensured popular anticipation of the event, and the excitement that accompanied the arrival of the vehicular caravan was orchestrated by the local *fascio* into demonstrations of concerted enthusiasm. An atmosphere of celebration pervaded the performance, and the public exhilaration spent itself only slowly in the days and weeks of discussion and comment that followed each event.

The telegrams sent to Mussolini and Starace after the passage of the Thespian Cars and following the first tour of the traveling cinemas in 1933–4 were naively spontaneous in their tone. Composed by the secretaries of the local *fascio*, the president of the *dopolavoro*, or by the *podestà* of the town, in the stilted phrases of provincials for whom Rome and the Duce were myths, the messages expressed "infinite gratitude to the Duce," and the "profound appreciation of the population as a whole for the marvelous initiative," praising "the magnificent entertainment."[35] The genuinely popular enthusiasm that, initially at least, inspired these gestures cannot be doubted; only when published by the fascist press, as customary acts of obeisance to the regime, did they lose their spontaneity. In provincial centers where daily life was ruled by dull routine and insular habits, these first contacts with the mass media left a small but immeasurably significant imprint on the consciousness of the community; organized by the OND under the auspices of the fascist government, they inevitably worked to raise public estimation of the regime's munificence.

The appropriation of popular recreation

The mass media, as truly modern forms of entertainment, had undeniable propagandistic value; and because their content was readily controlled by the state, they offered the regime a potential means of organizing leisure on an entirely new "totalitarian" basis. Yet there still existed, directly under the jurisdiction of the OND, an entire range of traditional popular pastimes. Games like bowls, amateur theatricals, the music of dance and marching bands, *orchestrine* and mandolin societies, were all activities that continued to flourish in small towns and urban neighborhoods; they were still protected, as it were, from the corrosive force of commercial entertainment, not only by the traditionalism of habits and the very real pleasure of creative participation as opposed to passive spectatorship, but also by the limited purchasing power of their sponsors, supporters, and members.

It was precisely the *popular* nature of these manifestations that presented both a problem and a potential resource for the fascist regime. As long as the institutional structures of the organizations that sponsored these activities remained intact, as they did in so many circles that had undergone "coordination" after 1926, what was to prevent people from continuing "to meet and find their accustomed pastimes," as workers in the mutual aid societies of Genoa were reportedly still doing in April 1930? Even if these gatherings did not lead to clandestine activities or even to open professions of "antinational sentiment" (police surveillance and neighborhood spies saw to that), they nevertheless presented the opportunity to sustain old allegiances. Indeed, the social activities themselves, as expressions of a distinctive class experience, inevitably reinforced the solidarity of the group, its exclusiveness, and its resistance to outside influence. Unless these were in some way detached from the social forms that shaped them, or infused with an entirely new meaning, the regime could not expect to break down resistance to its rule, much less inculcate in workers any new sense of national unity.

Accordingly, fascist functionaries recognized the need for a more persistent and subtle intervention in the life of the societies than the heavy-handed bureaucratic interference of "coordination." Each recreational form had to be subjected to the scrutiny of technical consultants in the apposite bureau of the national offices, its social purposes assessed in light of the national interest and its specific practice brought into line with an overall national directive. Activity by activity, fascism after 1927 gradually developed a de facto policy toward all existing popular recreational pastimes, from choral signing to plebeian bowls. An incessant publicity on behalf of formally organized activity was accompanied by vigorous promotional efforts to engage groups in *outside* events sponsored locally and nationally by the OND. Rules and regulations were imposed to "discipline" participants, while raising the quality of their activities to further their "moral education." Finally, OND propaganda attempted to "uplift" the status of popular pastimes, sanctioning their practice as contributing to the formation of a new national culture that would transcend class or regional boundaries.

Inevitably, the practical application of this policy of "appropriation" was fraught with intrinsic difficulties. Any too blatant tampering with pastimes that were entirely voluntary in character risked either driving away participants or at the very least dampening their enthusiasm. Such results were hardly desirable in any activity promising to improve workers' physical preparedness or with evident didactic potential.

The small theater was precisely the kind of "spiritual activity of the people" that, in the words of a fascist consultant on amateur drama, was "so delicate, yet so dangerous from every point of view" that it could not possibly be left unregulated. And yet, it was "so rich in artistic and social possibilities" that it had to be encouraged.[36] Small theater troupes had abounded in prefascist Italy, often affiliated with the democratic mutual aid societies or with socialist cultural circles. Their repertories, usually highly eclectic, were rarely overtly political; they included drama from the classical theater (in particular the farces of Goldoni), romantic comedies, short vernacular skits, and among the socialist clubs, the dramas of nineteenth-century realism adapted from the works of Victor Hugo, Eugène Sue, and Edmondo De Amicis. They held in common a reference to popular traditions, to common-sense, and an innate and sometimes explicit striving for social justice. Organized by energetic amateur thespians and supported with the contributions and goodwill of their neighborhood audiences, they provided genuine outlets for popular creativity. Sustained by voluntary efforts, they had led a precarious existence, and especially so as new kinds of recreation and entertainment – sports, movies, and radio – began to compete for popular attention.

Amateur theater was in fact the first popular recreational pastime to be subjected to comprehensive regulation by OND. Like all other associations the *filodrammatiche* were required to register with the OND. Subsequently, they were reorganized according to new internal rules. These were designed not so much to provide them with a specific content, as to ensure a "rigorous social and artistic discipline," eliminating the "anarchy of untrained egos" that ostensibly had plagued the small theaters before fascism, preventing them from realizing their full artistic potential.[37] The new-model drama society, inspired by a rarefied artistic ideal of "theater for its own sake," called for the group to be small and compact. Roles would be clearly specified and the artistic director invested with full authority to end, once and for all, the "tyranny of actors and actresses" by subordinating aspiring *prime donne* to the discipline of well-defined tasks. The group as a whole would be motivated by an unsullied passion for artistic expression; careerism of actors out to become celebrities was to be discouraged. Nevertheless, as befitting a theater worthy of its fascist affiliation, the stage setting should be "decent" and the actual production "decorous"[38] – a veritable microcosm of the ideal fascist society.

To achieve this ideal, the OND had to provide incentives and, first of all, tokens of official interest in the form of discounts on copyright fees and rebates on taxes paid on admissions. Neither of these was in

The nationalization of the public

itself a very generous measure, because few amateur societies had ever paid before being "coordinated." With the institution of provincial amateur theater federations in 1930, the OND undertook a more ambitious effort to organize drama societies on a new competitive basis. The provincial boards, each supplied with a special theater library of forty-four volumes, were responsible for recruiting new talent and refurbishing repertories. Sponsorship of special acting schools, contests for young authors, performances of award-winning plays (175 by eighty-five young authors in 1932) by the official provincial drama society (*filodrammatico-tipo*), all guaranteed a constant supply of new texts and talents, lacking, not only as a result of the old family troupes dying out as the OND claimed,[39] but also because the older generation of thespians resented the encroaching regulations.

Unquestionably the greatest stimulus to amateur theater production was provided by critical acclaim. Each year the OND sponsored numerous provincial and regional contests, and *Gente nostra* regularly carried news of the progress of single outstanding groups. Success in provincial competition brought the possibility of participation in regional contests and the prospect of subsidized trips to Rome for those qualifying for the final national round. The ideal envisaged by cultural organizers seemed to be fulfilled by 1935; according to the OND's leading expert on small theater, Luigi Chiarelli, one of the most esteemed of the prewar avant-garde playwrights, the several dozen groups convening in Rome were energetic, enthusiastic, and "coordinated and regulated like sporting teams," both on the stage and off. "All that," he concluded, was "very beautiful," as if *order* had become some ultimate aesthetic category, at least for judging the work of plebeian troupers.[40]

Of course not all groups went to Rome. But the significant numbers that aspired to do so, as evidenced by their energetic participation in local contests and by their supplications to Mussolini himself for a "few words of encouragement," is suggestive of the changes that had taken place in the organization of the popular theater under the dictatorship.[41] While stultifying regulations, permissions, copyright dispensations, and progress reports curtailed their autonomy, official recognition supported their endeavors. Repertories appear to have undergone a certain standardization, as well might be expected from this official tutelage. The plays recommended at the end of talent hunts, those publicized as prizewinners in contests, inevitably turned up as frequent choices in repertories, while the "socialistic" comedies deriving their inspiration from Sue, Hugo, De Amicis, and so forth, had of course been eliminated. The number of overtly fascist plays, on the

167

other hand, was small, reflecting both the lack of any significant production of fascist texts and the selective tastes of players and their public.[42] Perhaps the most important change, however, had occurred in the rapport between the small theater companies and their audiences and the relations of both to an emerging national theater network. Critical acclaim, by encouraging a professionalism of sorts, inevitably promoted a divorce between the players and their local public, while at the same time the OND's appropriation of the theater itself, nowhere more visible than in the official seal emblazoned on every proscenium, broke down the natural self-isolation of neighborhood audiences.

This highly mediated form of control was of course reinforced by the government censorship to which the small theater, like the press, cinema, and professional theater, was subject. The OND directives were seemingly draconian: One in 1933 imposed an "absolute prohibition on any play which in form or content conflicted with the political, educational, and cultural aims of the OND"; another prohibited the production of any script not explicitly approved by the censors; still other circulars banned plays in dialect and imposed quotas on the number of foreign plays any repertory could contain in a given season; finally, in 1935 all plays written by authors from the so-called Sanction nations were forbidden.[43] But the small theater proved far more difficult to control than the press, whose proprietors and contributors were readily identifiable. Moreover, the fascist censorship apparatus was never sufficiently well developed nor the criteria for "fascist aims" adequately defined so as to control effectively either content or form. Save where blatant antiregime propaganda was involved, explicit censorship was lax.[44] The threat of interference, together with official discrimination against foreign works and the absence of contact with the outside world, sufficed to foster the innate conformism of a parochial world.

The small theater took its place beside bands, choral groups, village orchestras, and marionette troupes as objects of the fascists' special concern – a concern no doubt intensified by the formation of the old guard fascists themselves in a cultural milieu that fostered a belief in the intrinsically edifying social virtues of theater and music. Other more lowly activities were marked for attention simply by virtue of their evident popular nature. For the fascists, these pastimes – *bocce*, dominoes, cardplaying – had no particular redeeming social value, yet they had in some way to be reconstructed because they were so closely identified with working-class sociability and its evident political implications. *Bocce*, for example, had initially been treated with immense disdain by fascist sports officials as having been "degraded by its close association with the taverns." Moreover, it was considered to lack a playing style suited to the vitality of the fascist era. Yet *bocce*, as they had begrudgingly come to recognize by the mid-thirties, was the "confirmed pastime of the popular classes"; *bocce* clubs, in fact, accounted for 6,434 of the nearly 8,000 sports sections enrolled in the OND in 1937.[45]

Precisely because the game was so popular, especially in the industrial suburbs and small towns of the North, the numerous players' groups had proved strongly resistant to coordination. Well into the late twenties, officials were complaining that the languid pace of the game and the clusters of men that watched its progress afforded ill-tolerated opportunities for "meeting and murmuring."[46] Unable to suppress the game, the OND dedicated itself to undermining its class specificity. Traditionally distinguished by its great number of local variations, the game in 1926 was subjected to a uniform national code of fifty-eight articles.[47] This was a first step toward organizing play on a new competitive basis. *Bocce* rallies, ever more numerous after 1931, brought the game out of the backstreet courts into the central *piazze*, where, feted by brass bands and surrounded by solicitously attentive fascist dignitaries, players competed for public recognition. The first regional competition was sponsored in Genoa in 1932 with 300 players. The step from regional to national affiliation was taken somewhat more haltingly, perhaps because sports organizers had lingering doubts about the appropriateness of bowls as a "fascist" pastime. Only in 1936, with all incongruities finally ignored, was the first national bowls championship convened in Rome to celebrate the foundation of the Italian Empire in Ethiopia.[48] Once *bocce*'s national affiliation had been established, the OND could claim to have eliminated the class distinctiveness of the game. In 1937 bowls was declared a "truly national sport," enjoyed by "people of all social classes," indeed the favorite pastime, as the journalist Ugo Cuesta pointed out, of such true Italians as Pius X, the composer Pietro Mascagni, and General Badoglio, the hero of the Ethiopian campaign.[49]

A similarly persistent and accentuated interference by the state can be traced in practically every other form of popular recreation – brass bands, orchestras, mandolin societies, choral singing, chess, even pushball, tug-of-war, and tamburin, "purely Italian games" as they were designated by the OND. In every case, activities that in prewar Italy had constituted the highly individual expressions of group sociability were federated at the provincial, regional, and national levels. Formal regulations for traditionally unstructured games and prescriptions on content and rules of conduct were enforced by official super-

Bocce playing in the confines of the Giovanni Paracchi Company of Turin. *Source:* OND, *I dopolavoro aziendali in Italia* (Rome, 1938).

vision and incentives in the forms of subsidies, critical acclaim, and a hierarchy of contests. In this way, the regime in effect appropriated as its own a whole series of popular pastimes, incorporating what had previously been experienced as autonomous expressions of class or community into the social life of the state, associating them with its official activities and infusing them with new competitiveness.

A public of participants and spectators

Sports were lavishly subsidized and from the late twenties increasingly propagandized by the fascist regime. At first glance, this would seem to have been the one area of national life that was thoroughly democratized as a result of government intervention. In one form or another, sports engaged the impassioned participation of millions, giving rise to an entirely new set of genuinely popular heroes. The gold medals won by Italian teams at the Los Angeles Olympics in 1932 and Berlin meets in 1936 were hailed by fans, regardless of class, as truly national victories. Such new symbols of national allegiance were fundamentally democratic in one sense, in that they evoked a common passion transcending class lines. Sports, commented Lando Ferretti, the first fascist president of the Italian Olympic Committee, served as "mixer and leveler of people from the most diverse social classes joined by a common passion and struggling for the same goal," and it offered, not incidentally, the "best distraction for youth otherwise tempted by political activities."[50]

The world of mass sports organized under fascism was far more complex, however, than the universally shared enthusiasm suggested.

Mass bocce competitions: the III Interregional Tournament at Vercelli, 1932. *Source*: Dopolavoro provinciale di Vercelli, *Il Dopolavoro nell' Anno X* (Vercelli, 1938).

171

The culture of consent: mass organization in fascist Italy

In reality there existed two levels of sports under fascism: the world of "high sports," of the well-funded and highly qualified Olympic teams, of the professional soccer circuit, of the glamorous technology of the trans-Atlantic air flights and the automobile racing tours; and, second, the world of "low sports," of *bocce* games, chess matches, tug-of-war contests, and gymnastic exercises. The two differed notably – in the purposes for which they were conceived, in the nature of the participation they encouraged, in the type of play they promoted, and especially in the resources each had at its disposal.

The fascist Sports Charter, drawn up in 1929 by Augusto Turati to end the bitter jurisdictional disputes between the OND and the Italian Olympic Committee (CONI), established these two realms as separate and distinct entities. CONI, founded in 1914 to prepare teams for the Olympics, was to supervise all professional and competitive sports as well as the various middle-class athletic clubs, which had been placed under its control by the government decree of 2 March 1927. The OND, on the other hand, was specifically prohibited from organizing "violent sports requiring unusual exertion or methodical training."[51] Its jurisdiction covered what were essentially noncompetitive games, as well as amateur associations and their activities. While this formulation contained some ambiguity – soccer, for example, which was both popular and competitive though not always professionally oriented, occasioned recurrent disputes between the two bureaucracies – the overall lines of jurisdiction were clear: CONI devoted its energies to promoting professional competitions while the OND was charged with developing an extensive "popular" program.

The organization of popular sports offered almost limitless possibilities, because workers had been given so few opportunities for physical education in the pre-fascist era. The liberal government had done little: The Daneo Law of 1909, which called for construction of gymnasia and sports fields in all new schools, was rarely respected. Most prefascist organizations, including the Federazione Italiana per il Gioco del Calcio, were oriented toward the middle and upper-middle classes. The Nationalists who founded *L'Atleta* and *La Gazzetta dello Sport*, like the cultural iconoclast Marinetti, who augured the "victory of gymnastics over books" in his Futurist program of 1913, were overwhelmingly preoccupied with the physical preparedness of the elites and of youth. The socialist movement had done little to promote workers' sports: partly because of the attitudes of workers themselves, most of whom being new to industrial town life displayed little interest for this unfamiliar habit; and partly because the intellectuals who were so prominent in the party organization maintained that sports were a

172

diversion from the class struggle. The Catholics were more attentive to the problem; the FASCI (Federazione Associazioni Sportive Cattoliche Italiane), founded in 1906 by Pius X in response to the burgeoning socialist party, had its own journal, *Stadium*, and 204 affiliates with 10,000 members by 1910.[52] But with the sole exception of *bocce*, which had been organized at the regional level in Piedmont in 1897, no network of sports associations comparable to those found in industrial towns in France, England, or Germany from the 1890s onward existed in prewar Italy. Soccer, the sport of contemporary English workingmen, although not unknown in prewar Italy, was at the time exclusively the sport of anglophile bourgeois gentlemen.[53]

The immediate postwar period saw a sudden upsurge in working class interest in sports. The number of workers' cycling societies, soccer clubs, and *bocce* circles increased, often promoted by the Socialist and Communist parties and by the Catholic Popular party, which all recognized that this spontaneous and enthusiastic participation reflected a genuine need for popular recreation, and that sports, rather than detracting from working class organization, enhanced its solidarity. So when the OND began to promote sports groups after 1926, it was able to capitalize on work begun by the opposition parties, although it still had ample room to organize enthusiasm for sports within its own associations and to lay claim to having brought sports to the masses for the first time.

"Many participants and few spectators" was the watchword of the OND sports promoter.[54] *Dopolavoro* sports, in Starace's words, "reached out to the masses," rather than "seeking champions or grooming exceptional athletes to break records." In contrast to the competitive sports handled by CONI, *Dopolavoro* sports were not supposed to encourage the ethos of aggressive individuality considered appropriate for training a dynamic new elite. They were intended instead "to teach the working masses in a practical way that, with relatively little effort, they can better their physical condition, strengthen and reinvigorate themselves, build up their resistance to diseases and, finally, ready themselves for the fatigue of work, and if necessary, that of war."[55] Team activity promoted by the *dopolavoro*, such as pushball, tamburin, and tug-of-war, required few skills, so that even the neophyte and the older worker could participate. But they were sufficiently competitive so as to "accustom people to strict discipline, thereby furthering their moral education."[56] The ideal *dopolavorista sportivo* was indeed the disciplined mass man: not overly competitive, yet with a well-developed "self-confidence and a sense of 'fair-play,'" "fit" and "virile," with a profound sense of team spirit.[57]

173

The OND developed its own peculiar reward system so as to encourage maximum participation, as opposed to selective perfectionism. *Brevetti* or certificates of participation, devised by Turati in May 1929, were awarded to individuals and teams participating in mass Sunday sports rallies, which in the PNF secretary's expectations were to be held nationwide with "mathematical regularity."[58] This most "efficacious" propaganda was designed to discourage individual competitiveness: Participants were never pitted against each other in any strict sense; they were awarded certificates according to their ability to pass fixed qualifying tests measuring their levels of fitness and skill. This system, as one athletic director explained to his charges (who, he claimed, responded with enormous enthusiasm) meant that the sports organizer could "honestly tell a group of one hundred individuals – among whom might be a perfect specimen – 'You are all equal'; the weak man consequently no longer felt as weak as he had before; nor did he feel overcome by discouragement and quit."[59] The *brevetti* also had the not incidental advantage of diminishing the enormous disparity in training between the highly competitive company sports teams and their self-trained and generally underequipped provincial competitors. Initially standards were quite rigorous, with no more than 35–40 percent of participants receiving *brevetti*. Gradually, however, perhaps to engender greater participation, they were relaxed, as is suggested by the number of certificates conferred at the Second National Gymnastics Contest in Rome in 1931: of the 207 teams present, 120 received first-class certificates of participation, 63 second-class, and 24 third-class.[60] In other words, no team returned home without some official recognition of its efforts.

Team competition was strongly encouraged, however, and the fascists, as we have seen, introduced to this end a high degree of formal organization into traditionally unstructured popular games. Competition of this kind had a twofold function: to encourage group solidarity and to promote a new sense of national identity. "The public authorities are well aware," the director of OND sports commented, "that sporting competition makes for camaraderie among employees and furthers community spirit among the workers."[61] Competitions forced club members to "defend their colors and the good name of the office, factory, or workshop where they are employed," in addition to upholding the banners of their neighborhood society. At the same time, the national organization of popular games encouraged team members to identify their sporting activities with the national organization, which acted both as sponsor and referee of their pastimes.

Sports promotion through this hierarchy of contests was undeniably effective in generating participation, especially in the early 1930s, when such competitions were still novel. By 1933 some 7,294 of the 19,029 *dopolavoro* sections were sporting societies, whereas the number of sports events was tallied at 191,773. The "working masses," as the OND leadership was solemnly to affirm in its 1935 yearbook, "prefer sports to all other activities."[62]

The OND sought further to determine the sporting preferences of its membership. In the intention of the OND leadership, *volata*, a hybrid game somewhere between soccer and handball, was to become the new national pastime of Italian workingmen. According to one account, *volata* represented party secretary Turati's personal reconstruction of classical football, a truly Roman and therefore fascist sport developed as an acceptable indigenous substitute for soccer, which was after all an import from England. *Volata*, unlike the game identified with "English degeneration," was in Starace's explanation more congenial to the Italian spirit; "more logical technically, and also more attuned to the Italian temperament" in that it was played with the hands – that is, "more rationally."[63] Other considerations clearly played into this impassioned espousal of *volata*, for no fascist leader ever invoked such nationalistic arguments when discussing professional soccer – a game not only accepted but fanatically promoted by fascist *gerarchi*. The OND itself was prohibited from promoting competitive soccer, which was under CONI's jurisdiction. Yet to appeal to working-class youth, many of whom were soccer fans, it had to offer a similarly dynamic sport, for few were attracted to the staid *bocce* games commonly preferred by the older generation. *Volata* offered a viable substitute. As a highly competitive game of skill, it seemed suited to the vitality of the fascist era. The "rationale of playing with the hands" had as well an important economic reason: *Volata*, unlike soccer, could be played competitively on rough terrain, that is, without need for expensive playing facilities.[64]

Beginning in 1929 *volata* was thus the main focus of OND sports promoters, receiving much publicity in the fascist press. The first national contest, held in Rome in 1930, was attended by 34 teams, the majority of which were company-sponsored, but with not a few finalists coming from the South, where they had been trained by the provincial boards. In 1931 there was a total of 809 teams. The next year, however, the number of teams began to decrease, first to 513 and then to 444 in 1933.[65] Whether because of a lack of competent trainers, the preference of younger workers for soccer, as opposed to a second-rate (if indigenous) substitute, or the resistance of older workers to a game requiring exertion and training, the OND was forced reluctantly to recognize that *volata* had failed to find a public: After 1933 all mention of the game was expunged from the annals of the OND.

Whereas the status of popular games was, so to speak, upgraded by competition (the case of *bocce* is exemplary), traditionally elite sports were only rarely "democratized." Soccer, which enjoyed great popularity as a spectator sport, did not engage mass participation, at least in any formal way, and much less did field and track, fencing, rowing, gymnastics, or swimming, all of which the OND claimed to be offering to *dopolavoristi*. It was in fact skiing that earned Mussolini's dictatorship much of its ill-deserved reputation for having "democratized" elite sports. Apart from being fashionable and upper class, skiing had a considerable mystique deriving from its association with the daring and prowess of Italy's crack alpine troops during the Great War. Military motives were in fact cited to justify the attention devoted by the OND to organizing mass ski rallies: Ostensibly these served to "remind Italians of the impelling need to prepare and train to defend Italy's vast alpine frontiers."[66] In reality, there was little militarism in the huge rallies organized annually at Limone Piedmont in northern Italy and Roccaraso in the South; they catered, as the plebeian *bocce* and tug-of-war contests did not, to a status-conscious petty bourgeoisie that flocked by the tens of thousands to enjoy a novel winter outing in the company of members of the royal family and party leaders. Fifty thousand persons attended the first annual outing in 1930 led by the Prince of Piedmont; by the end of the decade Italy was second only to Germany in the total number of registered skiers.[67]

With the single exception of skiing, which attracted large numbers of petty bourgeois women, the *dopolavoro* sports were overwhelmingly male oriented. When organizing sports for women, the regime confronted the intense hostility of the Catholic Church, which, although conforming to fascist morality in many other respects, was adamantly opposed to women's sports as violating public decency and imperiling motherhood. What little the OND did do was criticized by the Church as irresponsible, "encouraging the feminist ideal, masculinizing women and thereby estranging them from their maternal functions and kindling their eroticism."[68] The fascist government itself was considerably less forceful than it might have been in counteracting Church propaganda: Indeed, it even appeased Church criticism by censoring pictures of skimpily clad female athletes from the daily press.[69] Women's sports were nonetheless encouraged, especially as various experts on physical education and eugenics began offering persuasive arguments that if "administered in small doses they were of undeniable benefit in improving the race." The kinds of sports recommended, however, were those that "enhanced feminine grace and poise without the exertion pernicious to maternal functions": lawn tennis, swimming, rhythm dancing, and modified calisthenics.[70] But the OND focused primarily on the formalization of traditional popular games, like bowls; in the process, it actually tended to exclude women – as well as children – who, when the game was played informally in the neighborhood, took part or at least looked on with the men.[71] At the same time, it did little or nothing to provide the special facilities for those pastimes judged proper for women. Working women, unless they were employed in firms with unusually well-equipped sports facilities, were thus denied opportunities for physical recreation.

Participation sports were so high a priority item for the regime, especially in view of its growing concern for military preparedness in the thirties, that the generally low quality of OND sports seems curious. In theory, at least, the distinction stipulated by the fascist Sports Charter between professional and popular sports carried no apparent bias against the latter. Indeed, by differentiating between the two, Turati had expected to protect the world of popular sports from "contamination" by the competitive ethos and commercialization of professional sports. Protection of some kind was probably necessary in Italy. Popular sports involving physical participation were only beginning to find a public, and were open to being overwhelmed by audience events, the vast publicity for which might easily have engendered a passive mass of working-class spectators.

But an effective program of popular sports obviously presupposed an abundance of local recreational facilities and trained athletic directors. When the regime began to promote sports on a mass level, such amenities were lacking, significantly in the North and altogether in many regions of the South. Sports advocates spoke of the need for a "rational and totalitarian" planning of facilities to enable Italy to catch up with its more advanced northern neighbors.[72] But the government itself did little more than direct prefects to approve municipal expenditures on sports facilities and to authorize the General Director of Taxes to grant fiscal incentives for the purchase of land toward the construction of municipal sports facilities.[73] Because the political implications of sports were so great, the actual development of local facilities was left to the Fascist party, and handled through the special provincial sports councils set up in 1929. The party in turn used its authority to pressure municipalities to donate land, whereas all other expenses – sometimes subsidized by the PNF – were to be underwritten by private enterprises that logically expected a return on their investment.[74]

Party pressure produced striking results in the late twenties when

The culture of consent: mass organization in fascist Italy

Turati was party secretary and Arpinati, a soccer devotee, was undersecretary of the Ministry of the Interior. Between 1927 and 1930 more than 1,000 new sports fields were inaugurated; by 1930, the total number of playing fields amounted to 3,289, with marked increases in Piedmont and Lombardy and a not insignificant rise in the more prosperous southern regions, most notably Apulia.[75] These increases notwithstanding, the Dopolavoro of Florence complained in 1930 that it had no playing areas of its own and was being forced as a result to use the playing fields borrowed from the state railroads, whereas the *federale* of the Sicilian province of Messina reported to party headquarters in 1932 that only three playing fields were available to a population of 800,000 persons.[76]

Construction of new facilities, curbed by the economic crisis, failed altogether to keep pace with the increased rhythm of activities in the 1930s. As a rule, provincial organizers learned to maximize use of scarce local facilities, borrowing those provided by state ministries, especially the railroads, and the leading local industrial firms. So the *federale* of Florence reported in 1934 that *dopolavoro* members now had access to thirty-four playing areas.[77] Otherwise – and this was more normally the case in smaller towns – the *dopolavoro*, as we have seen, simply adapted their activities to the lack of sports facilities.

The regime itself, by officially sanctioning the division of sports into two categories – one professional and the other popular – inevitably discriminated against *dopolavoro* sports. "High sports" promoted by CONI, which won the regime international prestige and accolades at home, were financed both by lavish government expenditures and private sports promoters; the OND, on the other hand, was financed solely by membership fees and modest public subsidies.[78] Even if both, for different reasons, were high-priority items, exhibition sports, which guaranteed maximum returns in political propaganda for the regime and profits to commercial enterprise, were invariably privileged in the allocation of public funds and public attention.

Indeed, under fascism professional sports became big business, absorbing both public funds and private investment. The regime created a very favorable environment for professional sports and their big-time promoters. It underwrote the great public football stadia at Rome, Bologna, Turin, and Florence. It granted generous tax incentives to sports impresarios. The travel of professional teams was heavily subsidized.[79] The regime itself was so graft-ridden that little stigma was attached to the openly vested interests of many fascist *gerarchi* in sports promotion. Arpinati, undersecretary of the Interior, then undersecretary of the Corporations, in his capacity as president of the

Italian Soccer Federation and of CONI until 1932, was responsible for obtaining funds for the construction of the superstadium in his home-town of Bologna.[80] Giuseppe Marinelli, his successor at CONI, at the same time as being the PNF's administrative secretary, was also pres-ident of the Lazio, one of Rome's two professional soccer teams; all the way down the fascist hierarchy there appear to have been close ties between party officials and local sports promoters, ties that inev-itably resulted in the diversion of public funds into professional sports.

While Italy won medals and trophies in international champion-ships and mass exhibition sports flourished at home, popular partici-pation sports began to languish, and especially as the novelty of or-ganized bowls, tug-of-war, and other games promoted by the OND began to wear off. After reaching a peak of 191,773 events in 1933, the number of OND sports events declined dramatically to 102,547 in 1936, rising somewhat in 1937 to 130,017; these latter figures were in fact inflated by the addition of "chess events" – hardly a physical pastime.[81]

The triumph of mass spectator events over mass participatory ones was in no way uncongenial to the fascist leadership, at least in the short term. New symbols of national identity were as easily evoked by exhibition sports as by the hierarchy of competitions organized by the OND, and these certainly were no less effective diversions from politics than the activism of single teams of *dopolavoristi*. Spectator events further provided an outlet for aggressions that the regulated play of the *dopolavoro* did not: indeed, the incidence of violence at spectator events – of fans invading the fields, of protests against ref-erees' decisions, and assaults on foreign teams – was reportedly high. Spectator fanaticism of this kind, if not actively promoted by the fascist leadership, was certainly tolerated by the public authorities;[82] the im-passioned public of the mass spectator event served well the regime's propaganda purposes, at the expense, however, of the physical pre-paredness of its "working–soldiers," and the disciplined solidarity of its *dopolavoro* cohorts.

The "New Italy" as a mass commodity

By organizing a vast program of outings and tourism, the OND sought in the most tangible way possible to promote a new national identity. It worked toward a public in movement, so to speak, an active public as opposed to a passive audience. By 1937, when it sponsored some 50,000 foot marches, day outings, and tours[83] with an estimated three million "participations," the OND had successfully transformed the

Italian countryside, seashores, and mountains into the accessible and indisputably national commodities of a new mass leisure.

When the OND began to organize popular tourism, it had abundant resources at its disposal. Besides the inexhaustible variety of regional cultures, a wealth of historical monuments, and the priceless beauty of the Italian landscape, it inherited, or confiscated, an already well-developed network of outing clubs and touring societies dating from the early years of the century. The Italian Touring Club, founded in 1892 to promote the then-new sport of cycling, had by 1922 a membership of 200,000 drawn primarily from middle class adults and students. The Federation of Italian Excursionists enrolled thousands of middle and lower-middle class tourists. Even workers in many northern urban centers had set up their own excursion societies, which, organized in 1911 under the Workers' Union of Italian Excursionists (UOEI), founded by the Republican Ugolino Ugolini, counted tens of thousands of members by 1922.[84] The UOEI like all other "subversive" associations had been forced to disband in December 1926, and those of its members willing to change their political affiliation were readily absorbed into the OND. Two months earlier, *Il Dopolavoro escursionistico*, a monthly newssheet that always retained a more plebeian tone than the culturally pretentious *Gente nostra*, had begun publication as a replacement for the allegedly subversive *Vita uoeina*. The FIE, on the other hand, with its politically secure middle class constituency, was allowed to maintain its organizational structure intact until 1935, even though it was placed under the direction of the party secretary, and the OND took credit for the activities it sponsored.

The first significantly new impetus to mass tourism was provided by the famed "popular trains" inaugurated in August 1931. Even before this, *dopolavoro* members had received small discounts on travel, largely because the Minister of Communications Ciano, when setting up the highly efficient after-work organization for his own employees, thought to extend at least some of their numerous benefits to the constituency at large. The "popular trains" also resulted from Ciano's initiative, the outcome – as he frankly admitted – of a felicitous convergence of economic calculations and political considerations.[85] The discounts on group travel of up to 50 percent were designed to boost mass transit, thereby reducing the huge deficit of the state railroads as revenues declined during the depression; at the same time they provided the urban unemployed and poor a brief respite from the dismal depression atmosphere of the cities.

Accompanied by well-devised propaganda, the "popular trains" quickly became a new national institution, celebrated in popular ditties by a lower-class public that previously, had rarely, if ever, taken train trips for diversion. Between 2 August and 20 September 1931, more than half a million travelers took advantage of the discounts. The majority was drawn from the northern urban centers; Florence alone reported that during the first half of 1932, eighty-four trains carrying 70,000 travelers departed from the central station of Santa Maria Novella.[86] Even so, the cost of such "popular trains" was by no means as popular as their organizers claimed: The numerous trainloads of workers and employees brought to Rome for the celebration of the Decennale were generally subsidized by employers.[87] Once the initial euphoria had dissipated and the federations ceased organizing mass excursions, travelers on the "popular trains" declined to about 100,000 per year. At least some of those who used them were sufficiently status conscious to complain that no provisions were made for discounts in the more commodious second-class compartments.[88]

Mass tourism of the kind offered by the German "Strength through Joy" with its famed fleet of single-class cruise ships was a rarity in fascist Italy. Lacking the capital resources of the KDF, the OND simply concluded special agreements with private shipping agencies, such as the Florio Navigation Company, which offered discounts of 35 percent for groups of twenty-five or more on its Mediterranean cruises.[89] The prices negotiated were again hardly popular: The Latin Cruise sponsored by the Florentine Dopolavoro cost 550 lire for a seven-day trip, whereas the week-long cruise of the Levant was priced from 950 lire for a first-class cabin to 400 lire for a third-class berth. These prices, even when sweetened by installment payments, put cruises beyond the range of all but a relatively affluent public of petty functionaries drawn primarily from the northern cities: the 7,600 Milanese employees, for example, who enjoyed the Milan Dopolavoro's trip in 1933, or the 1,220 members of the Turin Civil Servants' After-Work Association, who toured the Mediterranean ports the same year.[90] The atmosphere aboard the ships was apparently less than egalitarian, if organizers of the 1935 Latin Cruise felt obliged to urge prospective excursionists to forego ostentatious cruise outfits.[91] This select public demonstrated few signs of becoming less exclusive: By 1937 the OND still sponsored only five cruises a year for 6,000 persons.[92] The less affluents' taste for the exotic was met by a variety of surrogates: numerous organized visits to the *Rex, Leonardo da Vinci,* and *Count of Savoy* at anchor, or in the case of the employees of one large Milanese electrical firm, by a day-long trip through the Milanese canals on a decorated barge dubbed by its 300 passengers the *Rex II*.[93]

The mass outing, as the one pastime almost every *dopolavorista*

could afford, was in contrast made as inclusive as possible, organized
– as an OND circular emphasized in 1933 – to offer "all workers, even
those not enrolled in the OND, the possibility of passing one or more
days in an atmosphere of happy diversion."[94] Bicycle touring was
particularly recommended as a "truly economic, popular, and rapid"
means of transportation for the "less well-to-do classes" and a special
badge of merit, the *audax ciclista*, was awarded for long-distance relay
racing. Especially after 1934, when the workweek in industry was
reduced to forty hours and the *sabato fascista* was instituted, Saturday
afternoon and Sunday occasioned the departures of thousands of workers into the surrounding countryside and groups of *rurali*, although to
a lesser extent, arrived – often for the first time – in the provincial
capitals or at the seaside. Mass excursions, bordering on national mo-
bilizations, celebrated an annual cycle of national holidays: the Feast
of the Assumption on 15 August, Armistice Day on 4 November, and
the fascist Labor Day of 21 April. This last, of course, was by far
the most carefully orchestrated of all, both because it was a fascist
holiday and because in the imposing demonstrations it evoked, it was
designed to eclipse altogether the memory of the May Day outing,
which had been among the most cherished traditions of the socialist
working class.

A great deal of inventiveness was employed to transform mundane
outings into memorable events, their great novelty thereby concealing
their infrequency. Fanfares, banners, contests, group singing, a few
speeches, were all added to embellish what was essentially poor man's
fare. One rally described by Andrea Gastaldi, *federale* of Turin, experimented with a "mass mobilization" of vehicles, obtaining twenty-
four trucks, forty-six automobiles, and forty-two motorcycles from
local industrialists and private individuals to transfer 1,500 peasants
and workers of the Canavesana zone of the province to Ceresole Reale
in the Alpine foothills. Along the Orco River the crowd visited the
important hydroelectric turbines supplying Turin. Free lunch was distributed and entertainment provided by a band contest entered by four
local bands. The outing, despite the poor weather, was in Gastaldi's
estimate a clear success. He ended the visit with a "brief speech"
explaining the significance of the trip, calling his audience's attention
to the "continual initiatives and measures taken by the regime to deal
with the problem of unemployment." The crowd of peasants and workers, he reported, followed him with "attention and enthusiasm" and
at the end gave "long acclaim to the Duce and the Regime."[95]

Mass outings were calculated to impress participants with the fraternal solidarity of all *dopolavoristi*. Those traveling from one city to another were often greeted by contingents of *dopolavoristi* from their host city; When the 2,000 Milanese workers visited the ocean liner *Rex* in 1932 they were provided with an abundant feast by the Genoese dockworkers.[96] Interregional rallies were promoted annually, with special effort made to involve groups from the surrounding provinces. The overriding aim of the second national bicycle relay race promoted by the FIE in 1931, besides preparing the contestants' "athletic-military prowess," was to instill a sense of fraternity among workers hitherto "divided by a stupid provincialism." By bringing over 2,000 cyclists to Rome, organizers anticipated that the northern contestants would "comprehend the great exertions made by their southern brothers," and especially those cycling from Sicily over the tortuous roads of the Mezzogiorno. They would thus return home with a "very different vision" of the southerners' "athletic and moral qualities."[97]

Although the rallies brought together workers from various occupational backgrounds and geographical locations, they were strictly plebeian affairs. Except insofar as the crowds were reviewed or addressed by local dignitaries, no effort was made to invite or encourage middle class participation. It was in fact exceptional for an employer to accompany his employees on outings: The general director of the General Electric Company of Milan was praised for the "exquisitely spontaneous gesture of kindness" that led him to join his employees briefly on board the *Rex II* and his "total departure from all traditional etiquette and conventionalism" in eating and drinking with his employees in the "most democratic of fashions." This one episode, concluded the observer, served as a "tangible sign of the collaboration, concord and, dare I say, brotherhood, that the regime by its continuous and persuasive work had created between capitalist and workers."[98] More usually the mass proletarian outings were simply to be shunned by the individualistic upper classes as yet another discomfiting display of the regime's immense vulgarity.

By breaking down a specifically provincial identity, thus familiarizing a parochial public with the geography of a "greater Italy," the fascist mass outing sought to politicize at the most primitive level. It was the ideal of any local functionary to bring his charges to the nation's capital at Rome, but in most cases this was not possible unless the rail trip was subsidized by employers. As local substitutes each region offered landmarks and monuments that evoked the unity and progress of the "new" Italy, and that by association were transformed into physical symbols of the fascist regime through the *dopolavoro* outing.

In the Veneto there were the battlefields of the Carso or the Piave, where the Italian nation had repulsed the Austrian invaders; in Latium the land reclamation projects of the Pontine Marshes where fascist technology had triumphed over the malarial swamplands, or the air-fields that testified to the might of fascist Italy; in Piedmont the great hydroelectric projects and the new speedways; in Tuscany the wealth of historical monuments; in Liguria the naval yards of Genoa and La Spezia. Each town in effect developed its own special goal: For the outlying districts, this was the provincial capital; for the landlocked city, the seaside; for the urban centers, the mountains and hills; and each trip brought participants a step closer to grasping, if not the whole geographical entity "Italy," at least a part that evoked the greatness of the whole.

Organizers themselves equivocated as to whether the excursion was a political rally or simply an outing. The departures of "popular trains" or special caravans of cars and buses occasioned special ceremonies. "Thirty-two thousand *dopolavoristi* departed for the lakes, mountains, and ski fields to the tune of 'Giovinezza,'" exulted Parenti, acclaiming "Snow Day" in a telegram to party headquarters in 1935.[99] But the smaller outing, the more routine trip, was less formalized. If the opportunity arose, or if the outing generated sufficient enthusiasm, it was easily transformed into a small political rally. And so the experience of the moment became fused with the image of the regime, rendered tangible through contact with the awesome potency of a new technology, the evocative sites of past patriotic feats, and the symbols of Italy's future might.

Although politics may not always have been explicit, the way in which the public was organized at least fostered conformity. The fact that all outings had to be registered with the provincial offices barred spontaneous group initiatives. "Improvised activities," in fact, were banned, as "failing to correspond to those fundamental principles of discipline that must guide every activity of the regime," and further, as not providing those "indispensable organizational guarantees required if the events were to attract the masses."[100] The authoritarian attitudes of party organizers tended as well to accentuate the regimentation of group travel. Although there are few indications that organizers generally achieved the desired level of discipline, some at least managed to militarize outings quite effectively: "*Dopolavoristi* or soldiers? The question is superfluous," one young *dopolavorista* was quoted as saying in August 1935: "I am just longing for the chance to go over there [Ethiopia] and take aim, just as we have been taught to do in the *dopolavoro* expeditions."[101]

Mass leisure in a class society

By the mid-thirties the OND had brought striking changes to the organization of popular leisure. Through policies designed at once to break down the class affiliation of leisure-time pursuits, to mediate access to new consumer patterns and recreational pastimes, and to extend the mass communications network, the fascist regime had acted as both promoter and sponsor of an emergent mass leisure. Thus popular recreational pastimes, which formerly constituted the highly individual expressions of group sociability, were subjected to increasing standardization, and the associations which sponsored them conferred with a new national identity through their common affiliation with the OND. Thousands of new *dopolavoro* centers had been set up where recreational facilities or even any organized leisure pastimes were previously lacking. Hundreds of thousands of persons who had little or no prior contact with organized recreational pastimes were involved in activities that brought them into contact with people from other regions and professional groups.

The organization of leisure activities on a mass scale was by no means unique to Italy; similar developments can be identified everywhere in western capitalist nations during the interwar decades, with the invention of new communication techniques, the extension of new consumer patterns, and the growth of commercial leisure industries. What distinguished the emergence of mass leisure in Italy was the high degree of state intervention in the process. Thus the forced "coordination" of thousands of autonomous popular cultural activities that had reinforced the cohesion of working class communities, dramatically accelerated their integration into national life. By curtailing their autonomy and prescribing rules of conduct for their activities, the OND constrained popular associations to participate in officially sanctioned national pastimes. Moreover, it acted to overcome a major obstacle to participation in public life, that is, the low level of popular consumption. If popular access to mass consumer habits had been left to free market forces, leisure habits – it may be assumed – would have remained largely traditional, popular wants would have remained unsatisfied and the regime itself deprived of an important means of assimilating the working population into national pastimes. As it was, the OND itself acted as a mediator arranging access to activities that many workers, because of their low purchasing power, could not possibly have obtained from commercial leisure industries.

The fascist organization of mass leisure was not at all inconsistent, however, with a profoundly inegalitarian social order. Indeed, for all

185

of the claims to have democratized leisure-time pursuits, the class nature of its programs was, as we have seen, pronounced. The public of the *dopolavoro* was relegated to the Saturday matinees or special performances, to the upper tiers of the theater, and to the third-class compartments on trains, and the recreational facilities for popular use were often rudimentary. Moreover, the fascist organization of leisure introduced a new status differentiation within recreational activities. Distinctions between the amateur and the professional, the dilettante and the expert, were accentuated; the "high theater" and elite sports were increasingly commercialized and professionalized, whereas the categories of the "amateur" sportsmen and the dilettante actors of "passion" not "ambition" – that is, of those pastimes identified as "popular" – were formalized. Nor did the OND seek to set up training programs or facilities that would provide access from one realm to another. Finally, low levels of popular consumption remained a barrier to participation and to the extension of facilities that state intervention could only partially overcome.

For all of the limits imposed on organizings by the very nature of the society in which it was operating, the OND nevertheless served fascist policy in a number of significant ways. The agency effectively regulated or replaced those traditional forms of proletarian cultural organization that had lent cohesiveness to the working class community. Even when these structures remained more or less intact, the OND in effect appropriated as its own a whole variety of games and pastimes. In this way it incorporated what had previously been seen as autonomous social expressions into the social life of the fascist state, infusing informal activities with competitiveness and associating them with the regime's official activities.

Workers may well have been served equally, if not better, under a liberal regime. The fact remains that in Italy the novel forms of consumption, organized recreational pastimes, and the mass media developed concurrently with fascism; if they were not actually attributed to the regime's benign intervention as fascist propaganda pretended, they were at least associated with it. Whereas in liberal–democratic societies the new forms of leisure were experienced as largely individual acquisitions, in fascist Italy they were, so to speak, conferred collectively and closely tied to state beneficence. Beyond satisfying social needs, although in a distorted way, the fascist organization of leisure provided the regime with a highly articulated institutional framework; this allowed it to purvey its own cultural production on a mass level. Through the local *dopolavoro* sections and the activities they sponsored, fascist cultural policy reached a vast popular audience.

7

The formation of fascist low culture

The monumentalization of culture

The fascist regime had early recognized the instrumental value of *la cultura* in the consolidation of its rule. Coming to power with all the rhetoric of an unfulfilled Risorgimento tradition, fascist and nationalist ideologues continuously paid homage to the idea of a unified and unifying national culture. The formation of a single dominant culture would, it was understood, not only help to mask the patent inequalities of Italian society, but also serve to legitimate the regime according to a traditional bourgeois and even a popular cultural sensibility. But this said, there remained a wide spectrum of "cultures" from which such a national culture might be forged, from the avant-garde to the popular; from the technological utopias of the Futurists, whose pugilistic tactics had made them especially suitable companions for the *squadristi*, to the verities of elitist practitioners of the old high culture; and, in theory at least, the stock of folk traditions of precapitalist Italy. The regime demonstrated itself willing to espouse any one of these according to its need for support, and as a whole its cultural pretensions remained extremely eclectic in content. But in practice, and especially in the formation of the institutions for the dissemination of one or another kind of culture, fascism was inevitably drawn toward the reproduction of the already class-defined divisions between "high" and "low."

From the mid-twenties, as the regime began to define a more or less autonomous cultural policy, Mussolini sought to disassociate himself from the avant-garde movements of the immediate postwar years. The euphoric iconoclasm of futurist thought, identified with the rise of fascism as Marinetti campaigned side by side with Mussolini, was gradually rejected in favor of positions that might receive the support of traditional academic culture.[1] At the same time, in its eagerness to earn a measure of cultural legitimacy, the regime adopted the traditional intellectual elite's disdain for the popularization of culture.

Fascism's ideal of culture was personified in the figure of Giovanni Gentile, the regime's greatest intellectual conquest. In common with many intellectuals who rallied to fascism, Gentile perceived the task of the new fascist intelligentsia as twofold: the renewal of elite culture by means of a dynamic new synthesis of the national heritage and fascist ideology, and, this accomplished, the utilization of the state as a positive educational force to impart national values to a citizenry that hitherto had perceived state institutions as "mere names or external, coercive forces."[2]

In practice, however, such a national cultural synthesis was never to be realized. Indeed, the cumulative effects of Gentile's influence in the early twenties and fascist cultural policy in general reinforced rather than broke down the traditional cultural division and class hierarchies inherited from the liberal era. Gentile's reform of the formal educational system perpetuated the old separation of elite education and popular instruction, while the organization of specifically fascist cultural agencies reproduced this dichotomy in separate institutions for a "high" and a "low" fascist culture.[3] "High" fascist culture was first and foremost associated with the monumental work of the Enciclopedia Treccani, published under Gentile's editorship in the early thirties, with the assembly of cultural notables in the pretentious Accademia Italiana, which was modeled on the French Académie and produced the first official dictionary of the Italian language, and with the lesser intellectual achievements of the Istituto Nazionale Fascista di Cultura.[4] Founded by the PNF in 1924 under the presidency of Gentile, the National Fascist Institute of Culture was specifically set up to reconcile traditional academic culture with the activism of the new generation of fascist intellectuals. Local branches, formed in the late twenties in numerous towns, had, according to official descriptions, "doctrinal purposes"; their programs were "specifically scientific and political, and their propaganda was to be directed to the middle class, that is, to the class that is capable of directly assimilating doctrine."[5]

For those classes incapable of "directly assimilating doctrine" there remained the "cultural" activities of the OND. Official propaganda followed Gentile in insisting that the expression of the true ideals of fascism, comprehensible solely to the elites, should be distinguised from "those simple slogans, appropriate to the masses, which practically and immediately distinguish friends from enemies, create myths, arouse blind support, and put into motion the forces of will and feeling."[6] In contrast to the Istituti Fascisti di Cultura, the *dopolavoro* was charged with "divulging doctrine by making it simple and accessible to the working class, together with elementary notions of general culture, fascist principles, and precepts."[7]

This hierarchical organization of the regime's cultural institutions inevitably had the result of removing more qualified intellectuals from any direct responsibility for the elaboration of OND cultural policy. In the regime's definition, "popular" culture simply involved the transmission of an already formulated body of precepts and information, whereas true culture was formed by the elite and purveyed to the masses. In keeping with this mechanistic division, "artistic education" for the masses and "popular culture" generally were treated as purely organizational questions. Cultural policy, to the extent that it existed, was relegated by default to a heterogeneous corps of intellectual collaborators: well-established cultural personalities at the national level; party functionaries, high-school professors, schoolteachers, and professional lecturers locally. By the thirties the resulting cultural *bricolage* had achieved an identity of its own, characterized by the institutions within which it was formed, as *cultura dopolavoristica*. In the end, distinguished less by its specific content than by its style, it was easily digestible, crudely propagandistic, and as eclectic as the background of its organizers and the mixed social composition of their audience might indicate.

The eminent *tecnici*, who were responsible for national "policy," were as a group completely detached from more vital cultural trends. The most prominent among them were the theater director Gioacchino Forzano; the noted playwright and critic Luigi Chiarelli, a leading exponent of the theater of the *grottesco* before the war who under the regime had become decidedly traditionalist; and the ex-nationalist Emilio Bodrero, professor of history of philosophy and president in the thirties of the Italian Society for Authors and Editors (SIAE).[8] Their affiliation with the OND conferred a certain cultural respectability to an organization otherwise staffed by intellectual mediocrities. But they were in fact little more than mediators between accepted cultural tastes and a new mass audience; they presided at juries, penned apologetics, and invented new techniques to impart the prevailing conventions to a mass audience. The OND, oblivious to the cultural iconoclasm of the "modernist" currents, thus remained practically impervious to the controversies that periodically swept the intellectual community.

The low-level conformism exhibited by OND cultural programs derived less from any explicit policy than from the cultural background of its local organizers. For the self-taught political cadre, the schoolmaster who lent his services to adult education classes, or the provincial professor who spoke at neighborhood conferences, "culture," whether traditional or fascist, was sacrosanct. Their own marginal position in a society where cultural traditions were revered and intellectuals held in high esteem encouraged respect, a respect that was reinforced by the accentuation of the class structure of education under fascism and the correspondingly heightened prestige attached to the diploma. Eager to vindicate their social function as intellectuals, and all the more because the nature of their employment alone no longer guaranteed them this status, they tended to monumentalize traditional culture. Indeed, their own prestige was inevitably heightened in proportion to the need for this culture to be explained and interpreted.

Inasmuch as their own status depended on the regime's need for mediators, cultural organizers were logically opposed to the democratization of a culture that they themselves had attained with such struggle. A "spineless democracy," wrote one cultural organizer, G. Pesce, specifically referring to the theater in *La Stirpe*, had reduced the problem of cultural appreciation to "a superficial and petty question of prices, seating, facilities, and repertories – the repertory – a democratic fetish!"[9] The problem was rather "profoundly intimate and spiritual"; it demanded the "spiritual education of the masses." The organizer's primary concern, he insisted, should not be "the creation of a popular theater for popular use and consumption," but "to bring love for the theatrical arts to the people and to bring the people to the theater." The theater building itself should make no concessions to its plebeian audience: "It must be beautiful and the balconies must frame the stage; the orchestra seats must be covered in velvet and the public must be well mannered and well dressed." The only defense against the cheapening of culture by contact with this new mass audience was, he recognized, economic. "The theater," he stressed, "must be the object of greatest respect," a respect that could only be encouraged by its monetary value. The theater had to be paid for so that the "worker feels that he is obtaining a valuable good for which any sacrifice is sweet: democratizing art by putting it in slippers with a broom in its hand has always been a most cretinous utopia." In this way the theater, highly idealized, was in the end to be marketed as a luxury product.

Culture, then, was a luxury and a privilege for which the worker had to struggle. The self-taught person was consequently ennobled as if to justify the sacrifices he was called on to make. "*Uomo faber*," as he was described by one cultural organizer, "loves books and libraries rather than the pulp magazine; loves the difficult because the difficult is an aspect of the heroic."[10] Yet cultural self-betterment did not imply social mobility; it was presented merely as a source of spiritual uplift. The artisan, the petty functionary, or the pensioner could acquire the trappings of culture during his spare time by emulating the cultural mores of his social superiors. Thus might social *gaucherie* be eliminated and social grace enhanced; even the most humble could embellish themselves with the ornaments of national culture.

The dominant themes of this *cultura dopolavoristica* were in the first place nationalistic. The innate parochialism of the provincial intellectual was deliberately reinforced by official images of the world abroad in which the excesses of democratic–liberal mass cultures were piously contrasted with solid national cultural traditions. This aversion to foreign influence, and especially to the twentieth-century cosmopolitan mass culture identified as "Americanism," was supported by high culture as well. Although fascist intellectuals were attracted by the image of a technocratic mass culture that apparently was also hegemonic, they were also fearful of its leveling, tolerant, and parvenu qualities. These latter aspects of Americanism were "endured" by the regime "with clenched teeth," as the antifascist novelist Cesare Pavese recalled, and authors like Caldwell, Steinbeck, and Saroyan found avid readers among many young intellectuals.[11] But these and all other manifestations of American culture, whether the "dissolute tunes of jazz bands" or the "sexual innuendo, American stimulants, and shameless Venuses" of the American-style tabloid press were repeatedly condemned in the fascist press as unfit for mass consumption. Even if such official disapproval had little practical effect – Hollywood movies enjoyed a wide popularity, and not only because of the immense power exercised by American capital in the film distribution networks – the intellectual habit that came from identifying foreign culture as a whole as alien and subversive had as its natural corollary the presumption that national culture, whatever its form, was a socially conservative force. In this way, the Italian cultural heritage was "nationalized" by fascism, integrated, as it were, into an imperialist image of Italy as "the country of Resurrected Romanism," in Pavese's words, "where even geometers studied Latin . . . the country of genius by the grace of God."[12] National origin was accordingly elevated into a crude, easily grasped esthetic category. Thus the "true" Italian, rejecting "exotic" music "coated with foreign froth," had finally learned to appreciate the "divine melodies" of Verdi, the "sublime harmonies" of Puccini, the "magnificently robust" choruses of Mascagni; with new-found respect, he now listened to those lesser-known bel canto composers who, like Donizetti, had not received the appropriate acclaim until "national values" had been illuminated by fascism.[13]

Artistic culture was likewise assembled from a list of the great masters: Bellini, Leonardo Da Vinci, Michelangelo – the "fathers of culture," as it were – who were presented to the public of the *dopolavoro* in humanizing anecdotes that recounted their eccentricities and quoted

191

their memorable sayings. Inevitably some concessions had to be made for modern art: The fascist regime, or so it was claimed, continued to nurture "modernism" in the pictorial arts. But the modern art held up for public appreciation through the weekly pictorial essays of *Gente nostra* was essentially provincial, untainted by the radical formalism of Carrà and De Chirico. The paintings illustrated were strictly figurative, frequently depicting still lifes or pastoral scenes; all subscribed to a trite academic classicism or to the sentimental evocations of a provincial "impressionistic" style. This "fusion of poetry and realism" extolled by *Gente nostra* was regularly reviled by the artistic avantgarde as philistine and reactionary.[14]

Thus the culture that was brought to the working public with such virtuous images was no more than the world of high culture as perceived and vulgarized by the organizers of low culture; the servants of culture and not its creators, they propounded it with all the pompous condescension and mystification of acolytes opening up the world of the occult to the uninitiated. In one sense, the "monumentalization of culture," achieved by their efforts, was similar to that aspired to on another level by the regime itself as it reconstructed the Imperial *fora*, isolating them from the fabric of the medieval city and destroying the historical continuum that united modern Rome with its ancient past. The national tradition was thus reduced to a roster of illustrious but essentially static and isolated cultural "monuments": Dante, Goldoni, Manzoni, Verdi, Puccini, D'Annunzio – an eclectic mixture, united solely by their similar packaging and consistent presentation to the public.

If embarrassing to the fascist cultural vanguard, as well as to academic culture, this distorted image of high culture at least allowed their world to remain intact. "Low-brow" culture could be readily dismissed as *roba da dopolavoro* (trash), whereas respect for official culture and the traditional status of the intellectual was reinforced. Even as the regime was willing to tolerate and even foster a measure of avant-garde iconoclasm to perpetuate fascism's image as a dynamic, modern, aggressive force, so it found in traditional culture a mode of imparting fascism's conservative social ideals to a mass public.

Educating to order

Nationalist ideologues had conceived of the state as above all a moralizing and educational force for forming the new model citizen–producer, and the programs they had drawn up before the March on Rome made educational reform a first priority of any postliberal regime. This general preoccupation with "education" persisted under fascist rule, although its practical effects were felt more immediately in the formal educational system than in the institutions for educating and instructing the working class. Thus the long-awaited reform of the schools, enacted in 1923 while Gentile was Minister of Education, addressed itself almost exclusively to the problem of forming the elites; it reinforced traditional class distinctions by increasing the number of requirements in the humanistic disciplines and by setting up an intensely competitive system of state examinations that restricted access to higher education. Whereas the separation of middle class students from the mass of petty bourgeois and working class children was thus confirmed, *instruction* in technical skills – as opposed to *education* in values – was itself systematically downgraded. The upper technical institutes had formerly provided an avenue for educational mobility; now university access was closed to their graduates and a new system of "complementary" technical schools was set up in which the majority of lower class students completed their education at age thirteen, having gained only a rudimentary knowledge of general cultural notions and a limited number of practical skills.[15]

The fascists did not of course exclude the idea of educating the masses. Indeed, fascist propagandists repeatedly described the ideological functions of the *dopolavoro* in terms of the "moral" and "intellectual" education of its members. At once social panacea, cure for class conflict, and reinvigorating tonic for the nation, this particular kind of education would, it was held, create a sober and disciplined working class by imparting the values of hierarchy, class collaboration, and patriotism. The appropriate mechanisms were detailed by the OND and included adult educational schools, conferences, local libraries, together with such modern pedagogical devices as correspondence schools, educational films, and slide shows.[16] But when it came to the practical task of devising a curriculum, fascist organizers demonstrated little vocation for teaching. The content of the courses and teaching methods was defined negatively in reaction to what was considered the "subversive" nature of the old Popular Universities.

The Popular Universities, first established at the turn of the century and about sixty in number by the immediate postwar period, had provided a meeting place for intellectuals of democratic and socialist persuasion and urban petty bourgeois and skilled workers. Originally inspired by the extension courses of English private universities, unlike their English counterparts they had been affiliated with the Chambers of Labor or mutual aid societies, or promoted by the Milan-based democratic Associazione per la Cultura Popolare.[17] With such overt

193

political affiliation and their expressed aim of combining political education with cultural preparation, the Popular Universities inevitably came under increasing attack from the fascist movement after 1922. According to nationalist intellectuals, their curriculum was riddled with a "morally sterile" positivism. The Popular Universities, as Mario Giani had written in 1924, were no more than "convenient pedestals" for "ambitious" professionals and "self-styled experts" who were "self-advertising" in search of clients; platforms for an "ephemeral exhibitionism" on the part of hack democratic politicians who duped the workers by deforming notions of high culture with "grotesque phraseology."[18]

But Giani had been enough convinced of their utility to propose an alternative. In his view, the old system of lessons and conferences based on "scholastic methods" had to be abandoned because "they were annoying and of little value to adults who had reached the age of reason and had acquired considerable practical experience." He proposed their replacement by meetings and instructive talks held in an informal environment so as to allow adults to state their own opinions and to reduce the "excessive hierarchical distinction between instructors and their audience." Similarly, the curriculum had to be revised to eliminate "impractical subjects." Scientific and literary conferences were simply "not convenient, given the scant leisure time of workers and employees," and the workers' "capacity to assimilate the formulas of high culture was inevitably wanting"; instructors who sought to impart such notions simply risked "fomenting chimeras."

When the Federation of Popular Universities was finally disbanded in 1926, the fascists were faced with the problem of disposing of the dozens of local institutions that remained. For some organizers, "fascistization" was the answer – whether under the auspices of the OND or the Istituto Nazionale Fascista di Cultura.[19] Gentile himself denounced the travesty of true culture implicit in the very idea of a "popular university." "The time has come to end the Popular University altogether," he affirmed in 1927 at the inauguration of the Neapolitan branch of the Istituto Nazionale Fascista di Cultura: "'Popular,' 'university': two words, a noun and an adjective, that are absolutely contradictory and incompatible. The university is not for the people. The people have so much work to do, so much to do for the well-being of the nation . . . ." Fascist culture, he reiterated, had as its crucial task the creation of a dynamic culture for the elites, for those alone who were capable of acquiring culture in its true sense: "We have no desire to work in extension; we refuse to deal with culture in quantitative terms; with a national culture as extended to the people or for the people; we deal solely with a culture of quality, which remains to be formed."[20]

With this unqualified condemnation, debate over a systematic re-organization of the schools came to a close. Some of the Popular Universities were reopened under the Fascist Institutes of Culture, some simply remained closed down, others were placed under the OND. Educational policy was left to the discretion of local organizers, with exceedingly eclectic results. A few, like Romano Stefanelli, president of the Turin Dopolavoro in the early thirties, suggested that popular education had no specific content. Its essential quality derived from its "accessibility"; the instructors' task was to "render culture comprehensible to the mentality and the psychological level of the organized." Others stressed that educational priorities should be dictated by what the workers could or should assimilate: "Hygiene and history" was how Carlo Scorza defined the format at Lucca. Speakers on the conference circuit at Ravenna were similarly advised to restrict their topics to what may be described as social and physical prophylaxis: They were to focus first of all on "an exact explanation of the Labor Charter, on the action and mandate of the trade unions, and class collaboration"; they might then include conversations on "the prevention of diseases particularly tuberculosis, and personal hygiene . . . in the home and the workplace."[21]

Political education was rarely mentioned openly by fascist organizers, who generally preferred the more neutral concept of "moral education" or "elevation" when alluding to the OND's propagandistic functions. In practice, political education was construed as the study of fascist institutions and legislation, with the OND supplying a model course under the auspices of its Corporate Correspondence School established in 1929. Each of the twenty-six biweekly lessons, printed in *Gente nostra*, contained propagandistic articles on some aspect of the corporate order; each was accompanied by a predictably biased essay question, the answers to which were to be submitted to the Central Office for grading. A self-conscious effort was made to encourage correspondents to relate their study to work experience. Thus, in an edifying lesson on fascist syndicalism, students were instructed to "choose a profession and illustrate the difference between the trade unions of the past, which lacked all legal rights and duties, and the present legally recognized trade unions." For the final examination, correspondents were told to use examples from their own "practical experience" to comment on this quotation from the Duce: "Only today have the working people in all their many pastimes and occupations been elevated through the fascist state to become active and conscious subjects [*sic*] of their own destiny."[22] The correspondents – 8,101 altogether, counting 1,282 peasants, 2,323 industrial workers, 2,641 employees, 842 shopkeepers, and 1,282 teachers and *dopolavoro* and union functionaries[23] – were either baffled by the byzantine complexity of corporate legalism or embarrassed to relate corporate precepts to daily practice. The OND complained that they simply regurgitated the lessons and seemed "totally lacking in any precise understanding of syndical laws, norms and regulations."[24]

The more common forum for political propaganda was provided by the occasional conference at which guest lecturers, usually lesser provincial luminaries, spoke on such subjects as "Fascism, religion and family," "The fascist penal legislation explained to the people," "Authority and liberty under fascism." Explicitly political talks, however, were far outnumbered by cultural "conversations" devoted to a variety of topics that, as chronicled in *Gente nostra*, ranged from "The forces of the occult" to "Scientific management."[25]

The insignificant use of the *dopolavoro* for overt political propaganda may be partly accounted for by the cultural formation of the volunteer speakers. Idealizing education, disdaining the subordination of a "pure" culture to crude propaganda, the lesser intellectuals who habitually lent their services to local groups did not conceive of themselves as political organizers, even when they supported the fascist order. "Sports rallies, ceremonies, and speeches all play their part," wrote G. Berlutti, a fascist "expert" on Popular Libraries, but "culture alone can create a profound and solid fascist consciousness." For small-time ideologues like Berlutti, the convoluted rhetoric of a vulgar idealism offered a more effective means of inculcating the masses with Italian values than the demagogic slogans of hack politicians.[26] "If the people had possessed a clear idea of what constitutes a race, a heritage, of that which is vital, natural, and immanent in history, of the laws governing economic forces," declaimed Ravenna's educational consultant, Professor Sante Muratori, "no myth from the Nirvanic east could possibly have perturbed the molecular structure of our solid, constructive, and Roman mentality."[27]

The fact remains that fascist politics was an essentially unpopular subject, not only because of its ideological content, but as a result of the form in which it was inevitably presented. Political education was essentially a catechism to be learned by rote: a gloss on the Labor Charter, a set of political aphorisms, or a smattering of abstract juridical notions. Unless students had a vested interest in comprehending the intricacies of corporate law – for career purposes or to file a claim in the Labor Courts – what incentive was there to learn? Any allowance for interpretation would undoubtedly have provoked unwelcome debate and comment; otherwise, the subject was quite simply boring. Crude political indoctrination could be used more readily in the schools, where attendance was compulsory, than in the essentially voluntary adult recreational activities. Politics was therefore a subject that the adept organizer avoided.

Opportunities for intellectual uplift in the *dopolavoro* were equally lacking. The number of educational courses offered by the local groups, having increased significantly between 1929 and 1931 in such subjects as stenography, foreign languages, and fine arts, declined thereafter from 878 courses with 15,138 students in 1931 to 384 courses with 12,581 students in 1937.[28] Considerable publicity was given to the OND's "mass distribution of books." But only one such distribution actually took place in 1928, when 118,000 books, or 1,270 for each province, were sent out for the purpose of setting up eight local libraries. Otherwise the OND limited itself to publicizing the availability of low-cost editions of the classics from the Vallecchi publishing house, which were available on the open market.[29] Occasionally it distributed political writings or recommended their purchase: Mussolini's *Vita di Arnaldo*, G. Gregori's history of the massacre of Sarzana, and pamphlets in the collection of the *Panorami di vita fascista*. By the OND's own rather generous count in 1934, only 1,569 of its 19,000 sections had their own libraries. Of these, according to official cultural statistics, a mere 264 were sufficiently well endowed to merit being classified as "popular libraries."[30]

Giani's exhortations notwithstanding, the much-denounced "theoretical method" of the Popular University was not replaced by an "exclusively practical method," nor was there any systematic use of modern teaching devices, films, or slides. The "conferences" that were the central feature of most cultural programs were conducted in the traditional fashion of the academy. Not infrequently, these offered an authoritative forum for the intellectually inept and politically servile. In his history of Lugo under fascism, Rignani recalled his intense embarrassment at one such talk, delivered by a certain Augusto Mele at the Alfredo Oriani Cultural Institute in the Dopolavoro of Via Garibaldi. In its course, Mele called James Joyce "a clown," "a pornographer," "an enemy of Latin civilization," and "a slave of international Judaism"; he concluded by invoking the Duce as "an antidote" against "this typical representative of modern decadence."[31] As guest speakers unfamiliar with and not necessarily sympathetic to a popular audience were brought into the *dopolavoro*, the formality even increased. The public response to one such conference held in 1937 at

the recreational circle of a Milan factory was described by an irate
trade union organizer: "An illustrious professor read aloud forty type-
written pages on scientific management, bristling with doctrine and
statistics"; the workers, he remarked, were "still terrorized from the
experience."[32]

Why in the end was so little achieved toward using this vast cultural
network for educational purposes? The cost of cultural facilities and
the scarcity of qualified collaborators doubtless played some part.
Equally remarkable, however, was the OND's own inability to develop
an educational curriculum. This was less the result of oversight than
the outcome of the inherently contradictory nature of the effort. From
the early thirties, syndicalist leaders preoccupied with the problem of
"why workers did not read" had admitted that there were in fact many
workers who expressed a wish to do so, but the syndicalists simply
did not know what to give them.[33] It was not until 1940 that the first
manual of popular culture was published and then not by the OND but
by the workers' education section of the fascist trade unions. Even
when fascist cultural organizers finally formalized a popular educational curriculum, the result was not education in the sense of providing
a critical framework, but indoctrination. The *Cultura dei lavoratori*
textbook, which, according to the syndicalist Capoferri, would provide
workers with "a clear vision of their duties, their functions, their material, and especially the ideal and political scope of their activities,"[34]
recalled an elementary school primer. It offered the usual pastiche of
historical notions and political aphorisms together with a methodolog-
ical admonition to workers that they should learn to feel history "in
the way one feels a religion." Only with such faith could the masses
be truly educated. Otherwise education, however elementary, was superfluous indeed. In a social order demanding uncritical acceptance
and only the most rudimentary familiarity with fascist ideals, it represented a potentially subversive force. In the end, a neglect of educational initiatives – a *diseducation* by default if not by intention – was
compatible with, and to an extent supportive of, the stability of the
fascist order.

Training the fascist worker

Failing to educate workers as fascist *citizens*, did the regime in compensation focus on making them model *producers*? In the late twenties,
the OND had been singled out by technocrats for its potential use as
a "gigantic school" for the "technical-social instruction" of adult
workers.[35] Single after-work clubs, and especially those set up in in-

dustrial centers, were to impart the precepts of rationalization while teaching the technical skills required by advanced industry. These semipublic initiatives were to compensate, at least partially, for the Gentile reform, which, by focusing exclusively on the humanistic disciplines, had relegated vocational instructions to a minor place in the national school curriculum.[36]

The need for a national system of adult instruction had hardly been lessened by the regime's own belated reform of the vocational instructional system carried out between 1928 and 1932 by Giuseppe Belluzzo. Appointed Minister of National Education in 1928, he devoted his energies to revamping the primary and intermediate vocational schools.[37] In 1929 the secondary training school was established to provide vocational instruction for children up to the age of fourteen. The act of 7 January 1929 subsequently provided for provincial advisory bodies (Consorzi Provinciali per l'Istruzione Tecnica) to supervise all local vocational instructional programs whether private or public. Finally in 1931 the intermediate instructional system was reorganized, with both state and private initiatives subjected to uniform government regulations.[38] Although all of these measures served to remedy the most glaring deficiencies of the Gentile reform, few working class children continued their schooling beyond the age of fourteen, and many ended their school career at nine. The problem of adult technical instruction thus remained acute.

Beginning in 1928 the OND had responded to technocratic expectations by organizing an energetic, if short-winded, campaign to "coordinate" the 280 schools that fell under its jurisdiction. These included the famed municipal school of Florence, Leonardo Da Vinci, which the OND took over in 1929, and Rome's oldest night school, the Maddalena, which was deeded to the OND in 1932.[39] But by the time Starace took command of the OND in 1931, this preoccupation with technical instruction, prompted by the rationalization movement in industry, had begun to wane. Starace himself, in any case, demonstrated little grasp of the complexities of machine culture. His primary concern, evidenced by his first directive on vocational instruction, was to introduce a proper level of political information into training courses. Teachers were encouraged to include lessons of the Labor Charter and the "fundamental principles of the corporate order" in their courses; these subjects were justified as having a "vocational utility" by helping workers engaged in labor disputes to comprehend the *action* of the trade unions.[40] Starace's second and last directive, issued in 1931, treated technical instruction like sports: It called for a national essay contest on such topics as "What can a nation rich in labor power like our own gain from the improved moral and technical abilities of its workers?"[41] Prizes for the best answers, thirty in all, consisted of a four-day, all-expense trip to Rome, where, in accordance with the "aims of the contest," the winners were to be given guided tours at the industrial, commercial, and agricultural enterprises of the city and surrounding province. The OND's subsequent failure to report the contest's outcome was suggestive of the response it evoked. Thereafter, Starace's interest in technical instruction flagged and with it that of the OND. By 1933 *Gente nostra* had ceased reporting on the progress of technical instruction among its member associations; that year the organization allocated a mere 50,000 lire for technical instruction, a twentieth of the sum lavished on the Thespian Car.[42]

The OND also neglected to impart the most basic skills of reading and writing, even though adult illiteracy rates (for persons over the age of forty) averaged some 30 percent nationwide in 1931, rising to 60–70 percent in the South. Although illiteracy rates did decline through the second decade of fascist rule, this was largely a result of the increased effectiveness of the elementary school system. The OND itself sponsored only 341 courses for illiterates or semiliterates in 1931 and 241 in 1932, whereas in 1933, 276 were conducted, conferring altogether some 10,000 certificates of reading proficiency. In 1937, 273 courses were reportedly offered with a total attendance of 7,030.[43] Its predominantly urban membership may well have been more literate than the national average, but it is clear that the OND did not perceive the *dopolavoro* as an appropriate setting for conducting literacy programs.

The character of the instructional programs set up under OND auspices similarly indicated the disparity between the technocratic ideal of the Nationalists and its fascist realization. Modern educational systems, as Gramsci commented in his *Prison Notebooks*, have tended to abandon the integrated nineteenth-century ideal of education, reinforcing the separation between a highly instrumental and specialized instruction in skills from the critical values at least implicit in education.[44] The fascists had in one respect set themselves against this trend by their efforts to inject politics into skill training – indeed, the very idea that technical instruction would lend itself so readily to such ideological manipulation was doubtless reinforced by the humanistic vocation of so many of the regime's cultural organizers. In practice, however, the very lack of an articulated conception of the importance of technical instruction in an industrializing society accentuated a narrowly instrumental organization of the instructional system. The OND, having absorbed a broad range of institutions, naturally construed instruction in a variety of ways: In the municipal schools, it was conceived as a public service, in certain lay and religious undertakings as a philanthropic initiative for the "uplift of the urban masses," in schools and training courses sponsored by industrial and commercial firms and government offices – by far the most numerous – strictly in function of career advance within that particular enterprise. In other words, instruction, insofar as it was available, was highly specialized, so much so that it prevented employees from easily seeking out new positions. In this way, it reinforced the immobility of the labor force, precisely at a time when the changing structure of the economy demanded increasingly versatile workers.

The demand for vocational instruction was in fact accentuated in the stagnant economy of the thirties. Syndicalist organizers repeatedly noted that the crisis had increased the need for adult instructional programs as it was unskilled workers who were most severely affected by the layoffs.[45] Industrial spokesmen, too, especially those for smaller firms unable to afford their own skill centers, called for an increase in training programs. The demand for skilled workers was heightened in 1934–5 when the machine industries, revived by armaments orders for the Ethiopian campaign, began to rehire. Even the Fiat management, which operated its own well-organized factory schools, complained that it was unable to find sufficient numbers of qualified workers.[46]

The OND's lack of response to what the Fiat management characterized in 1935 as a "problem of national dimensions"[47] in effect reflected policy choices that had been made as early as 1930–1. Opposing the trade unions, which claimed that with vocational instruction the worker would be rendered "a conscious element of production, with a keen desire to make progress and with a thorough grasp of his contribution to the productive process,"[48] the OND concluded that the problem of worker pacification was not subject to resolution by means of advance through the skill hierarchy or by promotion on the job. It was left to the fascist trade unions to establish special *scuole sindacali* and to conclude a series of agreements with industrial employers that provided special bonuses for workers engaged in training programs, regulated skill categories, and ensured the recognition of training certification in pay scales and job classifications.[49]

The return to traditions

Clearly rejecting a role in the development of a technological culture, the OND turned its organizational energies and ideological strategems toward sustaining those very folk traditions that were gradually disappearing with the spread of literacy, urbanization, and improved communications. This so-called return to traditions was first announced by Beretta in 1929,[50] when the regime, in its concern to reassure the crisis-stricken agricultural sector that its interests were being safeguarded, began to denounce the perils of urbanism and to defend sound rural virtues. By the early thirties the OND had become the leading celebrant of folk values, virtually ceasing its efforts to engender a more sophisticated identification with the fascist precepts. The term "popular culture," which was adopted by OND planners in the twenties to designate essentially modern cultural pastimes, came, at least until 1936, to be identified almost exclusively with folk traditions – whether genuine cultural survivals of the preindustrial community, long-extinct customs exhumed by diligent fascist ethnographers, or the many pseudo-popular festivities choreographed by the OND itself.

The apparent contradiction between the archaism and irrationality of folk custom and the commonly accepted notions of civil progress were reconciled by spokesmen in their explanations of the "genuine educational functions" of popular traditions. Beretta staunchly defended the "public utility" of popular customs against those "students of social pedagogy" who persisted in believing that they "constituted ancient and useless fossils that simply retarded the evolution of nations."[51] True education, now redefined to suit the reactionary social ideals of the regime, should not seek "to level what was impossible to level" nor to destroy the "perennial beauty of the race." When traditional customs, beliefs, and usages were "subjected to the unifying action of modern civilization," with its "tendency to standardize men and manners as if they were machines or implements," the national order inevitably deteriorated. A socially valuable education should have as its primary aim the retention of those traditions that lend cohesiveness to a nation and individuality to its people. Such national values had to be felt before being understood.

"To *educate* even before beginning to *instruct*"; such, in Beretta's words, was the OND's intention as it sought to "revive the intimate character of traditions."[52] As the "People" was inspired with a "devotion to the past," so folk traditions would be able to "carry out their true and effective social functions."[53]

In this way, according to Beretta, the masses would be given the possibility of "realizing their own unique individuality." Folk arts, religious cults, superstitions, legends – all of the manifestations of traditional folk culture – allowed the people to express their true natural emotions: "jubilation, exaltation, rejoicing, contrition, faith, sometimes fanaticism, as well as satire." As antidotes to the constraints of modern life with its routinized work habits, they would be granted at least an illusion of freedom in compensation for a real loss of autonomy. Even so, as the nationalist Bodrero stressed, folk festivities were not to be construed as mere "distractions tending to make the people forget the burden of their duties"; rather, they were "lofty means for their elevation." Indeed, if Bodrero were to be believed, they were the major means by which the Italian proletariat might understand its equal status in a higher "racial" unity. The restoration of traditions would finally "free the working man from his obsession with the difference between rich and poor" by placing within his reach "those many spiritual valuables that could not conceivably be acquired by wealth – including not least of all that pride in belonging to the Italian race, which is in itself an enviable acquisition." Once acquainted with "the natural and genuine treasures of popular art" and the "myriad charming local customs," the common man would "recognize that he possessed something the rich did not." The moral effect of the revived festivities would be immediate, their communal enactment and ritual forms "accustoming the people to order, to discipline, to feel the joy of their labors and the vigor of their bodies, securing them from idleness, frivolity, and vice."[54]

Having designated folk manifestations as the one cultural pastime where the people ostensibly gave spontaneous and free expression to its individuality, the OND tended naturally to obscure the degree to which it was actually involved in their revival. Sometimes it took full credit; more frequently, it emphasized that the "reflowering" of popular traditions responded to a "new spiritual need" and thus had not been "provoked artificially": "Judicious and vigilant propaganda" had sufficed to restore the "splendor of the past."[55] The reappearance of historical processions and religious cortèges, celebrated with triumphal floats, ceremonial ships, funerary biers, litters, lilies, fronds, candelabra, and plastic images was "in itself a manifestation of the innate religious devotion and patriotism of the people."[56]

In fact, however, folk ceremonial had in large part fallen into desuetude. Familiarity with urban habits through emigration, travel, the press, and military service had led – even in remote rural areas – to the replacement of customary dress by sober work garb.[57] Relatively few of the resplendent municipal festivals, at their peak in the late eighteenth century when sponsored by the royal courts and organized by local guilds, had survived into the postwar period, especially in the northern industrial towns. Those that remained had lost their traditional luster, through lack of municipal funding or public interest. The revival of traditions therefore required considerable artifice.

"No means has been neglected," acknowledged Beretta, to "utilize

Fascist Labor Day festivities on April 21, the so-called day of the Birth of Rome: the regime's substitute for the traditional socialist May Day outing; here the Vercelli Dopolavoro's outing to Piccolo San Bernardo, 1932. *Source:* OND, *I dopolavoro aziendali in Italia* (Rome, 1938).

popular traditions in a dignified way for purposes of national education." Beginning in 1928, folklore sections were set up within each provincial board, their organization entrusted to persons with "true competence," "profound knowledge" of local customs, and above all "a passionate interest" in the community heritage.[58] With the assistance of committees – made up of the traditional deputations responsible for managing municipal festivities, amateur historians, and ethnographers – the board sections sponsored meetings, competitions, and costume displays. The OND itself proved remarkably active, creating special choral groups (*camerate dei canterini*), organizing rustic bands playing traditional instruments, and promoting over 200 dramatic societies featuring plays in dialect, the most prominent among them being the Ruzzantini of Padua, which specialized in the works of the sixteenth-century popular dramatist Angelo Beolco, called il Ruzzante. The mass media were used extensively to popularize folk music and dances. The OND recorded popular songs for radio transmission, as

204

well as cooperating with the Istituto Luce in producing a series of sound films of the Canterini groups of the Romagna and Sicily; a widely distributed film, *La sentinella della patria*, portrayed the essential *Italianità* of the long-disputed northeastern border regions.[59] Although the OND made no pretense of engaging in "scientific activity," it nevertheless promoted the foundation of regional ethnographic museums, furnished them with local ethnographic lore and facsimiles of local costumes collected by its provincial boards.

In this one endeavor at least the OND obtained the full support of academic culture. Although the more qualified intellectuals were generally reluctant to involve themselves in strictly educational programs, they could easily endorse this "return to traditions." Folk culture represented a heritage free of the deforming influence of foreign ideologies.[60] Even when unabashedly manipulated for propagandistic pur-

Reaching out to the people: summer dance of the Dopolavoro of Collestatte, 1938.
Source: OND, *I dopolavoro aziendali in Italia* (Rome, 1938).

205

poses, it could still be perceived as a serious cultural form. Reenacted as living ceremonies by a robust populace, folk customs provided what for upper-class intellectuals was a comforting image – that of "the people" as the repository and bearer of true national virtues; for a positivist ethnographer like D'Ancona, who dominated the discipline under fascism, the original *gens* was indeed the very fount of cultural production, possessing a creative capacity lost in the modern popular classes. But whatever their specific school, ethnographers displayed their own class-deformed conceptions of the "people" and "culture" with what the cultural anthropologist Ernesto De Martino later characterized as a "most instructive ingenuousness."[61] Thus leading ethnographers, most prominently Raffaele Corso, editor of the scholarly journal *Folklore* and Professor of Colonial Ethnography at the University of Naples, put scholarship at the service of propaganda in contributing to *Gente nostra*, or serving on juries set up by the OND to judge the authenticity of reconstructed rustic costumes and dances. The National Committee for Popular Traditions, founded by Professor Paolo Toschi of Florence, served similarly as a cultural liaison between ethnographers and OND organizers. Its journal, *Lares*, founded in 1932 to promote scientific inquiry into folk custom, was jointly sponsored by the OND and demonstrated with scholarly precision the academic respectability of the fascist revival of folk culture.[62]

The event hailed by the OND as its "first manifestation of national propaganda"[63] was a giant costume rally held in Venice in August–September of 1928. The rally, initially conceived as a costume display for the Three Venices to demonstrate the distinctiveness of the region's people from the bordering populations of Teutons and Slovenes, was taken as an occasion to reaffirm the ethnic unity of the nation as a whole.[64] Its overriding purpose, in the words of the presiding officials, was to familiarize Italians with the "true Italy," personified in the 11,000 costumed peasants who, on 18–19 August and again on 8–9 September, paraded through Piazza San Marco in elaborate dress. Beyond evoking the "simple rural Italy, which cherished and preserved Italian traditions," the festival had a practical aim in fostering the reconstruction and use of folk costumes in daily life. In preparation for the rally, local artisans and ethnographers had been instructed to create a "model rustic costume, inspired by local motifs, yet adapted to modern work conditions so that it would be adopted where the traditional costume had disappeared forever."[65] This goal was not achieved by the overly fashion-conscious designs, most of which lacked authenticity and usefulness – as the jury acknowledged.[66] To the regret of the most adamant traditionalists, costumes were hardly acceptable as habitual dress, although with assiduous prompting they were adopted in religious and civic ceremonies of all kinds.

In a society where dress closely reflected the social status of the wearer, the widespread use of costume performed significant social and ideological functions. Dressing up was both a diversion from daily drudgery and a mode of affirming personal dignity, especially for those who could neither afford bourgeois fashion nor attain party uniform. The OND capitalized on this desire for ostentation, a desire further stimulated by the regime's own obsession with uniform. Decked out in the finery of an updated "traditional" dress, no longer the sign of civic backwardness, peasants and artisans were endowed with social dignity as participants and protagonists in the numerous folk festivities. In this sense the folk costume served as the "official dress," so to speak, of *dopolavoristi*, who, alone among the organized fascist groups, had no special uniform of their own.

The pictorial iconography of fascism quickly absorbed the revived folk costumes as images of national virtues. The comely peasant women who adorned the covers of *Gente nostra*, together with the sturdy peasant men who were "so mirthful, yet so indefatigable in their work and so sober and thrifty in their habits," symbolized "the People," whose costumes, in Corso's words, expressed that "passion and aesthetic sense" that "beautifies their existence even amid the daily misery and drudgery of their lives."[67] An essentially desolate world – and an unfamiliar one for most urban dwellers – was thus transformed into a rural haven; its undeniable but never-depicted hardships glossed over by an image of rejuvenating nature; its virtues, personified in solid patriarchs and "rural housewives," to be emulated by a promiscuous and frenzied urban world.

In 1930 the OND was instructed by the PNF to organize harvest and work festivals[68] as a means of promoting artisan and agriculture-based industries. As OND propaganda stressed, any effective protection of jobs had to be accompanied by the preservation of the traditions associated with them. The festivals were organized to reevoke the spirit of the rural community or the unity of the craft association in which professional activities and group social manifestations were closely intertwined. Whereas Tree Day, Fruit Day, Grape Day, and Mulberry Day were all declared to be minor national holidays, and as such to be organized nationwide, each single festival was celebrated according to specific local customs, generally using ritual forms derived from the traditional harvest festival or peasant *sagra*. Much emphasis was put on the pagan–Christian, that is, the nonclerical origins of such festivities in bacchanalian or dionysian fertility rites.

The overwhelming majority of such festivities were celebrated in rural towns and villages. In the countryside surrounding Rome, the months of August through October were marked by numerous fairs sponsored by the city's Dopolavoro dell'Urbe: feting peaches at Castelgandolfo, grapes at Marino, strawberries at Nemi, apples at Nerviano, vines at Ostia. At Marino a fountain set up in the central square flowed with wine, and grape clusters were freely distributed. The ceremonies generally incorporated symbols of traditional municipal solidarity. Thus in Marino the procession was held in honor of the town patron, Our Lady of the Rosary, and included the triumphal display of its historical trophy, which, according to local legend, had been captured from the Turks at the Battle of Lepanto by Marcantonio Colonna.[69] Such modern notes as a lottery and the electrical illumination of the public square, designed to attract tourists and thereby involve a larger public within the community circle, marked the transformation of traditional rustic fete into modern consumer spectacle.

In urban centers celebrations appropriating the forms of the harvest, although they evoked the solidarity of rural community, were manifestly consumer oriented. At Bergamo, the center of Italy's most important silk-producing province, the silk *sagra* was celebrated as called for by tradition one early summer Sunday when the silk cocoons had just been harvested and the peasant families were preparing to bring them to market. The festivities themselves centered around the merchandise fair in the sumptuous Frizzoni Palace, with displays of the finest artisan productions of chiffons, taffetas, and crepes; for the year 1934 the highlight of the display consisted of the presentation for public viewing – and potential purchase – of a particularly elegant silk blackshirt.[70] Even Milan, the nation's most modern city, had its version of Fruit Day, sponsored in 1934 by the Aeronautics Exposition. For the occasion the proper rural atmosphere was recreated within the city by importing contingents of costumed rustics from the surrounding provinces: The union of urban technology and rural fecundity was self-consciously celebrated in a central square by erecting an enormous iron scaffolding shaped in the futuristic form of the Littorial *fascio* and decorated with 1,000 kilograms of fresh fruit.[71]

Arts and crafts shows performed not dissimilar functions in attempting to reassociate the craftsman and his product in a celebratory and often distinctly nationalistic atmosphere. Bolzano, as the northernmost outpost of *Italianità*, was the site selected in 1930 for the first National Exposition of Arts and Crafts; the 50,000 objects exhibited there were advertised as "typical manifestations of the skill and versatility of the Italian race."[72] Numerous similar shows held at the regional and pro-

vincial level were devoted to glorifying artisan existence. The show
of art and rural craft that opened in the tiny Romagnuole town of
Voltana on 5 August 1931 took place in three rooms of the local nursery
school and, according to Rignani, who was one of its first visitors,
displayed furnishings, fabrics, pottery, pictures, and drawings, as well
as artifacts of all kinds from the surrounding province of Ravenna.[73]
The craft show for the region of Sicily held in Catania in 1934 was
devoted to shepherd's art and to the decoration of work tools as
"expressions of individuality and inventiveness."[74] Even the lowliest
occupations were dignified in this way: Catania's annual patron saint's
festival in 1937 featured among other attractions a special contest
among street vendors for the best hawker's cry.[75]

It cannot be shown whether such displays actually afforded spectators a measure of ideological reassurance that industrial modernization threatening the livelihood of the small producer and the autonomy and spontaneity of the individual was indeed being forestalled.
For the numerous visitors, especially in small towns, many of whom
were themselves of recent rural extraction, these shows were nevertheless a major cultural event. At Voltana, Rignani recalled, the towns-
people were "very interested" in this first review of local tradition and
"especially admiring" of the paraphernalia of the peasant "Al Mas-
serei": the wagons and oxcarts and the utensils (*caveie*) of all periods
and styles.[76] For the profascist ethnographer Emma Bona, the "most
agreeable aspect" of the thirty major provincial and regional shows
organized by the OND from 1930 to 1940 was the "passionate attendance" of the "people," who within the context of the shows themselves
repeatedly explained to the collectors the meaning and use of certain
artifacts and the traditions associated with them.[77]

The OND was at its most inventive when stage-managing the annual
municipal festivals and patron saint's days. Frequently the local organizing committees joined the OND. Otherwise, where festivals
played a particularly important role in civic life, as in Naples and
Rome, the provincial boards themselves took complete charge of the
manifestations, developing them on a new and more splendid basis.
With the backing of the OND and frequently with the support of local
chambers of commerce, which viewed the festivals as optimum means
of boosting tourist trade, additional funds were channeled into the
annual celebrations to such an extent that their preparation took on
the semblance of small-scale public works projects. By the mid-thirties,
all of the major cities were celebrating several resplendent festivals
including neighborhood festivals, which were frequently invested with
municipal pomp. Rome celebrated, among others, the festival of Saint

The culture of consent: mass organization in fascist Italy

John and the neighborhood festival of Noiantri; Florence had the Cricket festival, the festivals of San Rocco and the Patron Saint John, as well as the Easter celebration of the Scoppio del Carro; Naples, in Beretta's words, "let no religious anniversary pass by without some sort of festivity,"[78] whereas in Siena the renowned Palio was reinvigorated with numerous neighborhood fetes; Venice resumed its celebration of the festival of the Lagoons and Lido, and almost all of the seaboard towns held festivals in honor of the sea.

Festivities were choreographed to involve the greatest possible civic participation. The central event – usually a procession – was truly spectacular, complete with displays of cult figures, costumed peasants, caparisoned horses and oxen, allegorical floats, or, as in Venice and the other seaside towns, regattas with illuminated boats.[79] Numerous side events served to generate even more activity. Thus the Barbary races customary in many towns were updated in the form of cycling events, gymnastics contests, and soccer matches. The committees also sponsored contests for decorated booths, window displays, and for the ornamentation of candles. The public was further encouraged to take part in the reenactments of local legends that frequently commemorated either a heroic defense against or a miraculous rescue from a "hereditary enemy": the French were symbolically attacked in many small towns of Sicily, where the Sicilian Vespers of 1282 had entered into folk myth; bands of Turks were routed in ceremonies in towns along the Adriatic and southern Mediterranean seaboards; or feudal tyrants were defeated by the just wrath of outraged villagers in simulated battles. In Arezzo, on the day of the Joust of the Saracens, the city center was draped with hangings and banners to remind citizens of the chivalric traditions and the boldness, pride, and agility of their heroic antecedents. When suitable indigenous legends were unavailable, national myths were conjured up with fanciful scenarios: At Genoa one year the Dopolavoro had portworkers restaging the departure of Garibaldi's Thousand from the nearby village of Quarto, while during the festival of Piedigrotta at Naples, boatloads of fishermen set out to retrace Aeneas's route to Rome.

The OND not only respected the religious origin and nature of popular festivals and patron saints' days, but even fostered the religious fanaticism that sometimes characterized such manifestations. In areas of socialist and republican penetration especially, organizers readily capitalized on the divisions that had arisen between Catholic belief and a powerful anticlericalism, exploiting popular religiosity with the recognition that veneration for the traditional cult might be transferred to the new fascist order. This purpose was explicit in the fascist embel-

210

lishment on the festival of Noiantri in the artisan neighborhood of Trastevere in Rome. The celebration, originally a day-long event organized around the transfer of the Holy Image of the Madonna del Carmine to the church of San Crisogono, honored the neighborhood's protectoress, while at the same time marking the proud industriousness that distinguished this district on the right bank of the Tiber from other areas of Rome. In the late nineteenth century, this essentially religious characterization of the community's identity had gradually been superseded by a more secular consciousness; in the three decades after Rome became the capital, the procession had fallen into disuse. It was revived, and then only in a minimal way, in 1900, apparently to satisfy devout women parishioners – the men, that day, republican and intransigently anticlerical, withdrew to drink outside the nearby walls of the city. As socialist sentiment mounted in the neighborhood, competing processions were organized; one in 1905, beginning in Piazza Mastai and celebrating the taking of the Bastille, led to a pitched battle between priests and socialists from the nearby Aurora Club. Members of the Giordano Bruno and Tavani Arquati societies joined the counterdemonstration in 1907, drowning out the processional hymns with the Workers' Anthem.[80]

The neighborhood had put up such a strong resistance to the entrance of the *squadristi* in Rome in 1922 that fascist authorities subsequently were particularly solicitous of its pacification and welfare. The decision to organize a cycle of civic ceremonies alongside the original religious ceremonial was thus supported by Mussolini himself, who in 1927 personally authorized the use of special police funds for the purpose.[81] After 1927, the day-long festivity was transformed into a week-long midsummer festival in which Catholic ritual was fused with fascist ceremonial forms. The neighborhood fascist club, "Duilio Guardabassi," counseled by a local festival committee formed of merchants and fascist notables, was naturally concerned to find a "type" of festival organization acceptable to this refractory community. Accordingly, the new festivity had none of the pagan religiosity of the Palermitan Festival of Santa Rosalia, or the pandemonium of the Neapolitan Piedigrotta. Nor did it have the chaotic merrymaking of the Roman Saint John's Day, which was reorganized under the presidency of the Dopolavoro of the Urbe's "Righetto" Santamaria "to show off, to invent the unthinkable, to exaggerate beyond all bounds in order to impress the public."[82] The Festival of Noiantri still referred to the traditions of the neighborhood; among the major events were a commercial fair to revitalize the depressed artisan economy, a light show, plays in dialect, music, songs, "healthy and jocund visits" to the many local taverns, the posing of wreaths at a neighborhood monument in honor of the Sharpshooters (Bersaglieri) of Sciara-Sciat, and commemorations of Trastevere's own poet Belli, of "Er Pittor de Trastevere" Bartolomeo Pinelli, and, of course, of the local fascist "martyr" Guardabassi. The unifying note was nevertheless religious, from the opening processions and high mass attended by the city's most eminent officials to the fifty-foot-long banner that, draped over the archway entrance, declared in local dialect that the neighborhood was now under the beneficent dual guardianship of the Madonna and the Duce:

Trastevere, Trastevere	Trastevere, Trastevere
Brilli de nôva luce	Shining with new light
Ciaì la Madonna e'r Duce	The Madonna and the Duce
Che vejono su te.[83]	Keep you in their sight

More commonly, the fusion of Catholic ritual and secular celebration was achieved in the ceremonial forms themselves. In the ritual processions, side by side with the cult figures, candelabra, sarcophagi, and fronds might be found – if not the blackshirts – children outfitted in the uniforms of the Balilla, portrait effigies of the Duce, and the processional band playing "Giovinezza."[84] Overt symbols of the fascist order did not have to be present, however, for the manifestations to be construed as testimonies of awakened civic sentiment. The *trecento* revival held in the Oltrarno district of Florence in conjunction with the Festa of San Rocco in 1929 was celebrated – according to one contemporary description – with an unusual procession comprised of soldiers bearing standards and pikes, armored mace-bearers and pages, followed by ecclesiastics in full ceremonial dress chanting the psalms: The "mystical purity" of their chants symbolized for the observer that "arms and faith, wielded together, forge the greatness of nations."[85]

Whenever opportune, this syncretism of traditional and modern was embellished with social messages, if not outright celebrations of fascism's self-proclaimed achievements. A special contest with prizes of 2,000 lire was held annually at the Festa of Noiantri for the family with the most numerous offspring. Allegorical floats frequently represented themes from political life – the Battle of Grain or the fertility of Italy under fascist rule – or, as at the Roman festival of Saint John in 1934, illustrations of the slogan "Rome, Lighthouse of the World" with exquisitely constructed warships and factories. The Palermitan Festival of Santa Rosalia was celebrated in 1935 with a new fascist gloss when the OND sound truck toured the surrounding province with the film *Vecchia guardia*. The Neapolitan Festival of Piedigrotta, expanded in

1935 on the occasion of the mobilization for the war in Ethiopia, marked, according to OND reportage, the "genial alliance" between the "new Italy and the spirit of a most poetic people, whose songs exercise a suggestive sway over the masses." The main event consisted appropriately enough of a song festival that featured – in addition to a studied revival of tunes from the first unfortunate African campaigns of 1896 – a contest to refurbish the old repertory with a racist song incorporating the name of Haile Selassie; its aesthetic appropriateness was justified by Chiarelli, who noted that Haile Selassie was "a phonogenic name, easy to rhyme, and with a perfect last syllable for closing a strophe."[86]

The revival of carnival festivities was particularly appropriate in the austere depression years. The frenzied atmosphere of carnival time appears to have been deliberately stimulated by the local festival committees, so as to provide – as was true in mass spectator sports – a public catharsis in organized chaos. At Ivrea the Dopolavoro, with the aid of the local historical society, re-created a symbolic ceremony celebrated with great public din, in which the populace rebelled against arrogant feudal lords; at Novara the festival concluded according to tradition with the ritual burning in effigy of King Biscuit V, while at Syracuse the celebration culminated with the customary cremation of Carnival.[87] At Vercelli, organizers judged the public response to the return in 1934 of Bicciolano and his beautiful Majn to be "quite satisfactory," especially considering that he seemingly had been banished by the populace forever in the wake of the great crisis of 1898.[88] Viareggio's already famous carnival was considerably enlarged in 1934 by allegorical floats from all of the Tuscan provinces, the greatly increased crowds participating in the final all-night masked balls.

In keeping with carnival traditions, the OND had abandoned its strictures against public dancing in the *dopolavoro* in 1931; masked balls were authorized, it was affirmed, for the "sole purpose of providing *dopolavoristi* and their families with the proper amount of diversion."[89] The public feasts, which by custom had marked pre-Lenten rites, appear to have been celebrated with unusual gusto – and not a little self-consciousness as to their original social functions. At Verona in 1932 the traditional Bacchanal of the Gnoccho, which ended with the public cooking of gnocchi, was further celebrated by the town's Dopolavoro Corridoni with a special free repast for 300 of its impoverished citizens. Similarly, in the Varese, a procession of cooks carrying fifty large cauldrons concluded with a free distribution of bean and bacon soup, while in Alessandria thirty stalwart chefs concocted for public consumption a polenta weighing eighty kilograms and an omelette of 1,000 eggs. Not infrequently in the Veneto the traditional distribution of token portions of polenta and mortadella was followed by the distribution of somewhat more substantial food rations to the poor and unemployed.[90]

The overwhelmingly local and regional nature of these manifestations reinforcing, at least in appearance, the solidarity and self-consciousness of specific communities, in some respects conflicted with the essentially national orientation of the fascist regime. Encouragement of popular identification with the state, the nation, or race was – no matter how ancient the resurrected ceremony – hardly to be found in a "revival of traditions" based on regional or local distinctiveness. Regionalism itself, in its historical and political connotations, was associated with the divisions that had obstructed the Risorgimento. Moreover, in the eyes of many nationalists, it was synonymous with the democratic federalist programs of the postunification period, or worse, the proposals for decentralization advanced by socialists and *popolari* in the postwar years. Fascism, as Bodrero emphasized, had "no intention of reevoking or stimulating regionalism of this kind."[91] Purified of any inherited political significance, however, the regional ethnocentrism fostered by the "return to traditions," parochial and chauvinistic as it was, offered to the regime a partially acceptable surrogate for national allegiance, one infinitely preferable to class identification or what Bodrero dismissed as the "pernicious particularism of age-old political rivalries."

Fascist ethnographers and cultural organizers nevertheless attempted to extract from the myriad local customs some national or quasi-national overtones: the popular esthetic sense displayed in folk costumes; the religious fervor of patron saints' days; the crèche, pointedly contrasted with the Christmas tree of the "barbaric" North; the celebration of the Epiphany appropriately nationalized as the Befana Fascista. Beyond this, unity was molded out of the diversity of regional customs by numerous national shows.

The marriage of the heir to the throne, Humbert of Savoy, to the Belgian Princess Maria José in January 1930 was, although not a specifically fascist ceremony, seized on as a moment to develop a truly national festivity. The vast costume procession, "sponsored" by the head of government, was as if designed to evoke a new, yet semifeudal national hierarchy, with the fascist dignitaries, led by Turati (vassals to the royal dynasty), heading up a two-mile-long nuptial cortège composed of 300 contingents of lavishly costumed provincials.[92] As they passed beneath the reviewing stand in Piazza Quirinale, where the royal couple was ensconced beside the crowned heads of Europe, the peasant groups paid homage by depositing "gifts of the land": sheaves of grain, floral wreaths, baskets of fruit. Propitiary rites for the couple were then celebrated according to the local customs of the regional delegations: by some with candle-lit parades, by others with the release of augury doves, or with group dances or choral recitations of marriage songs. Combining as they did traditional peasant costumes, the military regalia of the House of Savoy, and the sober fascist uniforms, the images of the ceremony – among the most publicized national events before the Ethiopian campaign – suggested that for a brief instant the full fusion of popular customs, dynastic traditions, and fascist ritual had been achieved.

As the most spontaneous of activities organized by the regime, at least in their actual conduct, the revived festivities constituted a sphere where popular acceptance, but also rejection and even subversion, might be most freely displayed. Fascist accounts naturally emphasized the wholeheartedness of the people's response to the "return to traditions," and certain manifestations – as, for example, the *dopolavoro* INA's prize-winning Saint John's Day float for 1930 showing the *Ur-dopolavoristi* Adam and Eve astride a mastodon[93] – certainly displayed a creatively popular element in the highly manipulated *cultura dopo-lavoristica*. Whether the regime would have tolerated the translation of such self-irony into political satire seems most doubtful, however; the preparation of festivities was certainly far too well policed to allow the kind of pornographic exuberance displayed by the mid-eighteenth-century Neapolitan *popolino* in priapic images on masques and floats, an impulse that appalled public authorities and genteel society but was quite uncontrollable because of the breakdown of guild authority and Bourbon absolutism. Nevertheless, fascist festivities were the occasion for protests of sorts: some passive in the form of the withdrawal of participation that the police noted in Turin in the late thirties; some more overt in the "savage brutality of peasant bombardments" that, according to public officials in Pavia, had disrupted the distribution of grapes at the annual festival in 1933.[94] This particular popular "invention," whose main target was the assembled officialdom in the reviewing stand, obviously subverted the original fascist purpose behind the event: to consume peaceably and in a celebratory way the excess grape production that was ruining farmers by driving down market prices. But the very act of grape throwing was itself ritualized and so mediated through the festival form that it was completely cut off from any effective organized resistance to fascism. As such it could hardly

be characterized as in any way prepolitical, but rather primitively child-
ish, an act of insubordination within a structure that had been sub-
stantially accepted by the participants.

The politics of diversion

Perhaps the most striking aspect of the content of the *cultura dopolavoristica* as it emerged during the thirties was the absence of any
overt political appeals. Organization, more commonly than not, substituted for a positive cultural policy, whereas activity – however trivial
– served to compensate for the lack of explicit or consistent political
direction. From this perspective, the *cultura dopolavoristica* might be
understood better as a policy of diversion from political and social
concerns than as a cultural program designed to impart fascist
principles.

The diversionary effect was unquestionably most evident in sports.
By the mid-thirties sports, whether participatory or spectator, had
become a veritable obsession for tens of thousands of younger workers
enrolled in the fan clubs and sports sections affiliated with the OND.
Even the limited opportunities for social action provided in the trade
unions were eschewed for sports. The endless debates over the most
recent games and predictions for upcoming events were so time-con-
suming that syndicalist leaders remarked disconsolately on the virtual
impossibility of engaging young workers in syndical activities.

Similarly the movies, literature, and theater provided for consumption in the *dopolavoro* sections encouraged a form of cultural diversion
sanctioned by official policy. Costume epics and escapist sentimental
films presented their audiences with never-never lands of individual
happiness, artificially created worlds of mythical abundance, or, more
simply, with images of a satisfying and modest prosperity. The melodrama and farces of the amateur theater dealt with the humdrum,
with the trials and tribulations of a placid petty bourgeoisie far removed
from the imperialist ambitions of *Romanità*. The literary contributions
to *Gente nostra* ranged from exotic tales of adventure and travel to
domestic fables with predictably happy endings. All found common
ground in escapist dreams.

The cinemas of the *dopolavoro*, like the commercial movie houses,
were supplied by the major film distributors. From 1919 onward, the
Italian market was dominated by foreign and especially American
films.[95] Despite some government assistance to the domestic film industry that began in the thirties, Italian movies through 1935 rarely
accounted for more than 15 percent of the films annually available on

the market. Even when the government sought to curb the showing of foreign films – first as a political gesture in retaliation against the Sanctions, then after 1937 as an economic measure toward autarchy – 80 percent of the films passed by the censorship board were still foreign, most of which were American.[96] When the government finally did intervene, it was primarily for economic reasons rather than to promote a specific cultural or political line. With the significant exception of films such as Blasetti's *Vecchia guardia* and *1860*, and Alessandrini's *Luciano Serra pilota* – all produced in the second half of the decade – the fewer foreign imports were supplemented by an increased Italian production of films in the Hollywood style.

Most of the commercially available films subscribed to the conventions of the genre familiarly known as the "White Telephone," named after the white telephone of Jean Harlow film decors, which epitomized for Italian moviegoers the opulent chic of Hollywood and the escapist sentimental productions of Italy's counterpart, Cinecittà. The Italian versions, including most notably Mario Camerini's popular *Il signor Max* (1937), *Grandi magazzini* (1939), and *Gli uomini che mascalzoni* (1932), described a provincial world swept by the impelling passions of lovers' quarrels, small-time intrigues, and lottery victories.[97] They depicted the unpretentious aspirations of a lower middle class for comfortable livelihoods, security, and personal happiness, all of which conceived in the most individualist terms were readily satisfied with small gratifications.

Of the films made in what postwar critics have designated as the style of the *dopolavoro*, *Il signor Max* was the most significant in that it identified the ambience of the *dopolavoro* itself as symbolic of genuine popular social and cultural aspirations. Camerini, a foremost director of nonpolitical films, portrayed the futile attempts of a handsome newsvendor, Jonny, played by Vittorio De Sica, to enter the baffling world of high society by camouflaging himself in the fancy dress of the *alta borghesia*. Through this simplest of ruses, Jonny, decked out as the elegant Signor Max, is introduced to the luxuries of high society: the Casino of San Remo, the orchids and card games, international travel aboard trans-Atlantic liners. Impoverished by his adventures, he is soon forced to return to Rome, where, while attending his modest business, he encounters Loretta, his high-society paramour's maid. Denying that he is Signor Max, he begins to court her, seeking to sustain simultaneously his dual existence as elegant lady's man and sincere young lover. When both his mistress and her maid press for his attentions, he is forced finally to choose between frustrating aspirations and the security of his own class. In the end the two young

The culture of consent: mass organization in fascist Italy

lovers, Jonny and Loretta, find contentment in the ingenuous pastimes of the neighborhood *dopolavoro* and happiness ever after in a modest apartment, where the couple – reconciled to its real social milieu – settles down.

Although it might be argued that the escapist fantasies produced for commercial viewing conformed to, rather than shaped, popular aspirations, the same cannot be argued plausibly for the official media. No more than a third of radio broadcasting time was ever devoted to overtly political themes, while in the early thirties, before the regime tightened its control over the media, the amount was far less, with the bulk of radio time devoted to cultural programs, especially music of a popular nature, dance music, bands, regional folk music, light opera, and choral singing.[98] The content of the newsreels, produced by the Istituto Nazionale Luce, founded in 1924 and totally subsidized by the government, was not dissimilar. Only about 20 percent of the 61,416 meters of film footage produced in 1933 was devoted to propaganda films; another 19 percent was made into documentaries of a cultural nature;[99] of the remaining 60 percent presented in the form of the news shorts obligatory with every movie showing, most consisted of such scenes as trainloads of *dopolavoristi* en route from Rome to Littoria, children at play in the regime's seaside and mountain campsites, diversions such as motorboat racing, rhythm dancing, or folk festivals, and exotica in the form of American circuses or Austrian zoos.

The theatrical fare produced for the *dopolavoro* public was similarly devoid of explicit political themes. All of the one-act plays commissioned by the OND in 1929 to renew the repertory of amateur theater were moral tales, inspired by the conventions of a provincial and puritanical morality.[100] Ugo Falena's *Marriage of Arlecchino*, a banal imitation of the free-wheeling eighteenth-century commedia dell'arte, dramatized the encounter of two itinerant actors with a good-natured country priest. As the play unfolds, the priest's housekeeper, the kind-hearted yet irascible Emilia, discovers that the two are unmarried. Horrified that their promiscuity might desecrate the priestly abode, she informs the good father. He in turn presses them to get married, and when they resist he discloses his own illegitimate birth and the suffering of the child born out of wedlock. Overcome by emotion, the two actors consent to marry, a triumph of solid peasant morality over the corrupt mores of the urbanized harlequins. Oreste Poggio's *Un affare* used the conventions of the modern melodrama. Set in the petty bourgeois world of postwar Milan, the play recounts the trials of Margherita, a young woman of nouveau riche family, who in a moment of abandon in the closing months of the Great War had given herself to

218

her betrothed. Her passion is duly punished when he is killed in the Battle of Vittorio Veneto, but subsequently her honor is restored when she discloses her sin to a sympathetic young notary public who, as it turns out, is also a bankrupt count. With the marriage of his honor and her dowry, they are assured of a happy life ever after. The salon of the Countess Ghisela is the setting for Alessandro Varaldo's *Una scommessa*, which deals with the peccadilloes of courtesan life and the various wiles exercised by one young courtesan to arouse the jealousy of her frigidly aristocratic fiancé. She succeeds in her efforts; he becomes violently jealous, and the moral of the tale unfolds: Even aristocrats experience the same feelings of painful jealousy as plain folk.

The prizewinning entries in a short story contest held by the OND in 1929 for working class writers, although less polished, were replete with similar conventions.[101] Some of the stories were styled in the tradition of the tales of the *Decameron*, telling of popular wit and cunning, but altogether untainted by the ribaldry of the true *boccaccesco*. But the majority accepted the prevailing literary pieties. Antonio Mambelli, a Forlì mechanic, wrote of the fantasy-filled dream life of an Italian Walter Mitty; Mario Mancioli, a railroad employee from Padua, used his play *L'eterno donatore* to describe a stoic old peasant's unswerving loyalty to the land, faithfully transcribing in a precious Tuscan dialect the paternal denunciations of prodigal sons who had abandoned the land for the cheap diversions of the urban world.[102]

Admittedly, even when the OND sought to renew its repertory with plays of aesthetic or political distinction, it met with failure. The judges presiding over the 1930 contest for works for the Thespian Cars refused to award prizes to any of the 213 contestants on the grounds that they lacked sufficient artistic quality or political merit. None, they claimed, possessed the virtues of good propaganda by avoiding rhetoric or contrivance to "convey simply, clearly, and persuasively the new sense of life."[103] Those playwrights working in the traditional modes, they complained, were lacking in novelty or inspiration, thus suggesting that fascist achievements were insufficiently inspiring to generate a genuine popular literature. Because models from high culture were generally not encouraged for use in the *filodrammatici*, contestants were left with the trite rhetorical conventions of traditional melodrama and farce.

That even the plebeian litterateurs subscribed to the accepted conventions of the *cultura dopolavoristica* raises once again the question as to whether the petty strivings, frustrated expectations, and dreams of evasion commonly described were expressions of fascist ideology or simply the aspirations of their authors. The recurrent nature of the

219

themes suggests that they did indeed satisfy a petty bourgeois self-image. When encouraged by the OND, however, their themes were transformed into an officially sanctioned and highly publicized conformism, their implicit moralism was elevated into a pretentious and repressive public morality, and their personal visions of a happier life condoned as a politically acceptable social individualism. Appropriated as elements of official ideology, values that may well be described as quintessentially petty bourgeois received a public sanction. As such they pretended to a universal application they had neither claimed nor previously achieved in Italian society.

The petty bourgeois image of social relations purveyed through fascist cultural agencies was not immune to criticism, even from those who were otherwise cultural apologists for the regime. Fascist intellectuals, familiar with the French *cinéma-vérité* or the Soviet propaganda epic, condemned the Hollywood-influenced Italian film as both esthetically repugnant and politically unsound. Writing in Gentile's *Educazione fascista* in 1931, Anton Giulio Bragaglia, a leading film critic and theater director, deplored the persistent use by Italian directors of the "stale and standardized plots of the bourgeois comedy and American-style scripts with *femmes fatales.*"[104] Films, he stressed – citing the sociologist Ludwig Gumplowicz – should be used as a means of subtle social persuasion since "no other medium could so immediately sway the popular imagination." He held up for emulation the "marvelous works of Soviet propaganda," of Eisenstein, Pudovkin, Sutkevitch, and Dovshenko, which in his view effectively combined the highest artistic quality with a powerful propaganda message. The *Luce Cinegiornale*, he noted – like comparable Russian shorts of Vertov – selected the appropriate subjects: folklore, mass tourism, agricultural improvements, and sports. Italian directors, however, unlike their Russian counterparts, treated their subjects much too "dryly," failing sufficiently to editorialize about their material. Their audiences, as a result, were missing the newsreels' "profound" political significance as documents of novel collective experiences, perceiving them instead as innocuous, even laughable, diversions. The government, in Bragaglia's view, had to intervene more systematically, above all because the movie industry was capitalistic, and film-makers inevitably refused to experiment with those newer, riskier, and more politically sophisticated art forms that alone offered vehicles for expressing the new national spirit. Lacking incentives, directors would continue working in the traditional escapist mode. In the "battle between capital and intelligence" – he quoted René Clair – "intelligence would inevitably lose out."

Criticism of this kind, more persistent in the thirties with the heightened consciousness of a popular audience, which accompanied the populist strategy of "reaching out to the people," was subsequently – if only sporadically – reflected in the cultural directives of the OND. In 1933, for example, the agency announced peremptorily that amateur theaters could no longer choose works "associated with the bourgeois repertory, analytical, psychological, and thus antiquated and passé."[105] That summer, for the first time, the OND sponsored a contest to "modernize" the amateur theater repertory. Writers who expected to have their works considered were warned that "the trifling torments of petty bourgeois existence, the various endeavors to escape into an illusory better life . . . are altogether obsolescent and not corresponding to the vital needs of fascism."[106] The OND further reported the success of several new patriotic plays on the provincial circuit: Giuseppe Giambattini's *La prima ora*, drawing its inspiration from the March on Rome, was produced at Pola and Fiume; *Aquilotto* by Elia Lochman dramatizing the heroism of World War I pilots was put on at Bologna, Perugia, Verona, and Padua; G. Cucchetti's *Camicia rossa, camicia nera* reportedly received public acclamation when it toured the provinces of Verona, Venice, Rovigo, and Vicenza in 1933.[107]

But once the OND ceased recommending political works, interest waned. Normally, the bulk of plays produced consisted of melodramas or farces, and the preferred authorities were decidedly minor dramatists, protagonists of what Gramsci aptly called the "theater of insincerity";[108] they included authors as varied as the "naturalist" G. Giacosa and the playwright of the "grotesque," Rosso di San Secondo, and none of them demonstrated any particular interest in political thematics. The OND's own repertory for the annual tours of Thespian Cars was similarly selected with strict regard for "cultural and artistic merit";[109] in the year 1934 it was composed wholly of light comedies: S. Lopez's *La signora Rosa*; *Cicero*, a three-act comedy by Bonelli; Luigi Antonelli's *Il maestro*; *Serenata al vento* by Carlo Veneziani; *Equatore* by A. De Stefani, who was also a regular contributor to *Gente nostra*; and a prose rendition of *Lohengrin* by Aldo De Benedetti.[110]

Until the Ethiopian campaign there was no discussion of the content of a fascist popular art within OND circles. Beginning in May 1935, however, the editors of *Gente nostra*, recognizing the need to recall the masses from the fantasy world of sentimental comedies into the real world of national struggle, opened its columns to debate on cinema and theater. The contributions it received might best be characterized as the ingenuous proclamations of an exhilarated younger generation of intellectuals, inspired with the belief that enthusiasm alone could generate a new fascist culture. Contributors called for a "new mass theater," whose main protagonists, rather than being "the central focus of action," as in the traditional form, would serve as simple vehicles for the story line. Film directors similarly were admonished to produce truly popular epics:

> Photogenic women, "vamps," and "sex appeal," they belong to a different kind of film, the kind produced purely for diversion. We shall use the sunburnt faces of our peasants, of our workers, the healthy faces of our mothers.
>
> Let us encourage productions that examine labor in the fields and workshops; let us make a film that is closer to us and to the time we live in; with the people and for the people we shall give life to a new fascist film.[111]

By the spring of 1936 the proper thematic for a truly epic film was declared to be the "New Empire." Neither sentimental nor exotic, it would illustrate how fascism's "proletarian" ideal of colonial acquisition differed fundamentally from the anachronistic French and English notion of the "white man's burden."[112]

Gente nostra itself was used for the first time during the Ethiopian campaign as an organ for overt government political propaganda. Before then, occasional articles had dealt with colonialism – focusing, however, not on its political aspects, but rather on the pulchritude of native women and the exoticism of primitive customs.[113] When the Sanctions were imposed on Italy in November 1935, political cartoons suddenly appeared in *Gente nostra*, adopting an appropriately populist imagery to convey fascist aims to a mass public that had hitherto been left ignorant of high politics.[114] Italian war aims were couched in readily comprehensible terms: Italy was a proletarian nation, impoverished by the gluttony of plutocratic nations; these plutocracies, it was explained, had denied Italy its rightful place in the sun, despite the centuries of civilization, scarcity of natural resources, and abundant population that made it far more deserving. More specifically, who were the plutocracies? Grinning cowboys, dwarfish gendarmes, or Colonel Blimps, the latter caricatured as tight-fisted, high-handed tourists, picking their way through Italian ruins with disdainful condescension for a people reduced by its poverty to a servile status. What were Italy's intentions? Propaganda evoked a misplaced altruism. Italy, it would appear, was bent on a civilizing mission: The Negus had enslaved a Christian population that, starving and brutalized, eagerly awaited liberation. The gallantry of Italy's youth was fired by the picture of the exotic and oppressed Ethiopian maiden calling for deliverance. Once liberated and subjected to the ministrations of Italian culture and technology,

Ethiopia was destined to become a fertile land of prosperous settlers and happy natives, whereas Italy, its imperialist ambitions finally satisfied, would hold out a better life for its citizens. War – the ultimate diversionary strategy – lent itself well to the conventions of the diversionary tale.

Once the campaign was concluded, the debate over the contest of fascist popular culture disappeared together with the political cartoons from the pages of *Gente nostra*. Thereafter, the magazine occasionally would feature short stories referring explicitly to patriotic themes; and peasants or soldiers – rarely workers – appeared as protagonists. But, although the protagonists changed, the underlying values did not. The same petty bourgeois aspirations found as basic themes in earlier works were imputed to their more plebeian subjects. Film directors and authors continued to subscribe to accepted conventions, embellishing political themes with sentimentalism, rather than seeking to evoke a detached identification with the principles of fascism or with the new national collectivity.

That fascist low culture was essentially diversionary is not after all surprising. The full ideological assimilation of the popular classes into a new national consensus, which – as envisaged by fascist planners in the twenties – involved moral elevation, popular education, and vocational instruction, was in fact precluded by the very structure of the regime's cultural institutions. No amount of directives stipulating the content of a new "national" culture could be effective when the agencies of culture themselves, by reinforcing existing economic and social barriers, prevented their implementation. Youthful intellectuals, inspired during the Ethiopian campaign by their renewed faith in fascism's revolutionary possibilities, were no more successful than jaded OND functionaries: When seeking to apply the precepts of "reach out to the people" to the cultural domain, they too were frustrated by bureaucratic structures that, staffed by low-level cultural organizers, systematically segregated the intellectual elites from a mass public.

If not the unifying national culture aspired to by the younger generation, the *cultura dopolavoristica* nonetheless performed significant functions in legitimizing fascist rule. Although lacking the fundamental authenticity of "popular culture," fascist low culture did appropriate petty bourgeois ideological motifs, popular ritual forms, and, if only momentarily during the mid-thirties, a populist language with potential appeal to industrial workers. In this sense the *cultura dopolavoristica* mediated between "popular culture" and official ideology; it was responsive to – and at least partially an expression of – its popular audience, even while incorporating popular themes and forms as ele-

223

ments of official ideology. What had been essentially autonomous expressions of individual or group aspirations or prejudices were in this way transformed into cultural manifestations that were acceptable to, and to a certain extent supportive of, the dominant ideology.

The ideological inconsistency and slight political content of the *cultura dopolavoristica* perhaps belied its capacity to influence popular opinion. Cultural autarchy was unquestionably most complete at the lower levels of the society; ideological defenses were consequently weak. With the "coordination" of popular cultural institutions, workers were deprived of autonomous means of political expression and opportunities for contact with intellectuals on a more or less equal footing. They were cut off from the alternative sources of information available to the cultured elites through the foreign media and from the critical debates that were tolerated by the regime within intellectual circles. The petty bourgeois functionaries staffing the regime's cultural agencies were thus able to exercise a virtually uncontested authority over popular cultural manifestations. Susceptibility to the stultifying conformity they fostered varied, with workers with prior political experience proving most resistant. The petty bourgeois, that is, younger workers, and especially the peasants, whose previous contact with national political life had been highly sporadic, were far more impressionable. For an often ill-educated public, whose first introduction to national cultural and political events was mediated by fascist agencies, the terms of discourse were inevitably set by official ideology.

The fundamental eclecticism of *dopolavoro* pastimes, although an advantage in attracting a socially diversified audience, proved in the end highly disadvantageous in sustaining its support. As an essentially unstable cultural amalgam, fascist ideology required a monopoly if it was to retain its authority and credibility. Censorship to a certain degree protected it from the competition of more coherent ideological forms. The *cultura dopolavoristica*, however, contained within itself certain insoluble contradictions. The social attitudes it fostered – passivity, ignorance, individualism, traditionalism, evasion – were appropriate as long as the government's overriding concern was to ensure normality. They were compatible with bursts of uncritical enthusiasm, as evidenced at the time of the Ethiopian campaign. However, when the regime in the late thirties sought to sustain mobilization with a firmer identification with fascist principles, these same attitudes proved counterproductive: "A salubrious institution," as the *dopolavoro* was described by a former fascist, the journalist Emilio Radius, "yet a dangerous one for a regime seeking to mold the Italian people into a population of warriors."[115]

8

The limits of consent

Consent is as unstable as the sand formations on the edge of the sea.

B. Mussolini

The years between the close of the Ethiopian campaign and the outbreak of World War II present us with a series of seeming paradoxes. The period began with Mussolini apparently at the peak of his popularity, having just vindicated Italy's "proletarian" and "Roman" right to African colonies over the opposition of the "plutocratic" liberal democracies. Yet hardly a year later, the "exaggerated psychological exaltation" Morandi and other antifascists had observed during the seven-month campaign had degenerated into what police informers characterized as a "strange exhilaration," manifested not only in crowd rowdiness and rudeness toward fascist officials, but also in calls for a return to the ostensibly democratic *dicianovismo* of fascism's 1919 program and complaints over the regime's failure to act on any of its repeated promises for social reform.[1] By 1938, university students in the GUF had taken up the revolutionary slogans of the "first hour" and the fascist trade unions, responding to worker protests over inflation, after years of quiescence once again adopted a militant posture, seeking wage increases and recognition for the factory labor delegates. In September 1939, as fascist Italy's Nazi ally invaded Poland, public opinion, when not described as "discontent," was generally interpreted as "unresponsive," above all to the regime's militaristic bombast. After 1936, fascist propagandists repeatedly invoked the word "totalitarian" to characterize the fascist state, citing as evidence the centralization under the immediate authority of the Duce of the regime's mass organizations and the undeniably rapid increase in their extension and membership. Yet party activity in the provinces was reported to be increasingly "aimless," government inquiries exposed rampant corruption, and personnel of fascist mass organizations edured repeated shakeups, the most dramatic in October–November 1939, resulted in the ouster of Starace from the PNF secretaryship.

Was the fascist regime then on the verge of collapse by the time World War II started? "Crisis" is perhaps too strong a term for what were nonetheless obvious signs of instability. Nevertheless, it is clear, as Gramsci had so clearly perceived in 1926, that the conflicts arising within a totalizing system of rule were bound to reappear at the heart of the system itself, because they could find no other outlet for their expression.[2] Paradoxically, for a regime that had come to power over the shambles of the labor movement, the very organizations set up to suppress class conflicts forced it to an ever-increasing degree to respond to public opinion. To sustain a wartime economy required more than ever the active support of the working population. Whereas in 1926–7, the fascists had to create an entirely new organizational apparatus to generate such a support, there existed now one that in its extension at least was broad enough to mobilize practically all Italy. Yet this network, in addition to transmitting directives to the periphery, also relayed back to fascist officials the increasingly disturbing fluctuations in the public mood. The dictator himself may have dismissed out of hand all such expressions of popular disaffection – he had in any event long given up hope that the Italian "lambs" would ever become "wolves." What could not be ignored, however, was the frenetic political maneuvering that began as these discontents were exploited by the many competing groups within the regime itself to bolster their own particular interests. Thus by 1939, worker unrest in the big northern cities had led Catholic Action to revive its organizing efforts, undercutting the fascist neighborhood circles; it had caused some of the major employers to take their distance from the inefficient fascist federations and put all of their funds into operating their own self-enclosed social services; finally, it had aggravated the old rivalries between the fascist party and the fascist unions, with the PNF contending that syndicalist demagogy was provoking worker unrest, whereas the syndicalists claimed that the party was trying to "nazify" Italy by seeking to take control over trade union affairs.[3] Short of a full-scale war, there was no putting an end to these *beghe* or quarrels, for the regime now lacked any unifying domestic goals, such as were provided by the economic battles of 1926–7, the huge assistance effort mounted under the slogan "reach out to the people" in 1931–4, and the national defense against the Sanctions of 1935–6.

In this context, the very real limitations of the regime's mass organizations in rallying support for its policies were brought into focus. The "static acceptance" of the regime fostered by the OND's politically insipid policies was, as the fascists themselves belatedly recognized, fundamentally incompatible with that "dynamic expansionist and imperialist mentality"[4] more appropriate to the regime's foreign policy ambitions. The far-flung organization, previously so effective in engaging masses of production workers, clerical laborers, and peasants in officially sanctioned pastimes, now seemed to be an immensely unwieldy agency – "elephantine," as it was described by the political police in April 1937, "vaunting huge membership tallies and bountiful discounts for ski-lovers, *bocce* players, and movie-goers." But it conducted "no political propaganda whatsoever among the masses"; and consequently, it was increasingly incapable of diverting attention from the evident incompatibility between fascism's reckless militarism and its repeated, empty promises of social reform.[5]

Indeed, the contradictory relationship between the dictatorship and its mass base, "profound and immutable," as it was described by the PC d'I's leader Togliatti in 1934, had now been institutionalized, so to speak, within the organization itself, giving rise in the late thirties to a remarkable instability of form.[6] This was manifested not only in the regime's efforts, beginning in 1936, to codify the conduct of the organization – and which led to a further bureaucratization of the OND command – but also to an extraordinary dilation in the membership and repeated reshuffling of the top personnel. Already in July 1936, barely three months after the foundation of the Empire, Mussolini himself was apprised of "severe moral" and "alarming functional crisis" of the after-work organization. In a seven-page memorandum drawn up by his close advisor and friend, Ottavio Dinale, the Duce – who, deplorably "had to keep his eye on everything" (even the *dopolavoro*) – was informed that Puccetti, the new director of the OND, had uncovered administrative irregularities pervasive enough to warrant an audit of all records for the preceding decade.[7] Indictments for fraud were being drawn up against several former functionaries including the ex-director, Beretta. What truly worried Dinale, however, was the agency's "inexcusable" failure to adhere to its original goals: For several years, the organization had focused "almost exclusively" on theatricals and entertainments, to the virtual exclusion of education and social and economic initiatives. Its "absenteeism" in the economic sector was especially worrying in view of the government's renewed efforts to attain economic self-sufficiency. The "formidable strength" embodied in the organization was thus being wasted, Dinale concluded: If the regime was to capitalize effectively on the agency's "large popular base and capillary extension," it had necessarily to respond at all times to a "multiplicity of economic and political aims." Like other fascist reformers who repeatedly called for Mussolini to root out corruption in fascist bureaucracies, Dinale assumed that all past errors could be corrected by the appropriate administrative action. Specifically, he recommended that control be transferred from the party secretary to the President of the Council of Ministers – Mussolini himself – and that the technical council provided for by the 1925 statutes and dissolved in April 1927, when the PNF had taken command, be reinstituted for the purpose of supervising the agency.

Dinale's request for "energetic action" was speedily answered by the passage of a law modifying the OND's structure. The new statutes, promulgated on 24 May 1937, placed the agency under the direct control of the Duce; in reality, though, it continued to be presided over by the PNF secretary, who, as in the past, took all decisions regarding personnel and programs, delegating executive functions to a general director appointed with Mussolini's approval.[8] Although this new law thus introduced no substantive changes in administration, its real significance lay in its redefinition of the OND's juridical status. Article 4 recognized the "public utility" of the OND and granted it the same juridical and fiscal privileges of other branches of the state administration, exempting all of its events, even those open to the general public, from taxation. For all legal purposes, the OND had thereby become a public institution, subject solely to the head of state and lacking any juridical ties with the PNF. The statutes further clarified that properties confiscated under the fascist public security laws belonged by right to the OND and assured it an annual subsidy from the Ministry of the Corporations. By defining the OND by its real estate holdings and revenues, the measure had the curious effect of denying the value of the membership card. No mention was in fact made of membership, except to indicate that fees were to be used to defray operating costs; all citizens, it appeared, were now eligible to participate in this *public service*, although none of course had any say in its policies.[9] The law of May 1937, then, marked the consolidation of this mass recreational organization as a model totalitarian structure – at least in the fascist's sense of the term – with all of its local affiliates absorbed into the state apparatus. Barring a radical restructuring of the Italian state, this had the further effect of ensuring the OND's survival with or without a fascist government in power.

The OND, meanwhile, more and more bureaucratized, if somewhat less corrupt under Puccetti's leadership, was responsive neither to fascist aims nor to the wants of its constituents, devoting its energies to the lavish choreographic displays favored by Starace – displays that culminated appropriately with the inauguration of the OND's first national exposition in the Circus Maximus in September 1938. Local groups continued to amass new members: Altogether 800,000 between 1935 and 1937 and an additional 750,000 between 1937 and 1939, bringing the total to 3,831,331 on the eve of the war. But the vast majority of new members were entering into local groups that were, increasingly, fascist in name only. *Bettole* – dives – the disparaging word used by fascist social reformers fifteen years earlier to describe the socialist wine circles – now turned up in the inspectors' reports on rural meeting places; the moral tone of bourgeois city locales was if anything worse: Politics could not have been farther from the mind of the secretary of the OND in the resort town of Savona, who by 1940 had become so absorbed in operating the local casino that all other activities had come to a halt.[10] When the fascist government was forced finally to assess the nation's degree of military and economic preparedness following the invasion of Poland by its Nazi ally in September 1939, the OND, like virtually all other appurtenances of fascist rule, was found seriously wanting: "empty and mechanical," as it was described by the political police, and woefully neglected by party functionaries who "had long since lost sight of the principal aims of this great organization."[11]

If we ask what kind of ideological hold the fascist regime still had over the working population by the outbreak of World War II, the response is necessarily complicated. At one level, fascism had "disorganized" the workers, and as Emilio Sereni pointed out in 1946, "disorganized masses necessarily are and become less conscious masses."[12] At another, fascism had defined an entirely new framework of social and cultural reference; by obliterating the social forms that had sustained the utopian social vision of early twentieth-century socialism, it had changed the very terms in which workers conceived of their relations to the state and the prospects for any fundamental change within it. Twenty years earlier, the discourse of the working class had been characterized by bourgeois observers with words like "messianic"; its conception of its rights described as "hyperbolic" and "inflated." Italian workers, as the economist Prato had written in 1919, with typical conservative self-righteousness, conceived of "self-help as an astute bourgeois lie, self-betterment through skills or education as preparation for further exploitation, interclass solidarity as a sophism spread by economists and politicians who had sold out to the industrialists, and economic gain as having no value unless accompanied by political advantage or conquered by strikes, walkouts, or other forms of direct action."[13] By the late thirties, the struggles of the red years, whose "maximalist" rhetoric Prato caricatured, had still

The culture of consent: mass organization in fascist Italy

not been forgotten. "Just what socialism really meant to be and do" was the recurring topic of workers' conversations in the cafes of the small manufacturing center of Bordighera in 1938, according to Karl Walter. Yet it had become a "less animated post mortem than that of the last hand of *scopa*, best of all card games." Discontent there was, but it expressed itself in petty ways, as "hostility" and "resentment" – to use the common police terms – and it was a qualified hostility, no longer an intransigent opposition. At Bordighera, there was "much shaking of heads, with praise of the past, criticism of the present. The town was a livelier place in those days, but we didn't have this and that . . .": There was no asylum for the poor, and no *rancio del popolo* or people's mess provided by the *fascio*, no evening classes for the youth, and no *dopolavoro*, "that great competitor of the cafes, itself a glorified cafe, a people's club, where you can drink and play cards, billiards, tennis in the summer evenings, where there is dancing your girls can go to alone – but alone! and feel at home, peasant, shopkeeper, laborer, whatever their father may be, and regardless of member-ship."[14] If on the part of older workers, there was still a certain de-tachment from the regime's mass organizations, they nonetheless ac-cepted them, if not for their own pastimes, at least for those of their children.

Inevitably, as the permanence of the regime was accepted, it was also possible to conceive of changes occurring within it – not major structural changes, to be certain, but minor reforms, adjustments, as it were, that might make life and work more bearable. When queried by the union journal *Il Maglio* in 1938 for their opinions about the state of popular culture in Italy, Turinese workers responded that it was still elitist: Books were too costly and book publishers were "intolerant" of the culture of workers; professional instruction was too little avail-able and management tastes were too frequently imposed on their employees. With reforming zeal, the trade union delegate Alberto Ferrari asked why there was still no movie "truly worthy of the renown of the epic of the Littorial *Fascio*," which refuted Charlie Chaplin's *Modern Times* by portraying factory labor as "freely accepted and heroically experienced discipline" inspired by the political and eco-nomic themes of autarchy or told the story of the average worker at the Lingotto plant or at the Piedmontese Steel Mills or in the great textile works.[15] Admittedly the respondents – skilled workers all – were selected interlocutors, in Ferrari's case an especially ingratiating one. The point is that the fascists were confident enough to tolerate such debates at all, even in a closely controlled forum. Moreover, the

230

debate itself, regardless of whether it expressed how workers truly felt – although it was freewheeling and highly informed by the standards of trade unionism journalism anywhere – did not bring into question in any way the political regime that had produced such a trivialized pastiche. Rather than asking what functions this culture served, workers blamed the movie directors, the book publishers, and the theater producers, who had failed to abide by the high ideals of the regime; the employers, who had imposed their philistine tastes on their personnel; and obliquely the fascist party itself, whose corruption had led to the mismanagement of the regime's popular cultural policies. Logically it was assumed that all errors could be resolved within the framework of the fascist state, indeed within those very organizations established by the regime over the previous decade, through a process of "cultural renewal" perhaps with the participation of the new cultural elite in the student vanguards of the GUF. The foundry worker Francesco Cucini may have sounded disingenuous when he invited students to "pass hours of happiness" with the workers in "our magnificent company recreational centers," his enthusiasm rather forced. Nonetheless his reformist tone rang true.

This reformist outlet for worker grievances was naturally encouraged, not only by the syndicalists but also by the young fascist intellectuals. For the more progressive university students, as Ruggero Zangrandi recalled in his memoirs, "the way to approach the masses had long constituted a serious problem."[16] Consequently, in May 1936, when Starace instructed the GUF sections to involve themselves more actively in the cultural pastimes of the workers to create a "culture for all," students in the major industrial and commercial centers responded with giddy energy. For two years or so, students attended sports events with their "proletarian comrades," distributed *dopolavoro* cards at orchestrated mass rallies, and marched side by side with young workers in parades. Inevitably the artificiality and infrequency of these contacts prevented any sustained communication, and none, certainly, sufficient to break down either the class differences between students and workers, or what one student leader described as the "caste-like" structure of the regime's cultural organizations.[17] What is more, those contacts that did take place were enough to convince syndicalist leaders that student energies were better directed elsewhere. The students' "incomprehension of the worker mentality" – meaning, it may be supposed, their naive talk about the "second wave" of revolution – apparently provoked the sort of inflammatory discussion that only hindered trade union efforts to sooth restive workers.

231

The experiment was abruptly ended in late 1939, when a spokesman for the GUF announced that it "was premature to speak about fraternity between workers and students."[18]

Unlike the student groups – or the old guard fascists, who similarly called for a "reform in custom" – in the late 1930s the syndicalists insisted that reform had to be conceived in political rather than cultural terms. In July 1939 after two months of labor protests in the northern industrial towns, Mussolini appointed Pietro Capoferri, an ex-bricklayer from Bergamo and the head of the Milan Trade union federation, the new leader of the Fascist Confederation of Industrial Workers. As president of the CGFLI, Capoferri was in a good position to seek some highly visible reforms to bolster syndicalist authority. By November, as the pressures to mobilize for war were becoming increasingly urgent, Capoferri succeeded in persuading Mussolini that the syndicalists would be better able "to carry out their great and arduous tasks in a spirit of collaboration" if they regained some control over noncontractual issues.[19] By mid-November Mussolini agreed to give legal recognition to the factory fiduciaries, increase family bonuses, open new contract negotiations for office workers, and finally, grant the trade unions nominal control over the *dopolavoro*. Overriding the PNF's strong opposition, he appointed Capoferri to succeed Starace as the special commissioner of the OND, a position that he would hold until June 1940, when the new PNF secretary, Muti, was called up for army duty and Capoferri himself was appointed the temporary head of the party. At the February 1940 meeting of the representatives from the provincial *dopolavoro* in Milan – the first national meeting of organizers of labor held outside of Rome under the regime – Capoferri announced that the "union between work and after-work had been restored," thereby bringing about the "requisite revival of the workers' organizations in politics."[20] Purely in terms of its intended policies, the OND led by Capoferri was more responsive to worker needs; it even proposed special programs for women workers, who, with expanded rehiring for wartime production, were returning in large numbers into the factories. But with war a foregone conclusion, his main injunction was to prepare for "hard times": the promise that political rewards would be forthcoming with the return of peace turned out to be as empty as all of the earlier promises of the fascist syndicalists. By December 1942, in the face of military defeat and the collapsing war effort on the home front, the PNF reasserted its full control over the national network, claiming that syndicalist leadership had caused the local groups to become "disoriented."[21]

In the after-work organization generally, the line between state intervention and popular initiative had, of course, always been very thin, more so than in any other of the regime's organizations. The local groups were necessarily responsive to their membership, forming a common reference point for older workers and a strong associational bond among large numbers of younger people. But could they be made so responsive as to become centers of political opposition to the regime? Increasingly this question was posed by the antifascist resistance: Could not the process by which fascism had captured and regimented worker sociability now be reversed as the regime itself entered into crisis?

This possibility had been recognized by the Italian Communist party since 1933, when it had been forced to acknowledge the futility of urging workers to "boycott the bestial pastimes of the fascist bourgeoisie." An order of the day issued by the PC d'I's political office on 25 May 1933 identified the *dopolavoro* as the "most voluntary and least fascist" of the regime's mass organizations, and urged its cadres in Italy to "profit from these moments of meeting to mobilize the masses."[22] The party, in its effort to "breach fascist illegality," implicitly recognized that participation in itself, even in this fascist organization, indicated a predisposition to collective activity. Workers may have been "openly or imperceptibly subjected to a certain influence of the regime," as *Stato operaio* admitted they might be by virtue of belonging to the *dopolavoro*. But the very fact of their involvement raised the possibility that they had experienced first-hand the authoritarianism and corruption of fascism's social organizations.[23] In this sense, the *organized* under the fascist dictatorship were potentially more susceptible to a counterorganizational effort than the *unorganized*: the socially marginal above all, including peasants, women, and the unemployed and destitute, but also the socially passive, and, finally, even the self-excluding – the former worker – militants whose class experience, individualized by their refusal of any form of social participation under fascism, was lost to the younger generation of workers.

The Italian communists' own understanding of the social operations of fascist mass organizing had by 1935 been assimilated into the Comintern's "popular front" strategy. For Togliatti, who made a unique effort to apply this new strategy to the social reality of an established authoritarian regime in his lectures to party cadres at the Moscow Lenin School, the *dopolavoro* organization offered an ideal terrain for trying out "frontist" tactics. Admonishing communist organizers to join the local sections without "qualms and reservations," he urged that these be transformed into "centers of resistance, centers for the struggle against fascism." Naturally, he did not delude himself that the communists could in any way seek "worker control" of fascist institutions, something that clearly was not possible as long as the regime was in power. But single groups, in his view, might be "taken over" under the cover of legitimate activities. This meant moderation on the part of organizers: "they could not evidently demand that Mussolini be shot; that would get them expelled from the clubs"; nor could most afford to be as daring as members of one group from Trieste who, on the pretense of an outing abroad, had traveled as far as Odessa, made contacts with Soviet comrades, and returned home to be arrested en masse by the police. Organizers could, however, arouse doubts about the probity of administrators by requesting audits of the accounts, provoke discussions using those books with a class content permitted under the censorship laws, and generally exploit the residual democratic forms left in the old circles or whatever latent democratic tendencies might be present in the new ones to seek a greater voice for members in determining club policies.[24] In this way, the workers themselves would gradually develop a stronger sense of group solidarity, a higher level of self-consciousness regarding their relations with the fascist supervisors, and a greater autonomy with respect to government and party bureaucracies.

The tactic of "legal infiltration" was treated as a serious threat by the fascist authorities: "How many opportunities this system offers!" noted one police official in 1936. "Agitating around local questions, stirring up rancors against this or that administrator, pointing out eventual shortcomings – all of this done casually, yet with intelligence and method, by somebody who appears to have the best interests of the organization at heart, cannot fail to split the organizations apart."[25] But in the end it proved far less effective than the communists had anticipated or the police feared. By the time "popular frontism" had been fully approved within party circles, the Civil War in Spain had already begun to divert communist energies away from Italy. Meanwhile, the attentive Bocchini, chief of the political police (OVRA), had developed a counterstrategy to deal with this effort at subverting fascist institutions, a "preventive action," as he described it in a long memorandum to his subordinates, to complement the "repressive measures" already in effect.[26] Orders issued on 31 July 1936 called for "close and cordial" contacts between the political police and the local *questure*, full cooperation of fascist organizers with the OVRA, more assiduous surveillance of all former emigrants and ex-political prisoners, and a more extensive deployment of informers. Heightened police vigilance could not really prevent communist sympathizers from stirring up trouble in the circles to which they belonged. But the periodic roundups and interrogations of suspects after 1936 and thousands of arrests effectively prevented party sympathizers from sustaining contacts with comrades in other clubs or from carrying on any regular correspondence with the Communist party headquarters in Paris.[27]

However, the very structure of the fascist organization of leisure posed obstacles that were only partly appreciated by the left. Relying on reports from party cadres within Italy, Togliatti had virtually discounted any possibility of infiltrating company recreational groups on the grounds that employers treated even the most modest request for a voice in administrative decisions as an outright breach of management authority. Workers who dared to make such demands were immediately branded as troublemakers and subject to dismissal. But at the same time, Togliatti greatly underestimated the number of workers in the company groups or their numerical weight within the OND network as a whole, holding, incorrectly, that their membership was comprised overwhelmingly of incorrigibly petty bourgeois salaried employees. As we have seen, however, the management-sponsored circles embraced a constantly growing number of industrial workers; this tendency was further reinforced in the late thirties as rearmament spurred rehiring and the vitality of neighborhood groups waned. Although employers unhappy with the regime's adventurous foreign policy and heavy levies on business may have become less cooperative with fascist functionaries, none relaxed their tight grip over their recreational groups.[28]

Togliatti's optimistic appraisal of the *dopolavoro* as a potential domain for communist agitation was in fact based on the memory of the old worker circles, with which the communists, from past experience, were most familiar – organizations that had once subsumed the totality of workers' pastimes from political activism to economic defense. The fascist clubs were in reality innately parochial structures, far removed from the groups they had supplanted: The very separation of leisure associations from job-related concerns inevitably limited the issues that could be effectively exploited to gain worker sympathies or raise their political awareness. Within the clubs, demands for the ouster of a particularly invidious administrator, for more sports or free sports, and more generally for greater responsiveness to worker preferences, could be raised and even satisfied to a degree without undermining fascist legitimacy.

It is clear that the left, while understanding the importance of the fascist organizing effort as a key factor for building resistance against the fascist regime, had not fully understood the specificity of its form, nor the way in which the changing relations between work and after-work had modified the terms in which class struggle had to be conceptualized. The thrust of fascist organizing outside of the workplace had been, first, to break the cohesiveness of worker sociability and, subsequently, to undermine the trade union structure by capitalizing on the formation of a mass-based party organization and the mechanism of an emerging mass market. This did not mean that the left should have posited leisure itself as an autonomous area of class struggle, but it did mean having to consider the sphere of recreation and consumption together with the sphere of production in analyzing class position and the articulation of class attitudes. Although the left was quite correct in not dismissing the *dopolavoro* organizations as mere class expressions of the bourgeoisie, neither could it accept them as empty or autonomous structures of power potentially turned to the purposes of whoever happened to be participating or organizing within them.

By 1939, in any event, the communists, as if sensing the futility of organizing within after-work groups, turned their attention instead to the fascist unions. Whether under peacetime conditions these would have offered more fertile terrain for agitating against the regime is of course difficult to say, for by June 1940 the contradictions within the fascist system were being played out on a far grander scale. After no more than a year of Italian participation in a profoundly unpopular war, the communists were able to move their center for clandestine operations back into Italy, and the first allied bombardments of the northern towns in March 1943 almost immediately sparked mass strikes in industry. Nonetheless, it would take the allied landing in Sicily in early July 1943, followed by a palace coup on July 25, to bring about the fall of Mussolini's regime.

Like so many of the government structures inherited by the fascists from the liberal era or established by the regime to consolidate its power, the OND survived Mussolini's fall. On 11 October 1944 Vincenzo Baldazzi, an ex-republican imprisoned by the fascists in 1927, was appointed as special commissioner for the OND by the social democrat Ivanoe Bonomi, the head of the first government of national liberation. In his first directive, Baldazzi promised a "truly democratic direction" to the OND: Its preeminent functions, as clarified by subsequent orders, were to prevent the dispersal of the agency's property and to provide relief for the war-stricken population.[29] In September 1945, as if to mark the OND's irrevocable break with its fascist past, the agency was reinaugurated as ENAL, the National Organization for

Worker Assistance, a name more consistent with its immediate tasks in postwar national reconstruction.

In its present form, ENAL is no more than a government social service funded by revenues from a national lottery, Enalotto, and promoting on a far less magnificent scale the same kinds of pastimes sponsored by the OND. Its base organizations – *CRAL*, or worker recreation assistance circles – have been considerably reduced in number as the major political parties, beginning with the Christian Democrats in 1947, withdrew their circles to found their own autonomous networks. As a parastate agency, ENAL is considered above politics: "one of the government's instruments for planning . . . not free time itself, [but] by the appropriate facilities for the use of free time in the public interest." Public interest, of course, has been determined largely by the parties in power; and although ENAL has not been a conspicuous force in democratizing Italian public life, it has been used on occasion against the left. Thus the Christian Democratic ministry of Mario Scelba banned "politics" from the *CRAL* in 1954, enforcing its directives by ousting the party sections (mainly communist) from their premises and suspending the liquor licenses of recalcitrant circles.[30]

Memory of ENAL's past has dimmed in the meantime. Its functionaries today deny that the OND was ever fascist in any strict sense. The regime is said simply to have provided a favorable ambience in which the genial plan of a well-meaning and insufficiently recognized philanthropist took hold and flourished. Some recall that the agency functioned more efficiently under fascism, receiving as it did ample fiscal exemptions and subsidies from the government, full cooperation from employers, and of course the undivided support of the workers. Still others hold that it was a good plan put to bad use by a corrupt government.

In retrospect, there does indeed appear to be much that was not specifically "fascist" about the regime's organization of leisure-time activities – that is, if single facets of its development are examined in isolation. In conception, certainly, the *dopolavoro*, as it was originally proposed by the technocrat Giani, belongs to a tradition of industrial planning that, extending from Robert Owen's New Lanark to the schemes of "Americanizers" in the early twentieth century, envisaged a rational conflict-free community in which all social relations were ultimately functional to productive efficiency. In its application, too, the OND, at least through to 1927, preserved an ostensibly apolitical quality as an ambitious experiment in social engineering designed to modernize the archaic social organizations of a conflict-ridden society. Its functions after 1927 might also be considered in effect, if not in purpose, nonfascist: the assimilation of previously autonomous working class associations into the mainstream of national life; the homogenization of popular culture through contact with the mass media; the separation of recreational clubs from job-related organizations and union halls; the depoliticization of leisure pursuits. All of these might in fact be compared to similar trends in nations under liberal-democratic rule during the interwar period, as much a product of capitalist advance as of any government-directed policy. In some respects at least, this analysis of the transformation of worker leisure-time activities under fascism had yielded a picture very similar to that drawn by the American sociologists Robert and Helen Merrell Lynd, who, at their return to "Middletown, U.S.A." in the early thirties, found that leisure was "becoming more passive, more formal, more organized and more commercialized, taking on, in those phases where it remained active, more of the competitive emphasis so characteristic of the culture as a whole."[31]

From the perspective of the thirties, the intervention of the fascist regime in the organization of worker leisure certainly appears far less anomalous than it does today. For in identifying it as a major target of organizing, the fascists were, in their own terms, addressing what in post–World War I Europe was familiarly known in business and governing circles as the "problem of worker leisure." By 1918, the eight-hour day/forty-eight-hour week had become the "war cry of the masses" in all the western nations; and elsewhere, as in Italy, after intense agitation by organized labor, the shortened work week had been accepted as a measure of capitalist reform. Initially, it had been assumed, although with a certain conservative skepticism about "what *they* would do with their leisure time," that any increase would be beneficial to the recipients: Reassured of their stake in the society as consumers and citizens, workers would lend their "wholehearted support to the greatest production of goods."[32] However, the actual institution of the "eight hours," whether by legislation or contract, aroused elsewhere many of the same apprehensions that in Italy had led Giani to found his institute for the study of worker leisure in 1919. Workers, it appeared, would be presented with the same old near-occasions of social sin, for rarely were shorter hours accompanied by wage gains that were commensurate with productivity increases. Consequently they might "rot with drink," rather than seek out "harmless and entertaining commercial entertainment," as the American reformer James Sizer feared; or they might waste their energy in militant actions rather than engage in constructive politics.[33] In the early twenties, in the liberal democracies, there was thus what Gustave Méquet of the ILO described as a widespread feeling that "events should not be allowed to get out of control." But a consciousness of the appropriate countermeasures did not extend much beyond reiterating the dangers to the social order of what the World Committee of the YMCA characterized as "self-indulgence, sloth, social inefficiency, and a craving for unhealthy excitement." Not even the most conservative official could realistically do more than endorse the sentiment behind the YMCA's 1924 report. The "solution" to the problem, it maintained, lay in "the establishment of a right relationship between state, voluntary, and commerical endeavors, resolving the possible conflicts of interest and seeing that the ground is covered without overlapping."[34]

In the fascist dictatorships, by contrast, the problem of leisure was addressed by direct government intervention; and the solution generally took the form of a special national institution. In the five years after the Nazis inaugurated their "Strength through Joy" Organization (KDF) in November 1933, centralized national agencies on either the Italian or German model were established by all of the right-wing dictatorships in Europe. From 1935, Salazar's Portugal had its own Fundaçao Naçional para Algeria no Trabaljo. The Ergatixi Estia or "Workers' Hearth" founded by the Greek dictator Metaxas in 1937 purported to bring discipline to the leisure of the Hellenic workers. The Bulgarian regime had its own "Strength through Joy," as did Romania, which placed its central agency under the National Ministry of Labor. Finally in Spain in late 1938, conservatives working with the Franchist Fuero del Trabajo established a special bureau for Educaçion y Descanso that was closely modeled on the OND. These institutions naturally were not all of the same kind; because each was confronted with different economic and political conditions and widely different social traditions, the implementation of any rationalizing project inevitably took a variety of forms and had varying effects. Thus in Nazi Germany, the establishment of the KDF was supported by the wholesale appropriation of the rich institutional heritage of German social democracy; it thrived in an area of relatively high mass consumption and full employment under the Labor Front, which in turn was under the Nazi party. Wholly self-financing by the mid-thirties, with its much publicized cruises and advertisements for Volkswagens, it resembled nothing so much as a giant national tourist office. Like all such interventions, it too claimed suprapolitical goals: By the "sound organization" of leisure time, the KDF "increased efficiency, thereby contributing to national strength and national wealth."[35]

The culture of consent: mass organization in fascist Italy

In the capitalist democracies too, as the effects of the economic depression began to be felt in persistent unemployment, social unrest, and constitutional crisis, there was a rethinking of the pragmatic liberalism of the twenties. Even in Britain, where conservatives still clung to the tenets of laissez-faire, preferring support for individual philanthropic initiatives to any costly state intervention, this one aspect of fascism inspired considerable interest. Some, like the Reverend Fox, although heartily approving of any system that "kept workers from wasting their money and muddling their heads in the wine shops when they came back from the fields and the factory at the end of the day," suspected that postwar Italy especially "needed a paternal government in order to re-create the nation," and that its system might not be "applicable" to other countries.[36] Others, however, were more willing to experiment. One educator, for example, noted that "while Italy may well be fascist we must take into consideration all that is of importance and innovative in dealing with worker spare time." In assessing the operations of the OND, he hoped that there were no fundamental contradictions between liberal ideology and fascist organizing principles, and wherever common areas of concern could be identified a new "British synthesis" might be developed from the fascist experience.[37]

By the mid-thirties, there thus existed a general consensus that the traditional liberal policy of giving free reign to the individuals' use of free time was suspended, at least insofar as worker pastimes were concerned. In 1935, when the ILO's governing board met to discuss the question, representatives of government, employers, and organized labor discussed the issue with the "liveliest interests, as well as with the greatest understanding." Nobody, as the president of the body, the Italian De Michelis, reported, "suggested that workers' spare time was a purely personal matter."[38] Indeed by the late thirties, however reprehensible the authoritarian organization of leisure in fascist countries may have appeared, nowhere in the international conferences or in the reports and studies on workers' spare time was their leadership in the field seriously disputed. Assessments of the effectiveness of state intervention focused exclusively on the techniques of organizing itself: The political implications were ignored. As if to mark this fact, all international conferences on leisure between 1936 and the outbreak of the war were convened in the fascist countries: in Hamburg in 1936, in Rome in 1938, and in Tokyo in 1940. When after the war, social scientists returned to the subject, it is true that the "problem" – of *mass* leisure – was no longer identified as specific to the working class or subject to any totalizing state intervention.[39] Whether this return to laissez-faire assumptions resulted from a refurbishing of belief in democratic procedures; or came from the realization that the costs of any special intervention far outweighed the possible political benefits; or grew out of the understanding that with capitalist advance and the erosion of the traditional worker community, leisure pastimes had indeed become the integrative forces that had been hoped for, must be the subject of another study.

But the specificity of the organization of leisure in Italy between the wars cannot finally be separated from an understanding of the historical function of fascism in the consolidation of Italian capitalism. The historical role of fascism had been posed by a number of fascist leaders at the outset as that of bridging the void between the state and the masses, between the "legal" and the "real" Italy. This void, partially filled by the workers' own associations after 1900, could never have been overcome either by the exercise of violence alone, or the insistent pleas of a propaganda apparatus. In Italy, the process by which the "primitive" structure of worker associationalism was broken down and popular sociability "captured" by the state was *fascist* for the very reason that a high degree of state involvement was required to achieve what in other industrializing nations in the West was accomplished gradually through essentially pluralistic means. The formation on a wide scale of new mediating institutions that were at once capable of engaging popular participation and disseminating dominant values would have been difficult, if not inconceivable, except within the context of fascist coercion; for, as we have seen, neither employer welfare facilities nor the fascist syndicalist circles could effectively compete with the workers' own associations. Nor did the market mechanism, further unbalanced by fascist curbs on consumption, function effectively enough to dissolve traditional social habits. It was only after force had been systematically deployed to break up the institutional centers of working class opposition to fascism that less openly oppressive methods of impressing the dominant values of the society on the working masses could be contemplated.

This did not mean that fascism was completely intolerant of other voluntary initiatives. The regime's respectful attitude toward Catholic associational activity underscores the selectivity of fascist totalitarianism. From the late twenties, the Church and the regime subscribed to a series of mutual agreements, the net effect of which was to "catholicize" civil society while depoliticizing the social organizations under Catholic leadership. Thus, although the Church agreed to dissolve the Catholic national sports federation in 1927, Catholic Action, its adult laymen's organization, had been allowed to retain control over diocesan cultural events, and its women's groups to continue competing

241

with fascism's own *Fasci Femminili*. With the Lateran Agreements of March 1929, the Church had agreed to dissolve its children's groups, the Catholic Explorers, thereby yielding the task of organizing Italian children exclusively to the fascist *balilla*. In compensation religious instruction was introduced into the state school system. However, the efforts by social Catholic activists to found "worker secretariats" during the early years of the Depression led to open confrontation between the Church and the regime that resulted in a temporary ban against all Catholic Action activities in the summer of 1931. The crisis was not overcome until Catholic Action agreed to curb the political activities of the ex-*popolari* and to testify its allegiance to the national state by adopting a tricolor insignia and displaying the flag at all of its events.[40] In this conservative form, the Catholic circles very occasionally provided a forum for persons critical of the morality if not the actual politics of the regime, and they may well have protected their members from the most virulent motifs of fascist propaganda. But on the whole, these circles were probably as repressive of popular initiatives as the regime's own groups, perhaps more so, because they were responsible for their conduct to censors in the Church hierarchy who, it was well known, were far more experienced in their work than any parvenu fascist official. Thus, although parish circles may well have competed with the fascist clubs for membership, they themselves proposed no active resistance to the regime. That this very conservative form of social Catholicism should have become so strongly entrenched under fascism; that it ultimately constituted the only relief from fascist organizations is perhaps the best measure of the regime's hold on Italian society: "The definition of alternatives," as one political theorist has written, is truly "the supreme instrument of power."[41]

In the final analysis, much of the credibility of the culture of consent formed under fascism depended on the lack of familiarity with any coherent alternative. By the late thirties, it is likely that at least a large minority of the membership in the fascist mass organizations were young people, born in the post-1919 baby boom. Unless they had grown up in antifascist households, or had contact with communist organizers, or had emigrated abroad, they were familiar solely with the associations and publications of the regime. Their use of leisure, as much as any other aspect of their lives, separated them from the struggles of the "red years," and from the social experiences of the "generation of the irreconcilables." This was not because their recreation was "fascist," but rather because it was alien to the experiences of the older workers: a consumer item, rather than the natural extension of the comings and goings of women, men, and children in the neighborhood *circolo fa-*

migliare; showy and relatively costly compared to the austere outings and amusements of the old clubs; organized from above as "signs of a better life" rather than the pillars of the "new world of justice and civilization" built through struggles and self-sacrifice. The popular culture of reformist socialism, of the militant working class movement of the "red years," like the *bocce* games for old folks, must have seemed dull and old-fashioned to the young workers. The older generation, in turn, disapproved of the pastimes of youth, who appeared to care "only about having a good time." "All they have to do is see four kicks at a soccer ball," one pensioner was overheard saying to two friends in a Rome streetcar, "and they forget everything about what we are living through now."[42] The gap between generations was of course nothing new, or peculiar to Italy, above all in this period of transition to a mass culture. But under fascism, it acquired a special political significance because it was institutionalized through the fascist mass organizations and so distanced the young worker as well as the young intellectual from the cultural and political experiences of the "red years."

To argue that fascist organization of leisure was supportive of fascist rule is not to say, however, that it was unswervingly responsive to fascist aims. The organizational strategies of a regime that styled itself mediator of Italian capitalist interests were themselves fraught with contradictions. Even the best-conceived plans of fascist functionaries could not evidently compensate for the remarkably low level of popular consumption, official deference to traditional concepts of culture, government's solicitous respect for private enterprise, or the regime's alliance with reactionary groups within the agrarian elites. Organizers could at most mediate between the often conflicting demands of vested economic interests and the regime's own need for a politically responsive mass base. They could not overcome that insuperable obstacle to popular participation in official activities posed by the increasing impoverishment of the working classes under fascist rule. Nor, finally, could they resolve the problem inherent in the very nature of the depoliticized consensus achieved by the regime: Without politics there could be no real legitimacy; yet any thoroughgoing political mobilization risked slipping out of fascist control and was virtually impracticable in any event as a result of the ossification of the party apparatus by the late thirties.

In these circumstances, the ideological consensus engendered by the diversionary pastimes of the fascist organization of leisure was bound to be superficial and, in the end, fragile. It might even be said that, over the long run, such a highly visible state intervention in civil society had a quite contradictory effect: It accentuated bourgeois dependency on the state apparatus of social and ideological control at the same time as it left many sectors of the working population with a profound – and healthy – skepticism about the apparently classless and apolitical nature of national cultural modes.

Abbreviations

Archives

ACS	Archivio Centrale dello Stato
CO	carteggio ordinario
CR	carteggio riservato
D	Direttorio
MI, PS	Ministero dell' Interno, Pubblica Sicurezza
PNF	Partito Nazionale Fascista
PCM	Presidente del Consiglio dei Ministri
SPP	Situazione politica delle provincie
SPD	Segretaria Particolare del Duce
ACSF	Archivio Centro Storico Fiat

For full references and explanations, see Note on Sources. Unless otherwise noted in specific citations, the folder, volume, or carton number is designated by b. (busta, or envelope or box), f. (fascicolo, or folder or file), sf. (sottofascicolo, or subfolder or file).

Newspapers and periodicals

ASI	*Annuario statistico italiano*
ASInd	*Assistenza sociale nell'industria*
BLPS	*Bollettino del lavoro e della previdenza sociale*
GN	*Gente nostra*
LF	*Lavoro fascista*
OND, *BU*	*Bollettino ufficiale*
OND, *BM*	*Bollettino mensile*
OSL	*Organizzazione scientifica del lavoro*

Political, economic, and labor groups

CGL	Confederazione Generale del Lavoro
CGFLI	Confederazione Generale Fascista dei Lavoratori Italiani
CGII	Confindustria or Confederazione Generale dell'Industria Italiana
CONI	Comitato Olimpionico Nazionale Italiano
CRAL	Cirocoli Ricreativo-Assistenziali Lavoratori
ENAL	Ente Nazionale Assistenza Lavoratori
EOA	Ente Opere Assistenziali
FIE	Federazione Italiana deli'Escursionismo

Abbreviations

GUF	Gruppi Universitari Fascisti
ILO	International Labor Organization
KDF	Kraft durch Freude
MVSN	Milizia Volontaria Sicurezza Nazionale
ONB	Opera Nazionale Balilla
ONC	Opera Nazionale Combattenti
OND	Opera Nazionale Dopolavoro
PC d'I	Partito Comunista d'Italia
PNF	Partito Nazionale Fascista
PSI	Partito Socialista Italiano

Notes

1. The organization of consent

1 Luigi Einaudi, *La condotta economica e gli effetti sociali della guerra* (Bari, 1933), pp. 313–317; also, Max Weber, *Economy and Society*, ed. G. Roth and C. Wittich (New York, 1968), I, 153; and in a similar vein, J. M. Keynes, *Essays in Persuasion* (London, 1931), passim. The "crisis of transformation and direction" that accompanied bourgeois recovery after World War I has been studied most recently by Charles S. Maier, *Recasting Bourgeois Europe: Stabilization in France, Germany and Italy in the Decade after World War I* (Princeton, 1975), and in Alan Wolfe's *The Limits of Legitimacy* (New York, 1977), pp. 108–78. See also Karl Polanyi's *The Great Transformation* (Boston, 1957), esp. pp. 227–44.

2 In individual countries, the chief characteristics of this process varied, as did its specific social objects and the terms used in its study. On Germany see George L. Mosse, *The Nationalization of the Masses* (New York, 1975); on France, Eugen Weber, *Peasants into Frenchmen* (Berkeley, 1976); on England, Bernard Semmel, *Imperialism and Social Reform* (New York, 1968), and especially Gareth Stedman Jones, "Working Class Culture and Working Class Politics in London: Notes on the Remaking of the Working Class," *Journal of Social History*, vol. 7, no. 4 (Summer 1974), 460–508; on Americanization and assimilation in the United States, see Gerd Korman, *Industrialization, Immigrants and Americanizers* (Madison, 1967).

3 On liberal "voluntarism" see especially Kathleen Woodroofe, *From Charity to Social Work in England and the United States* (London, 1962); and Donald Rohr, *The Origins of Social Liberalism in Germany* (Chicago, 1964).

4 For a history of the redefinition of culture under industrial capitalism, see Raymond Williams, *Culture and Society, 1780–1950* (New York and London, 1958). The changing social-ideological dimension of the "politics of culture" is perhaps best captured in Jurgen Habermas, *Strukturwandel der Öffentlickheit* (Neuwied, 1962) (The Structural Transformation of the Public Sphere). The significance of this new political culture for worker participation in the state has naturally been subject to very diverse interpretations: from that of post–World War II American sociologists like Clark Kerr et al. (*Industrialization and Industrial Man* [New York, 1972]) and Gabriel Almond and Sidney Verba (*The Civic Culture* [Princeton, 1963]), who maintain that it gave workers a "language in which to couch their demands and the means to make them effective" (Almond and Verba, p. 6) to that of the critical theorists of the Frankfurt School, including Max Horkheimer and Theodor W. Adorno (*Dialectic of Enlightenment* [New York, 1972]) and Herbert Marcuse (*One-Dimensional Man* [Boston, 1974]), who argue that it has completely obliterated any meaningful expression of an autonomous working class culture.

247

5 On the various meanings of the word, see Raymond Williams, *Keywords* (London, 1974), pp. 67–8.

6 See especially the formulation of the fascist Dino Grandi, "Le origini e la missione del fascismo," in *Il fascismo*, ed. A. Zerboglio and D. Grandi (Bologna, 1922), p. 70; for a detailed treatment of this aspect of fascist ideology, see David D. Roberts, *The Syndicalist Tradition and Italian Fascism* (Chapel Hill, 1979).

7 Maier, passim; on the difficult consolidation of fascist power in the 1920s, see Adrian Lyttelton, *The Seizure of Power: Fascism in Italy, 1919–1929* (New York, 1973). Using index 100 = 1913, wages in 1921 stood at 127, in 1927 at 98; in 1933 at 101. In general, on workers' wages and consumption levels, see: Cesare Vannutelli, "Les conditions de vie des travailleurs italiens au cours de la periode 1929–1939," in *Mouvements ouvriers et depression économique de 1929 à 1939* (Assen, 1966); and most recently, Vera Zamagni, "La dinamica dei salari nel settore industriale," in Pierluigi Ciocca and Gianni Toniolo, eds., *L'economia italiana nel periodo fascista* (Bologna, 1976); Renato Giannettini and Aldo Rustichini, "Consumi operai e salari negli anni '20 in Italia," *Movimento operaio e socialista*, vol. 1, no. 4 (n.s.) (October–December 1978), pp. 347–72.

8 B. Mussolini, "Il discorso dell'Ascensione," (26 May 1927), *Opera omnia* (hereafter *OO*, ed. Edoardo and Duilio Susmel, 36 vols. (Florence, 1951–63), 22, p. 384.

9 On the functions of "consumerism" as a participatory ideology, see Stuart Ewen, *Captains of Consciousness* (New York, 1976), in addition to the "philosophy" of the father of public relations, Edward Bernays, in his *The Engineering of Consent* (Norman, Okla., 1955).

10 Italian liberalism's notoriously obstinate neglect of the "social question" is examined in Christopher Seton-Watson, *Italy from Liberalism to Fascism* (London, 1967); Maurice Neufeld, *Italy: School for Awakening Countries* (Ithaca, 1961); and Alberto Caracciolo, *Stato e società civile: problemi dell'unificazione italiana* (Turin, 1960).

11 Antonio Stefano Benni, Speech before the First Intersyndical Committee, 10 July 1929, Palazzo Viminale, ACS, Carte Cianetti, b. 4.

12 On Mussolini's own ambiguous views toward labor, see his speech of 15 March 1923 (cited in Angelo Tasca, *Nascita e avvento del fascismo*, 2 vols. (Bari, 1965), 2, p. 306, and Chapter 2.

13 Antonio Salandra, *La politica nazionale e il partito liberale* (Milan, 1912), esp. pp. xvii–xviii.

14 Giuseppe Prato, quoted in *Italia industriale*, vol. 1, no. 2 (October–December 1919), p. 48.

15 Alfredo Rocco, "Crisi dello Stato e sindacati," *Politica*, vol. 2, no. 19 (December 1920), p. 8.

16 The literature on such "intermediate" associations, by U.S. authors especially, is vast. It is usually subsumed under the notion of "voluntary" associations. For the most complete summary of the various typologies used, none of which is wholly satisfactory for a study that is comparative and historical, or seeks to analyze these institutions as "mediating" institutions within a specific kind of economic development, see Constance Smith and Anne Freedman, *Voluntary Associations: Perspectives on the Literature* (Cambridge, Mass., 1972). For an analysis of Tocqueville's views as well as other national studies, see J. Roland Pennock and John W. Chapman, eds., *Voluntary Associations* (New York, 1969).

17 For a prehistory of late-nineteenth-century philanthropy, see Arnoldo Cherubini, *Dottrine e metodi assistenziali dal 1789 al 1841: Italia, Francia, Inghilterra* (Milan, 1958). For the period 1890–1914, see Elia Boschetti, *La beneficenza come è e come*

deve essere (Bologna, 1911); Matteo Maggetti, *La genesi e evoluzione della beneficenza* (Rome, 1880); also Guido Vitali, *Per la pace sociale* (Florence, 1900). The reform of philanthropy in Italy is discussed in Enrico Martini, *Dall'assistenza alla solidarietà* (Turin, 1933).

18 In his study of Franco's Spain, the sociologist Juan Linz goes so far as to suggest that "authoritarianism provides a welcome relief from overpoliticization in democratic societies that had not developed apolitical voluntary associations in proportion to the number of fiercely conflicting political groups" (J. Linz, "An Authoritarian Regime, Spain," in Erik Allardt and Stein Rokkan, eds., *Mass Politics: Studies in Political Sociology* [New York, 1970], pp. 251–83, esp. p. 263). Following a similar line of reasoning, William Kornhauser (*The Politics of Mass Society* [New York, 1964]) sees "totalitarianism" arising out of "mass societies," that is, out of societies that, lacking sufficient voluntary associations to prevent anomie, become susceptible to demogogic appeals.

19 Antonio Gramsci, "Americanismo e fordismo," in *Quaderni del carcere* (hereafter *Quaderni*), ed. V. Gerratana, 4 vols. (Turin, 1975), 3, p. 2140.

20 Boschetti, p. 203.

21 Woodroofe, p. 22.

22 Among others, the nationalist Alfredo Oriani, in *La rivolta ideale* (Naples, 1908). The expert British observers Thomas Okey and Bolton King concurred in their *Italy Today* (London, 1909). All of the Italian reformers agreed that Italy was behind: old-fashioned "filantropia," "beneficenza," and "assistenza" had to give way to a modern "solidarismo sociale" – that is, to a social welfare system or to a nationwide set of Poor Laws.

23 The failure of Italy's industrial leadership to undertake philanthropic initiatives, equal to those established on a private and local basis by employers in other industrial nations is discussed in Guido Baglioni, *L'ideologia della borghesia industriale nell'Italia liberale* (Turin, 1973); see also Chapter 3.

24 On the formation of this highly articulated club life, descendant of the nineteenth-century mutual aid societies, see Neufeld, esp. pp. 171–6, and, in greater detail, the reformist labor leader Rinaldo Rigola's *Storia del movimento operaio italiano* (Milan, 1957), esp. pp. 9–22; also Alfredo Angiolini and Eugenio Ciacchi, *Socialismo e socialisti in Italia* (Florence, 1919). Specifically on the organization of industrial workers, see Stefano Merli, *Proletariato di fabbrica e capitalismo: il caso italiano, 1880–1900*, 2 vols. (Florence, 1972), 1, pp. 582–613. For the classic study of the Italian Socialist party, its social inclusiveness and strength as the sole modern mass party in prewar Italy, see Roberto Michel's *Il proletariato e la borghesia nel movimento socialista italiano* (Turin, 1908). On the political and social character of socialism's vast network of local organizations, see Giuliano Procacci, *La lotta di classe in Italia agli inizi del secolo XX* (Rome, 1970); also Donald H. Bell, "Worker Culture and Worker Politics: The Experience of an Italian Town, 1880–1915," *Social History*, vol. 3, no. 1 (1978), pp. 1–21.

25 ACS, MI, PS (1903–49), G 1, b. 57, f. Vercelli, sf. Bianzè (Vercelli), Società operaia di mutuo soccorso, founding statutes, 1894.

26 On the well-documented fascist expeditions against the socialist associations, see: *Fascismo. Inchiesta socialista sulle gesta dei fascisti in Italia* (Milan, 1963), esp. p. 112, the results of an inquiry conducted by the Italian Socialist party for Parliament in 1921; also the official history of the Fascist party by Giorgio A. Chiurco, *Storia della rivoluzione fascista*, 4 vols. (Florence, 1929), 3, passim; and the most thorough analysis of all in Tasca, 1, pp. 143–221.

27 For the most thorough study of the origins of fascist syndicalism, see Ferdinando Cordova, *Le origini dei sindacati fascisti* (Bari, 1974); also Chapter 2.

28 Polanyi, pp. 227–44; also Maier, passim.

29 Cited in Renzo De Felice, *Mussolini il fascista: l'organizzazione dello stato fascista, 1925–1929* (hereafter De Felice, vol. 3), 5 vols. (Turin, 1968), 3, pp. 232–3.

30 On the political economy of fascism, see in addition to Pietro Grifone, *Il capitale finanziario in Italia* (Turin, 1968), the synthesis of recent historical studies by Valerio Castronovo in *Storia d'Italia, dall'unità a oggi. La storia economica* (Turin, 1974), pp. 267–84. Single aspects of the economy, from sectoral growth to workers' wages, are studied in the special issue of *Problemi del socialismo* ("Capitalismo, fascismo e sviluppo economico"), vol. 14, nos. 11–12 (September–December 1972), and in Ciocca and Toniolo, eds. Cf. a more traditional liberal view, which holds that curbs on free market forces in support of social stability inevitably restricted economic development, in A. F. K. Organski, "Fascism and Modernization," in S. J. Woolf, ed., *The Nature of Fascism* (New York, 1969), pp. 14–91.

31 Mario Saibante, *Il fascismo e l'industria (Panorami di vita fascista)* (Milan, 1940), p. 4.

32 Quoted from a draft speech prepared for the Fascist Grand Council in early November 1927, and then apparently discarded as too pessimistic in ACS, SPD, CR, b. 27 Gran Consiglio, sf. 5, 1927 inserto C, November 1927. For police accounts of the unrest in 1927, see De Felice, vol. 3, pp. 240–1.

33 As recalled in his "Speech of the Ascension."

34 *OO*, 22, p. 287.

35 On European receptivity to the ideology of rationalization, see Charles S. Maier, "Between Taylorism and Technocracy: European Ideologies and the Vision of Industrial Productivity in the 1920s," *Journal of Contemporary History*, vol. 5, no. 2 (1970), 27–61. For national variations see Paul Devinat, *Scientific Management in Europe* (ILO, *Studies and Reports*, ser. B, no. 17 [Geneva, 1927]) and his *Les conséquences sociales de la rationalisation économique* (Vienna, 1927). The actual process of rationalization in Italy, understood in its most restricted sense as standardization and mechanization of plant, was in fact singularly absent. See Paola Fiorentini, "Ristrutturazione capitalistica e sfruttamento operaio in Italia negli anni '20," *Rivista storica del socialismo*, vol. 10, no. 30 (January–April 1967), 134–54; also Giulio Sapelli, "L'organizzazione 'scientifica' del lavoro e innovazione tecnologica durante il fascismo," *Italia contemporanea*, vol. 28, no. 125 (October–December 1976), 3–28. In general, on the concept of rationalization under fascism, see in addition to Gramsci's notes on "Americanism and Fordism": Enzo Santarelli, "Dittatura fascista e razionalizzazione capitalistica," *Problemi del socialismo* vol. 14, nos. 11–12 (September–December 1972), 704–8.

36 B. Mussolini, *OO*, vol. 23, p. 302.

37 Quoted in the Confindustria's *Organizzazione industriale*, vol. 7, no. 18 (15 September 1927), p. 242.

38 Quoted in Lyttelton, p. 345.

39 Lello Gangemi, "La concentrazione e la razionalizzazione delle industrie in Italia," *Economia*, vol. 8 (1930), p. 361.

40 Carmen Haider, *Capital and Labor under Fascism* (New York, 1930), p. 224.

41 "Al popolo napoletano," *OO*, vol. 25, p. 48.

42 ACS, MI, PS, Pol. Pol. (1926–45) cat K 35, b. 109, f. 1, PNF 1932–4, "Propaganda fascista," Rome, 6 April 1932, 7 April 1932.

43 "Andare al popolo," *Stato operaio*, vol. 6, nos. 1–2 (January–February 1932), p. 49.

44 Giuseppe Bottai, "Ordinamento e sviluppo dell'Opera Nazionale Dopolavoro," *Gerarchia* (February 1928), p. 99.
45 Quoted in *Il Dopolavoro fiorentino*, vol. 2, no. 4 (1–15 March 1929).
46 Cited in Smith and Freedman, p. 228.
47 Gaetano Salvemini, *Under the Axe of Fascism* (New York, 1936), pp. 333–4.
48 "Discorso dell'Ascensione," p. 363.
49 On Spain, see Linz, p. 255; on Germany, Franz Neumann, *Behemoth: the Structure and Practice of National Socialism* (New York, 1944), p. 51; for a comparative study of fascism in a sociological and historical perspective, see Walter Laqueur, ed., *Fascism: A Reader's Guide* (Berkeley and Los Angeles, 1976).
50 Cf. Renzo De Felice, *Mussolini il Duce: gli anni del consenso* (Rome, 1975); also Philip V. Cannistraro, *La fabbrica del consenso* (Bari, 1976).
51 See especially *Quaderni*, vol. 2, 865–6; vol. 3, 1614–16, 1624–6, 2172–3. Among the exemplary uses of Gramsci's concept of hegemony in recent historical writing are Raymond Williams, *Marxism and Literature* (London, 1977), esp. pp. 75–127; Perry Anderson, "The Antinomies of Antonio Gramsci," *New Left Review*, no. 100 (November 1976–January 1977), pp. 1–78; Eric Hobsbawm, *The Age of Capital* (London, 1975), esp. pp. 248–50; and Eugene D. Genovese, *Roll Jordan Roll* (New York, 1974), pp. 25–28.
52 See, for example, Carl J. Friedrich et al., *Totalitarianism in Perspective: Three Views* (New York, 1969).

2. The politics of after-work

1 On the beginnings of fascist syndicalism, see Ferdinando Cordova, *Le origini dei sindacati fascisti* (Bari, 1974), esp. pp. 42 ff.; also Roland Sarti, "I sindacati fascisti e la politica economica del regime," *Problemi del socialismo*, vol. 14, nos. 11–12 (September–December 1972), 746–65.
2 On Nationalist ideology, see Francesco Gaeta, *Nazionalismo italiano* (Naples, 1965); also Ferdinando Perfetti, *Il nazionalismo italiano dalle origini alla fusione con il fascismo* (Bologna, 1977); on the Nationalists' relations with high finance and heavy industry, see Richard Webster, *Industrial Imperialism in Italy* (Berkeley, 1975), esp. pp. 37–40, 338 ff.
3 On the "revisionists" and the technocratic aspirations of early fascism, see A. Aquarone, "Le aspirazioni tecnocratiche del primo fascismo," *Nord e Sud*, vol. 11, no. 4 (April 1964); also Adrian Lyttelton's cogent observations on the reform program of urban middle-class fascism in *The Seizure of Power: Fascism in Italy 1919–1929* (New York, 1973), pp. 153–4; see also the views of its leading spokesman, G. Bottai, in his own account, *Vent'anni e un giorno* (Milan, 1949), and now A. De Grand, *Bottai e la cultura fascista* (Bari, 1978), esp. pp. 1–70; also Camillo Pellizzi, *Una rivoluzione mancata* (Milan, 1948).
4 For the syndicalist program, see the CNSF leader Edmondo Rossoni's presentation in *Le idee della ricostruzione* (Florence, 1923); also Mario Vaina, *Sindacalismo* (Bari, 1923).
5 By 1923, the CNSF had a large following of its own, though not in industry; initially it was drawn mainly from assorted "economic" unions formed after 1919 primarily among public employees. But by January 1922 about half of the total 458,284 members belonged to the Corporation for Agriculture, the majority being rural laborers

from the Po valley region who had been coerced into joining after the destruction of their own socialist leagues by the fascists in 1920–1 (Cordova, pp. 58, 242, 326 n. 41).

6 Rossoni and Gino Olivetti, the general-secretary of the Confindustria, had met at least once before the March on Rome to discuss Rossoni's proposals for cooperation between their respective organizations (Roland Sarti, *Fascism and the Industrial Leadership in Italy, 1919–1940* [Berkeley, 1971], p. 37). From March 1923 on, the syndicalists had proposed setting up workers' courses (*corsi di maestranza*) in "close collaboration" with employers, sponsored by management though staffed by volunteers from the fascist Federation of Vocational School Instructors (*Lavoro d'Italia*, 30 March 1923, 21 April 1923, 6 May 1923, 28 July 1923, 18 August 1923; also Giusti, "Per l'educazione tecnico-professionale delle maestranze," ibid., 25 August 1923; r.s., "Turismo e sport sindacale," ibid., 22 February 1923).

7 The Nationalist Association, which fused with the PNF in 1923, was especially adamant about developing vocational instruction along with a new "ethical" education for the "masses": see especially *Il nazionalismo italiano e i problemi del lavoro e della scuola*, Atti del secondo convegno di Roma della Associazione Nazionalista Italiana (Rome, 1919); also *L'Idea nazionale*, 20 March 1919, 15 June 1919.

8 The first eight-hour pacts negotiated between the socialist metallurgical unions (FIOM) and the Association of Machine and Metallurgical Employers (AMMA) in February 1919 marked labor's first victory following the armistice, a "utopia become reality" in the words of Rigola, then secretary of the CGL; the demand had spread like "wildfire" (see the PSI leader Turati's parliamentary report, *L'orario di lavoro delle otto ore*, preface by G. Prato [Milan, 1920]), so that by the end of 1919 more than two million workers were covered by similar contracts (on Mussolini's decision to enact the law, see Cordova, p. 130). The text accompanying the decree-law indicated that it was enacted with "reservations": under no circumstances was it to "feed illusions that a reduction of hours was to be accompanied by higher salaries" (*BLPS*, no. 39 [January–June 1923], pp. 1–362). Statistics compiled for August–September 1924 after the law was put into effect indicated that the number of industrial enterprises respecting the eight-hour day/48-hour week had dropped since July 1923 from 83 to 74.5 percent of the 16,189 enterprises surveyed, and from 88 to 77.5 percent of the workforce (*BLPS*, no. 41 [January–June 1924], pp. 1–481 passim; no. 45 [January 1926], pp. 1–80).

9 A. C., "Le otto ore di lavoro," *Lavoro d'Italia*, 15 March 1923; also E. Rossoni, quoted in *Il Dopolavoro*, vol. 1, no. 3 (1–15 March 1923).

10 Biographical notices on Giani are scant since after his fall from favor under fascism, he became a "nonperson"; for his prefascist formation, see: L. Pezzoli, "Una lunga fatica e una bella vittoria," *La Stirpe*, vol. 3, no. 6 (June 1925), 371; also *Dopolavoro ferroviario*, vol. 1, no. 1 (January 1926). From the content and style of his writings, Giani was certainly familiar with William H. Tolman's pioneering work on personnel management, *Social Engineering: a record of things done by American industrialists employing upwards of one and one-half million of people*, with an introduction by A. Carnegie (New York, 1909). On the technocratic environment he encountered in the United States, see Samuel Haber, *Efficiency and Uplift: Scientific Management in the Progressive Era, 1890–1920* (Chicago, 1969); Milton J. Nadworny, *Scientific Management and the Unions, 1900–1932* (Cambridge, Mass., 1955), esp. pp. 1–42; H. G. J. Aitken, *Taylorism at Watertown Arsenal* (Cambridge, Mass., 1960);

and Stuart D. Brandes, *American Welfare Capitalism, 1880–1930* (Chicago, 1976). In the United States, there had initially been conflict between moral reformers who advocated the older humanitarian tradition of "welfare work" and management experts who sought a "scientific" organization of after-work that was free of any benevolent overtones (see D. Nelson and S. Campbell, "Taylorism versus Welfare Work in American Industry: H. L. Gantt and the Bancrofts," *Business History Review*, vol. 46, no. 1 [Spring 1972], 1–16); such distinctions were ignored in Italy, though Giani himself clearly propended for the "scientific" notion when discussing the potential "profits" from industrial betterment (see Chapter 3).

11 According to Pezzoli (p. 371), a meeting with the liberal prime minister Giolitti in early 1921, arranged by a friend, the Catholic deputy Pallastrelli, then under-secretary of agriculture, had proven equally fruitless; the prime minister declared Giani's project unfeasible, reasoning that state financial resources were too limited and that, in any case, the socialists would be adamantly opposed to any government meddling in worker pastimes.

12 M. Giani, "Per il dopolavoro," *Lavoro d'Italia*, 22 March 1923; *Il Dopolavoro. Rivista quindicinale illustrata*, vol. 1, no. 1 (1–15 February 1923), a fortnightly review absorbed by the syndicalist monthly *La Stirpe* in December 1923; the same title was used for a new series, vol. 4, no. 1 (January 1926)–vol. 6, no. 8 (February 1929), as well as for an edition published under the fascist "Republic of Salò" at Vicenza from late 1943 to early 1945.

13 M. Giani, "Per il dopolavoro," *Lavoro d'Italia*, 22 March 1923; also "Il problema del dopolavoro," 8 March 1923.

14 E. Rossoni, "Per il dopolavoro," ibid., 5 May 1923; M. Giani, "Gli orizzonti del dopolavoro," *La Stirpe*, vol. 1, no. 1 (December 1923), p. 39.

15 *La Stirpe*, vol. 1, no. 1 (December 1923), p. 54–5.

16 *Il Dopolavoro*, vol. 1, no. 2 (16–31 July 1923), vol. 1, no. 14 (1–15 September 1923), 11. On fascist squadrism in Piacenza province, see *Fascismo. Inchiesta socialista sulle gesta dei fascisti in Italia* (Milan, 1963), pp. 316–55.

17 *La Stirpe*, vol. 2, no. 4 (April 1925), 3–8; Palmiro Togliatti, *Lectures on Fascism*, trans. D. Dichter (New York, 1976), p. 78.

18 *Lavoro d'Italia*, 21 February 1924, 8 March 1924, 29 March 1924; also *Idea nazionale*, 22 February 1924; on Lojacono, ibid., 20 March 1919.

19 *La Stirpe*, vol. 2, no. 4 (April 1924), 312–13; also *Lavoro d'Italia*, 8 May 1924.

20 Reports carried in ACS, MI, PS (1903–49), G. 1, b. 22, f. Genova, part 2, sf. Sezione APE, 1923; also, sf. APEF, 1923; G. Tagliaferri, *Comunista non professionale* (Milan, 1977), p. 29; S. Provvisionato, "L'esperienza di 'Sport e proletariato,'" *Sport e società* (Rome, 1976), pp. 109–17; F. Felice, *Storia dello sport in Italia* (Rimini–Florence, 1977), pp. 80–90.

21 *La Stirpe*, in addition to publicizing the social virtues of foreign models of personnel management (from Robert Owen's New Lanark to the more recent philanthropic initiatives of Andrew Carnegie, John D. Rockefeller, and Henry Ford), closely followed employer initiatives in Italy in its "notiziario dopolavorista."

22 The one example cited (*La Stirpe*, vol. 2, no. 6 [June 1924], 479) was sponsored by a paper mill at Romagnano Sesia (Novara). Coercion probably played some part in an arrangement that had the employer constructing a two-story center and then placing it in syndicalist hands.

23 Preface, E. De Angelis, *Che cosa è e che cosa vuole il dopolavoro: l'organizzazione in provincia di Pavia* (Pavia, 1929), p. ii.

24 M. Giani, "Per l'elevazione delle classi operaie: il dopolavoro," *Lavoro d'Italia*, 15 March 1924; Cordova, p. 238.

25 Cordova, pp. 242, 247, 263–7; Lyttelton, pp. 309–10.

26 "Relazione dell'Ufficio Centrale del Dopolavoro al III Consiglio delle Corporazioni," *La Stirpe*, vol. 2, no. 6 (June 1924), pp. 479–81.

27 "Fascismo e dopolavoro," *La Stirpe.*, no. 7 (July 1924), pp. 643–4; "Gli enti nazionali e il dopolavoro," *La Stirpe.*, no. 9 (September 1924). M.G., "Per un ente nazionale del dopolavoro," *La Stirpe.*, no. 11 (November 1924).

28 Cordova, p. 403; see also Rossoni's comments in *La Stirpe*, vol. 3, no. 11 (November 1925).

29 ACS, PCM, 3, 3–6, 3200 sf. 1–1, Nava to Mussolini, 29 January 1925; Nava to Mussolini, 11 February 1925.

30 Ibid., report Pezzoli, n.d., but early April; Mussolini to Nava, 16 April 1925; ACS, PCM, *Verbali*, 6 April 1925, p. 98 bis; also *Lavoro d'Italia*, 26 April 1925, and *Il Popolo d'Italia*, 29 April 1925.

31 On the legal and other advantages of this variant on the *ente parastatale*, see G. Frignani, *Istituti parastatali e problemi d'assistenza e previdenza sociale. Discorsi alla Camera dei Deputati* (Rome, 1926).

32 R. D. Law 582, 1 May 1925, published in *Gazzetta ufficiale del Regno*, 846 (14 May 1925).

33 ACS, PCM, 1939–43, 3, 3–6, 3200, sf. 3–1, Mussolini to Duke of Aosta, 6 June 1925.

34 In addition to its initial endowment, the OND received an emergency grant of 400,000 lire annually for 1925–6 and 1926–7; after 1927 it obtained a regular subsidy of 1.07 percent of the obligatory dues paid to the trade unions and employer associations and administered by the Ministry of Corporations, a sum that amounted annually to approximately 4 million lire. For annual budgets, OND, *I primi cinque anni d'attività dell'OND* (Rome, 1931), pp. 205–26; ACS, PNF, Direttorio, b. 205, f. pratiche generali, OND, *Esercizio finanziario*, 1933–4; PCM, 1939–43, 3, 3–6, 3200, sf. 14, 1925–6; sf. 2, 1926–7; sf. 3.2, 1927–8, 1929–30; sf. 33, 1930–1, 1934–5, 1936–7. The semivoluntary character of OND financing was immediately underscored by Minister of Communications Ciano, who, urging Mussolini to authorize special railroad travel reductions to encourage membership in the *dopolavoro*, noted that the state's contribution "would suffice solely to cover the costs of organization and propaganda; the workers themselves and private initiative will have to provide for the actual institution of the local sections" (PCM, 1939–43, 3, 3–6, 3200, sf. 7, 30 October 1925).

35 *Lavoro d'Italia*, 20 April 1925; OND, *BU*, vol. 1, no. 1 (Janaury 1927), preface.

36 *La Stirpe*, vol. 4, no. 7 (July 1926); *Lavoro d'Italia*, 18 April 1925, 1 October 1926; PCM, 1931–3, 3–36, f. 8554/2, Turati to D'Alessio, 2 February 1926.

37 By the end of 1926, boards had been set up in only seventeen out of seventy provinces: Trent, Milan, Brescia, Como, Venice, Piacenza, Modena, Florence, Siena, Ravenna, Rome, Naples, Palermo, Turin, Novara, Alessandria, and Genoa; the number of members recruited directly by the OND amounted to 125,901, while 134,687 others came from the associations established within the state services (OND, *L'attività dell'OND dal maggio 1925 al marzo 1927* [Rome, 1927], p. 25; also OND, *BM*, vol. 1, no. 4 [April 1927]). On the particular difficulties Giani's appointees faced in the party squabbles of 1925–7, see: ACS, PCM, 1939–43, 3, 3–6, 3200, sf. 4, Suardo to Mussolini, 8 February 1926; 26 February 1926; sf. 6–4, Concini de Concin, avv. Franco. Ispettore della OND: suo ricorso avverso l'esonero di detto

incarico; also 1931–3, 3, 3–6, n. 8555, various letters from Giani to Mussolini 1926–7 and in particular Giani to Mussolini, 23 February 1926, annotated by Mussolini.

38 In September 1920, at the time of the factory occupations, the CGL counted 1,930,000 members in industry and agriculture. Its postwar maximum in 1921 was 2,200,000; see P. Spriano, *L'occupaziane delle fabbriche* (Turin, 1964), p. 1; on the syndicalists in the late twenties, see Carmen Haider, *Capital and Labor under Fascism* (New York, 1930), passim; also S. Tranquilli's "Gli sviluppi e funzioni del sindacalismo fascista," *Stato operaio*, vol. 2, no. 11–12 (November–December 1928), 693–705.

39 Lyttelton, pp. 277–92, 345.

40 OND, *BM*, vol. 1, no. 4 (April 1927), p. 11; ACS, PCM, 3, 3–6, 3200, sf. 2 Council of State, meeting 29 October 1926; sf. 3–1, note Ferrari-Pallavicino to Suardo, 24 November 1926; note Giani to Suardo, 20 November 1926; sf. 1–5, memorandum Ferrari-Pallavicino to Suardo, 5 November 1926; sf. 1, Ferrari-Pallavicino to Suardo, 8 November 1926. According to Haider (p. 220), who interviewed leading fascist officials in 1927–8, both Turati and Bottai, in consideration of the agency's technical-administrative functions, recognized that the "organization should rather be attached to the Ministry of Corporations and will be ultimately surrendered to it, or at least become a state and not a party institution."

41 OND, *BU*, vol. 1, no. 1 (January 1927), p. 39.

42 ACS, PCM, 1939–43, 3, 3–6, sf. 1, Ferrari-Pallavicino to Suardo, 8 November 1926, with note by Mussolini. ACS, PCM, 1939–43, 3, 3–6, n. 8555. A nasty rumor campaign about Giani's alleged malfeasance while in charge of the OND preceded his ouster; see one main font in ACS, SPD, CR.,b. 71, f. Carlo Lodi, a confidant of the PNF's administrative secretary Chiavolini, placed in the OND in early 1927. That these allegations were completely trumped up was implicitly acknowledged by the regime in May, when Ferrari-Pallavicino, with Mussolini's approval, wrote to reassure the Duke that the change in the administration had nothing to do with "irregularities" as "had been rumored" (ACS, PCM, 1939–43, 3, 3–6, 3200, sf. 3–7, Ferrari-Pallavicino to Mussolini, 15 May 1927; on the Duke's resignation: ACS, PCM, 1939–43, 3, 3–6, 3200, sf. 304, Duke of Aosta to Mussolini, 16 March 1927; Mussolini to Duke of Aosta, 4 April 1927; ACS, PCM, 1939–43, 3, 306, 3200, sf. 3–6, Turati to Suardo, 3 June 1927; sf. 8556, Giani to Mussolini, 27 April 1927; Duke of Aosta to Suardo, 22 May 1927; Giani to Duke of Aosta, 7 April 1927; *Il Dopolavoro dell'urbe*, vol. 1, nos. 6–7 [July 1930]).

43 ACS, PCM, 1939–43, 3, 3–6, 3200, sf. 3–7, Turati to Suardo, 6 May 1927. On the OND structure, OND, *BM*, vol. 1, nos. 11–12 (November–December 1927): "Ordinamento – programmi e regolamenti dell'OND" (hereafter OND, "Ordinamento"). On the ambiguities in the OND juridical structure resulting from this rapid changeover in its administration, see R. Richard, *La figura giuridica dell'OND* (Pavia, 1940), esp. pp. 40–78.

44 ACS, PCM, 1939–43, 3, 3–6, 3200, sf. 6–2, Turati to Mussolini, 17 December 1928, 19 December 1928. *LF*, 1 January 1930; also E. Savino, *La nazione operante*, 2nd ed. (Milan, 1934), p. 72.

45 OND, "Ordinamento", passim.

46 Some of the more active fascist federations, including Ravenna, Modena, and Florence, promptly began publishing their own bulletins. As the provincial party press developed in the later twenties, recreational activities were generally allotted a special *pagina del dopolavoro*. See, for example, *Bollettino del dopolavoro provinciale di Modena*, numero unico (30 September 1927); *Dopolavoro fiorentino*,

1928–31, irregular publication. *Gente nostra*'s circulation was mainly in the *dopolavoro*: 25,000 weekly, rising in 1939 to 115,000 with 40,000 subscriptions (ACS, SPD, CO, OND, f. 509. 016, sf. 3. Mino Somenzi to O. Sebastiani).

47 OND, "Ordinamento," p. 8.

48 OND, *BU*, September 1929, prot. n. 31148, 1 September 1929, p. 91; OND, "Ordinamento," p. 13.

49 M. Giani, "L'azione educativa dei dopolavoro," *La Stirpe*, vol. 3, no. 1 (January 1929), 42. OND, "Ordinamento," circular no. 301, 26, December 1927; also R. D. Law, 19 January 1928, no. 201. In 1927, Minister of Public Instruction Fedele had "invited" teachers to hold talks and lessons in the *dopolavoro*, urging them "to adapt their educational experience to the level of the particular public in each place" (OND, *BM*, vol. 1, nos. 11–12 [November–December 1927], p. 99). Teacher cooperation was essential; by the early thirties 1,772 held the positions of directors of local groups and 2,030 of technical collaborators according to the *Associazione fascista della scuola, foglio di disposizione*, vol. 4 (31 December 1933) 1229; the degree to which the party depended on these professionals for its cadres can be appreciated in the complaint of the *federale* of Trent, 21 October 1930, regarding the "scarcity of school teachers . . . almost the only element on which we can rely in the small municipalities" (ACS, PNF, SPP, b. 26, Trento).

50 ACS, PCM, 3, 3–6, 3200, sf. 2, Council of State, general meeting, 29 October 1926. In 1937, when the OND was legally made an extension of the state apparatus, fascist jurists were perplexed as to how to redefine the concept of *aderenti*, since citizens could in no juridical sense "adhere" to their own state, and especially now that they had been totally brought into the state by fascism.

51 *GN*, 22 December 1929.

52 *GN*, *Atti*, III Congresso Internazionale dell'Organizzazione Scientifica del Lavoro, Parte II, Memorie, p. 1155; OND, *BM*, vol. 1, no. 4 (April 1927), p. 27; quote from *GN*, vol. 2, nos. 5–6 (June–July, 1928), p. 17.

53 *GN*, vol. 1, nos. 9–10 (September–October 1927), p. 8.

54 *GN*, p. 37.

55 "Women's Work in Fascist Countries," *The International Trade Union Movement*, vol. 18, nos. 8–10 (August–October 1937), 84–85; see also: Maria Castellani, "Lavoro femminile e disoccupazione," *LF*, 17 November 1934; for the best introduction to fascist policy toward women, see A. De Grand, "Women under Italian Fascism," *Historical Journal*, vol. 19, no. 4 (1976), pp. 947–68.

56 OND, *BU*, vol. 1, no. 1 (January 1927), p. 17.

57 Quote from *OSL*, vol. 2, no. 5 (October 1927), 347; for a general characterization of the movement, see "Il movimento italiano per l'economia domestica," *OSL*, vol. 3, no. 1 (January 1928), p. 47; ENIOS, the sponsor of *OSL*, also promoted *Casa e lavoro* (Rome, vol. 1, no. 1 [April 1929]), while yet other proponents of household rationalization founded *La mia casa: rivista mensile di organizzazione scientifica applicata alla economia domestica*, vol. 1, no. 1 (November 1927). On the U.S. movement, see B. Ehrenreich and D. English, "The Manufacture of Housework," *Socialist Revolution*, vol. 5, no. 4 (October–December 1975).

58 Quote from N. Pende, a fascist "expert" on the sociology of women ("Le radici del male dell'iponatalità," *Gerarchia*, vol. 10, no. 8 [July 1929] pp. 519–20).

59 *Supplemento del Bollettino dell'Unione Femminile Cattolica Italiana*, ser. 4, no. 2 (December 1929); endorsing this new arrangement, the UDCI exhorted its members to work within local *dopolavoro* organizations to ensure a larger role for a "more

Christian and therefore more honest spiritual education of the masses'' (p. 1). Fearing that their organization would be deprived of any specific function once the Piccole Italiane and Giovani Fasciste were placed under the ONB in 1929, the Fasci's leaders had originally sought permission to set up their own Opera Assistenziale Femminile Fascista (see ACS, SPD, CO, b. E/47, f. 509.006/2.1, petition dated 5 October 1929). This request was naturally turned down. For 1930, the last year separate statistics were kept by the OND, 154,000 women were enrolled, equal to 10 percent of the total membership (*BLPS*, no. 55 [1931], p. 177).

60 G. Bertinetti, *Il libro del Dopolavoro* (Turin, 1928), p. 14.

61 *GN*, 29 September 1929.

62 *Civiltà fascista*, ed. G. Pomba (Turin, 1928), p. 413.

63 OND, "Ordinamento," pp. 40–41.

64 ACS, MI, PS (1903–49), G 1, b. 56, sf. Germigna (Varese), Circolo Cordialità, 1929. For a typical example of "evasion," to use the term adopted by prefects in their reports, see the case of the mutual aid society Eugenio Valzanzia. According to the prefect, it; "touted itself as being a welfare association; but it was in fact a section of the Republican party and under the pretext of mutual aid, members kept alive their faith and perhaps even nourished the secret hope of reconstituting the party" (ACS, MI, PS [1920–45], G 1, b. 96, f. Ancona, sf. Società mutuo soccorso Eugenio Valzanzia, 1929).

65 Circular, 5 January 1927, B. Mussolini, *OO*, vol. 22, p. 468; for the full text of the January 1924 law on working class associations, see ILO, *Legislative Series*, 1924, It 1, Decree: Supervision of Worker Associations; for an example of its use, see ACS, MI, PS (1920–45), G 1, b. 138 Treviso, sf. Sant'Ambrogio di Fiera, sezione Dopolavoro fascista, 1929; there the prefect, using the pretext that the club had allowed young girls to dance after hours, removed the director, a former communist named Novella. By May, Mussolini claimed his prefects had already shut down 25,000 of Italy's 187,000 taverns; his government, he boasted, could permit itself the "luxury of closing down these purveyors of ruinous happiness," since it no longer had "to solicit the votes of innkeepers and their clients as had been the case in the democratic-liberal middle ages" (*OO*, vol. 22, p. 363).

66 ACS, MI, PS (1903–49), G 1, b. 56, sf. Germigna (Varese), Circolo Cordialità, 1929.

67 ACS, MI, PS (1903–49), b. 35, f. Novara, sf. Arona (Novara), Società della Tazza, 1928.

68 ACS, PCM (1927), b. 3–18, n. 3233, memo Turati to President of the Council of Ministers, 20 July 1927; memorandum Suardo to President of the Council of Ministers, 18 September 1927.

69 ACS, MI, PS (1920–45), G 1, b. 102, f. Como, sf. Como, Dongo, Circolo Operaio Ricreativo, prefectorial report 6 December 1932.

70 ACS, MI, PS (1920–45), G 1, b. 141, f. Vercelli, sf. Borgo Isola (Vercelli), prefectorial report 7 October 1929.

71 ACS, PNF, Direttorio, b. 205, f. pratiche generali, OND, *Esercizio finanziario*, 1933–4.

72 ACS, MI, PS (1903–49), G 1, b. 45, f. Roma, Casa del Popolo. "Appunti per il gabinetto di S. E. il Ministro," 23 March 1927; ACS, *Mostra della Rivoluzione fascista*, b. 17, f. 37 "Casa del Popolo"; *LF*, 4 May 1929.

73 *LF*, 18 December 1931.

74 *Vita e lotta delle case del popolo della provincia di Firenze, 1944–1956* (Florence, 1956); Alleanza per la Ricreazione Popolare di Firenze, "I rapporti fra l'amministrazione

finanziaria dello Stato e le case del popolo della provincia di Firenze, lettera a S. E. Ezio Vanoni, Ministero delle Finanze" (Florence, 1953). A mere 100 of the more than 2,000 members of the venerable Florentine Mutual Aid Society of Rifredi attended the general assembly, and many of those who did come voted under duress to "donate" the property to the PNF. Società di Mutuo Soccorso Rifredi, "Riccorso avverso lo sfrattamento amministrativo con breve storia della vita e della attività del sodalizio" (Florence, 1955). Pamphlets courtesy of Signorina Albertina Baldi.

75 OND, *BM*, vol. 1, no. 4 (April 1927), pp. 48–52.

76 Circular Turati to *federali* and *dopolavoro* commissars, 28 May 1927, cited in OND, "Ordinamento," p. 45.

77 OND, Dopolavoro provinciale di Ravenna, *Il dopolavoro, istituzione fascista* (Ravenna, 1929), pp. 21, 65–9.

78 *65 anni di vita della casa del popolo di Pignone*, a cura del Comitato di Difesa (Florence, 1954). Pamphlet courtesy of A. Baldi.

79 See, for example, the statute of the Dopolavoro Agricolo of Montalbano Elicona (a rural center in the province of Messina) in ACS, MI, PS (1920–45), G 1, f. Messina, sf. Montalbano Elicona, taken as a model for all the agricultural *dopolavoro* circles in that province.

80 Merli, p. 848; OND, "Ordinamento," p. 68.

81 ACS, PCM, 1927, 14, 3, f. 244, Giani to Suardo, 3 December 1926; Circular Turati to provincial boards, 22 June 1927, in OND, "Ordinamento," p. 46.

82 ACS, PNF, SPP, b. 22, La Spezia, "Gran rapporto delle Camicie Nere della Lunigiana," 9 June 1929; MI, PS (1927–33), 1930–1, sezione seconda, G 1, b. 75, sf. Genova – sindacati: fiduciary report, 3 August 1930.

83 Ibid.

84 *GN*, 9 June 1929; also 1 September 1929.

85 The summer of 1931 was particularly agitated: In June, vast strikes broke out among women rice weeders in several northern provinces; from late spring, rioting against Catholic Action groups induced by fascists took place; and in June–July at least fifteen bombing incidents occurred. See: Rome-based *Herald Tribune* correspondent D. Darrah's *Hail Caesar* (Boston, New York, 1936), pp. 170–2, 194. The results of a nationwide fascist inquiry into Catholic Action indicated the organization's extraordinary growth over the preceding year; see A. Parisi, "L'azione cattolica nel 1931: organizzazione e atteggiamenti politici," *La Chiesa del Concordato*, a cura di F. Margiotta Broglio (Bologna, 1977), pp. 591–681; also P. Ranfagni, *I clericofascisti* (Florence, 1975); and F. Schianchi, *La università cattolica del Sacro Cuore* (Milan, 1974). On Communist party activity, see P. Spriano, *Storia del partito comunista italiano*, 5 vols. (Turin, 1967–76), vol. 2, pp.287–307; De Felice, vol. 4, pp. 77–80, 82, and especially P. Secchia, *L'azione svolta dal partito comunista in Italia durante il fascismo, 1926–1932. Annali Feltrinelli*, vol. 8, 1966.

86 In 1932 Mussolini introduced a bill authorizing the government to ratify the Washington Convention of 1919 on the eight-hour day/48-hour week. By the time the bill became law on 16 May 1933, replacing the legislation on hours of work of 15 March 1923, and 30 June 1926 (ILO, *Legislative Series*, 1933, It. 5, "Act: Hours of Work"), it was already an anachronism; in July 1934, 28.7 percent of all industrial workers were on part time or working under 40 hours per week (*Bollettino mensile di statistiche*, September 1934, p. 794). According to C. Vannutelli's estimates ("Les conditions de vie des travailleurs italiens au cours de la periode 1929–1939," *Mouvements ouvriers et dépression économique* [Assen, 1966], p. 314, table 3), the average number of working hours per month among

industrial workers decreased by 25 hours between 1929 and 1936:

Year	hours/month	Year	hours/month	Year	hours/month
1929	182	1933	174	1937	163
1930	175	1934	172	1938	159
1931	170	1935	159	1939	160
1932	168	1936	157		

87 De Felice, IV, pp. 170–1; Castronovo, pp. 296–333; L. Rosenstock-Franck, *Les Etapes de l'économie fasciste italienne du corporativisme à l'économie de guerre* (Paris, 1939).
88 *OO*, vol. 25, p. 72, and De Felice, IV, p. 226; "Consegna a Parenti" (dated 24 June 1933), in *Forze civili*, vol. 2, nos. 7–8 (July–August 1933); and the perceptive communist analysis in "Andare al popolo," *Stato operaio*, vol. 6, nos. 1–2 (January–February 1932), p. 49.
89 *GN*, 26 October 1930; "enthusiasm" was the keynote of Starace's acceptance speech. He was subsequently appointed head of the FIE (*GN*, 13 November 1930). On Starace's activity in Milan, see *Popolo di Lombardia*, 9 March 1929; on the first national meeting, see *LF*, 16 January 1931.
90 For biographical notices: ACS, SPD, CR, b. 90, A. Starace, sf. rilievi a suo carico, and sf. varie; also D. M. Tuninnetti, *Il partito fascista nella vita nazionale* (Rome, 1933), p. 176.
91 Cited from Mario Rivoire, "Fascismo e partito," *Critica fascista*, vol. 9, no. 22 (15 November 1931), 422–5. There is no history of the PNF in the thirties, although many studies (e.g., Germino) refer generically to the changes in structure taking place in that decade; the articulations of local party organizations after 1930 can be clearly seen in G. Sapelli's *Fascismo, grande industria e sindacato: il caso di Torino 1929–1935* (Milan, 1975), pp. 71–84; as well as in M. Palla's *Firenze nel regime fascista, 1929–34* (Florence, 1978), esp. pp. 206–30; for a perceptive overview, see E. Ragionieri, *Storia d'Italia dall'unità a oggi: la storia politica e sociale* (Turin, 1978), pp. 2223–5. The term "party of a new kind" was coined by Lenin and copied by Mussolini, as Togliatti noted in his Moscow Lectures, pointing out that the PNF might properly be considered the Italian bourgeoisie's "party of a new kind" (Togliatti, *Lectures*, pp. 13–43; for PNF statutes: Aquarone, pp. 518–29).
92 *LF*, 18 December 1931.
93 "Una visita al dopolavoro tramvieri di Roma," *LF*, 24 April 1932.
94 A. Starace, *L'Opera Nazionale Dopolavoro* (Rome, 1933), p. 94.
95 Indeed, the OND'S membership drive, which had been so successful in the late twenties (at least as measured by membership tallies), slackened off with the great crisis; for 1930 an increase of only 176,914 members was registered; for 1931, 149,945; and for 1932 a mere 3,485. The declining rate of enrollment was most seriously felt in the industrial sector, where, after increasing at an annual average rate of 80 percent between 1926 and 1929, it fell off to 14 percent in 1930 and to 12 percent in 1931; between 1931 and 1932 membership barely rose from 683,851 members to 684,413. In Piedmont the numbers of industrial workers enrolled actually fell between 1930 and 1932 from 119,150 to 111,055, as in Lombardy in 1931–2 from

219,865 to 215,480. At least some of this decline in membership could of course be ascribed to layoffs in the industrial concerns through which many members were enrolled. The OND was still ill equipped to enroll the unemployed or to launch an effective recruitment drive for new members outside the state employees' organizations and private industrial and commercial firms that had accounted for the overwhelming number of members in the late 1920s (OND, *Realizzazioni e sviluppi dell'Opera Nazionale Dopolavoro* [Rome, 1933], Appendix: "Ripartizioni per zone dei tesserati secondo le diverse categorie di lavoro").

96 OND, *BU*, February 1931, prot. n. 10909, 25 February 1931; OND, *BU*, October 1931, prot. n. 37720, 20 October 1931; also *LF*, 18 December 1931. ACS, PNF, SPP, b. 22, La Spezia, report of the *federale* to party secretary, March 1931.

97 Communiqué no. 4, Starace, in *Santa milizia*, January 24, 1931.

98 ACS, MI, PS (1927–33), b. 75, Torino, 1930–1, seconda sezione, f. Torino–sindacato: report 8 August 1931. The essentially voluntary nature of participation in the *dopolavoro* was recognized by the Communist party of Italy as early as 1933; for a first nuanced appraisal, see F. Furini, "Per la conquista delle masse dopolavoriste," *Stato operaio*, vol. 7, no. 8 (August 1933), p. 502; also Archivio Partito Comunista, 1933, 1123/88–Q 1, ufficio politico, 5 May 1933, o.d.g.: "Lavoro delle organizzazioni di massa giovanili e nel Dopolavoro," signed R. di Marcucci; in addition to Togliatti's *Lectures*. Nevertheless, as Furini correctly pointed out, participation was not unanimous: "There are numbers of workers who have always been, and still are, opposed to the *dopolavoro*, who do not want to enroll, and if forced to do so, refuse to participate in any of its activities" – but these workers were a "minority" and generally to be found among the older generation (p. 502).

99 OND, *Annuario* 1937, p. 249. According to the 1936 population census (as analyzed by Paolo Sylos Labini, *Saggio sulle classi sociali* [Bari–Rome, 1974] table I, 1), the salaried petty bourgeoisie, including teachers, state and private employees, numbered 990,000, whereas workers in industry and construction numbered 4,200,000. Fascist estimates (OND, *BU*, October 1935, prot. n. 61301), according to which 3,479,200 small proprietors, sharecroppers, tenants, and common laborers were eligible to join, clearly understated the total number of peasants; according to the 1931 population census (analyzed by O. Vitali, *La popolazione attiva in agricoltura attraverso i censimenti italiani, 1861–1961* [Rome, 1968], pp. 190–8), the population active in agriculture numbered 8,168,876; excluding women (4,004,601) and large and medium proprietors (approximately 20 percent), the fascist estimate is perhaps a realistic assessment of "eligibles."

100 OND, *Annuario*, 1936, p. 14: according to ENAL, "Legge 24 maggio 1937, portante modificazione alle norme sull'ordinamento dell'OND," the total regular staff in the central administration numbered 200.

101 Savino, p. 252.

102 ACS, PNF, D. II, Servizi amministrativi, b. 275, Ufficio Legale, sf. 22 L: Inchiesta OND. Most irregularities resulted from falsifying accounts and sales of membership cards. Also on alleged and actual corruption in the OND: ACS, SPD, CO, b. 49, OND, f. 016.518, Dinale to Mussolini memorandum, p. 2; also ACS, MI, PS, Polizia politica, M 3, b. 158, f. 5, 1935–6, containing police reports on firings in the OND bureaucracy, not least of all that of Beretta, who, his corruption notwithstanding, was subsequently appointed a high-level trade union inspector. A commission of inquiry, appointed in late 1935, found that "accounts had been kept in a disorderly and chaotic state for several years," and estimated outright theft at 1.8 million lire

or approximately $144,000 (ACS, PCM, 1939–43, 3, 3–6, 3200 sf. 33, Min. delle Corporazioni, Commissione di disciplina, Minutes, 15 July 1937).

103 On Parenti, see: ACS, SPD, CR, b. 45, Rino Parenti, sf. fiduciary reports of 4 June 1932 and 4 July 1933; also ACS, PNF, SPP, b. 7, Milano, 3 October 1931 and 16 February 1934; other prominent *federali* active in the provincial *dopolavoro* organizations included A. Gastaldi at Turin and Carlo Parenti at Florence.

104 On Battigalli, ACS, PNF, SPP, b. 14, f. Pescara; OND, *BU*, December 1939, foglio di comunicazione, no. 207, 16 December 1939. On the appearance of this "new middle class" in the fascist bureaucracies see, in general, R. Michels, *First Lectures in Political Sociology*, trans. A. de Grazia (Minneapolis, 1949), pp. 113–14; also Harold D. Lasswell and Renzo Sereno, "The Fascists: The Changing Italian Elite," in Laswell and D. Lerner, eds., *World Revolutionary Elites*, pp. 179–93. Whether the OND ever sought to exploit the potential insights of "ex-subversives" in any systematic way is unlikely. The example of one Virgilio Poletti, an "ex–ardito del popolo" and secretary of the Dopolavoro of Parma in 1934–5, praised by his superiors for his solicitous attention to the "figli del popolo" of the proletarian Oltretorrente district, appears altogether exceptional (ACS, PNF, SPP, b. 12, Parma); the risks of recruiting such figures (without of course assuming that they even sought such positions) obviously outweighed the possible political benefits.

105 An example, the board of Ariano (Avellino), a rural center with 20,747 inhabitants, included altogether seventeen men: three doctors, three professors, two lawyers, an engineer, a merchant, a photographer, salesman, builder, clerk, architect; two were unidentified as to profession, though one, the treasurer, certainly had accounting skills (*LF*, 23 July 1929).

106 Emilio Radius, *Usi e costumi dell'uomo fascista* (Milan, 1964), p. 314. On the changing function of the "intellectual" in the 1930s, see S. Grussu, "Modificazione delle funzioni intellettuali dal 1936 a oggi: una analisi," *Critica marxista*, vol. 15, no. 6 (1977), 37–72.

107 *BLPS*, 54 (31 July 1930–31 December 1930), p. 158. Although the training desirable for "organizers" of leisure was never even discussed, the regime did undertake efforts to train professional organizers for youth (*balilla*) and labor. On 5 February 1928, it set up the Accademia Fascista per la Preparazione degli Insegnanti di Educazione Fascista, a two-year course to train *balilla* leaders. The *scuole sindacali* for the new syndical cadres began operation in 1930. The OND manuals, with meticulous instructions on how to organize amateur theater, orchard gardens, cinema and radio services, and so forth, were evidently for the benefit of cadres, whether amateur or self-styled professionals.

108 For accounts: *LF*, 17 November 1935, 20 December 1935, 21 December 1935, and passim, October 1925–May 1936; also *GN*, 5 January 1936, 12 January 1936; on Fiat, *Bianco e rosso*, passim, October 1935–May 1936.

109 Spriano, III, p. 45.

110 Report dated May 1936, in S. Merli, ed., "La ricostruzione del movimento socialista in Italia e la lotta contro il fascismo dal 1934 alla seconda guerra mondiale," Istituto Giangiacomo Feltrinelli, *Annali*, vol. 5 (1962), 192.

3. Taylorizing worker leisure

1 See Chapter 2, note 10. For an analysis of the character of employer paternalism in pre–World War I Italy, its paucity and autocratic implementation, see: S. Merli,

Proletariato di fabbrica e capitalismo industriale: il caso italiano, 2 vols. (Florence, 1972–3) vol. 1, pp. 357–72; also Baglioni, passim. On the mentality of the "exceptional" philanthropist, see G. Baglioni: "La costruzione del paternalismo organico del pensiero di un imprenditore d'eccezione, A. Rossi," *Studi di sociologia*, vol. 9, nos. 3–4 (July–December 1971); and on the first stirrings of reformism, his "La prima organizzazione di classe del padronato italiano: la Lega di Torino," ibid., vol. 10, nos. 2–3 (April–September 1972).

2 R. Sarti, *Fascism and the Industrial Leadership in Italy, 1919–1940* (Berkeley, 1971), pp. 10–32; also V. Castronovo, "La grande industria: giochi interni e linea di fondo," *Il Ponte*, vol. 26, no. 10 (31 October 1970), 1198 ff.

3 See *Organizzazione industriale*, 1922–5, passim; CGII, *Annuario*, 1922–6; *Bollettino della "Cotoniera,"* 1922–6, passim; *Bollettino della "Laniera,"* 1922–5, passim. On Benni: Piero Melograni, "Antonio Stefano Benni," *Dizionario biografico italiano*, vol. 8, pp. 558–61; Adrian Lyttelton, *The Seizure of Power: Fascism in Italy, 1919–1929* (New York, 1973), pp. 212–13. In post–World War I America, the term "welfare work" continued to be used (as it was in England; see E. Kelly, ed., *Welfare Work in Industry* [London, 1925]), although more modern (and neutral) terms, for example "personnel management" and "social engineering," were preferred by employers. In Italy, the term "welfare work," meaning all of the employer-initiated benefits for workers, came to be translated as "assistenza sociale nella fabbrica," in France, as "oeuvre sociale"; see for example R. Pinot, *Les Oeuvres sociales des industries metallurgiques* (Paris, 1924).

4 M. Fassio, *L'organizzazione industriale moderna* (Turin, 1922), cited in Castronovo, *Agnelli* (Turin, 1971), p. 328; Fiat's expensive paternalism was justified to its stockholders in its annual stockholders' report (Archivio Centro Storico Fiat, *Relazione del consiglio di amministrazione e dei sindaci*, 20 March 1923, p. 7); whatever it cost was certainly offset by the 30 percent reduction in labor costs from 1920 to 1923 (Castronovo, p. 336).

5 Quoted in Fiat, *Le mutue interne* (Turin, 1940), p. 30. ACS, MI, PS (1903–49), G 1, b. 50, Torino (part II) sf. società mutuo soccorso Fiat: prefectorial report, 26 May 1926. As a further concession in 1924, Fiat had increased its regular contribution to the fund to 10 lire per worker per year (400,000 lire) and promised to pay work fines into the fund.

6 "Fascismo e sindacalismo," *Gerarchia*, vol. 4, no. 5 (May 1925), p. 274.

7 M. Giani, *Quaderni del dopolavoro*, "Il dopolavoro nelle industrie" (Rome, 1925), no. 2, p. 5.

8 Ibid, p. 3.

9 Ibid, p. 2; Di Nardo, p. 403, in *Civiltà fascistà*, ed. G. Pomba (Turin, 1928); also OND, *BU*, vol. 1, no. 1 (1 January 1927), p. 32 for complaints about industry's fear "even of a parastate agency" and its lack of cooperation.

10 One of the most significant outcomes of this industrial reorganization after 1927 was a general increase in firm size. In industrial Turin the average size of the labor force in machine and metallurgical firms nearly doubled between 1928 and 1931; by 1938 it had tripled, reaching an average of 100 employees per firm. For Italy as a whole between the industrial censuses of 1927 and 1938, the number of large firms employing 250 or more persons jumped by 75 percent: from 1,724 with altogether 1,067,863 employees to 2,153 with 1,522,671. The most striking growth occurred in "gigantic" firms with more than 1,000 employees; these increased in number from 224 in 1927 with 375,350 workers or 9 percent of the industrial labor force, to 345 in 1938 employing 717,418 persons or 20 percent of the total (Unione Fascista degli

Industriali della Provincia di Torino, *Torino industriale* [Rome, 1939], pp. 13, 17; *Censimento degli esercizi industriali e commerciali*, 1927, vol. 8, p. 36; *Censimento, 1937–1940, Risultati generali, I, Industria*, part 2, pp. 16–17). Because this latter census used somewhat different criteria, I have relied on M. Saibante's interpretation of the 1937–40 industrial statistics in *Il fascismo e l'industria* (Verona, 1940), p. 64. Generally, on the effects of rationalization on labor, see H. Braverman's excellent *Labor and Monopoly Capital: the Degradation of Work in the Twentieth Century* (New York, 1974), esp. pp. 1–52.

11 CGII, *Relazione all'assemblea* (Rome, 14 February 1930), p. 130.

12 Renzo De Felice, *Mussolini il fascista: l'organizzazione dello stato fascista, 1925–1929* (hereafter De Felice, vol. 3) 5 vols. (Turin, 1968), 3, p. 452; ACS, SPD, CR, b. 27; Gran Consiglio, sf. 5, 1927, inserto C. Ministero dell'Interno, Capo della Polizia, Note for the head of the Cabinet of Ministers, containing fiduciary reports on strikes among textile workers, 24 and 27 October 1927. In the four months following the first wage cuts, police reported twenty-three slowdowns, seventeen major strikes, and seven sitdown protests; in late October 1927, 15,000 workers in the textile centers of Legnano and Valle Olona struck against the new national contract. According to various police reports from the fall of 1927, workers struck "in support of those punished or fired for disciplinary reasons; to oblige employers to restore the old work systems; because they had not been paid justly; or for reasons generally having to do with the employer's failure to abide by the contracts." The fascist trades proved unable to stop the strikes.

13 G. Bottai, *Il dirigente d'azienda in regime corporativo* (Città di Castello, 1929), p. 22.

14 C. Tarlarini, "Relazione al Consiglio Superiore dell'Economia Nazionale," *BLPS* (March 1926), pp. 86–8.

15 F. A. Liverani, *Gli spacci operai, come nacquero e come si diffusero* (Milan, 1928), p. 10.

16 Ibid., p. 17.

17 *Il Popolo d'Italia*, 9 December 1926.

18 *Lavoro d'Italia*, 19 September 1926.

19 OND, *BM*, "Il dopolavoro e le opere assistenziali nelle industrie," vol. 1, nos. 7–8 (July–August 1927), pp. 7, 26–8.

20 O. Bellucci, "Il fattore umano nell'organizzazione scientifica del lavoro," *Organizzazione scientifica del lavoro* (hereafter OSL), vol. 2, no. 6 (December 1927), 484; for an example, see P. Audibert, "L'organizzazione razionale del lavoro nelle miniere," *Organizzazione scientifica del lavora*, vol. 3, no. 4 (July–August, 1928), pp. 545–6.

21 "Il dopolavoro e le opere assistenzioni nelle industrie," p. 15. The more receptive climate for industrial welfare work was reflected almost immediately in the number of firms listed by the OND as having some kind of social service for workers. By the end of 1927, 479 firms with 64,757 employees had enrolled, while another 633 firms sponsored services independently and an additional 35 were planning new initiatives. See OND, *BM*, vol. 2, no. 1 (January 1928), 84, for a complete list of the enterprises with social services.

22 *La Stirpe*, vol. 5, no. 6 (June 1927), 372; Lyttelton, p. 69.

23 OND, *I dopolavoro aziendali in Italia* (Rome, 1938), pp. 245–68; ASInd (March–April 1932), p. 194; LF, 4 April 1940; Montecatini, *La Società Montecatini e il suo gruppo industriale* (Milan, 1936); Montecatini, *Il Dopolavoro Montecatini* (Milan, March–April 1942).

24 OND, *I dopolavoro aziendali*, pp. 301–12.
25 *Informazione industriale*, 30 December 1929.
26 Quoted in De Felice, vol. 3, p. 453
27 Speech of 22 June 1929, quoted in CGII, *Annuario*, 1929, p. 40.
28 *LF*, 9 July 1929.
29 Fiat, *Le istituzioni Fiat*, p. 31, citing the OND's communiqué of 14 March 1928. This turned out to be a relatively minor concession: Fiat retained uncontested control over its mutual funds and professional schools as well as over the staffing and planning of its recreational programs.
30 *Santa milizia*, 21 April 1928; 26 July 1930; OND, *I dopolavoro aziendali*, p. 17. The number of company groups increased from 3 to 10 between 1928 and 1930, rising to 22 by 1937.
31 According to the Confindustria, the total number of firms with *dopolavoro* was: 1927, 861; 1928, 1,239; 1929, 1,670; 1930, 2,130; 1931, 2,938; 1937, 3,000 (CGII, *Annuario*, 1937). The absence of statistics for 1932–6 might suggest that firms supplying social services tapered off in those years because of the economic crisis. For a general pictorial description of industrial social services, see: CGII, *L'industria e le opere sociali* (Rome, 1937); also ASInd, vol. 12, no. 3 (May–June 1938). The OND claimed nonetheless that 8,000 medium-sized firms could potentially set up *dopolavoro* facilities (OND, *BU*, February 1937, prot. no. 9594 Puccetti to *dopolavoro provinciali*).
32 For example: ACS, PNF, SPP, b. 19. Rome, fiduciary report of 4 December 1934; ibid., fiduciary report, 1935.
33 ACS, PNF, SPP, b. 24. Terni, report *federale* to party secretary, 1931; report *federale* to party secretary, August 1931.
34 ACS, PNF, D. Carte delle Federazioni, b. 209, Florence, f. Lecore Signa, Marinelli to Donegani, 29 January 1937; Donegani to Marinelli, 11 February 1937.
35 CGII, *Annuario*, 1937.
36 *Informazione industriale*, 3 May 1929; ibid., 7–14 December 1934.
37 *LF*, 3 April 1937.
38 Quoted in ASInd, vol. 7, no. 4 (July–August 1933).
39 CGII, *Relazione all'assemblea generale dei delegati* (Rome, 30 June 1933), p. 112.
40 OND, *BM*, vol. 1, nos. 7–8 (July–August 1927), p. 32.
41 See the Dopolavoro director Vandone's report of 1934 in *Bianco e rosso*, vol. 3, no. 5 (May 1934).
42 In 1937 employees at Benni's Magneti Marelli Company complained to Capoferri that the company was subtracting 10 lire per month, claiming that the deduction had been officially approved. When Capoferri referred the complaint to the fascist federation of Milan, he pointed out that the company might well try to deny that it was forcing membership, "but in effect, joining was obligatory because employees who objected [to the deductions] were suspect." The unauthorized quota had to be eliminated, he insisted, in view of the rising cost of living and because otherwise the *dopolavoro* "ran the risk of being hated" (ACS, SPD, CO, OND, f. 509.016, sf. varia, police wiretap, 16 April 1937).
43 OND, *BM*, vol. 1, nos. 7–8 (July–August 1927), p. 22.
44 *Organizzazione industriale*, August 1929; ASInd, vol. 7, no. 1 (January–February 1933); G. Gobbi, "Clima politico," ASInd, vol. 5, no. 2 (March–April 1931), p. 24.
45 On the "Beauty of Work," see A. G. Rabinbach, "The Aesthetics of Production in the Third Reich," *Journal of Contemporary History*, vol. 2, no. 4 (October 1976), 43–74; also T. Mason, *Sozialpolitik im Dritten Reich: Arbeiterklasse und Volks-*

gemeinschaft (Opladen, 1977), passim. Run by the ambitious young architect Albert Speer, it had reportedly sponsored by 1939 the redecoration of 26,000 workshops and the institution of 24,000 washing and changing rooms, 18,000 canteens and recreation rooms, 17,000 gardens in industrial plants, and 3,000 sports fields.

46 G. Gobbi, "Sviluppo del servizio sociale in Italia," ASInd, vol. 10, no. 4 (July–October 1936), 33–35; ibid., vol. 11, no. 2 (March–April 1937), 15–18. On the absence of innovation in health care under the regime, see: Ministero per la Costituente, Commissione per lo Studio dei Problemi del Lavoro, *Atti*, vol. 3 (Rome, 1946), 104.

47 *Censimento industriale*, 1937–40, vol. 1, part 2, 17. CGFI, *Relazione*, 1938, p. 28.

48 On the Fiat works under fascism, see V. Castronovo's *Agnelli*; also G. Sapelli, *Fascismo, grande industria e sindacato; il caso di Torino, 1929–1935* (Milan, 1975); S. Bologna, "Quando la storia della classe operaia Fiat?" *Quaderni piacentini*, vol. 11, no. 46 (March 1973), 170–4; International Labor Office, *Studies and Reports*, ser. A, no. 35, Studies in Industrial Relations, vol. 2, The Fiat Establishment (Geneva, 1932), pp. 22–73 for a description of the plant and social services. ACSF is a main source of information, specifically b. 14 and b. 10.

49 Fiat, *Le istituzioni Fiat a favore dei propri addetti: il dopolavoro* (Turin, 1929), p. 16.

50 ACSF, *Relazione del consiglio di amministrazione e dei sindaci*, Assemblea ordinaria degli azionisti, 20 March 1923, p. 7.

51 On the introduction of the Bedeaux system, see Castronovo, pp. 485–6; on the inauguration of the Dopolavoro, ACSF, b. 10, *La nuova grandiosa sede del dopolavoro Fiat*, 1928.

52 *Bianco e rosso*, vol. 2, no. 4 (June 1933); vol. 3, no. 9 (November 1933); vol. 3, no. 5 (May 1934).

53 ACSF, Biografie, f. U. Gobbato; f. Aristide Follis.

54 For a description, see Fiat, *Le istituzioni Fiat*, pp. 34–6; *Bianco e rosso*, vol. 3, no. 5 (May 1934).

55 Sapelli, p. 114.

56 Ibid.; OND, *I dopolavoro aziendali*, p. 16.

57 ACSF, b. 14, *Cassa mutua interna operai Fiat* (Turin, 1928); *Le mutue aziendali Fiat* (Turin, 1940); also ILO, "Fiat Establishment," pp. 58–64. On children's camps: ACSF, b. 10, *Cassa mutua operai Fiat, 1924–1936*. Children reportedly gained an average of 2 kilograms during their month's sojourn (p. 17). Besides recreation, children also received an hour of instruction per day on patriotic and fascist themes. On the fringe benefits of the office employees, see *Mutua impiegati Fiat* (Turin, 6 July 1942).

58 ACSF, b. 14, *40 anni della Scuola Alunni Fiat*; ILO, "Fiat Establishment," pp. 54–55.

59 *Bianco e rosso*, vol. 3, no. 1 (January 1934); vol. 3, no. 5 (May 1934); Fiat provided scholarships for students and attendance was obligatory for those enrolled.

60 ILO, "Fiat Establishment," pp. 63–64; plans in *Le istituzioni Fiat*, pp. 26–30. On Mirafiori, see *Rapporto 28 Ottobre, 1939: Dopolavoro aziendale Fiat*; for management's view of the services at Villar Perosa, see *Villar Perosa: il villaggio Agnelli*, 1931. According to the press release in honor of its twenty-fifth anniversary, the village demonstrated "the degree to which modern mechanized civilization can develop not only without repressing or diminishing, but indeed increasing and even exhalting the traditional social and moral values."

61 ACS, MI, PS (1927–33), 1928, b. 164, f. Torino, prefectorial telegram, 7 June 1928.

62 *Bianco e rosso*, vol. 2, no. 11 (November 1933); *Le istituzioni Fiat*, pp. 57–63.
63 See especially: ibid., pp. 32–34, 65–70.
64 Ibid., p. 40.
65 *Bianco e rosso*, vol. 3, no. 5 (May 1934).
66 *Bianco e rosso*, vol. 6, no. 10 (October 1937).
67 *Bianco e rosso*, vol. 4, no. 4 (April 1935). According to Cianetti (CFLI, Series Ab, 1, *Convegno nazionale dei dirigenti dei sindacati fascisti dell'industria*, Rome, 17 March 1934, p. 10), 1,000 copies of *Lavoro fascista*, the least conformist newspaper of the regime, were delivered weekly to the Fiat works and there were numerous complaints when the number was temporarily reduced. This is not to say that management did not have difficulties organizing this cultural interest. In 1934 Vandone noted that "we must be frank in acknowledging the difficulties encountered in organizing conferences that spark the interest of the people who work, or at least it is difficult to find topics that truly interest the masses." To boost participation, organizers were seeking more attractive topics and more convenient scheduling (*Bianco e rosso*, vol. 3, no. 5 [May 1934]).
68 *Bianco e rosso*, vol. 1, no. 3 (May 1932); vol. 1, no. 5 (July 1932).
69 *Bianco e rosso*, vol. 2, no. 4 (June 1933); vol. 2, no. 6 (August 1933); vol. 3, no. 1 (January 1934).
70 *Bianco e rosso*, vol. 3, no. 10 (October 1934).
71 *Bianco e rosso*, vol. 1, no. 8 (December 1932).
72 *Bianco e rosso*, vol. 2, no. 4 (June 1933).
73 ACSF, b. 14, Biblioteca Fiat, *Supplemento al catalogo generale*, April 1934.
74 *Bianco e rosso*, vol. 4, no. 10 (October 1935); vol. 5, no. 11 (November 1936).
75 *Bianco e rosso*, vol. 4, no. 4 (June 1935); vol. 6, no. 4 (April 1937); OND, *I dopolavoro aziendali*, pp. 106–7.
76 SIP, *Grande dizionario enciclopedico*, vol. 17, p. 433. SIP was absorbed by the state holding company IRI in 1933.
77 *Sincronizzando*, vol. 1, no. 1 (February 1922), p. 69.
78 *Sincronizzando*, vol. 9, no. 1 (January 1930), p. 61.
79 Ibid., p. 62.
80 *Sincronizzando*, vol. 8, no. 12 (December 1929), p. 871.
81 *Sincronizzando*, vol. 7, no. 12 (December 1928), p. 816; vol. 9, no. 1 (January 1930), p. 63.
82 *Sincronizzando*, vol. 9, no. 1 (January 1930), p. 61.
83 *Sincronizzando*, vol. 8, no. 6 (June 1929), p. 425.
84 R. Tremelloni, *L'industria tessile italiana, come è sorta, come è oggi* (Turin, 1937), pp. 225–36. According to Tremelloni (pp. 230–3), only 2.3 percent of the textile labor force was engaged in sales or clerical capacities as compared to Fiat, where in February 1929, 14.7 percent of the personnel was salaried (ILO, "Fiat Establishment," p. 34).
85 For the examples of this early industrial paternalism see, in addition to Merli and Baglioni, R. Romano, "Il cotonificio Cantoni dalle origini al 1900," *Studi storici*, vol. 16, no. 2 (April–June 1975), esp. pp. 489–94; the halting shift to more methodical management systems is especially well illustrated in C. B. Tosi, *Dieci anni coi miei operai* (Milan, 1933).
86 G. Bullo, "Piani regolatori di borgate e villaggi industriali," *Bollettino della "Cotoniera,"* vol. 21, no. 2 (February 1926), pp. 483–5.
87 L. di Stefani, "Selezione psicotecnica dell'operaio laniero," *Bollettino della "Laniera"*, vol. 47, no. 9 (1933), pp. 517–19.

88 For example: Cotonificio Fratelli Turati with 700 workers (*Torino*, April 1928, p. 226); Cotonificio Anselmo Pomo (ibid., p. 228); Borgesesia (ibid., November 1928, p. 811); Cotonificio Paolo Mazzonis (ibid., January–February 1928, p. 155).
89 *La Stirpe*, vol. 4, no. 10 (October 1926), p. 577.
90 *Bollettino della "Cotoniera,"* vol. 24, no. 7 (July 1929), p. 487.
91 On Valli di Lanzo: *Torino*, January–February 1928, p. 154; on Strambino: ibid., April 1928, p. 222; on Borgesesia: ibid., November 1928, p. 811.
92 K. Walter, *The Class Conflict in Italy* (London, 1938), p. 98; also OND, *I dopolavoro aziendali*, pp. 337–8; *ASInd*, January–February 1931, pp. 10–11; *ASInd*, March–April 1935.
93 *ASInd*, January–February 1931, p. 8.
94 On the closing of socialist circles at Schio and Valdagno, ACS, MI, PS (1920–45), G 1, b. 142, Vicenza, sf. Schio (Vicenza) 1928; sf. Circolo operaio, Vicenza, 1932.
95 *Bollettino della "Laniera,"* vol. 46, no. 10 (1932), p. 609.
96 Ibid., vol. 44, no. 10 (1930), p. 852; *Informazione industriale*, 18 February 1932.
97 *Bollettino della "Cotoniera,"* vol. 24, no. 4 (April 1929), p. 268.
98 William H. Tolman, *Social Engineering* (New York, 1909), p. 357; For similar attitudes among French workers see J. Beaudemoulin, *Inquête sur les loisirs de l'ouvrier français* (Paris, 1924), p. 18.
99 ACS, PNF, SPP, b. 25, Torino, sf. 3, fiduciary report, 11 December 1937.
100 G. Giugni, "Esperienze corporative e post-corporative nei rapporti collettivi di lavoro in Italia," *Il Mulino*, January–February 1956, p. 4.
101 *LF*, 9 April 1929.
102 Ibid., 2 July 1929.
103 ACS, Carte Cianetti, b. 4, Minutes of the Central Intersyndical Committee, Meeting of 6 July 1929, Viminal Palace, Rome.
104 Ibid.
105 Ibid.
106 Ugo Manunta, "Spacci di fabbrica," *LF*, 8 September 1932.
107 Walter, p. 98.
108 *LF*, 7 November 1931; one among several "reports from the field" carried in *LF* on 29 October 1931, 1 November 1931, and 3 November 1931 as well.
109 Ibid., 14 May 1931.
110 G. Casini, "I giovani operai e i sindacati," *LF*, 20 July 1934.
111 OND, *BU*, December 1929, prot. n. 48158, Beretta to *dopolavoro provinciali*; *Informazione industriale*, 12 April 1934. ACS, Carte Cianetti, b. 5. Conference of the CGFLI, 16 November 1938.
112 Antonio Gramsci, *Quaderni del carcere*, ed. V. Gerratana, 4 vols. (Turin, 1975), 3, p. 2146.
113 CGII, *Relazione*, 1933, p. 88.

4. The penetration of the countryside

1 A. Serpieri, "Il fascismo e i ceti rurali," *Gerarchia*, vol. 4, no. 1 (January 1924), 9; on Serpieri, a disciple of Pareto, who saw fascism as a revolution by the new elite against the speculators, see Adrian Lyttelton, *The Seizure of Power: Fascism in Italy, 1919–1929* (New York, 1973), pp. 349–50.
2 On the agrarians' attitudes toward fascism, see: G. Pesce, *La marcia dei rurali* (Rome, 1929); also A. Serpieri and N. Mazzocchi Alemanni, *Lo stato fascista e i rurali*

Notes to pp. 96–103

(Milan, 1935), p. 98. On fascism's accommodation of the large landowners, see Carl Schmidt, *The Plow and the Sword* (New York, 1938), pp. 40–4; also the results of recent research: E. Fano, "Problemi e vicende dell'agricoltura tra le due guerre"; A. Cadeddu, S. Lepre, and F. Socrate, "Ristagno e sviluppo nel settore agricolo italiano (1918–1939)"; P. Corner, "Considerazioni sull'agricoltura capitalistica durante il fascismo," contained in *Quaderni storici*, nos. 29–30 (May–December 1975).

3 For a general analysis of conditions in the Italian countryside see: Schmidt, pp. 2–35; E. Sereni, *Il capitalismo nelle campagne, 1860–1900*, rev. ed. (Turin, 1968); also his *La questione agraria nella rinascita nazionale italiana* (Rome, 1946); also M. Bandini, *Cento anni di storia agraria italiana* (Rome, 1963).

4 B. Mussolini, *OO*, vol. 22, p. 321; on the rural sector in the 1926–7 crisis, see D. Preti, "La politica agraria del fascismo: note introduttive," *Studi storici*, vol. 14, no. 4 (October–December 1973), pp. 809–16; also P. Corner, "Rapporti tra agricoltura e industria durante il fascismo," *Problemi del socialismo*, vol. 14, no. 11–12 (September–December 1972), pp. 734–8.

5 Lyttelton, p. 352.

6 Serpieri and Mazzocchi Alemanni, p. 98.

7 Lyttelton, pp. 351–3.

8 On prewar emigration see R. Foerster's classic, *The Italian Emigration of Our Times* (Cambridge, 1919), pp. 7, 15. For the interwar patterns, see Maurice Neufeld, *Italy: School for Awakening Countries* (Ithaca, 1961), Table 3, p. 521; and especially Anna Treves, *Le migrazioni interne nell'Italia fascista* (Turin, 1976).

9 In a speech before the Senate on 17 February 1928, cited in Preti, p. 820.

10 B. Mussolini, *OO*, vol. 23, pp. 257–8.

11 E. Fano Damascelli, "La 'restaurazione anti-fascista liberista': ristagno e sviluppo economico durante il fascismo," *Movimento di liberazione in Italia*, vol. 23, no. 104 (July–September 1971), p. 57.

12 According to figures cited in ibid., p. 56, emigration in 1881–1901 absorbed 35 percent of the natural population increase; in 1901–11, 43 percent; in 1911–21, 18 percent; in 1921–31, 25 percent; and in 1931–6 only 15 percent. The population as a whole increased from 37,452,000 to 42,503,000 between 1921 and 1936 or 336,900 annually, as compared to 239,000 annually in 1901–11, and 154,700 annually in 1911–21 (Neufeld, Table 2, p. 520).

13 A. Serpieri, *Problemi della terra nell'economia corporativa* (Rome, 1927), p. 99.

14 OND, *I primi cinque anni*, p. 13.

15 Serpieri, *Problemi*, p. 101.

16 Paul Corner, *Fascism in Ferrara, 1915–1925* (Oxford, 1975); also Lyttelton, pp. 63–64, 70–71, 352.

17 Schmidt, pp. 37–38; on syndicalist activity in the South, see Simona Colarizi, *Dopoguerra e fascismo in Puglia, 1919–1926* (Bari, 1971).

18 See Figure 1, "Dopolavoro Members in Agriculture by Region."

19 Protocol no. 33103, 21 December 1927, Turati to *dopolavoro provinciali*, cited in OND, *BM*, vol. 1, no. 11–12 (November–December 1927), p. 94.

20 "Per il dopolavoro rurale," *GN*, 10 November 1929; the "traveling chairs" or schools date back to the late nineteenth century in Lombardy and Emilia; these were reorganized under the Ministry of the National Economy in February 1927 to increase vocational instruction in rural districts.

21 OND, *I primi cinque anni*, pp. 62–63.

22 Ibid., p. 63.

23 P. Cannistraro, "The Radio in Fascist Italy," *Journal of European Studies* vol. 2, no. 2 (June 1972), pp. 134–6.
24 *L'Agricoltore d'Italia*, 26 January 1929.
25 M. Pompei, "Il dopolavoro rurale," *LF*, 14 June 1936.
26 *LF*, 25 November 1931.
27 OND, *Annuario*, 1937, p. 142.
28 "Piemonte," *Enciclopedia Treccani*, vol. 27, pp. 175–6; O. Vitali, *La popolazione attiva in agricoltura attraverso i censimenti italiani, 1861–1961* (Rome, 1968), Table 3, pp. 190–1; statistics for 1931 indicate that 66.3 percent of the male population active in agriculture were proprietors, 9.1 percent tenants, 4.7 percent sharecroppers, 18.1 percent day laborers, and 0.2 percent others (Vitali, *Popolazione*, Table 4, p. 200).
29 "Lombardia," *Enciclopedia Treccani*, vol. 21, p. 422; statistics for 1931 indicate that 32.1 percent of the male population active in agriculture were proprietors, 19.5 percent tenants, 12.0 percent sharecroppers, 35.4 percent day laborers, and 1 percent others (Vitali, *Popolazione*, Table 4, p. 200).
30 See Chapter 2, p. 28.
31 *Il Popolo di Pavia*, December 11, 1932; E. De Angelis, *Il dopolavoro in provincia di Pavia* (Pavia, 1929), pp. ii, 6; also his *Cinque anni di organizzazione a Pavia* (Pavia, 1931).
32 "Piemonte," p. 179; between 1931 and 1936 the number of proprietors in Piedmont declined from 66.3 to 55 percent of the total, while in Lombardy it dropped from 32.1 to 27.4 percent (Vitali, *Popolazione*, Table 4, p. 200); on the police measures to halt immigration in these areas, see Gaetano Salvemini, *Under the Axe of Fascism* (New York, 1936), pp. 7–9.
33 ACS, PNF, SPP, b. 13, f. Pavia, report *federale* to Turati, October 1930. Of the 117,558 persons employed in agriculture in Pavia, 50.6 percent were *braccianti* and 44.6 percent landowners (*VII Censimento, 1931*, vol. 3, f. 17., p. xiii.)
34 *Il Popolo di Pavia*, 10 November 1936.
35 "Varese," *Enciclopedia Treccani*, vol. 34, p. 994; *VII Censimento, 1931*, vol. 3, f. 19, p. xi; Gallarate was the scene of the great textile strikes in 1927 and repeated disturbances in 1930–1.
36 L. Mattei, *I dopolavoro agricoli in provincia di Varese, 1930–1937* (Varese, 1938), p. iii.
37 Ibid., p. 14.
38 Ibid., p. 17; this figure is likely to have represented nearly all eligible peasants, since that year the Fascist Union of Agricultural Laborers in the province counted 4,885 members and the Fascist Union of Agriculturalists (including proprietors, tenants, and sharecroppers) numbered 7,300.
39 Ibid., pp. 26–39.
40 Ibid., p. 16; *VII Censimento, 1931*, vol. 3, f. 19, p. xi.
41 According to Mattei, p. 18, 7,000 out of 10,800 members in 1937 were day laborers.
42 According to the 1931 census, of the active male population in agriculture, 23.5 percent were proprietors; 8.6 percent tenants; 32.8 percent sharecroppers; 34.0 percent laborers; and 1.1 percent others (Vitali, *Popolazione*, Table 4, p. 201); specifically on Ravenna, see *VII Censimento, 1931*, vol. 3, f. 4, Ravenna; of the total agricultural population of 78,840 persons (representing 63 percent of the active population), 18.5 percent were proprietors, 39.4 percent sharecroppers or tenants, and 41.4 percent *braccianti*.

43 Lyttelton, p. 78; G. Geminiani, *L'assalto del fascismo alla cooperazione ravennate* (Lugo, 1951), passim.

44 OND, Dopolavoro provinciale di Ravenna, *Il dopolavoro, istituzione fascista* (Ravenna, 1929) (report of the first provincial congress of the *dopolavoro* at Ravenna, 21 April 1929), pp. 21, 65, 67, 69.

45 *Santa milizia*, 15 February 1930.

46 OND, Dopolavoro provinciale di Ravenna, *Il dopolavoro, istituzione fascista* (Ravenna, 1930); *Santa milizia*, 26 July 1930.

47 Rignani, *Lugo durante il periodo delle guerre fasciste 1932–luglio 1943* (Lugo, 1973), p. 40; *Santa milizia*, 27 December 1931; 8 January 1931; 24 January 1931; recalcitrants were threatened with expulsion from all organizational activities and the publication of their names in the fascist press. Suspensions were few. *Dopolavoro* enrollments for 1928–37 were: 1927, 357; 1928, 2,416; 1929, 7,035; 1930, 13,053; 1931, 7,281 (February); 1934, 11,162; 1935, 12,000; 1936, 11,781; 1937, 15,593 (figures derived from annual reports in *Santa milizia*, 1930–7).

48 *Santa milizia*, 3 May 1930; also 22 July 1939.

49 On this aspect of fascist social policy and the landowners' economic as well as social reasons for supporting it, see Corner, "Rapporti," pp. 740–6.

50 According to Schmidt (p. 115), rural laborers in the neighboring province of Forlì worked an average of 95 days in 1934, earning perhaps 1,297 lire annually.

51 At the Second Congress in 1930; see above, n. 46.

52 Lyttelton, p. 71.

53 See Table 1, Chapter 2, on Florence, *Il Bargello*, 27 October 1934; also OND, *Il dopolavoro in Toscana* (Florence, 1935).

54 G. Dusmet, "Spare time organizations for agricultural workers in Italy," *International Labor Review*, vol. 33, no. 2 (February 1936), p. 235; ACS, PCM, 1928–30, f. 4, 1. 11968; f. 1, 7.4834.

55 Dusmet, p. 236.

56 Schmidt, pp. 61–65, 159–63.

57 "Come il fascismo ricostruisce il Mezzogiorno," *LF*, 30 August 1929. The history of fascism's penetration of the South remains to be studied; for a beginning, see Lyttelton's perceptive insights into the early alliance between *squadrismo* and the southern clientele groups (pp. 188–201); on the pre-1926 period, see also Colarizi, passim.

58 On the structure of the southern clientele system, see S. Tarrow, *Peasant Communism in Southern Italy* (New Haven, 1967), who deals with it in the context of another mass party's often beleaguered efforts to adapt to a society permeated with traditional values and loyalties.

59 On fascism's struggle against the mafia: Mori's memoirs, *Con la mafia ai ferri corti* (Verona, 1932); M. Pantaleone, *Mafia e politica* (Turin, 1962); also E. J. Hobsbawm's discussion of the mafia in *Primitive Rebels* (New York, 1962).

60 ACS, PNF, SPP, b. 12, Palermo, report Paternostro to Turati, 30 June 1929.

61 ACS, MI, PS (1920–45) G 1, b. 123, Ragusa, f. Associazioni disciolte, 1928; also prefectorial report, 31 August 1928.

62 See, for example, the report of the *federale* of Reggio di Calabria contained in a letter from A. Melchiori, vice-secretary of the PNF, to M. Bianchi, undersecretary of the Ministry of the Interior, noting that "numerous circles survive throughout the province attracting all of the malcontents and even some opponents"; their political "hue" was indicated by such typical masonic names as "New Era," "Free Thinkers," and

"Country and Liberty" (ACS, PNF, SPP, b. 17, letter Melchiori to Bianchi, 27 December 1928).

63 Paternostro, 30 June 1929.

64 ACS, PNF, SPP, b. 16, Ragusa, letter (probably C. Lodi) to Turati, 14 November 1928.

65 ACS, SPD, CR, b. 71, f. Carlo Lodi, letter Lodi to Chiavolini, 18 October 1930.

66 ACS, PNF, SPP, b. 12, Palermo, report Di Belsito to Turati, October 1928.

67 Contained in the PNF, *Fogli d'ordine dal 31 luglio IV al 28 ottobre XIII* (Rome, 1935); for 1930 figures: OND, *I primi cinque anni*, p. 198.

68 ACS, PNF, SPP, b. 5, Messina, report L. Zannardini to G. Giuriati, 24 October 1930.

69 ACS, PNF, SPP, b. 15. Ragusa, report Prefect Marca to G. Giuriati, 30 June 1931. Lupis was removed in 1931; however, he would return to power as *podestà* of the town of Ragusa in 1938.

70 ACS, PNF, SPP, b. 12, Palermo, fiduciary report, July 1932.

71 ACS, MI, PS (1920–45), G 1, b. 113, f. Messina, sf. San Salvatore di Fitalia, petition A. Masurra to Minister of the Interior, 30 August 1929.

72 Ibid, sf. San Salvatore di Fitalia, prefectorial report signed A. Guerresi, 23 October 1929.

73 ACS, MI, PS (1920–45), cat. G 1, b. 113, f. Messina, sf. Montalbano Elicona, petition Giuseppe Pantano to Minister of the Interior, 10 September 1929.

74 Ibid, sf. Montalbano Elicona, prefectorial report, 15 July 1929; Sf. Montalbano Elicona, prefectorial report, 3 December 1929.

75 Ibid, sf. Montalbano Elicona, Commissar F. Occhino to prefect, 2 November 1931.

76 Carried in OND, *I dopolavoro aziendali*, passim.

77 "Basilicata," *Enciclopedia Treccani*, vol. 2, p. 189.

78 ACS, PNF, SPP, b. 16, Potenza, commander MVSN to Giuriati, 21 March 1931; also commander MVSN to Starace, 8 February 1934; prefectorial report, December 1932.

79 Ibid, b. 16, Potenza, Rautiis to Starace, 30 November 1934.

80 Ibid, b. 16, Potenza, Rautiis to Starace, 28 June 1935.

81 As reported before the Chamber on 1 March 1933 by Catalani, still protector of the province in his role as deputy; cited in Salvemini, p. 303.

82 ACS, PNF, SPP, b. 4, Matera, Sandicchi to Starace, 25 November 1934.

83 Ibid. Complaints regarding the difficulty of recruiting fresh cadres were frequent in the South and the Islands; thus the *federale* of the province of Nuoro (Sardinia) reported in 1952 that the Sardinian population, although "patriotic" and "disciplined," had failed to "realize that fascism was a revolutionary movement." The "feudatories of the prefascist period had grabbed up all of the party and governmental offices so that it seemed that one had to have either belonged to the masonry, be at least fifty years old, or have been a marshal of the *carabinieri* in order to make a political career" (ACS, PNF, SPP, b. 10, Nuoro, f. 20, report O. Sellani to Starace, 25 June 1935; ibid., 23 January 1936).

84 ACS, PNF, SPP, b. 4, Matera, Sandicchi to Starace, 25 November 1934.

85 Ibid, b. 4, Matera, Starace to Sandicchi, December 1934; Sandicchi to Starace, 31 May 1935; *Lavoro agricolo fascista*, 30 November 1930, cited in Salvemini, p. 304.

86 OND, *I dopolavoro aziendali*, p. 389.

87 ACS, PNF, D. Servizi amministrativi, b. 204, f. OND, letter Starace to Marinelli, 22 November 1930, 1 August 1931, 13 July 1931 requesting special contributions from party funds for OND use in the South.

88 ACS, PNF, SPP, b. 4, Matera, report S. Pirretti to Minister of the Interior, 28 January 1939.

89 Protocol n. 61301, Starace to *dopolavoro provinciali*, cited in OND, *BU*, October 1935.
90 Protocol n. 55682, Puccetti to *dopolavoro provinciali*, cited in OND, *BU*, July 1937.
91 Foglio di communicazione, n. 85, cited in OND, *BU*, July 1937.
92 See Table 2, Chapter 4; also OND, *Annuario*, 1937, nn.; *Annuario*, 1938, p. 236.
93 *GN*, 26 February 1939.

5. Privileging the clerks

1 The insignificance of Italy's new middle class as an autonomous political force in the postwar period (compared, say, to the workers in the socialist movement or Catholics in the popular party) may account for the paucity of contemporary studies: R. Mondolfo's "Il problema delle classi medie," *Critica sociale*, vol. 35, no. 9 (1–15 May 1925), 120–4; vol. 35, nos. 11–12 (1–30 June 1925), 132–5, is the earliest effort to undertake such a study. See also Giuliano Pischel, *Il problema dei ceti medi* (Milan, 1946); the nationalist Nello Quilici's *La borghesia italiana* (Milan, 1946) and Antonio Fossati's *Le classi medie in Italia* (Turin, 1938), both profascist, contain nonetheless some perceptive observations. The "problem" has become the subject of discussion in Italy only since the publication of Paolo Sylos Labini, *Saggio sulle classi sociali* (Bari, 1974).

2 Elsewhere the "problem" of the new middle class has generated works that remain indispensable preparation for any national study, including: Karl Dreyfuss, *Occupation and Ideology of the Salaried Employee* (New York, 1938), 2 vols.; Emil Lederer, *The Problem of the Modern Salaried Employee; Its Theoretical and Statistical Basis* (New York, 1937; originally published in 1913); also his *The New Middle Class* (New York, 1937), written with Jacob Marschak in 1926. For a review of these and other studies, see Michel Crozier, *The World of the Office Worker*, trans. D. Landau (Chicago, 1971), whose own study of petty functionaries in Paris of the Fifties in this and in his "Employés et petits fonctionnaires parisiens: le loisir comme moyen de participation aux valeurs de la société bourgeoise," *Esprit*, vol. 27, no. 274 (June 1959), 934–54, offers a lucid analysis of their cultural habits. For the United States see C. Wright Mills, *White Collar: the American Middle Class* (New York, 1953); a comparative historical perspective is in Arno J. Mayer, "The Lower Middle Class as Historical Problem," *Journal of Modern History* vol. 47, no. 3 (September 1975), 409–36. On the new middle class and Nazism, see D. Schoenbaum, *Hitler's Social Revolution* (Garden City, New York, 1967), pp. 6–10, 67–8, 108–9, 245–6.

3 On the civil service under fascism, see T. Cole, "Italy's Fascist Bureaucracy," *American Political Science Review*, vol. 32, no. 6 (December 1938), pp. 1143–57; a view from inside by the liberal functionary C. Petrocchi, *Il problema della burocrazia* (Rome, 1944); a critical appraisal by a reforming fascist expert, R. Spaventa, *Burocrazia, ordinamento amministrativo e fascismo* (Milan, 1928); and, finally, a standard fascist presentation of the functions of the civil servants under the regime: S. Di Massa, *Burocrazia fascista* (Rome, 1937).

4 Di Massa, p. 69.

5 According to Spaventa, p. 38. Adjusted statistics for 1 July 1923–1 July 1928 indicate that there were 544,088 state employees in 1923 (before cuts began, reaching a low of 507,241 in 1925; the main loss was in the railroads (see Chapter 5, "Making the model railroad corps"). F. A. Repaci, "Il costo della burocrazia dello Stato," *Riforma sociale*, vol. 39, no. 3 (May–June 1932), 259–90; the corporatist character of fascist

reforms in the early twenties was underscored by the communist deputy F. Lo Sardo in his April 4 speech before the Chamber, "Sul provvedimento per il caro viveri . . ." (Rome, 1925).

6 Sylos Labini, pp. 47–51, 155–61; Francesco Demarchi, "Dimensioni della burocrazia e sua evoluzione storica," in Sabino Cassese, ed., *L'amministrazione pubblica in Italia* (Bologna, 1974), pp. 105–8; also his *L'ideologia del funzionario* (Milan, 1968), pp. 65–6. The General Accounting Office (Ragioneria Generale dello Stato) did not publish records of expenditures or personnel increases in parastate offices or political and trade union bureaucracies, though these apparently accounted for significant increases in personnel.

7 B. Barberi, *La dinamica del trattamento economico dei dipendenti dello Stato nel periodo 1913–1931* (Rome, 1935), p. 58; Sylos Labini, p. 59. G. Moccia, *Il trattamento economico del personale statale* (Rome, 1936), pp. 19–22; Cole, p. 1154; ASI, 1932, p. 441; 1939, p. 267.

8 Mussolini, cited in Di Massa, p. 54; on the generally unsuccessful effort by the PNF to extend its control over the bureaucracy, see Dante Germino, *The Italian Fascist Party in Power* (Minneapolis, 1959), pp. 84 ff.; Renzo De Felice, *Mussolini il fascista: l'organizzazione dello stato fascista, 1925–1929*, 5 vols. (Turin, 1968), 3, pp. 344–6.

9 *Forze civili*, September 1931.

10 For the debates concerning the definition of the juridical status of public employees, see B. Dente and S. Cassese, "Una discussione del primo ventennio del secolo: lo Stato sindacale," *Quaderni storici*, no. 18 (1971), pp. 943–70. On the effects of the fascist legislation on the contractual status of state employees, see Cole, pp. 1155–6.

11 The main source for prewar employee associationalism is Ministero di Agricoltura, Industria e Commercio, Ufficio del Lavoro, *Le organizzazioni di impiegati, notizie sulle origini e lo sviluppo delle organizzazioni di miglioramento degli impiegati pubblici e privati in Italia* (Rome, 1910).

12 On the postwar organizations, see *ASI*, 1919–21, p. 394; in December 1921, 329,900 of the total enrolled belonged to local federations, some of which certainly were affiliated with profascist groups; in addition, 45,446 persons, mainly in the railroad and postal services, were enrolled in the Confederazione italiana dei sindacati economici, which early supported the Fascist party. According to Jens Petersen, "Comportamento elettorale e basi sociali del fascismo italiano tra il 1919 e il 1928," *Studi storici*, vol. 16, no. 3 (July–September 1975), p. 666, clerks in private and public employ made up 14.6 percent of total PNF enrollment in November 1921, though only 4.5 percent of the population; see also Ferdinando Cordova, *Le origini dei sindacati fascisti* (Bari, 1974), pp. 29–38, on the attractions of fascist syndicalism for "intellectual workers."

13 Germino, pp. 54–55, 91–92.

14 *Forze civili*, October 1931.

15 *Forze civili*, September 1931.

16 *L'organizzazione degli impiegati*, p. 7.

17 Decree Laws no. 1908, 25 October, 1925, founding the Railroad Dopolavoro; no. 1271, 9 July 1926, founding the Post and Telegraphic Service Dopolavoro; no. 743, 12 May 1927, setting up the Dopolavoro for Employees of the State Monopolies; no. 300, 21 February 1929, founding the Colonial Dopolavoro for dependents in Libya and East Africa.

18 As, for example, in England; C. V. Humphreys, *Clerical Unions in the Civil Service* (Oxford, 1958).

19 Although railroad workers played a key role in the reformist socialist labor movement,

the history of their organizations, especially after the turn of the century, has been little studied: for an introduction, see L. Guerrini, *Organizzazione e lotte dei ferrovieri italiani* (Florence, 1957); E. Finzi, *Alle origini del movimento sindacale: i ferrovieri* (Bologna, 1975); also passing comments in Italo Briano, *Storia delle ferrovie italiane*, 3 vols. (Milan, 1977), 1, pp. 142–5, 198.

20 In its concern for railroad efficiency, the regime displayed a preoccupation more typical of a mid-nineteenth-century European bourgeoisie. On the innovations in the service, many of which had been planned in the decade before the fascists took power, see, in addition to Briano's even-handed account: Ministero delle Communicazioni, *Le ferrovie dello stato nel primo decennio fascista, 1922–1932* (Novara, 1933); Ciano's *Dieci anni di attività al Ministero delle Communicazioni* (Rome, 1940); F. Tajani, *Storia delle ferrovie italiane* (Milan, 1939); A Crispo, *Le ferrovie italiane: storica politica e economica* (Milan, 1940); as well as the technical history by M. Kalla-Bishop, *Italian Railways* (London, 1971).

21 Ministero delle Communicazioni, *Le ferrovie dello stato*, p. 8. I. Briano, "Interview," 4 May 1978.

22 F. A. Repaci, *La gestione delle ferrovie dello stato nel sessennio 1923–1924–1928–1929* (Turin, 1930), pp. 25–27, 61, 288; for salary averages, see Ministero delle Communicazioni, Amministrazione delle ferrovie dello stato, *Relazioni*, 1924–5 to 1939–40; analyzed in Barberi, p. 45.

23 F. A. Repaci, 1938–9; also Ministero delle Communicazioni, *Le ferrovie dello Stato*, passim.

24 Cited in *Lavoro d'Italia*, 17 August 1926; statements of expenditure on the Railroad Dopolavoro contained in *Relazioni*, 1925–6, etc.

25 Statuto, *Dopolavoro ferrovario*, 1926.

26 Dr. U. Fasciolo, "The Problem of Sites for Dopolavoro Houses for the Italian State Railways," Kraft durch Freude, *World Congress for Leisure Time and Recreation: Report of the Second International Congress on Leisure* (Hamburg–Berlin, 1936), pp. 310–15; also his "Recreation in the Italian State Railway System," pp. 182–5.

27 *Relazioni*, passim.

28 Briano, "Interview."

29 Ministero delle Communicazioni, *Le ferrovie dello Stato*, p. 12.

30 Briano, I, p. 210.

31 Ministero delle Communicazioni, *Le ferrovie dello Stato*, p. 7.

32 Crozier, *World*, p. 17.

33 Lolini, a frustrated exponent of the original "technical council" on administrative reform, remained a leading critic of the shortcomings of fascist administrative reform, with almost no audience by the thirties. See his *Per l'attuazione dello Stato fascista* (Florence, 1929) with a preface by G. Gentile, pp. 67–8, as well as his first study: *La riforma della burocrazia* (Rome, 1919), runner-up in a contest for essays on "the defects and inconveniences of the present bureaucratic order" sponsored by the Italian Society for Joint Stock Companies immediately after World War I.

34 On the rationalization of office work, see, in addition to Braverman, *Labor and Monopoly Capital* (New York, 1974), esp. pp. 293–409, W. H. Leffingwell, *Scientific Office Management* (New York, 1917), a work that apparently was little known in fascist Italy; also D. Lockwood, *The Blackcoated Worker* (London, 1966). The only treatises on the scientific management of office work in Italy were by R. Numeroso, a lawyer and high functionary of Naples, founder of the local Gruppo Amici Razionalizzazione (GAR) and a bit of a crank in his exalted conception of rationalization; see his *L'organizzazione scientifica del lavoro nella pubblica amministrazione* (Na-

ples, 1933); *Psicotecnica e ufficio del personale nelle pubbliche amministrazioni* (Naples, 1935); also *Dall'individuo all Stato: sintesi dell'organizzazione scientifica del lavoro nell'individuo, nella famiglia, nella scuola, nell'azienda* (Naples, 1935); *Critica fascista* was a leading advocate of reform: see especially: S. Alessi, "Intorno all'ordinamento burocratico," vol. 10, no. 16 (15 August 1932), pp. 308–9. On the lack of administrative innovation, see also Cole, pp. 1147–52; Spaventa, pp. 98–103. On hiring practices that aggravated the inefficient use of personnel, see Barberi, pp. 99–100, in addition to De Stefani's observations about the "illustory savings" made by using temporary help.

35 *Sommario di statistiche storiche dell'Italia 1861–1965* (Rome, 1968), p. 129; also the detailed analysis by Barberi, pp. 39, 58.

36 Cited in S. Caruso, *Burocrazia e capitale in Italia* (Verona, 1974), p. 62.

37 Pischel, pp. 164–5; in a similar vein, see also Petrocchi, p. 152.

38 *I dopolavoro aziendali*, p. 1181.

39 For example: ACS, PCM, 1940–3, 3, 3–6, no. 1495, sf. 5, P. Casorati to Avv. G. Gasperini; Gasperini to Rossoni, 19 November 1932; also sf. 3, M. Carta to Segretario Gabinetto PCM, 29 December 1936 containing the records of the Dopolavoro of the Presidency of the Council of Ministers.

40 ACS, PCM, 3, 3–6, no. 1495, sf. 3, "Relazione sommaria della attività svolta nel periodo dal 28 ottobre 1934 al agosto 1943"; also Carta, 29 December 1936.

41 *Famiglia nostra* [I, no. 1 (April 1930–40)], February 1932; in general on INA, see A. Scialoja, "L'INA ed il progetto giolittiano di uno monopolio di Stato delle assicurazioni sulla vita," *Quaderni storici*, no. 18 (1971), pp. 971–1027; also "Regolamento per il personale, approvato dal Consiglio di Amministrazione nell'adunanza del 27 marzo 1935" (Rome, 1935); "Tabelle degli stipendi del personale" (Rome, 1927); "Ruoli di anzianità del personale dipendente dall'Istituto Nazionale delle Assicurazioni per l'anno 1935" (Rome, 1935), all courtesy of the Personnel Department of INA; on the structure and financing of INA's Dopolavoro, see annual administrative reports in *Famiglia nostra*.

42 *Famiglia nostra*, esp. November 1930, February 1933.

43 *Famiglia nostra*, June 1930.

44 Alessi, p. 309.

45 Crozier, "Employés," p. 951.

46 *Famiglia nostra*, April 1931.

47 *Famiglia nostra*, May 1930.

48 *Famiglia nostra*, January 1931.

49 The publication of Turin's *ATM* (from 1925) preceded by three years the foundation of its Dopolavoro for tramway workers; see also *ATAG: rivista mensile del dopolavoro tramviario*, published in Rome from December 1930 under the direction of Nicola Leuzzi, as well as ATM's Milanese *Rivista mensile* published from 21 April 1932 under the direction of Dr. Biaggini; see especially *ATM*, July–December 1930, p. 215; *ATAG*, July–August 1929, p. 2.

50 A. Iurilli, "Passato e presente," *Famiglia nostra*, March 1934.

51 *Famiglia nostra*, June 1931.

52 *Famiglia nostra*, February 1932.

6. The nationalization of the public

1 *Il Dopolavoro provinciale, rivista mensile*, Bologna, 18 August 1930; *Il Dopolavoro fiorentino*, 15–30 November 1929.

2 According to the official list these included 6,140 medical discounts, 3,465 on furnishings, 2,510 on clothing, 1,085 on hotels and *pensioni*, 969 on cinema and theater, 730 on food, 452 on transportation (*BLPS*, 56 [1931], p. 916).

3 On the Venice Exposition, see: A. Pellegrini, *Il dopolavoro a Venezia* (Venice, 1929), pp. 157–68 OND, Circolare no. 771 bis. "Concorsi nazionali per l'ammobiliamento e l'arredamento economico della casa popolare" (Rome, 1928); sales totaled 300,000 lire in the first 15 days (approximately $17,000) (OND, *I primi due anni*, p. 51). In his "Ordinamento e sviluppo dell'Opera Nazionale Dopolavoro," *Gerarchia* (February 1928), p. 101, Bottai cites the show as the OND's most significant contribution to date to national reconstruction (*Il Dopolavoro fiorentino*, numero unico, December 1928).

4 "Individual thrift and parsimony" alone would guarantee "an adequate tenor of life," according to OND advertisements for the Alta Italia company (*GN*, 19 October 1930).

5 OND, *BU*, vol. 2, nos. 5–6 (May–June 1928), pp. 55–8, and especially Turati's circular to southern Italian prefects dated 9 June 1928 regarding "uncoordinated" societies. *BLPS*, (1930), p. 168; also *LF*, 21 June 1930, which announces R.D. 28 July 1930, no. 980, creating the *dopolavoro* postal savings booklet.

6 *GN*, 5 October 1930, 14 September 1930. The OND, in cooperation with the Assicurazione d'Italia Company, further offered a "popular" insurance program against extravocational risks. This was conceived by Turati out of the conviction that "the insurance habit among the most humble categories of the Italian working classes is not equal to the actual necessities of their economic security"; it provided two standard forms of policy: against extravocational risks and against risks outside working hours, for a 6-lira annual premium, 5,000 lire in case of death; 10,000 lire in case of total permanent disability, payment according to percentages fixed by article 95 of the law of 31 January 1904; the second called for an annual 10-lira premium and provided 5,000 lire in case of death, 10,000 for total permanent disability, and 8 lire per day for leave from the sixth day following the date of accident up to a maximum of 60 days (OND, *I primi cinque anni*, p. 60) (1930 lira = 6 cents). This was supplemented in 1931 by the OND's own compulsory insurance program covering *dopolavoro* activities, designed to "enhance the value of the card" and spread "a firm sense of the problem of social insurance, to which the majority of Italians were [ostensibly] wholly oblivious until the fascist period" (*LF*, 3 April 1933). In fact about 95 percent of the annual fees were used to cover OND operating expenditures.

7 On the development of radio, see Cannistraro, "The Radio," p. 130, and his more recent *La fabbrica del consenso: fascismo e mass media* (Bari, 1975), pp. 225–71; also A. Papa, *Storia politica della radio in Italia*, 2 vols. (Naples, 1978). By comparison, see the spectacular rise in the numbers of licenses in Great Britain, France, and Germany: Great Britain at the end of 1926 counted 2,178,000 and in 1939, 8,900,000; Germany at the beginning of 1926 counted 1,022,000 and in 1939, 13,711,000; France in 1934 counted 1,308,000 sets declared and in 1939, 4,992,000 sets declared (source: D. Landes, *The Unbound Prometheus* [Cambridge, 1969], pp. 427, 429).

8 Cited in R. Loffredo, "Dopolavoro rurale," *GN*, 20 October 1935.

9 *BLPS* (1930), p. 152; OND, *BU* (1 December 1929), p. 38; also E. De Angelis, *Che cosa è e che cosa vuole il Dopolavoro: l'organizzazione in provincia di Pavia* (Pavia, 1929), p. 232.

10 OND, *Annuario* (1938), nn.; the reasons accounting for this relative underdevel-

opment lay – according to Cannistraro (pp. 134–5) – in the constant wrangling among the fascist bureaucracies, the OND, the EIAR (a semipublic utility for broadcasting and programming), the Ente Radio Rurale set up under the Ministry of Communications in 1933, and the Opera Nazionale Balilla; the OND's own failure to supply radios to its affiliates appears attributable, as in the case of the cinema, to its reluctance to infringe on private distributors; see, for example, OND, *BM*, vol. 2, nos. 11–12 (November–December 1928), pp. 8–9, statements affirming the OND's intention not to compete with private distributors.

11 *GN*, 22 February 1931: as claimed by the OND itself!
12 *GN*, 12 January 1930.
13 *GN*, 29 September 1935.
14 *GN*, 1 December 1929.
15 *GN*, 9 December 1929.
16 *GN*, 6 March 1932.
17 *GN*, 13 March 1932.
18 OND, *BU* (January 1932); protocol no. 5390 (18 January 1932); Starace to *dopolavoro provinciali.*
19 *Annali di statistica*, ser. VI, XV (1933), "Statistica di alcune manifestazioni culturali italiane nel periodo, 1926–1930," pp. 80–84. Figures are for mid-1929; "movie theaters" appear to include all Church-related, commercial, and party-run establishments.
20 *GN*, 4 August 1929.
21 OND, *BM*, vol. 2, nos. 11–12 (November–December 1928), p. 32.
22 Ibid., pp. 102–3. "Norme per le proiezioni cinematografiche": Protocol e/22864 (27 July 1927).
23 OND, *Annuario* (1938), nn. *Annuario statistico italiano* (1939), p. 324; as compared to 2,700 commercial theaters with 1,283,921 seats; 546 Church theaters with 143,399 seats; 125 PNF-related (ONB, etc.) with 37,327 seats; and 125 belonging to other *enti* with 39,587 seats (as of 1 October 1937). Of the OND cinemas 41 played full time, 28 played less than five times per week, 298 only on holidays and Sundays, 5 varied, and 5 were unspecified.
24 A. Starace, *L'Opera Nazionale Dopolavoro*, pp. 65–6, for his reassurances that the OND had no intention of encroaching on the theater industry.
25 In general on Italian theater during the interwar years, see G. Pullini, *Teatro italiano fra due secoli, 1850–1950* (Florence, 1959); also A. Alberti, *Il teatro nel fascismo* (Rome, 1974). On Mussolini as theater director and actor, see U. Silva, *Ideologia e arte del fascismo* (Milan, 1973), pp. 89–98, and esp. p. 89 for Pirandello's comments on Mussolini as "True man of the theater . . . actor, author, and protagonist in the Theater of History." As a public figure, Mussolini was particularly adept at making the transition from stage to silent films to sound movies, in other words as a political personality he was well suited to an era of transition in the mass media.
26 *GN*, 6 February 1932.
27 L. Antonelli, "Sabato teatrale," *GN*, 26 February 1936; *LF*, 1 January 1936.
28 On participation, *Il Popolo d'Italia*, 10 January 1937; on restrictions on the public, OND, *BU* (1 January 1937), protocol no. 537 (5 January 1937) signed Alfieri, head of Minculpop, and directed to the prefects; more explicitly on the means to prevent the *Sabato teatrale* from "infringing on legitimate theater," OND, *BU* (1 March 1937), protocol no. 20198 (11 March 1937).
29 *Il Bargello*, 16 May 1937.
30 *GN*, 28 June 1932.

31 For descriptions, see *GN*, August 1930; 2 October 1932; OND, *L'Opera Nazionale Dopolavoro* (Rome, 1937), pp. 39–40.

32 *GN*, 6 May 1934; 24 August 1930; 6 May 1934.

33 *BLPS* (1931), p. 170.

34 OND, *Esercizio finanziaro*, 1933–4: income from tickets amounted to 293,709 lire, while expenditures were 2,045,902.45 lire.

35 Ibid., 10 August 1931; 13 September 1931; 14 August 1933; 21 October 1934; 23 December 1934; also *LF*, 10 February 1935.

36 A social history of the rich tradition of popular theater remains to be written: see the brief study of a former participant in the small theater movement of Florence, U. Bardi, "Le piccole ribalte durante il fascismo," in *La Toscana nel regime fascista* (1922–39), 2 vols. (Florence, 1971), 2, pp. 657–66.

37 De Angelis, pp. 47–48. In general, on the fascist guidelines for the small theater, see OND, *BM* ("Scopi ed organizzazione del movimento filodrammatico dell'OND") vol. 1, no. 2 (1 February 1927).

38 G. Pesce, "La filodrammatica e il dopolavoro," *La Stirpe*, vol. 2, no. 6 (June 1924), p. 561.

39 *GN*, 9 April 1933; A. Starace in ibid., 31 October 1935.

40 L. Chiarelli, "I dilettanti ed il teatro di prosa," ibid., 25 August 1935.

41 Reports on the numbers of small theaters varied considerably even by the OND's own ostensibly meticulous counts. That of 1937, apparently the most accurate, indicated 1,500 drama societies, with 23,000 participants who altogether performed 14,000 times: This represented a significant increase over the 700 groups identified when the OND began "coordinating" local societies in 1927. Official figures taken from *BLPS*, 1930–5, and OND, *Annuario*, 1937, 1938, indicate: 1926, 113; 1927, 460; 1928, 1,053; 1929, 1,095; 1930, 1,901; 1931, 1,994; 1932, 2,205; 1933, 2,226; 1934, 2,305; 1935, 2,500; 1936, 1,519; 1937, 1,553. In general, 1936–7 figures, assessed after Beretta's ouster at a time when the OND's forces were under review, approximate the real extent of OND activities. The OND's network of theaters (owned or run by the OND) was considerable: OND, 443; private, 458; Church (*oratori*), 382; municipal, 299; various *enti*, 265; PNF, 84. Of the OND's theaters, 62 had less than 250 seats; 239, 250–499; 69, 500–749; 8, 750–999; and 4, over 1,000 seats. To be remarked and requiring much further study are the considerable number of Church facilities (see Chap. 8, pp 241–2.) Source: *ASI* (1940), p. 85; theaters existing as of 1 March 1939.

42 Bardi, p. 661.

43 OND. *BU*, February 1932, citing the law on theater censorship of 6 June 1932, also protocol 9332: Beretta to *dopolavoro provinciali*, 11 February 1932, directing amateur theaters to choose from a precensored list drawn up by the Minister of the Interior; ibid., May 1933, protocol 27527; Starace to *dopolavoro provinciali*, 10 May 1933, restricting the quota of foreign plays to 25 percent of the total; ibid., March 1935, protocol 19387: Beretta to *dopolavoro provinciali*, prohibiting works in dialect; ibid., November 1935, foglio di communicazione, 2, prohibiting works of the "Sanction" nations.

44 Bardi, p. 666.

45 OND, *Annuario* (1937), p. 43.

46 See, for example, OND, *BU* (November 1929), protocol 15574 (25 November 1929) pointing out the difficulties in "coordinating" circles in "areas with many players," probably Piedmont and Liguria, where the game was particularly popular.

47 "Bocce," *Enciclopedia Treccani*, vol. 7, p. 233.

48 OND, *Annuario* (1937), p. 45.
49 Ugo Cuesta, *Il libro del dopolavoro* (Rome, 1937), p. 123.
50 Quoted in A. Ghirelli, *Storia del calcio italiano* (2nd ed., Turin, 1967), p. 63. In general, on sports under fascism, see: F. Fabrizio, *Sport e fascismo: la politica sportiva del regime, 1928–1936* (Rimini–Florence, 1976), also his *Storia dello sport in Italia* (Rimini–Florence, 1977) esp. pp. 65–120; also S. Provvisionato, *Lo sport in Italia* (Rome, 1978).
51 OND, *I primi due anni d'attività*, p. 9; also Augusto Parboni, "Lo Sport nel dopolavoro," *Sport fascista*, vol. 1, no. 1 (June 1928).
52 Fabrizio, *Storia*, pp. 1–112; also S. Provvisionato, "L'esperienza di *Sport e proletariato*," pp. 109–19; L. Martini, "Sport e movimento cattolico," both in *Sport e società* (Rome, 1976), pp. 119–27; "Sport," *Enciclopedia Treccani*, vol. 30, p. 502; L. Mineo-Paluello, *Education in Fascist Italy* (London 1946), pp. 34–8.
53 On sports in France, see E. Weber, "Gymnastics and Sports in *Fin-de-Siècle* France: Opium of the Classes?" *American Historical Review*, vol. 76, no. 1 (February 1971); Ghirelli, *passim*.
54 P. Jelmini, "Recreation and Physical Fitness among the People," in World Congress for Leisure Time and Recreation, *Reports* of the Second International Congress on Leisure (Hamburg–Berlin, 1936), p. 431.
55 Starace, p. 47.
56 Jelmini, p. 432.
57 Description carried in Bertinetti, *Il libro del Dopolavoro* (Turin, 1928), pp. 61–2. Recent Marxist studies on the nature of sports in capitalist society – P. Hoch, *Rip Off the Big Game, the Exploitation of Sports by the Power Elite* (Garden City, New York, 1972), and G. Vinnai, *Fussballsport als Ideologie* (Italian trans. *Il calcio come ideologia* [Milan, 1970]) – have stressed that capitalist societies generally promote a high degree of individual competitiveness in sporting pastimes; this assessment should be revised to take into account cases where working-class sports are used to promote a sense of discipline, as opposed to the aggressive individualism desired in the elites, or in the upwardly mobile sectors of the society.
58 *GN*, 11 August 1929.
59 OND, Dopolavoro provinciale di Vercelli, *Il dopolavoro provinciale di Vercelli nell'anno X* (Vercelli, 1933), p. 20.
60 *GN*, 11 August 1929; *LF*, 5 June 1931.
61 Jelmini, p. 433.
62 OND, *BU* (1 January 1934), p. 8; OND, *L'Opera Nazionale Dopolavoro* (Rome, 1935), nn.
63 Starace, p. 48.
64 As underscored in *Santa milizia* (5 January 1929).
65 *GN*, vol. 2, no. 24 (15 June 1930); OND, *BU* (1 January 1934), p. 7.
66 Starace, p. 48.
67 *LF*, 5 June 1931; as reported in a general review of sports in ACS, MI, Polizia Politica, b. 217, f. 3, cat. G 7, Sport.
68 Quoted in *Civiltà cattolica*, vol. 89, no. 3 (1938), 230.
69 Emilio Radius, *Usi e costumi dell'uomo fascista* (Milan, 1964), p. 319.
70 U. Gabbi, "Gli esercizi sportivi e la donna," *Educazione fascista* (1930), p. 19; *dopolavoro* sports for women did not really begin to be organized until the thirties; the example of Nazi Germany may well have proved a stimulus to the regime to intervene more actively in their promotion.

71 "Cultura operaia e vita quotidiana in Borgo San Paolo," in Città di Torino, Assessorato per la cultura, ed., *Torino tra le due guerre* (Turin, 1978), pp. 22–4.
72 F. Muzi, "Educazione sportiva totalitaria," *Italia augusta*, vol. 5, no. 11 (November 1928), p. 18.
73 F. Muzi, "Si costruisce," *Sport fascista*, vol. 2, no. 2 (November 1929), p. 37; also OND, *BM*, I, nos. 11–12 (November–December 1927), circular 19, Turati to sports offices of local *dopolavoro* (17 August 1927).
74 Muzi, "Si costruisce," p. 38; also "Gli enti sportivi fascisti e i loro compiti nelle provincie," *LF*, 8 September 1929.
75 Muzi, "Si costruisce," indicated that 405 fields were opened in 1929: in Piedmont 87, Lombardy 83, Veneto 29, Julian Venetia 1, Tridentine Venetia 4, Liguria 7, Emilia 34, Tuscany 17, Umbria 5, Latium 8, Marches 7, Abruzzi–Molise 7, Campania 22, Apulia 36, Basilicata 1, Calabria 21, Sicily 17, Sardinia 19.
76 *Il Bargello*, 9 February 1930; ACS, PNF, SPP b. 5, Messina, report, 26 June 1932.
77 *Il Bargello*, 4 November 1934.
78 The CONI was financed by a 15 percent tax on all tickets to spectator games.
79 See Ghirelli on fascism and soccer, pp. 73–76.
80 On Arpinati, ACS, SPD, CR. b. 75, f. Arpinati, Leandro.
81 1931, 89,632 events; 1932, 156,022 events; 1933, 191,773 events; 1936, 130,017 events; 1937, 102,547 events; chess games added 11,164 "events" in 1936 and 6,953 in 1937. Source: OND, *BU* (January 1934); OND, *Annuario* (1937, 1938).
82 See ACS, MI, PS (1927–33), 1932, 2nd section, b. 64, cat. D 14, *gare sportive*; reports from various provinces all indicating a high incidence of violence at games and police complaints on the difficulty of controlling the fans; in particular, the report of the *questore* of Naples (f. Naples, 9 March 1931) noting that the championship game between Rome and Naples was "awaited with a passion that outstripped the habitual, degenerating into a veritable racism"; for a month prior to the game the police had been conducting "an action of propaganda and pacification," so as to isolate the more hot-headed fans.
83 OND, *Annuario* (1930), p. 237; "participations" indicated the incidence of attendance, not obviously the actual number of different persons attending.
84 Minio-Paluello, pp. 36–8, 154.
85 Ciano, *Dieci anni di attività*, p. 318.
86 Ibid., p. 319; *Il Bargello*, 18 December 1932. Initiatives similar to the "popular trains" were found in other European countries; see for an interesting comparison, the "Billet Lagrange," instituted by the Popular Front in France in 1936; it offered much higher discounts of 40–60 percent as compared to the Italians' 25–50 percent because the French government "overrode all objections to the contrary from railroad operators": 600,000 tickets were sold in the first month of operation, and in July 1936 a million and a half Parisians departed from the city taking advantage of the discounts and vacations instituted by the government; on this, see M. Dommanget's introduction to P. Lafargue, *Le Droit à la paresse* (Paris, 1972), pp. 79–80.
87 *GN*, 5 March 1933, on the management-sponsored trip of General Electrical Company of Milan; ibid., 7 October 1932, trip of 11,000 Milanese workers to Rome; ibid., 8 October 1933, 2,000 Fiat workers and 1,000 miners from the Valdarno to Rome.
88 *Il Bargello*, 18 December 1932.
89 On the KdF's large subsidies from the Labor Front and its own well-placed investments in cruise ships and other vacation facilities, see Schoenbaum, *Hitler's*

Social Revolution (Garden City, New York, 1967), pp. 104–5; OND, *Annuario* (1937), nn.
90 Prices quoted in *GN*, 13 January 1935, and *Popolo delle alpi*, 14 March 1935 (the 1935 lira = approximately 6 cents). As reported in ACS, PNF, SPP, b. 6, Milan, fiduciary report (24 June 1932); also *GN*, 7 June 1932.
91 OND, Ispettorato Superiore V Zona Toscana, *Crociera latina* (1935).
92 OND, *Annuario* (1938), p. 237; for that year it reported only 2,000 travelers abroad; by comparison the costs and quantity of travelers on KdF-sponsored trips: a six-day trip through the Norwegian fiords departing from Hamburg cost 41.50 R.M. (50 cents) per day; for a twenty-day sea trip to the Azores, 82 R.M. or a dollar per day; this policy allowed 130,000 persons to travel abroad in 1934 (prices quoted in L. H. Weir, *Europe at Play* [New York, 1937], p. 560). Travel within Italy was also costly, e.g., a week's trip from Turin to Apulia cost 850 lire in 1930 (*Informazione industriale*, 5 September 1930).
93 See for example *GN*, 10 June 1934, on the trip of 1,200 workers from Lecco to visit the *Leonardo da Vinci* at Genoa; also 8 July 1934, 28 April 1935; for the CGE's outing, see *GN*, 6 November 1932.
94 *GN*, 18 August 1933.
95 ACS, PNF, SPP, b. 15, Torino, f. 3, report Gastaldi to Giuriati, 21 August 1931; this same report contains accounts of worker unrest and the inability of the trade unions to stem it, pointedly contrasting this with the success of the *dopolavoro*.
96 *GN*, 28 April 1935.
97 *GN*, 20 September 1931.
98 *GN*, 6 November 1932.
99 Quoted in *GN*, 16 February 1935.
100 OND, *BM*, vol. 1, nos. 11–12 (November–December 1927); 26 June 1927, "Disposizioni per escursionisti."
101 *GN*, 11 August 1935.

7. The formation of fascist low culture

1 On the relationship between futurism and fascism, see Adrian Lyttelton, *The Seizure of Power: Fascism in Italy, 1919–1929* (New York, 1973), pp. 370–4.
2 On Gentile, see his *Fascismo e cultura* (Milan, 1928); and the recent essay by G. Semerari, "Il neoidealismo nella filosofia del primo '900: Neoidealismo e fascismo," *Matrici culturali del fascismo* (Bari, 1977); also Lyttelton, pp. 374–7.
3 Most historians of fascist ideology have either ignored the different levels of fascist cultural policy or dismissed "low" cultural policy as propaganda: see for example N. Bobbio, "La cultura e il fascismo," in *Fascismo e società italiana* (Turin, 1973), who describes fascist culture as "a huge factory of stereotypes, produced to indoctrinate the masses and youth, of watchwords transmitted through newspapers, schools, and radio" (p. 241); also E. Tannenbaum, *The Fascist Experience* (New York, 1973), who, separating "literary and artistic trends" and "intellectual and cultural life" from "popular culture and propaganda," tends to equate low cultural policy with popular culture itself. For a perceptive analysis of what I have designated as "high" fascist cultural policy, see Lyttelton, chapter 14, "Ideology and Culture," pp. 364–93. A provocative overview of the formation of the "mass" or middle-brow intellectual is contained in E. Galli della Loggia, "Ideologie, classe, e costumi,"

L'Italia contemporanea, 1945–1975 ed., V. Castronovo (Turin, 1976) pp. 379–434. For comments on the dangers posed by fascism's distinction between high culture and low culture, especially in view of the traditional divorce between elite and popular cultures in Italy, see a pro-Nazi German, H. Hartmann's otherwise sympathetic appraisal: *Der Fascismus dringt ins Volk: eine Betrachtung über das Dopolavoro* (Berlin 1933).

4 On the function of the *Enciclopedia* in the organization of Italian bourgeois culture, see G. Turi, "Progetto della *Enciclopedia Italiana*: l'organizzazione del consenso fra gli intellettuali," *Studi storici*, XIII, no. 1 (January–March 1972), pp. 93–152. The Istituto's role in the regime's cultural policy remains to be studied; for brief notes, see Lyttelton, p. 383; also G. Gentile, "Il nostro programma," *Educazione fascista*, vol. 5, no. 5 (May 1927), pp. 257–63.

5 Cited in E. De Angelis, *Che cosa è e che cosa vuole il Dopolavoro: l'organizzazione in provincia di Pavia* (Pavia, 1929), p. 84, as well as other bulletins published in 1928–30 distinguishing the cultural functions of the fascist institutes from those of the *dopolavoro*.

6 Cited in Lyttelton, p. 377.

7 De Angelis, p. 84.

8 On Bodrero, see E. Savino, *La nazione operante* (3rd ed.; Rome, 1937), p. 278.

9 G. Pesce, "Teatro del popolo," *La Stirpe*, vol. 2, no. 36 (June 1924), 483.

10 G. Farina d'Anfanio, "I problemi della cultura e gli operai," *La stirpe*, vol. 9, no. 3 (March 1933), 122; also Bertinetti, *Il libro del Dopolavoro* (Turin, 1978) passim.

11 C. Pavese, *American Literature: Essays and Opinions*, trans. E. Fussell (Berkeley, 1970), pp. 196–7.

12 Ibid., p. 196.

13 Characterizations from *GN*, 25 August 1929, 2 February 1931, 15 March 1931: also Cuesta, *Il libro del Dopolavoro* (Rome, 1937), pp. 27–28.

14 On artistic trends, see Lyttelton, pp. 384–8; also C. Sanguineti Lazagna, "La concezione delle arti figurative nella politica culturale del fascismo," *Movimento di liberazione in Italia*, vol. 14, no. 4 (1967).

15 On the Gentile reform, see Lyttelton, pp. 406, 508; also D. Bertoni Jovine, *Storia dell'educazione popolare in Italia*, rev. ed. (Turin, 1965), pp. 269–96; and L. Minio–Paluello, *Education in Fascist Italy* (London, 1946). On the distinction between education and instruction, and the growing divorce between the two, see the analysis by Gramsci, *Gli intellettuali e l'organizzazione della cultura* (Turin, 1966), pp. 106–14. On the effects of the reform, the fine study of M. Barbagli, "Sistema scolastico e mercato del lavoro: la riforma Gentile," *Rivista di storia contemporanea*, vol. 2, no. 4 (October 1973), pp. 456–92.

16 OND, *Ordinamento*, passim.

17 On the Popular University: Bertoni Jovine, pp. 247–50; A Cabrini, "Popular Education in Italy," *Industrial and Labor Information*, vol. 10, nos. 3–4. (21–28 April 1924), pp. 49–52; most recently, M. G. Rosada, *Le università popolari in Italia, 1900–1918* (Rome, 1975); also her "Biblioteche popolari e politica culturale del PSI tra ottocento e novecento," *Movimento operaio e socialista*, vol. 23, nos. 2–3 (April–September 1977), pp. 259–88.

18 "L'educazione degli adulti nei Dopolavoro," *La Stirpe*, vol. 2, no. 3 (March 1924), 214.

19 U. Gabbi, *L'università popolare in Italia* (Parma, 1926), pp. 7–8.

20 Cited in F. Boffi, "Le università popolari e gli istituti fascisti di cultura," *Educazione fascista*, 1928, pp. 341–2.

21 R. Stefanelli, *Dopolavoro: norme e pratiche per i dirigenti* (Turin, 1935), p. 52; F. Fioretti, "L'attività dei commissariati del Dopolavoro," *La Stirpe*, vol. 5, no. 3 (March 1927), p. 173; OND, Dopolavoro provinciale di Ravenna, *Il dopolavoro: istituzione fascista*, II Congresso provinciale del dopolavoro (Ravenna, 1930), p. 30.
22 *GN*, 28 July 1929, 11 August 1929, 19 January 1930.
23 *LF*, 27 October 1929.
24 *GN*, 3 November 1929.
25 Topics as listed in the weekly *notizario* of *GN*, 1929–34, passim.
26 G. Berlutti, "Le biblioteche e la cultura popolare," *Bibliografia fascista*, no. 10 (1928), pp. 1–4; generally on the resistance of teachers to overt propaganda in the curriculum, see Lyttelton, p. 411.
27 *Dopolavoro, istituzione fascista*, p. 106.
28 OND, *BU*, January 1934, p. 12; OND, *Annuario*, 1937; OND, *Annuario*, 1938, p. 238.
29 *BLPS*, no. 56 (1931), p. 173; *GN*, 27 March 1932.
30 As reported by Dusmet, "Spare time organizations for agricultural workers in Italy," *International Labor Review*, vol. 40 (February 1935), p. 234; OND, *BU*, January 1934, p. 11; the OND counted in 1926, 178; 1927, 225; 1928, 313; 1929, 1,943; 1930, 2,398; 1931, 2,307; 1932, 2,365; 1933, 2,298. *Annuario statistico italiano*, 1937, p. 277, containing statistics for 31, December 1934: OND, 265; schools, etc., 977; Associazione Nazionale Combattenti, 69; PNF, 143; ONB, 88; religious, 372; private, 195; for a total of 2,109. On the organization of the popular libraries, see: "Les bibliothèques du dopolavoro," *Bibliothèques populaires et loisirs ouvriers, Enquête faite à la demande du BIT*, ed. Institut International de Cooperation Intellectuelle (Paris, 1933), pp. 177–200.
31 P. Rignani, *Lugo durante il periodo delle guerre fasciste, 1932–luglio 1943* (Lugo, 1973), p. 65.
32 A. Ferrari, "Problemi di cultura operaia," *Il Maglio*, 9 March 1938.
33 T. Cianetti, quoted in CGFLI, *Convegno dei dirigenti*, p. 15.
34 Confederazione generale fascista dei lavoratori dell'industria, *La cultura dei lavoratori* (Florence, 1940), p. ii.
35 See A. Giambitto, "La valorizzazione del lavoro italiano mediante la diffusione e l'organizzazione scientifica dell' insegnamento professionale-serale," *Atti* del III Congresso dell'Organizzazione Scientifica del Lavoro, II, p. 1155.
36 According to Lyttelton (p. 406), Mussolini's eagerness to gain the approval of traditional culture, together with his concern to demonstrate his government's effectiveness in pushing through a major piece of legislation, explains his willingness to pass a reform conflicting with the regime's pretentions to modernity. Industry's response to the regime's neglect of a basic prerequisite of industrializing society bears further analysis; for the reform's effects on the vocational instructional system, see L. Borghi, *Educazione e autorità nell'Italia moderna* (Florence, 1950), pp. 250–1.
37 Belluzzo's appointment, coinciding with the rationalization movement, earned praise from industry and the trade unions; see for example: G. Revere, "Scuola di cultura e scuole professionali," *OSL*, July–August 1928; N. Giammartino, "Riforma tecnica della scuola," *LF*, 27 January 1928.
38 R. Sottilaro, "Vocational Education in Italy," *International Labor Review*, vol. 24, no. 4 (October 1936), pp. 460–7; legislative decree of 17 June 1928, no. 1314, transferred all vocational schools attached to the Ministry of the National Economy to the Ministry of National Education; Act of 7 January 1929, no. 8, set up the *scuola*

secondaria d'avviamento professionale; the intermediate schools were reformed by the Act of 15 June 1931, no. 889.
39 *BLPS*, no. 56 (1931), p. 174. In 1929, 382 *dopolavoro* sections reportedly offered their members vocational instruction, while only a year later, 546 sections reportedly sponsored 1,100 courses with a total attendance of 42,000.
40 *GN*, 15 November 1931; Dusmet, p. 234.
41 *GN*, 29 November 1931.
42 ACS, PNF, D, b. 205, f. pratiche generali, OND, *Esercizio finanziario*, 1933–4; OND, *BU*, January 1934, p. 14; OND, *Annuario*, 1937, p. 238. By 1933 the number of sections promoting instruction had declined to 409; in 1937 *dopolavoro* sections offered 751 courses as compared with the 1,100 in 1930, while total enrollment had fallen off to 28,853 persons.
43 OND, *BU*, January 1934, p. 12: OND, *Annuario*, 1937, p. 238.
44 Gramsci, *Gli intellettuali*, pp. 106–14.
45 Sottilaro, p. 469; also L. Begnotti, "Per una nuova classe dirigente: l'educazione dei lavoratori," *LF*, 22 November 1934.
46 *Bianco e rosso*, 12 March 1936, p. 11; also 7 March 1935, p. 8.
47 Ibid.
48 Sottilaro, p. 476.
49 Ibid., pp. 473–7; also report of the Ministero della Educazione Nazionale, Direttore Generale per l'Istruzione Media Tecnica, "La formazione ed il perfezionamento dei lavoratori," in Reports of the Seventh International Management Congress (Washington, D.C., 1938), pp. 61–4; also CGFLI, *Organizzazione fascista dei lavoratori*, I (Rome, 1935).
50 OND, *BU*, vol. 3, no. 9 (November 1929), circular 22 November 1929, Beretta to *dopolavoro provinciali*. By this time, government directives of 1926–7 suspending certain holidays and festivities in order to concentrate civic energies on fascism's "economic battles" had evidently been nullified.
51 Cited in "Report, Presented to the First International Congress of Popular Arts, Rome, October 30, 1929," in OND, *Popular Italian Costumes, Music, Dances and Festivals* (Rome, 1931), p. 66 (hereafter Beretta, vol. 1).
52 Ibid.
53 Cited in "Report Presented to the Second International Congress of Popular Arts, Antwerp, September 1930" (hereafter Beretta, vol. 2) in ibid., p. 78.
54 Ibid., pp. 78–9.
55 Giacomo Nunès, "Rapport de la Commission Italienne de Cooperation Intellectuelle," in *Art populaire et loisirs ouvrières, enquête faite à la demande du BIT*, ed. Institut International de Cooperation Intellectuelle (Paris, 1934), p. 165.
56 Beretta, vol. 2, p. 79.
57 See *Art populaire* for a general analysis of the decline of traditional folk manifestations in Europe; the intellectuals' preoccupation with the decline of folk culture was evidently not confined solely to fascist regimes; the different approaches to the problem in the thirties merit fuller study.
58 Beretta, vol. 1, p. 1, passim, for a description of activities.
59 *GN*, 29 September 1929; also Beretta, vol. 2, p. 70.
60 For an introduction to this significant and as yet unstudied aspect of fascist cultural policy, see E. De Martino, "Intorno a una storia del mondo popolare subalterno," *Società*, vol. 5, no. 31 (September 1949), pp. 411–35; also Lyttelton, pp. 371–2.
61 De Martino, "Intorno a una storia del mondo popolare subalterno," p. 49.
62 See for example R. Corso, "I dopolavoristi d'Italia convenuti a Roma . . . ," *GN*,

8 January 1930; *Lares*, vol. 1, no. 1 (June 1930), Organo del Comitato Nazionale per le Tradizioni Popolari. The danger that politics would pervert science (and thereby affect the "authenticity" of folk customs) was apparently debated, and the differences quickly resolved in a resolution taken at the Congress on Popular Traditions held in Florence in May 1929 urging that "all measures be taken to maintain the 'purity' of traditions and to preserve 'authenticity' in their revival" (A. A. Bernardy, *Rinascita regionale* [Rome, 1930], p. 49). OND interference was more marked beginning in 1935 with injunctions to substitute the "indigenous" term *la popolaresca* for the foreign *folklore* (circular Bodrero to *dopolavoro provinciali*, 24 April 1935, *Lares*, vol. 6, nos. 1–2 [March–June 1935], p. 160). On ethnologists in the service of the Ethiopian campaign, see the recent studies of M. Lospinoso, A. Rivera, et al., in *Matrici culturali del fascismo* (Bari, 1977).

63 "Report of the Jury," display of Italian Costumes at Venice, in *Popular Italian Costumes*, p. 96.

64 OND, *BU*, vol. 3, 9 November 1929, protocol no. 43582; 29 November 1929, Turati to *dopolavoro provinciali*.

65 Beretta, vol. 1, p. 68.

66 See the querulous remarks on the fickleness of fashion-conscious modern women by a leading female anthropologist, A. Bernardy (p. 48): "The tendency to modify, alter, and banalize costume style is too typical of a modern female sensibility, which is iconoclastic rather than conservative, admiring and ardent in support of the latest fashion sensation rather than of modest continuity; sacrificing the pompons on shoes to make the foot look smaller, removing pleats from full petticoats to slim down the figure, altering the line of the bodice or headdress – presumably, or rather presumptuously – to make it suit better individual looks, unreflecting of the fact that every one of these changes is a deformation, that when dealing with tradition, every emendment is a solecism, personal innovation disfiguring, and modernization itself trivializing, if not downright sacrilegious." Bernardy failed to remark the paradox that the very habit of awarding prizes as incentives for participation in this "revival" inevitably provoked rivalries, and thereby embellishment, showiness, and the change she so deplored.

67 *GN*, 8 January 1930.

68 OND, *Costumi, musica, danze e feste popolari in Italia*, rev. ed. (Rome, 1935), p. 78.

69 *Costumi*, pp. 78, 94.

70 "Le giornate della seta," *GN*, 24 June 1934.

71 A. Curcio, "Frutta d'Italia," *GN*, 4 November 1934.

72 Beretta, vol. 2, p. 88.

73 Rignani, p. 23.

74 Beretta, vol. 2, p. 94.

75 OND, *Annuario*, 1938, p. 43.

76 Rignani, p. 23.

77 E. Bona, "Attività dell'OND per le arte popolari italiane dal congresso di Trento all'anno XVII," *Atti* del IV Congresso Nazionale di Arti e Tradizioni Popolari (Venice, 1940), p. 9.

78 Beretta, vol. 1, p. 70.

79 Descriptions in annual calendar of events, *Costumi*, pp. 13–82.

80 *Il Dopolavoro dell'urbe*, vol. 1, nos. 6–7 (July 1930); ACS, PCM, 1934–6; f. 14, 2, n. 966, memorandum E. Santamaria to Pres. Council Min., 14 June 1928; 969/1 prov. secretary OND to Min. Interior, 16 July 1927.

81 Ibid.; 969/1 letter Prefect Garzaroli to secretary, Pres. Council Min., 20 July 1928; also 1931–3, f. 14, 2, no. 5671.
82 *Il Dopolavoro dell'urbe*, vol. 1, no. 5 (June 1930).
83 *Il Dopolavoro dell' urbe*, vol. 1, nos. 6–7 (July 1930).
84 The use of fascist ritual bears more systematic study, especially in the light of the often commented-upon phenomenon of *Ducismo*, the veritable cult of Mussolini so marked in the Italian South. C. G. Chapman's anthropological study of a small Sicilian town, *Milocca: a Sicilian Village* (Cambridge, Mass., 1971), based on field-work conducted in 1928–9, describes the unusual first sight in 1929 of small girls in fascist uniform participating in the local patron saint's procession (p. 177).
85 *GN*, 25 August 1929.
86 For accounts of the preceding, see ibid., 30 July 1933, 1 July 1934, 25 August 1935, 8 September 1935, and 15 September 1935.
87 Ibid., 6 March 1932, 25 March 1933, and 4 February 1934.
88 *La Provincia di Vercelli*, 13 February 1934.
89 *GN*, 1 March 1931.
90 Ibid., 27 March 1932; Beretta, vol. 2, p. 87; at Ponti (Alessandria), *Costumi*, p. 18; *GN*, 6 March 1932, 27 March 1932.
91 *Costumi*, p. 294.
92 Descriptions in *GN*, 8 January 1930 and 12 January 1930; also "Adunata nazionale del costume di Roma, facsimile del programma," in *Costumi*, pp. 255–88.
93 *Famiglia nostra*, July–August 1930.
94 ACS, PNF, SPP, b. 25, Torino, Sf. 4, fiduciary report, 10 February 1939; *Il Popolo di Pavia*, 25 August 1933.
95 In general on the Italian cinema see G. Tinazzi, ed., *Il cinema italiano dal fascismo all'antifascismo* (Padua, 1966); also Tannenbaum, pp. 230–9.
96 As judged by films presented for censorship, listed in *Annuario statistico italiano*, 1936, p. 228; 1937, p. 278; 1938, p. 286; 1939, p. 324; 1940, p. 85.
97 For a lively description of these films see Tannenbaum, pp. 232–8.
98 Cannistraro, "The Radio in Fascist Italy," *Journal of European Studies*, vol. 2, no. 2 (June 1972), p. 145.
99 *ASI*, 1934, p. 221; analysis based on *Italia tra le due guerre, antologia di cinegiornali prodotti dall'Istituto Nazionale Luce* (series of thirty newsreels released in 1973 by the Institute); see also the catalogue, edited by I. Guasti and M. Sperenzi, *Propaganda di regime e giudizio della storia* (Florence, April–May 1973).
100 OND, *Collana del Carro dei Tespi: commedie in un atto* (Rome, 1929).
101 OND, *Spighe: novelle per dopolavoristi* (Rome, 1928).
102 These stories were representative of selections found in later anthologies as well. See, for example, OND, *Novelle di operai* (Rome 1935); ibid. (Rome, 1939); also Dopolavoro provinciale di Pavia, *Germogli: novelle di dopolavoristi* (Pavia, 1934).
103 *GN*, 14 September 1930.
104 A. G. Bragaglia, "La cinematografia politica ovverosia il cinema 'quinto potere,'" *Educazione fascista*, November 1931, pp. 989–90.
105 *LF*, 16 July 1933.
106 Quoted in *Santa milizia*, 27 May 1933.
107 *GN*, 9 April 1933.
108 G. Davico Bonino, *Gramsci e il teatro* (Turin, 1972), pp. 37–40.
109 *GN*, 28 June 1931.
110 *GN*, 6 May 1934.
111 *GN*, 12 May 1935.

112 *GN*, 2 August 1935.
113 See for examples: "Donne e fanciulle in Etiopia," *GN*, 18 October 1931; A. Castaldi, "Donne d'Abissinia," *GN*, 13 February 1932; U. Imperatori, "Somalia," *GN*, 6 March 1932; A. Castaldi, "Il fertile Tigre," *GN*, 11 August 1935.
114 *GN*, 24 November 1935; 1 December 1935; etc. Cartoons were signed by the noted cartoonist Bepi.
115 Radius, p. 317.

8. The limits of consent

1 R. Morandi, "Il movimento socialista risorge," in S. Merli, ed., *La ricostruzione del movimento socialista in Italia e la lotta contro il fascismo dal 1934 alla seconda guerra mondiale*, Istituto G. G. Feltrinelli, *Annali*, V, 1962, p. 712; on public opinion see Renzo De Felice, *Mussolini il Duce: Gli anni del consenso* (hereafter De Felice, vol. 4), 5 vols. (Turin, 1974), 4 pp. 776–8. Pending the appearance of the fifth and final volume of his biography of Mussolini, there is still no thorough study of the later years of the regime. For an overview, see E. Santarelli, *Storia del movimento e del regime fascista* 2 vols. (Rome, 1967), 2, 221–359.
2 In the Lyon Congress Theses of the PC d'I, in A. Gramsci, *Sul fascismo*, ed. E. Santarelli (Rome, 1974), pp. 304–11.
3 This aspect of PNF–trade union relations awaits further study. For a fine contemporary analysis, see the report written by Eugenio Curiel in January 1939 for the PC d'I in Merli, pp. 283–90.
4 Quoted from *Stato e impero*, the regime's official journal of colonial affairs founded in 1938 and cited in Luigi Preti, *Impero fascista, africani ed ebrei* (Milan, 1968), p. 110.
5 ACS, MI, PS, Polizia Politica, b. 158, f. 5, cat. M 3, PNF (1935–7), police report, Milan, 17 April 1937.
6 P. Togliatti, "What Are the Sources of Fascism's Strength?" in *Lectures on Fascism*, trans. D. Dichter (New York, 1976), p. 145; see also Ernesto Ragionieri, *La storia d'Italia, dall'unità a oggi: la storia politica e sociale* (Turin, 1976), pp. 2225–7.
7 ACS, SPD, CO, b. 59, f. 209.016, sf. Ottavio Dinale, "Un problema del Regime: il Dopolavoro," 9 July 1936.
8 *Atti parlamentari*, Legislature XXIX, Sessione 1937, Senato, p. 1437; Camera dei Deputati, Discussione 12 maggio 1937, pp. 3637–42.
9 For a thorough discussion of the juridical implications of the Law of May 1937, see R. Richard, *La figura giuridica dell'OND* (Pavia, 1940), esp. pp. 40–82. According to the PNF statutes of 1938, modified in December 1939, the OND was classified as an organization dependent *on* the PNF; cf. its preceding characterization as an organization *of* the PNF. However, the PNF statutes were not legally binding under Italian law.
10 According to a memorandum sent by Puccetti to Mussolini on 31 May 1931, the construction of *dopolavoro* had ceased keeping pace with membership increases, "for want of impelling cause and regular financing" with the result that "many towns had failed to accomplish anything to date" (see ACS, PNF, D, b. 204, f. pratiche generali, OND, "Proposta per la costruzione di un ente immobiliare del PNF," 31 May 1939). His concern with the collapse of organizational activity was echoed in reports of police and party informers: see, for example, ACS, PNF, SPP, b. 11, Padua, fiduciary report, 20 January 1938; b. 14, Piacenza, fiduciary report, 27 October

1939; b. 25, Torino, fiduciary report, December 1939; also of interest, the reports of the OVRA on the slackening attendance at spectator sports events in ACS, MI, PS, Polizia Politica, b. 217, f. 3 cat. G 7 (Sport) 1939–40; on Savona, see ACS, PNF, SPD. b. 20, Savona, fiduciary report, 31 August 1940.

11 ACS, MI, PS, Polizia Politica, cat. M 3, PNF (1938–9), police report, September 1939; for the fascist leadership's own perceptions of Italy's total state of military and economic unpreparedness for war, see Galeazzo Ciano, *Diaries, 1939–1943* (Garden City, N.Y., 1946), esp. pp. 117–64; on opposition to the war as manifested in police reports on public opinion, see Alberto Aquarone, "Lo spirito pubblico in Italia alla vigilia della Seconda Guerra Mondiale," *Nord e sud*, vol. 11 (January 1964), 117–22.

12 Sereni, *La questione agraria nella rinascita nazionale italiana* (Rome 1946), p. 260.

13 G. Prato, "Verso la giornata di sette ore e ultra," quoted in *Italia industriale*, I, no. 2 (October–December 1919), p. 48.

14 Walter, *The Class Conflict in Italy* (London, 1943), p. 46.

15 Quoted in *Il Maglio*, organ of the fascist federation of industrial workers of Turin, 30 March; see also 5 January, 19 January, 9 February, 9 March, 27 March, 11 May, and 25 May 1938. For protests against managerial control, see ibid., 15 June and 20 December 1939.

16 Ruggero Zangrandi, *Il lungo viaggio attraverso il fascismo* (Milan, 1962), pp. 201–16, esp. p. 201.

17 On the so-called generation of the Littorial, see E. Tannenbaum, *The Fascist Experience* (New York, 1972) pp. 128–32; also various articles appearing in *Critica fascista* in 1938–9, esp. E. Leoni, "Rendere popolare la cultura," vol. 7, no. 4 (13 December 1938), p. 56; and "Ancora rendere popolare la cultura," vol. 17, no. 18 (15 July 1939), p. 42; also E. Capaldo, "Gruppi universitari fascisti e Gioventù Italiana del Littorio," vol. 17, no. 1 (1 November 1938), pp. 6–8.

18 G. Guizzardi, "Funzione della gioventù universitaria e propaganda operaia, *Critica fascista*, vol. 18, no. 4 (15 December 1939), 62–64; for the syndicalist view, see F. Fusini, "GUF e sindacati operai," *Il Maglio*, 14 September 1938; also I. Bucca, "I sindacati e GUF," 19 April 1939. On the close police surveillance of these contacts, see P. Spriano, *Storia del partito comunista italiano*, 5 vols. (Turin, 1967–75), 3, pp. 196–201.

19 Pietro Capoferri, *Venti anni coi sindacati* (Milan, 1951), pp. 194–7; also OND, *BU*, 10 October 1939, *foglio di disposizione* no. 1442, 29 October 1939.

20 *Lavoro fascista*, 14 December 1939; see also L. Fontanelli, "Il dopolavoro col lavoro," *Lavoro fascista*, 19 November 1939 and 28 November 1939; *GN*, 7 December 1939. *Testo del discorso, pronunciato dal consigliere nazionale P. Capoferri, 19 febbraio, 1940* (Treviso, 1940); according to Capoferri (*Venti anni*, p. 197), more than 160 "home economics" centers for women were set up in 1939–40.

21 *LF*, 12 December 1942; OND, *Attualità*, vol. 2, (9 December 1942).

22 Archivio Partito Comunista, 1933, 1123/88-Q1, Ufficio politico, 25 May 1933, o.d.g.: "Lavoro nelle organizzazioni di massa giovanili e nel Dopolavoro," signed R. di Marcucci.

23 Furini, "Per la conquista delle masse dopolavoriste," *Stato operaio*, VII, no. 8 (August 1933), p. 500.

24 Togliatti, pp. 73–86; citations from pp. 82, 84.

25 ACS, MI, PS, Polizia Politica, b. 136, f. 12, cat. k 35, "Propaganda comunista nei sindacati fascisti e dopolavoro," report of 26 June 1936.

26 ACS, MI, PS, Polizia Politica, b. 136, f. 12, cat. k 35, "Propaganda comunista nei sindacati fascisti e dopolavoro," 31 July 1936.

27 Spriano, III, pp. 103–6.
28 On big business's increasing estrangement from the regime on the eve of the war, see Sarti, *Fascism and the Industrial Leadership in Italy* (Berkeley, 1971), pp. 125–33; on the growth of the *dopolavoro aziendale*, ACS, MI, PS, Polizia Politica, cat. M 3, PNF, (1938–9) police report, n.d.
29 For a judicious analysis of the continuities between the fascist state and postwar liberal democratic institutions, see Claudio Pavone, "La continuità dello Stato: istituzioni e uomini," in *Italia, 1945–1949: le origini della repubblica* (Turin, 1973), pp. 137–288; specifically on the OND, see OND, *BU*, Circular I, prot. no. 137464, 11 October 1944; also G. Malavisi, *ENAL* (Rome, 1948); A. Jacomelli, "L'ENAL: una bandita chiusa," *Attualità*, no. 13 (1956), pp. 1–18.
30 "I lavoratori e il tempo libero," supplement to no. 11 (November 1968) of the review "*Vita italiana – Documenti, informazioni*," published under the auspices of the President of the Council of Ministers (Rome, 1968), p. 47, Jacomelli, p. 15; on the struggle of the Case del Popolo of Florence to regain their properties, see: "I rapporti fra l'amministrazione finanziaria dello Stato e le Case del popolo della provincia di Firenze, Lettera a S. E. Vanoni" (Florence, 1954); also *numeri unici* (single publications) issued by various *case del popolo* in 1953–6, protesting evictions; pamphlets courtesy of A. Baldi.
31 Robert S. and Helen Merrell Lynd, *Middletown in Transition* (New York, 1937), p. 245.
32 As augured by the British Laborist and Minister of Labor George Barnes in the ILO, International Labor Conference, *Proceedings*, First Annual Meeting (Washington, D.C., 1919), p. 41; for a brief history of the movement for the "eight hours" from 1889 to 1919, see Stephen Bauer, "The Road to the Eight Hour Day," *Monthly Labor Review*, no. 2 (August 1919), pp. 41–65. On the attitudes of employers, government officials, and representatives of organized labor in the early twenties, see ILO, 6th Session, *Proceedngs*, 2 vols. (Geneva, 1924); also Report of the Director, "Utilization of Workers' Spare Time" (Geneva, 1926), pp. 256–64. For an overview of the ILO studies and congresses on the subject, see A. A. Evans, "Work and Leisure, 1919–1969," *International Labor Review*, vol. 99, no. 1 (January 1969), 35–99. Cf. the attitudes toward leisure under early capitalist industrialism in E. P. Thompson, "Time, Work Discipline and Industrial Capitalism," *Past and Present*, no. 38 (December 1967), pp. 56–97.
33 G. Méquet, cited in ILO, Studies and Reports, ser. G (Housing and Welfare), no. 4, *Recreation and Education* (Geneva, 1936), p. 131. Although the concept of leisure has been examined in historical perspective, the actual organization of worker leisure activities has only recently begun to be studied. For selected studies and a recent bibliography, see Michael R. Marrus, ed., *The Emergence of Leisure* (New York, 1974). A fine overview of trends in American business is given in Robert Goldman and John Wilson, "The Rationalization of Leisure," *Politics and Society*, vol. 7, no. 2 (1977), pp. 157–87. Contemporary studies abound, however, almost entirely from the point of view of business managers and moral reformers. See for example, James Sizer, *The Commercialization of Leisure* (New Haven, 1926); in addition to the surveys by Herbert May and Dorothy Petgen, *Leisure and Its Use* (New York, 1928), and Yvonne Bécquet, *L'organisation des loisirs des travailleurs* (Paris, 1939).
34 Report, World Committee, YMCA, "The Leisure of the Younger Worker," *International Labor Review*, vol. 9, no. 6 (June 1924), pp. 829–35.
35 KdF, World Congress for Leisure Time, *Reports* of the Second International Congress on Leisure (Hamburg–Berlin, 1936), p. 30; and the various reports from the countries

represented; see also Richard, pp. 13–28. On Spain, see Juan Bta. Viza Caball, *Valorisaçion del descanso (dopolavoro español)* (1937).

36 *The Spectator*, 6 February 1932.

37 *International Quarterly of Adult Education* (May 1935), p. 47.

38 Méquet, p. 133.

39 See Eric Larabee and Rolf Meyersohn, eds., *Mass Leisure* (Glencoe, Ill., 1958).

40 On the relations between Church and regime, see De Felice, IV, pp. 246–75; also the recent work of S. Pivato, "L'organizzazione cattolica della cultura di massa durante il fascismo," *Storia contemporanea*, vol. 13, no. 2 (July–September 1978) in addition to Chapter 2, n85.

41 E. E. Schattschneider, *The Semi-Sovereign People* (New York, 1960), p. 68.

42 On the generation gap under fascism, see *Torino tra le due guerre*, pp. 22–28; also ACS, MI, PS, Polizia Politica, cat. G 7, Sport, (1939–40), report of 31 January 1939.

Bibliography

Note on sources

The documentation available for the study of the mass organization of leisure in fascist Italy simply confirms how little the subject lends itself either to treatment according to the canons of a traditional institutional history or to a social "history from below." The first thing that strikes the eye is the absence of a more or less spontaneous vox populi. Anybody familiar with the Italian labor movement or with the organization of working class associational life before the march on Rome knows how very rich the sources are for their study: the statutes of workingmen's clubs duly registered with the public authorities, the many bulletins deposited according to copyright law in the National Library of Florence, the police reports which are especially meticulous just after the Great War, the reports and the press of the left parties, even the journals of the industrial elites, pig-headedly against reforms, yet outspoken and not unlucid in their observations on public life. Until very recently, only the work of D. H. Bell, "Work Culture and Worker Politics," vol. 3, no. 1 (1978) had suggested the susceptibility of the many Italian sources to what might be described as an Anglo-American social history. Unfortunately the older English-language literature, including M. F. Neufeld, *Italy: School for Awakening Countries* (Ithaca, 1961) and S. Surace, *Ideology, Economic Change and the Working Classes: the Case of Italy* (Berkeley, 1966), is lacking the subtlety of analysis of the classic Italian-language studies: A. Angiolini and E. Ciacchi, *Socialismo e socialisti in Italia* (Florence, 1919), R. Michels, *Il proletariato e la borghesia nel movimento socialista italiano* (Turin, 1908), and R. Rigola, *Storia del movimento operaio italiano* (Milan, 1947); nor does it reflect the archival richness of the more recent work; that of G. Procacci, *La lotta di classe in Italia agli inizi del secolo XX* (Rome, 1970), of S. Merli, *Proletariato di fabbrica e capitalismo: il caso italiano, 1880–1900*, 2 vols. (Florence, 1972), and of the numerous local studies appearing over the last several years in the journal *Movimento operaio e socialista* (Genoa).

Contrasted with this abundance, the period after 1925–6 is bleak. As the *squadristi* unleashed their attacks on working-class circles, the antifascist opposition was outlawed and, finally, the clubs, cooperatives, and mutual aid societies were "coordinated" by the fascist syndicates, the OND, and the fascists' national cooperative and mutual aid confederations. The working class voice was dimmed; except for brief moments, in 1926–7 during the crisis of stabilization and in 1930–1, when the Great Depression hit Italy, it seems silent, until the resurgence of working-class militancy at the close of the decade.

The problem of sources is compounded by the loss of the central administrative records of the OND in the chaotic years between the fall of fascism and the formation of the Republic. Whether their disappearance was caused by wartime bombardments, theft, or aggravated bureaucratic oversight is unknown: No conspiracy theory is needed to explain the loss, though it is perhaps not beside the point to note that no similar mishaps befell the records of the Confindustria or most other agencies destined to play a more obvious technical function in the continuity of the Italian state. Postwar administrators too considered the *dopolavoro* as having relatively little political importance and therefore no evident historical interest. Consequently, the local records were in most cases quite literally relegated to the dustbin of history; or given the acute paper shortage in the immediate postwar years, they were recycled. In Florence, for example, some fragments of the OND's administration survived as scrap paper, now the carbon copies of letters filed away as part of the archives of the Partito d'Azione at the Istituto per la Storia della Resistenza.

Other archival documentation is remarkably sparse at least on a national level. Indeed, from the contents of the files of the Council of State, of the Fascist party directory, and of the Ministry of the Interior, there emerges such an impoverished record of what was happening among the lower classes that one is led to conclude either that the fascist regime was exceptionally inefficient or that it practiced malign neglect to a fine art, deliberately ignoring the ordinary fluctuations of public opinion. The latter conclusion is the more plausible one. The ostensibly apolitical, seemingly frivolous nature of the *dopolavoro*, at least as perceived from the vantage point of leaders preoccupied with the conduct of "high politics," made it of low priority, if not negligible interest, best left to low-echelon functionaries and organizers of culture. Moreover, Mussolini's policing agencies were always more interested in ferreting out political nonconformity than with weighing systematically the quality of political consensus. Consequently, once working-class outings, small theater benefits, or choral singings were conducted with what seemed a purely social or recreational purpose, prefects, policemen, and party spies generally lost interest. The result was workers, much like women and other powerless groups, seemed to disappear from history; that is, they disappeared from readily documented politics into the less visible social and private spheres of life.

In this study, policy aims and activities have thus had to be reconstructed through diverse sources, the apparent eclecticism of which is perhaps the best testimony of the extraordinary complexity of organization that touched so many aspects of social life. Scattered through the Central State Archives (ACS) there is much valuable information on official policy and working-class associational life: in the reports on the "political situation of the provinces" (SPP), collected by the PNF federations on behalf of the national directory; in police reports, especially those filed in the section G 1 (or miscellaneous associations) at the Ministry of the Interior or gathered by the political police

(Pol. Pol.); and, finally, in the many memos, letters, and clippings catalogued by subject in the confidential and ordinary correspondence (*carteggio riservato* or CR and *carteggio ordinario* or CO) of Mussolini's personal secretariat (SPD). The fascist press too can prove a surprisingly rich source, although only after decoding its monotonously opaque rhetoric. The syndicalists' newspaper *Lavoro d'Italia* and its successor, *Lavoro fascista*, along with *Il Maglio* of Turin, are especially useful inasmuch as they, more than any other official publications – except perhaps for fascist intellectuals' *Critica fascista* – were forced to air debates in order to maintain their working-class readership. A capitalist truth, different in some respects from that of the regime, can be found in its numerous variants in company newspapers and bulletins, making these useful sources for understanding the operations of institutions in single enterprises. The profusion of publications edited by the OND itself, some regular, some ephemeral, are similarly good indicators of the complexity of local situations since they were the main vehicles for articulating policy. All of these official sources, with their implicit if not ostentatious celebration of fascist normality, must be read in light of the often subtle, rarely overly optimistic, analyses of the antifascist resistance; those made by the Communist party of Italy, which in its effort to reconstitute its clandestine bases after 1927 carefully scrutinized the strength of the fascist mass organizations, can be found in articles in the monthly *Stato operaio* and in internal reports available in the party archives at the Gramsci Institute in Rome. Finally, there exists a wide range of national and international inquiries into the use of worker leisure conducted under the auspices of the International Labor Organization and by state and private agencies and even single reformers. The use of this material to develop a cross-national and comparative perspective on the organization of leisure, together with studies of the provincial networks and even single institutions within Italy will, I believe, add important new dimensions to the general framework that this documentation affords for the study of the operations of the institution as a whole within the fascist state.

I. Archival sources

Archivio Centrale dello Stato,
  Carte Cianetti
  Ministero dell'Interno, direzione generale pubblica sicurezza, divisione polizia politica, fascicoli di materia, 1926–45,
    categories: G, G7, K, K3, K8, K11, M3.
  divisione affari generali e riservati,
    (1914–26) category: G1.
    (1927–33) category: G1.
    (1920–45) category: G1, associazioni diverse per provincia.
  serie diverse,
    (1903–49): G1, associazioni.
  Partito Nazionale Fascista, direttorio nazionale,

Bibliography

situazione politica delle provincie.
Segreteria Particolare del Duce,
carteggio riservato.
carteggio ordinario.
Archivio Centro Storico Fiat,
Biografie.
Busta 10, Opere sociali, assistenziali, turistiche.
Busta 14, Servizi sociali.
Archivio Partito Comunista Italiano

II. Government publications

Gazzetta Ufficiale del Regno
Istituto Centrale di Statistica. *Annuario statistico italiano*, 1930–40.
    Censimento degli esercizi industriali e commerciali al 15 ottobre, 1927. Vol.
    viii. Relazione generale.
    Censimento industriale e commerciale, 1937–1940. Parte seconda, risultati
    generali. Vol. I. Industria.
    VII Censimento generale della popolazione, 21 aprile, 1931. Relazione
    generale.
    Sommario di statistiche storiche italiane, 1861–1955. Rome, 1955.
Ministero per la Costituente, Lavoro, commissione per lo studio dei problemi
    di. *Atti*. Vols. II–III, Rome, 1946.
Ufficio di Politica Economica, *Opere e leggi del regime fascista*. Rome, 1927.

III. PNF, labor, and trade associations: publications and reports

Confederazione generale fascista dei lavoratori. *Organizzazione fascista dei
    lavoratori*. Vol. I, Rome, 1935; vol. II, Rome, 1936.
Confederazione fascista dei lavoratori dell'agricoltura. *Dopolavoro, radio, ci-
    nema rurali*. Rome, 1939.
Confederazione fascista dei lavoratori dell'industria. *La cultura dei lavoratori*.
    Florence, 1940.
Confederazione generale fascista dell'industria italiana. *L'industria e le opere
    sociali*. Rome, 1937.
    L'industria italiana. Rome, 1929.
    L'industria nell'Italia fascista. Rome, 1939.
    Relazione all'assemblea generale. Rome, 1930, 1932, 1933.
Confederazione generale italiana dell'industria. *Annuario*, 1922–39.
Partito nazionale fascista. *Fogli d'ordine, dal 31 luglio IV al 28 ottobre XIII*.
    Rome, 1935.
Unione fascista degli industriali della provincia di Torino. *Torino industriale*.
    Rome, 1941.

294

IV. Opera Nazionale Dopolavoro

A. Periodicals and reports

Il Dopolavoro: rivista quindicinale illustrata, vol. I, no. 1 (15 February 1923); ceased publication with vol. I, no. 18 (15 November 1923); continued from 15 December 1923 to December 1925 as a section in *La stirpe*.
Quaderni del dopolavoro. 4 vols., Rome, 1925.
Il Dopolavoro, vol. IV, no. 1 (n.s.) (January 1926); ceased publication with vol. VI, no. 8 (February 1929).
L'attività dell'OND dal maggio al marzo 1927. Rome, 1927.
Bollettino ufficiale: scopi ed organizzazione, vol. I, no. 1 (1 January 1927).
Bollettino mensile: scopi ed organizzazione del movimento filodrammatico dell'OND, vol. I, no. 2 (February 1927).
Bollettino mensile: scopi ed organizzazione del movimento musicale dell'OND, vol. I, no. 3 (March 1927).
Bollettino mensile: sviluppo ed organizzazione del movimento per gli orto-giardini domestici, vol. I, nos. 5–6 (May–June 1927).
Bollettino mensile: il dopolavoro e le opere assistenziali nelle industrie italiane, vol. I, nos. 7–8 (July–August 1927).
Bollettino mensile: la partecipazione dell'OND ai congressi nazionali e internazionali durante il 1927, vol. I, nos. 9–10 (September–October 1927).
Bollettino mensile: ordinamenti, programmi e regolamenti dell'OND, vol. I, nos. 11–12 (November–December 1927).
Bolletino mensile: l'attività dell'OND nel corso dell'anno 1927, vol. II, nos. 1–2 (January–February 1928).
Bollettino mensile: norme pratiche per l'allevamento del bacco da seta, vol. II, nos. 3–4 (March–April 1928).
Bollettino mensile: le attività assistenziali dell'OND, vol. II, nos. 5–6 (May–June 1928).
Bollettino mensile: orto-giardini domestici, iniziative e realizzazioni del dopolavoro, vol. II, nos. 7–8 (July–August 1928).
Bollettino mensile: il servizio cinematografico e radiotelefonico dell'OND, vol. II, nos. 9–10 (September–October 1928; ceased publication).
Il Dopolavoro escursionistico: Rassegna quindicinale della commissione centrale per l'escursionismo dell'Opera Nazionale Dopolavoro, vol. I, no. 1 (17 February 1927). After 1930 it became the *Rassegna Quindicinale della Federazione Italiana dell'Escursionismo*.
Gente nostra: illustrazione fascista, vol. I, no. 1 (3 March 1929). Called "organo ufficiale dell'OND" beginning 13 March 1931; absorbed *Il Popolo d'Italia*'s weekly *Illustrazione fascista* 5 April 1931; ceased publication 17 July 1943.
Bollettino ufficiale, 1930–44.
I primi cinque anni di attività dell'Opera Nazionale Dopolavoro, 1926–1930. Rome, 1931.
Dopolavoro provinciali e organizzazioni dipendenti. Rome, 1932.

Bibliography

Realizzazioni e sviluppo dell'Opera Nazionale Dopolavoro. Rome, 1933.
L'Opera Nazionale Dopolavoro. Rome, 1936, 1937, 1938.
Annuario. 1937–9.
Attualità: la settimana del dopolavoro. Irregularly published 1941–3.
Il Dopolavoro: settimanale dell'Opera Nazionale Dopolavoro, vol. I, no. 1 (May 1944). Published at Vicenza through February(?) 1945.

B. Special publications

Collana del Carro dei Tespi: commedie in un atto. Rome, 1929.
Circular, n. 771-bis (ufficio centrale assistenza): Concorsi Nazionali per l'ammobilamento e l'arredamento economico della casa popolare. Rome, 15 February 1928.
Costumi, musica, danze e feste popolari italiane. Rome, 1931 (2nd rev. ed., Rome, 1935).
I dopolavoro aziendali in Italia, edito dalla direzione generale dell'OND in occasione del congresso mondiale del dopolavoro a Roma. Rome, 1938.
Mostra I del dopolavoro: catalogo-guida ufficiale, settembre 1938 (XVI) Circo Massimo. Milan, 1938.
Novelle di dopolavoristi premiati al secondo concorso del dopolavoro. Milan–Rome, n.d. [1930].
Novelle di dopolavoristi. Rome, 1938, 1939, 1940.
Novelle di operai. Rome, 1931.
Spighe: novelle di operai dopolavoristi. Rome, 1928.
Testo del discorso pronunciato dal consigliere nazionale Pietro Capoferri al Teatro Lirico di Milano in occasione del rapporto dei dirigenti provinciali dell'OND, 19 febbraio, 1940. Treviso, 1940.

C. Local organizations

ATAG: rivista mensile del dopolavoro tramviario. Rome, 1930–9.
ATM: rivista della azienda tramviario municipale di Torino. Turin, 1925–40.
ATM: rivista mensile dopolavoro tramviario di Milano. Milan, 1932–40.
Dopolavoro provinciale di Como. *Il dopolavoro, istituzione fascista: programmi, istruzioni e norme.* Como, 1930.
Dopolavoro provinciale di Firenze. *Il dopolavoro fiorentino: organo ufficiale del dopolavoro provinciale di Firenze,* vol. I, no. 1 (31 December 1928). Ceased publication 31 December 1931.
Dopolavoro provinciale di Livorno. *Rassegna della attività dopolavoristiche provinciali di Livorno.* Livorno, 1934.
Dopolavoro comunale di Lodi. *Relazione,* 3 aprile, 1927. Lodi, 1927.
Dopolavoro Modena. *Bollettino del dopolavoro provinciale di Modena, numero unico* (30 ottobre, 1927). Modena, 1927.
I concorso regionale dei burattinai. Modena, 1930.

Montecatini. *Il dopolavoro Montecatini.* March–April 1942.

Dopolavoro provinciale di Parma. *Relazione.* Parma, 1933.

Dopolavoro provinciale di Parma. *Relazione.* Parma, 1934.

Dopolavoro provinciale di Pavia. *Germogli: novelle di dopolavoristi.* Pavia, 1934.

Rassegna delle opere. Pavia, 1932.

Dopolavoro provinciale di Ravenna. *Il dopolavoro, istituzione fascista, I Congresso provinciale del dopolavoro a Ravenna, 21 aprile, 1929.* Ravenna, 1929.

Il dopolavoro, istituzione fascista, II Congresso provinciale del dopolavoro a Ravenna, 27 aprile, 1930. Ravenna, 1930.

Dopolavoro provinciale di Torino. *Dopolavoro, norme pratiche per i dirigenti.* Ed. Romano Stefanelli. Turin, 1935.

Dopolavoro provinciale di Vercelli. *Dopolavoro, norme pratiche per i dirigenti.* Vercelli, 1933.

Il dopolavoro nell'anno X. Vercelli, 1933.

Ispettorato dell'OND, V Zona, Toscana. *Il dopolavoro in Toscana,* numero unico. Florence, 1935.

Il dopolavoro dell'urbe: rassegna quindicinale. Rome, 1930–1.

D. Studies on the dopolavoro

Baldi, Albertina. "Il dopolavoro strumento di propaganda del fascismo." *La Toscana nel regime fascista, 1922–1939,* 2 vols. Florence, 1971. Vol. I.

Bertinetti, Giovanni. *Il libro del dopolavoro.* Turin, 1928.

Credaro, L., and M. Bernabei. "L'Opera Nazionale Dopolavoro in Italia: organizzazione ed attività." *International Quarterly of Adult Education,* II (May 1935).

Cuesta, Ugo. *Il libro del Dopolavoro.* Rome, 1937.

De Angelis, Emanuele. *Che cosa è e che cosa vuole il dopolavoro: l'organizzazione in provincia di Pavia.* Pavia, 1929.

Cinque anni di organizzazione a Pavia. Pavia, 1931.

de Grazia, Victoria. "La taylorizzazione del tempo libero operaio nel regime fascista." *Studi storici,* II (1978).

"Disciplina del lavoro e mediazione sociale sotto il regime fascista." *Annali,* Fondazione Giangiacomo Feltrinelli, XX, 1980.

Del Vescovo, Michele. *Che fare con l'ENAL? situazione e progetto di riforma.* Rome, 1970.

Dusmet, Giacomo. "Spare time organizations for agricultural workers in Italy." *International Labor Review,* vol. XXXIII, no. 2 (February 1936).

Galli, Giovanni. "Un'organizzazione ausiliaria del P.N.F.: l'Opera Nazionale Dopolavoro in provincia di Arezzo." *Studi Storici,* III (1975).

Harrison, Randolph. "Italian National Leisure Time Society." *Monthly Labor Review,* XL (February 1935).

Hartmann, Hans. *Der Faschismus dringt ins Volk: eine Betrachtung über das Dopolavoro.* Berlin, 1933.

Bibliography

Jacomelli, Alberto. "L'ENAL: una bandita chiusa." *L'Attualità*, XI (November 1956).

Leicht, Pier Silverio. *L'Opera Nazionale Dopolavoro*. Rome, 1937.

Luconi, S. *Il dopolavoro italiano*. Turin, 1929.

Maffei, Luigi. *I dopolavoro agricoli in provincia di Varese, 1930–1937*. Varese, 1938.

Malavisi, Gioacchino. *ENAL*. Rome, 1948.

Mércier, Jean. *L'Oeuvre nationale des loisirs: institut de droit public italien*. Annales de l'Université de Lyon, troisième série, Droit, fascicule 1. Paris, 1936.

Pellegrini, Antonio. *Il dopolavoro a Venezia ed i raduni dei costumi italiani: sviluppo ed azione cronografica illustrata*, anno IV–anno VI [1926–8]. Venice, 1929.

Perulli, Virgilio. *L'Opera Nazionale Dopolavoro nel sistema giuridico*. Padua, 1934.

Richard, Riccardo. *La figura giuridica dell'OND*. Collezione della Facoltà di Scienze Politiche della R. Università di Pavia, Pavia 1940.

Starace, Achille. *L'Opera Nazionale Dopolavoro*. Panorami di vita fascista, collana edita sotto gli auspici del PNF, II. Rome, 1933.

Ufficio di Politica Economica. *The "Opera Nazionale Dopolavoro" (National Welfare Work) and the Social Protection of the Workers*. Rome, 1927.

V. Contemporary newspapers and journals

L'Agricoltore d'Italia: Organo dell'Associazione fascista degli agricoltori italiani [1926–2].

L'Assistenza sociale nell'industria: Organo dell'ufficio d'assistenza della Confederazione generale fascista dell'industria [1928–9].

Il Bargello: Settimanale della federazione provinciale fascista fiorentina [1929–9].

Bianco e rosso: Bollettino mensile del Dopolavoro Fiat [1932–42].

Bollettino del lavoro e della previdenza sociale [1919–33; title changes to *Sindacato e Corporazione* in January 1933].

Bollettino della "Cotoniera": Rivista tessile mensile [1925–35].

Bollettino della "Laniera": Supplemento commerciale-settimanale a cura dell'Associazione dell'industria laniera italiana [1925–35].

Civiltà cattolica [1922–39].

Critica fascista [1923–39].

Economia [selected issues].

Educazione fascista: Rivista mensile di cultura politica [1927–37].

Famiglia nostra: Rivista mensile dell'Istituto nazionale assicurazioni [1930–40].

Forze civili: Rassegna mensile delle Associazioni fasciste del pubblico impiego . . . [1931–6].

Gerarchia [1922–39].

L'Idea nazionale [selected issues].

L'Italia industriale: Organo della Confederazione generale dell'industria italiana [1919–21; superseded in 1921 by *L'Organizzazione industriale*].

Lares: Organo del Comitato nazionale per le traditioni popolari [1930–9].

Lavoro d'Italia: Organo della Confederazione delle corporazioni e sindacati fascisti [1922–8; superseded by *Lavoro fascista* in December 1928].

Lavoro fascista: Organo quotidiano della Confederazione generale fascista dei lavoratori italiani [1929–39].

Il Maglio: Settimanale dei lavoratori dell'industria di Torino [1937–40].

Notiziario Breda [1923–5].

L'Organizzazione industriale: Organo della Confederazione generale dell'industria italiana [1921–39].

Organizzazione scientifica del lavoro: Organo mensile dell'Ente nazionale italiano per l'organizzazione scientifica del lavoro [1926–30].

Il Popolo delle alpi: Giornale della federazione fascista di Torino [1934–9].

Il Popolo d'Italia [selected issues].

Il Popolo di Pavia [1929–35].

La provincia di Vercelli [1930–5].

Santa milizia: Settimanale della federazione provinciale fascista di Ravenna [1928–39].

Sincronizzando: Rivista mensile di elettrotecnica e varietà [1922–31].

Sport fascista [1928–39].

La Stirpe: Rivista della corporazioni fasciste; critica e cultura, sindacale, dopolavoro, illustrazione dell'attività economica-politica-artistica d'Italia [1923–39].

Stato operaio: Rassegna di politica proletaria [monthly publication of the Communist party of Italy, 1927–39].

Torino: Rivista mensile illustrata del movimento letterario-artistico-industriale piedmontese [1925–39].

VI. International Labor Office: publications and reports

Cabrini, Angelo. "Memorandum on the Use of Spare Time in Italy." *Industrial and Labor Information*, vol. X, nos. 3–4 (21–28 April 1924).

Evans, Archibald A. "Work and Leisure, 1919–1969." *International Labor Review*, XCIX (January 1969).

"Fascisti Programme for the Utilization of Workers' Leisure." *Industrial and Labor Information*, no. 7 (6 July 1923).

Institut International de la Cooperation Intellectuelle, *Art populaire et loisirs ouvriers*, enqute faite à la demande du BIT. Paris, 1934.

Bibliothèques populaires et loisirs ouvriers, enquête faite à la demande du BIT. Paris, 1933.

International Labor Office, International Labor Conference. Eighteenth Session. Geneva, 1934. *Reduction of Hours of Work*, First Item on the Agenda. Geneva, 1934.

Bibliography

Minutes of the Commission on Hours of Labor. Geneva, 1920.

Report, first Washington, D.C., meeting of organizing committee. London, 1919.

Sixth Session. Geneva, June 1924. *Development of Facilities for the Utilization of Workers' Leisure (Questionnaire I).* Geneva, 1924.

Sixth Session. Geneva, June 1924. *Report on the Development of Facilities for the Utilization of Workers' Leisure. Item I on the Agenda.* Geneva, 1924.

Sixth Session. Geneva, June 1924. *Report of the Committee on the Utilization of Workers' Spare Time,* 2 vols. Geneva, 1924.

Legislative Series, 1922–1939.

Report of the Director, 1925. "Development of Facilities for the Utilization of Spare Time." Geneva, 1925.

Report of the Director, 1926. "Utilization of Workers' Spare Time." Geneva, 1926.

Report of the governing body of the International Labor Office upon the working of the convention limiting hours of work of industrial undertakings to eight hours in the day and forty-eight in the week. Geneva, 1931.

Report of the governing body of the ILO upon the working of the convention concerning the application of the weekly rest in industrial undertakings. Geneva, 1933.

Report to the Preparatory Conference, Hours of Work and Unemployment, January 1933. Geneva, 1933.

Second Supplementary Report on the Development of Facilities for the Utilization of Workers' Leisure. Geneva, 1924.

Studies and Reports. ser. A, no. 35, Studies on Industrial Relations, II. "The Fiat Establishments." Geneva, 1932.

Studies and Reports. ser. B, no. 17, Studies on Economic Conditions. "Scientific Management in Europe," by Paul Devinat. Geneva, 1934.

Studies and Reports. ser. G, no. 4, Studies on Housing and Welfare. "Recreation and Education": reports presented to the International Conference on Workers' Spare Time. Brussels, 15–17 June 1935; Geneva, 1936.

Studies and Reports. ser. G, no. 5, Studies on Housing and Welfare. "Facilities for the Use of Workers' Leisure during Holidays." Geneva, 1939.

Supplementary Report on the Development of Facilities for the Utilization of Workers' Leisure. Geneva, 1924.

Utilization of Spare Time. List of documents received by the International Labor Office and placed at the disposal of delegates to the Sixth International Labor Conference Geneva, 1924.

Sottilaro, Rosario. "Vocational Education in Italy." *International Labor Review,* vol. XXXIV, no. 4 (October 1936).

"Utilization of Spare Time in Italy." *Industrial and Labor Information,* no. 14 (22 June 1925).

"Workers' Education in Italy." *International Labor Review,* vol. III, nos. 1–2 (July–August 1921).

Index

Académie Française, 188
Acerbo, Giacomo, 28
AGIP (Agenzia Generale Italiana
    Petrolio), 135
Agnelli, Edoardo, 36
Agnelli, Giovanni, 62, 70, 74, 75, 78, 81
agriculture
    backwardness of, 12
    crisis in, 96–8, 100, 106
    modernization of, 14, 18, 94–100,
        108–9, 112–3, 124
Albarese (Grosseto), 114
Alleanza Cooperativa (Turin), 65
Alta Italia Insurance Company, 154
americanism, vii, 13, 191, 237
Ansaldo Ironworks, 12
antifascism and antifascists (*see*
    resistance)
antiurbanization campaign, 98–9
Antonelli, Luigi, 221
APE (Associazione Proletaria
    Educazione Fisica), 30
APEF (Associazione Anti-alcolica
    Proletaria Escursionistica), 30
Apulia, 100
Arpinati, Leandro, 178
Assistenza sociale nell'industria, 66, 72
Associazione per la Cultura Popolare,
    193
associazioni di impiegati, 131
Avezzano, 31

Badoglio, Pietro, 169
Balbo, Italo, 81, 110
Baldazzi, Vincenzo, 236
balilla, 13, 16, 212, 242
    see also Opera Nazionale Balilla
Banca Popolare (Milan), 143
Barbiellini Amidei, Bernardo, 28
Bargello, 113
Bariola (Caronno Milanese), 108
Basilicata, 100, 121–3

Battigalli, Emilio, 56
"Beauty of Work" Office, 73, 262–3 n.
    45
Bedeaux system, 75
Befana Fascista, 70, 214
Belli, Giuseppe Gioacchino, 212
Belluzzo, Giuseppe, 12, 42, 96, 199
Benni, Antonio Stefano, 62, 91, 93
Beolco, Angelo (il Ruzzante), 204
Beretta, Enrico, 38, 56, 202, 203, 227
Bergamo, 208
Berlutti, Giorgio, 196
Biagi, Bruno, 92
Bianco e rosso, 79
Blasetti, Alessandro, 217
Bocchini, Arturo, 234
Bodrero, Emilio, 189, 203, 214
Bollettino della 'Laniera', 85
Bolognini, Commendatore, 67
Bona, Emma, 209
Bonelli, Luigi, 221
bonifica integrale (integral land
    reclamation act), 96, 97, 114
Bonomi, Ivanoe, 236
Bonservizi, Nicola, 48
Bordighera, 230
Borgosesia Wool Works, 85, 86
    Papà Magni Award of the, 87
Borsalino Company, 86
Bottai, Giuseppe, 17, 37, 53, 64, 91, 142
braccianti (agricultural day laborers, 106,
    109, 110, 112, 120, 122, 123
Bragaglia, Anton Giulio, 220
Brescia, 36, 37, 106
Briano, Italo, 139, 140
Bullo, Gustavo, 84, 85
Busto Arsizio, 108

cagoiani, 123
Caldwell, Erskine, 191
Calzolari, Engineer, 148
camarate dei canterini, 204, 205

Index

Camerini, Mario, 217–8
Cantoni Coats Company, 87
capitalism
    end of laissez-faire, 1
    under fascism, 5, 248 n. 30
    stabilization of Italian, 4, 11–12
    welfare, vii, 67–70
    see also economy
Capoferri, Pietro, 92, 198, 232
Carafa D'Andria, Andrea, 29
Carbonari societies, 115
Carrà, Carlo, 192
Carta, Mario, 144
Casalini, Armando, 25, 27, 32
Casa del Popolo of Borgo Isola
    (Vercelli), 46
Casa del Popolo of Rome, 46, 47
case del popolo (peoples' houses), 9, 10,
    113
Catalani, Don Vito, 118
Catalano, Giuseppe, 119
Catholic Action, 19, 226, 241–2, 256 n.
    85
Catholic Church and Catholics, 176, 241
    activism during the Depression, 14, 51,
    95
Catholic Explorers, 242
cattedre ambulanti (travelling chairs of
    agriculture), 40, 266 n. 20
Cengio, 67
censorship, 168, 224
Central Intersyndical Committee, 90
CGE (Compagnia Generale Elettricità or
    General Electric Company), 67, 183
Chatillon Synthetics Company, 67
Chiarelli, Luigi, 167, 189, 213
Christian Democracy, 236
Cianetti, Tullio, 92
Ciano, Costanzo, 36, 136, 137, 140, 180
Cinecittà, 217
Cinegiornale Luce, 220
Cinema,
    content of, 216–8
    discount policies for, 159–60
    rural, 104, 111
circolo dei civili (or dei capeddi),
    115–19
Circolo operaio, Dongo (Como), 46
Circolo Pio X (San Salvatore Fitalia), 120
civil service
    dopolavoro in 127–8, 134–50
    growth of 129–30
    juridical status of, 130–3
    standard of living of, 128–32
CONI (Comitato Olimpionico Nazionale

Italiano or Italian National Olympic
    Committee), 79, 172–8, passim.
Committee for the Battle of Grain, 97
Committee of Eighteen, 130
Communist party of Italy (Partito
    comunista d'Italia or PC d'I), 30,
    173, 227, 233–6
    activism during the Depression, 14–15,
    51, 106
    organizing in the dopolavoro, 233–5
Comintern, 233
Confederation of Agricultural Employers,
    111
Confederazione Generale Fascista dei
    Lavoratori Italiane (CGFLI), 232
    see also fascist syndicalism
Confederazione Generale del Lavoro
    (General Confederation of Labor), 6,
    25, 37, 100, 139, 253 n. 38
Confederazione Nazionale dei Sindacati
    Fascisti
    move to nationalize dopolovoro, 32–3
    see also fascist syndicalism and
    syndicalists
Confindustria, 64, 68, 153
    and fascist syndicates, 91
    and industrial philanthropy, 62, 70
    Office of Welfare Work of, 66
    and PNF, 72
    see also industry
congregations of charity, 7
consent
    contradictory character of, 225–6,
    243–4
    definitions of, 3–5, 99–100, 226
    government by, 1–3
    and hegemony, 20–1
    in liberal democracies, 2–4
    and public opinion, 20
Consorzi Provinciali per l'Istruzione
    Tecnica, 199
coordination
    definition of, 47
    impact on workers' associations,
    48–50, 165
Cordiality Club of Varese Railroad
    Workers, 45
Corporate Correspondence School, 195
corporatism or corporativism, 25
    institutions of, 5, 10–11
Corriere della Domenica, 39
Corso Raffaele, 206, 207
Council of Ministers, President of, 34
CRAL (Circoli Ricreativi-assistenziali

lavoratori or Worker Recreational-Assistance Circles), 237
Cremona, 105
Crespi Management, 87
Crisafulli Mondio, Michele, 119
Critica fascista, 13, 142
Crozier, Michel, 141, 147
Cucchetti, Gino, 221
Cucini, Francesco, 231
Cuesta, Ugo, 169
cultura dopolavoristica, (*see* culture *see also* OND, cultural policies of
Cultura dei lavoratori, 198
culture
  of consent, 1–5
  definitions of, 2, 187, 279 n. 3
  civic, 5
  diversionary, 216–24
  and folk traditions, 201–16, 282 n. 62
  high vs. low, 187–92
Cup Society of Novara Railroad workers, 45–6

D'Alessio, Francesco, 36
Daneo Law, 1972
D'Annunzio, Gabriele, 192
De Amicis, Edmondo, 166, 167
De Benedetti, Aldo, 221
De Chirico, Giorgio, 192
Decree-Law of January 24, 1924 on Associations, 45, 46
De Martino, Ernesto, 206
De Michelis, Giuseppe, 240
Democrazia Sociale, 121
Depression, 14, 159
  and fascist mass organizing, 51–4
  impact on consumption, 158–9
De Sica, Vittorio, 127
De Simone, Eugenio, 145
De Stefani, Alberto, 141, 142
De Stefani, Alessandro, 221
Dinale, Ottavio, 118, 227–8
Dinamite Nobel (Lecore Signa), 69
Di Nardo, Giuseppe, 44
Di Segni, Riccardo, 149
Donegani, Guido, 69
dopolavoro in agriculture, 18, 42, 94–5, 100–26
  company (or *aziendale*), 18, 41–4, 60–3, 66–7, 70–88, 174, 235
  as fascist syndicalist organizing tool, 26–33
  fascist syndicalist rivalry with, 54–5
  and foreign initiatives, 36, 239–41

goals of local, 40
  as mediating institution, vii, 16–18
  participation in, 19, 54–5
  and salaried workers, 51, 127–8, 134–50
  staffing of, 40–1
  in state administration, 18, 134–50
  technocratic origins of, 24–6
  in tertiary sector, 42, 127–8, 134–50
  women's programs of, 42–4
  wartime mobilization of, 58, 161, 224, 225–7, 229, 232
  see also Opera Nazionale Dopolavoro
  civil service
  working class
Il Dopolavoro, 26, 39
Il Dopolavoro escursionistico, 180
Dopolavoro
  of Cutignano, 112–13
  of Florence, 152, 178
  of Genoa, 29, 210
  of Milan, 181
  of Montalbano Elicona, 120–1
  of Naples, 29–30
  of Roman Transit Company, 54, 148
  of the Presidency of the Council of Ministers, 144–5
  of the State Railroads, 134, 135–140
  dell'Urbe (Rome), 208, 211
  of the Turinese Civil Servants' Association, 181
D'Orio, Giovacchino, 156

economic battles, 226
  of autarchy, 58
  of grain, 97
economy
  and capital accumulation, 154
  and consumerism, 152–9
  and consumption, 14
  state intervention in, 11, 12
  and foreign competition, 11, 156–8
  rationalization of, 12–13
  stabilization of, 4, 11, 154, 245 n. 1
  war, 232, and working class standard of living, 5, 246 n. 7
  see also capitalism
  agriculture
  industry
Educaçion y Descanso, 239
education
  in *dopolavoro* circles, 192–8
  and instruction, 193
  syndicalist definitions of, 27–8
  nationalist conception of, 192–3

Index

Educazione fascista, 320
eight-hour legislation: *see* hours of work
1860, 217
Einaudi, Luigi, 1
Eisenstein, Serghei, 220
emigration, 98–9, 106, 266 n. 12
Emilia-Romagna, 100, 110–12
Emmanuel Philbert (duke of Aosta),
    34–5, 37–8
ENAL (Ente Nazionale Assistenza
    Lavoratori or National Agency for
    Worker Assistance), 236–7
Enalotto, 237
Enciclopedia Treccani, 188
Ente Opere Assistenziali, 52, 69
Ente Radio Rurale, 103
Ergatixi Estia (Workers' Hearth), 239
Ethiopian campaign, 58, 154, 169, 221
    explained to public, 221–4

Falcioni decree-law, 96
Falena, Ugo, 218
Famiglia nostra, 146, 147
family
    in fascist planning, 42–3
    effects of mass leisure on, 43, 242
Farina, Antonio Luigi, 132
Farinacci, Roberto, 160
Farmers' Hour (L'Ora dell'Agricoltore),
    103, 113
Fasci Femminili, 13, 16, 42, 43, 106, 242
Fasciolo, Umberto, 138
fascism
    compared to liberal pluralism, 22–3
    instability of, 226–7
    policing under, 20
    and *squadrismo*, 8–9, 110
    see also violence and intimidation
Fascist Association of Employees in
    State Industrial Enterprises, 132
Fascist Association of Postal and
    Telegraphic Employees, 132
Fascist Association of Public Employees
    (AFPI or Associazione Fascista per
    il Pubblico Impiego), 132
Fascist Association for Small Industries,
    153
Fascist Chamber of Deputies, 93
Fascist Federation of Artisan
    Communities, 153
Fascist Labor Day (also Birth of Rome,
    21 April), 33, 182
Fascist party (PNF or Partito Nazionale
    Fascista)
    allegiance to, 51, 100, 121

and the civil service, 132
    curbed by Mussolini, 33
    in economic battles, 41, 100
    and industry, 68–9
    as party of a new kind, 53, 257 n. 91
    relief programs of, 69
    and School of Social Work at San
        Gregorio a Celio
    and sports promotion, 177–9
    and syndicalism, 25, 37–8
Fascist Railroad Employees Association
    (Associazione Nazionale dei
    Ferrovieri Fascisti), 132, 134, 137–8
Fascist Star of Merit, 87
fascists of the first hour, 3
Fassio, Mario, 62
Fascist syndicalism
    class collaboration of, 24–5
    constituency of, 94, 100, 249–50 n. 5
    after March on Rome, 31–2
    militancy of in late thirties, 225
    undercut by industrial welfare work,
        88–92
    takeover of OND by, 232
Federation of Popular Universities, 194
Federazione Associazioni Cattoliche
    Italiane Sportive (FASCI or Catholic
    National Sports Federation), 49–50,
    173
Federazione Italiana per l'Escursionismo
    (FIE or Federation of Italian
    Excursionists), 180, 183
Federazione Italiana per il Gioco del
    Calcio (Italian Soccer Federation),
    172, 179
Federazione Italiana Operai Metallurgici
    (FIOM or Italian Federation of
    Metallurgical Workers), 31, 62
Fedi, Enzo, 114
Ferrara, 31, 100
Ferrari, Alberto, 230
Ferretti, Lando, 171
Ferrovie dello Stato (State Railroads)
    Dopolavoro of, 137–40
    fascist obsession with, 135–6, 271–2 n.
        20
    social services in, 135–40
festivals
    carnival, 213–14
    in Naples, 210, 212, 215
    of Noiantri, 210–12
    patron saints, 210–12, 215
    of San Rocco, 212
Fiat Motor Company, 31, 58, 66, 89, 139
    and fascism, 68, 70, 81

instructional programs at, 201, 264 n. 67
Lingotto plant of, 230
militarization of, 81
and Workers' Mutual Fund, 62, 77
social services at, 74–81
filodrammatiche: see theater
Fioretti, Armando, 90, 91
First Interprovincial Congress of Fascist Syndicates, 90
Florence, 113, 161, 162
Florio Navigation Company, 191
Folklore, 206
Follis, Aristide, 76
Ford, Henry, 26
fordism, 13, 64–5
Forzano, Gioacchino, 160, 162, 189
Forze civili, 132
Fox, Reverend H. W., 240
Frankfurt School, 3
freemasonry, 29, 116, 119, 123
Fuero del Trabajo, 239
Fundação Nacional para a Alegria no Trabalho, 239
futurism and futurists, 149, 172, 187, 188

Galileo Machine Works, 58, 162
Gallarate, 108
Gambacciani, Lorenzo, 48
Gangemi, Lello, 13
Gastaldi, Andrea, 182
Gazzetta dello Sport, 172
General Director of Taxes, 159, 177
Genoa, 29, 31, 51, 165
Gente nostra, 39, 112, 206, 207
advertising in, 153, 156, 157, 159
cultural pretensions of, 180, 192, 216
politics in, 221, 222, 223
and technical instruction, 195, 200
and theater, 167
Gentile, Giovanni, 187–8, 193, 194–5
Giacosa, Giuseppe, 221
Giambattini, Giuseppe, 221
Giampaoli, Mario, 52
Giani, Mario
managerial background of, 24, 25, 250 n. 10, 251 n. 11
ouster from OND, 37–8
seeks state support, 32
as spokesman for industrial reform, 60, 63
on worker education, 194
Gilbreth, Frank and Lillian, 42
Gillette Company, 156
Gioise giornate del decennale, 111

Giordani project-law, 90
Giugni, Gino, 89
Giuriati, Giovanni, 36
Gleichschaltung, 19–20
Gobbato, Ugo, 76
Gobbi, Guelfo, 72
Goldoni, Carlo, 83, 166
Gramsci, Antonio, 1, 7, 21–2, 92, 200, 226
Grandi, Dino, 110
Gregori, Giuseppe, 197
Gruppi Universitari Fascisti (GUF or Fascist University Youth Groups), 16, 225, 231–2
Guardabassi, Duilio, 211, 212
Gutermann Silkworks, 87

Haider, Carmen, 14
Haile Selassie, 213
hegemony, 1, 21–3, 92–3,
holidays, 207 (*see also* festivals)
hours of work, 239–40, 250 n. 8, 256–7 n. 86
and eight-hour day, 239
1923 legislation on, 25
Hugo, Victor, 166, 167
Humbert of Savoy, 214

ILVA Steel Mills, 66
industry
acceptance of *dopolavoro*, 67
expenditures on social services, 67–70
influence over fascism, 6
growth under fascism, 5, 260–1 n. 10
and fascist unions, 65, 89–92
and party relief work, 68–70
and labor relations, 60–1
rationalization of, 64, 67
relations to agriculture, 96–7
and social legislation, 61–3
and vocational instruction, 250 n. 6
and welfare work, 25–6, 89–92, 247 n. 23
instruction, 198–201
downgrading of, 281 n. 36
intellectuals
changing social definition of 189–90, 146–7
and their conflicting interpretations of culture, 191–2, 196–7
influence on fascist cultural programs, 55–6, 128, 224, 168, 196–8
support for the dopolavoro, 189–90, 205–6

Index

International Labor Office (ILO), 239, 240
Istituto di Cultura Alfredo Oriani, 197
Istituto Luce, 160, 204, 218
Istituto Nazionale Assicurazioni (INA or National Insurance Institute), 32
  social services in the, 135, 143, 145–7, 148–9
Istituto Nazionale Case Impiegati Statali (INCIS or National Institute for State Employee Housing), 143
Istituto Nazionale Fascista di Cultura, 188, 194
Italian Consortium of Manufacturers (CIM), 133
Italian Popular Party (PPI or Partito Popolare Italiano), 36, 126
Italian Society for Authors and Editors (SIAE or Società Italiana Autori e Editori), 189
Italian Touring Club, 180

Joyce, James, 197

Kraft durch Freude (KDF or Strength through Joy), 72, 181, 239

Labor Charter, 44, 195, 196
Labor Front, 92, 239
Lacava, 122
Lares, 206
La Scala Opera House, 161, 192
La Spezia, 51, 54
L'Atleta, 172
Lateran Accords, 242
latifundia, 115, 118, 122, 124
Lavoro fascista, 92, 115, 291
Lazio, 179
Lazzari, Costantino, 47
League of Nation Sanctions, 58, 168, 217
leisure
  as arena of worker resistance, 235–6
  class distinctions in the use of, 185–6
  fascist conceptualization of, 44, 51–2
  problem of worker, 238–41
  rationalization of, 44
Leuzzi, Nicola, 54
liberalism and liberals
  neglect of the social question by, 246 n. 10
  weak presence in pre-World War I civil society, 5, 7
Liguria, 28–9
literacy, 109, 200
Liverani, Ferdinando, 65–6
Lochman, Elia, 221
Lodi, Carlo, 118, 123, 126

Lojacono, Luigi, 28–9
Lolini, Ettore, 141, 272 n. 33
Lombard Consortium of Machine and Metallurgical Industries, 65
Lombardy, 100, 105, 106–9, 178
Lomellina, 106
Lopez, Sabatino, 221
Luciano Serra pilota, 217
Lugo, 111
Lupis, Luigi, 119
Lusignuoli, Aldo, 145
Lynd, Robert and Helen Merrell, 238

mafia, 116, 119
Maglio, 230
Malnati, Linda, 49
Malusardi, Edoardo, 90
Mambelli, Antonio, 219
Mancioli, Mario, 219
Manifatture Cotoniere Meridionali (Nocera), 85
Manunta, Ugo, 91
Mantua, 105
Manzoni, Alessandro, 192
Marconi, Guglielmo, 13
Marelli Company, 155, 157, 158
Maria Josè, 214
Marinelli, 69, 179
Marinetti, Filippo Tommaso, 172, 187
Marzotto Woolworks, 85, 86, 91
Mascagni, Pietro, 169, 192
mass media
  under fascism, 185–6
  see also radio, cinema
mass organizing and organizations
  centralized under Mussolini, 225
  definition of, 16
  during the Depression, 14–15, 51–4
  and hegemony 21–3
  limits of effectiveness, 226–9
  obstacles to in the Mezzogiorno, 115–24
  productivist model of, 14, 24–5
  and self-organization of elites, 21–2
  see also entries on specific organizations
Matera, 122–4
Mattei, Luigi, 109–10
Matteotti assassination, 12, 32
May Day, 33, 182
Mazzoni, A, 138
mediating institutions, 7
Mele, Augusto, 197
Messina, 119, 120–1, 178
Metaxas, Joannis, 239
Mezzogiorno, 95, 114–24

306

Index

Michelin Company, 31
"Middletown, USA," 238
Milan, 52, 153, 161, 208
Ministry of Communications, 136
Ministry of the Interior, 121, 144
Ministry of the National Economy, 31, 34, 41
Ministry of Popular Culture (Minculpop), 20
Ministry of the Press and Propaganda, 161
Modern Times, 230
Modigliani, G. E., 47
Montalbano Elicona, 120
Montecatini Conglomerate, 69, 70
Morandi, Rodolfo, 58, 225
Mori, Cesare, 116
Morigi, Renzo, 110, 111, 112
Muratori, Sante, 196
Musarra, Antonino, 120
Mussolini, Arnaldo, 26
Mussolini, Benito as actor, vii, 275 n. 25
  as americanizer, 13, 98
  on the civil service, 129, 130, 132
  cultural pretensions of, 160, 187–8
  on the *dopolavoro*, 91
  and labor relations, 6, 62–3, 66, 68, 90–1, 232
  on land reform, 96, 98
  after Matteotti crisis, 37
  as Minister of the Interior, 45
  political opportunism of, 6, 32
  popular response to, 164
  as populist, 52–3
  and revaluation crisis, 11–13
  Speech of the Ascension of, 98
Muti, Ettore, 232

Naples, 153, 161
Narducci, R., 138
National Association of Movie Producers, 159
National Bloc, 116
National Bureau of Labor (Ufficio Nazionale Superiore del Lavoro) abolition of, 34
National Committee for Popular Traditions, 206
National Confederation of Fascist Syndicates (CNSF or Confederazione Nazionale Sindacati Fascisti), 24
National Fascist Confederation of Agriculturalists, 103, 125
National Fascist Syndicate of Agrarian Technicians, 102

National Silk Board, 102
National Socialist Party, 130
  regime, 229
  see also Kraft durch Freude Labor Front
Nationalism and nationalists, 7
  conception of the state, 192
  on education, 192–3, 200, 250 n. 7
  "nationalization of the masses," 2
Nava, Cesare, 33
Necchi Sewing Machine Company, 156, 195, 197
Nervi, Pier Luigi, 138
New Lanark, 26, 237
Nicolato, Alfredo, 31
Nitti, Saverio Francesco, 123
Novara, 28, 31, 105, 106

opera, 32–3
  del duomo, 34
Opera Bonomelli, 34
Opera Nazionale Balilla (ONB), 34
Opera Nazionale Combattenti, 16, 34
Opera Nazionale Dopolavoro
  as advertising agency, 152–9
  in agriculture, 101–4, 125
  consumer programs of, 152–9
  corruption in 227–8, 253 n. 42
  crisis of, 226–9
  cultural policies of, 188–90
  educational programs of, 193–8
  elite support for, 36
  financing of, 35, 252 n. 34, 228
  foundation of, 32–4
  goals of, 34–6, 41–4, 53
  group membership in, 50–1, 54
  instructional programs of, 198–201
  juridical status of , 228, 285 n. 9
  and Kraft durch Freude, 72
  membership in by sector of the working population, 55, 229, 257 n. 95
  1937 reform of, 228–9
  organization of, 228
  participation in, 41, 258 n. 98, 262 n. 42
  publications of, 39
  and recreation, 164–70
  reorganization under PNF, 38–40
  and revival of traditions, 201–16
  sources for the study of, 290–3
  staff of, 36, 55–7, 189–90, 252–5 n. 37, 254 n. 49, 259 n. 104–5, n. 106, 260 n. 83
  under Starace, 52–5
  technical commissions in the, 39

307

Index

Opera Nazionale Dopolavoro (*cont.*)
and tourism, 180–4
and wartime programs, 232
Opera Nazionale Maternità ed Infanzia
(ONMI), 13, 34
operas, 104, 163
opere pie, 7
oratori, 7
Organizzazione industriale, 62
Organizzazione scientifica del lavoro, 66
Oriani, Avvocato, 29
OVRA, 234
Owen, Robert, 26

Padua, 31
Palermo, 119
Panorami di vita fascista, 197
Pantano, Giuseppe, 120–1
Parenti, Rino, 52, 56, 84
Paternostro, Roberto, 116–17
patron saints days, *see* festivals
Patronato Nazionale d'Assistenza, 37
Pavia, 31, 105, 106, 215
peasantry
emigration of, 98–9, 106
fascist policy toward the, 94–100
standard of living of, 97–9
unrest among, 105
Pesce, Giovanni, 190
Pezzoli, Liberato, 33
philanthropy
Italian compared to British and
German, 8
and Poor Laws, 8
prefascist organization of, 7–8
247 n. 22
Piacenza, 28, 31
Piedmont, 100, 105–6, 178
Piedmontese Steel Mills, 230
Pignone Union of Florence, 48–9
Pinelli, Bartolomeo, 212
Pirelli Company, 70
Pirretti, S., 124
Pischel, Giuliano, 142
Pistoia, 113–14
Pius X, 169, 173
Poggio, Oreste, 218
Ponte All'Olmo, 28
Ponti, Gian Giacomo, 82, 83
Popolo d'Italia, 66
Popular Libraries, 196–7
Popular Front, 233
Popular trains, 180–1
Popular Universities, 192–5
Potenza, 118, 112–3
Prato, Giuseppe, 229

prefects, 102
action against worker clubs, 44–9, 255
n. 65
Prince of Piedmont, 176
Prince of Piedmont Club, 118, 119
Prison Notebooks, 21
productivism, 199
influence on fascism, 24–5
syndicalist, 10
propaganda, 58
in education, 196–8
relative absence of overt, 216–224,
226–7
in technical instruction, 199–200
Public Security Laws of November 1926,
12, 44, 47
Puccetti, Corrado, 56, 125
Puccini, Giacomo, 163
Pudovkin, V., 220

quota novanta, 11

radio
ownership of, 155–6, 274 n. 7, n. 10
Radius, Emlio, 57, 224
Raghianti, Piero, 147
Ragusa, 115, 117
rationalization movement, 41–2, 242 n.
35, 254 n. 57, 256 n. 64, 272 n. 34
Italian compared to American, 13–14,
64–5
in the state administration, 141–2
Rautiis, Filippo, 122, 123
Ravenna, 48, 68, 195
"reach out to the people," 14–15, 51–5
recreation (*see* OND, recreation)
Red Cross, 32
regionalism
and folk traditions, 214
resistance, 165
antifascist, 168, 225
Catholic, 226
communist-organized, 233–6
to coordination, 49–51
to management-sponsored social
services, 88–9
prepolitical, 215–16
and working-class unrest, 20, 226, 256
n. 85, 261 n. 12
Restoration Act of the Civil Service
(Nazi), 130
Rignani, Pasquale, 111, 209
La Rinascente, 133
Risorgimento, 6, 187, 214
Rocco, Alfredo, 7, 131

Index

Rocco Laws (*see* Syndical Laws of 3
April, 1926)
Rome, 100, 128, 167, 169
Rosselmini Gualandi (count), 36
Rossi Wool Mills, 86, 87, 157
Rosso di San Secondo, Pier Maria, 221
Rossoni, Edmondo, 10, 24, 32
and leadership of the CNSF, 27
support of for *dopolavoro*, 27
Rotary Clubs, 7, 19
Royal Athletic Club, 86
Royal Family, 113
Rural Housewives Organization (or
massaie rurali, 16
ruralization, 99–104

sabato fascista, 57–8, 182
Sabato teatrale, 161–2
Sagra dei Tessitori (Weavers' Festival),
87
sagre, 104, 207, 208
Saibante, Mario, 12
Salandra, Antonio, 6
Salvemini, Gaetano, 19
Sandicchi, Vittorio, 122–3
San Salvatore Fitalia (Messina), 120
Santamaria, Enrico (Righetto), 211
Saroyan, William, 191
Savona, 229
Savoy, House of, 215
Scelba, Mario, 237
scientific management, 13
see also rationalization movement
Scorza, Carlo, 36, 195
Sellani, Orfeo, 123
Sentinella della patria, 205
Sereni, Emilio, 229
Serpieri, Arrigo, 95, 96, 97, 99, 100
sharecroppers (*mezzadri*), 109, 112–13
Sicily, 31, 95, 100, 114–21
Signor Max, 217–8
Sincronizzando, 82
Sindacato dei Lavoratori Intellettuali,
147
Sindacato rosso, 30
Sizer, James, 238
Snia Viscosa, 67, 70
social insurance, 90, 154, 274 n. 6
socialism and socialist movement, 126
club-life and culture before the March
on Rome, 8–10, 27, 112, 166, 247 n.
24, 211
club-life and culture under fascism, 28,
106
confiscation of properties of, 46–7
and German Social Democracy, 9

and Second International Unionism, 89
social composition of, 9
Terzini faction of, 30
Società Idroelettrica Piemontese (SIP or
Piedmontese Hydroelectric
Company), 31
and cultural programs, 83–4
social services at, 81–4
Società Operaio-Agricola Montalbano
Elicona, 120
Sorrentino, Arturo, 29
Soviet Union, 76, 80, 234
Sport e proletariato, 30
Sports
bocce, 168–9
brevetti for, 174
under capitalism, 277 n. 57
Charter of 1929, 172, 177
facilities for, 177–9
Olympic, 171
organization of 170–9
participatory and spectator, 179
professional, 172, 177–8
skiing, 176
violence in, 179
and women, 176–7
Spreti Palace, 46, 110
Stadium, 173
Starace, Achille, 161, 164
directives of to *dopolavoro*, 124, 159
directives of to GUF, 231
as mass organizer, 14, 164
as OND special commissioner, 52–4
ouster of from PNF secretaryship, 226
state
nationalist conception of, 24, 59
transformation of, 59
State Tobacco Monopoly, 157
Stato operaio, 14, 30, 233
Steel and Iron Works (Novi Ligure), 66
Stefanelli, Romano, 195
Steinbeck, John, 191
Steinmetz, Alfred, 82
Stige Gas Works, 67
Stirpe, 190
Stolypin Plan, 96
Strambino Cotton Mills, 85
Sue, Eugenè, 166, 167
Sutkevitch, 220
Syndical Laws of 3 April, 13, 37, 64, 89
Syracuse, 115

Tagliaferri, Gino, 30
Tarlarini, Carlo, 64, 65
taylorism, 64, 142
see also rationalization movement

309

Index

Terni Steel Mills, 69
tertiary sector
  growth of, 126–8
  and growth of new middle class,
    127–28, 270 n. 1, n. 2
  standard of living of employees in the,
    127
  and white collar cultural habits, 146–9
textiles industry
  composition of labor force, 84
  social services in, 85–7
theater, 190
  content of amateur, 218–19, 221
  organization of amateur, 166–8, 276 n.
    41
  organization of professional, 160–4
Thespian Cars, 109, 123, 162–4, 200, 219,
  221
Third International Conference on Home
  Economics, 42
Third International Congress on
  Scientific Management, 13, 42
Tocqueville, Alexis de, 7
Togliatti, Palmiro, 227, 233, 235
Tolman, William H, 88
tourism, 180–4
totalitarianism, vii
  and the *dopolavoro*, 19
  Italian compared to Spanish and Nazi,
    19–20
Tremelloni, Roberto, 84
Turati, Augusto, 172
  as head of the OND, 37–8, 102
Turchi, Francesco, 117–18, 119
Turin, 31, 54, 161, 215
Tuscany, 100, 112–14

Ugolini, Ugolino, 180
Ulzoga, Cherubino, 113–14
unemployment, 97
Union of Fascist Metallurgical Workers,
  66
Unione Donne Catholice Italiane
  (UDCI), 43
Unione Operaia-Escursionistica Italiana
  (UOEI or Workers' Union of Italian
  Escursionists), 180

Valli di Lanzo Cotton Mills, 85
Vandone, Ernesto, 76
Varaldo, Alessandro, 219
Varese, 106, 108–9
Vecchia guardia, 217
Venetia, 100

Venice, 153
Vercelli, 171
Verdi, Giuseppe, 191, 192
Vertov, Dziga, 220
Victor Emmanuel III, 47
Vidoni Palace Agreements, 76, 89
violence and intimidation, 3, 8–9, 10, 28,
  30, 100, 247 n. 26
Visocchi Decree-Laws, 96
Vita di Arnaldo, 197
Vita uoeina, 180
Vittoria, 118
volata, 175–6
Volpi di Misurata, Giuseppe, 11, 98
Voltana, 209
voluntary associations
  and business elites, 7
  fascist impediments to, 114
  in liberal polities, 7
  as mediating institutions, 7
  politicization of, 247 n. 18

Walter, Karl, 86, 91, 230
war veterans, 29, 121
Webb, Beatrice, 8
welfare work (*see* industry, welfare
  work) *see also* philanthropy
Westinghouse Corporation, 29, 31
"wine circles," 30
women
  Catholic organizing of, 241–2
  fascist policies toward, 42–3, 254 n. 55
  participation of in *dopolavoro*, 122
  and revival of traditions, 283 n. 66
  and sports, 176–7, 277 n. 70
working class
  associationalism before the March on
    Rome, 8–11, 27–8, 30, 229
  coordination of workers' circles, 47–9
  divisions within the, 133–4, 139, 235
  generation gap in, 243
  repression of the, 3, 8–9, 10, 28, 30,
    100, 247 n. 26
  response to the *dopolavoro*, 49–51,
    54–5, 58, 88–90, 138–40, 233
  standard of living of, 12, 14, 51–2,
    64–5
World War II, 236

Young Italians (Giovani Italiane), 16
Young Men's Christian Association
  (YMCA), 7, 17, 60, 239

Zangrandi, Ruggero, 231